Gareth Stedman Jones
Michael Löwy
Göran Therborn
John Merrington
André Gorz
Ronald Aronson
Norman Geras
André Glucksmann
Lucio Colletti

Verso

Western Marxism

A Critical Reader

Edited by New Left Review

© *New Left Review*, 1977

Verso Edition, 1978

Verso, 7 Carlisle Street, London W1

Printed by Unwin Brothers Limited,

The Gresham Press, Old Woking, Surrey

ISBN 902308 29 7

PH 3-11-80

Contents

Contents

Editorial Note

The essays printed in this volume were, in their majority, first published in *New Left Review*. They were designed to form a series that would answer to two needs: firstly, clear exposition of the major theoretical systems within the tradition of Western Marxism, from the aftermath of the October Revolution to the present day; and secondly, critical assessment of these legacies, from the standpoint of a younger generation of Marxists. This two-fold programme accounts for the structure of the volume published here. The selection of thinkers discussed is not exhaustive of figures within the Western Marxist tradition: the criterion for inclusion has been the production of a distinctive *system* of thought. In the case of Lukács, the Frankfurt School and Althusser, exposition and critique are combined in the same essays. In the case of Sartre, one essay is an elucidation, the other an assessment. In the case of Gramsci, the essay published here is essentially expository. The lack of a critical evaluation of Gramsci's work is thus the main omission from the volume. The absence is remedied elsewhere, in an essay to be published after this volume went to press: Perry Anderson, *The Antinomies of Antonio Gramsci* (NLB edition, 1978). Another, lesser lacuna is any treatment of Althusser's political writings in the seventies. These are the object of an assessment by Valentino Gerratana, 'Althusser and Stalinism', in *New Left Review* No. 101. These two 'external' texts can thus be read as extensions to the main architecture of the work assembled here. Finally, the interview with Lucio Colletti that ends the book has a character of its own. In the form of questions and answers, it contains at once an account of the main theses of the theoretical school of which Colletti is now the most eminent representative, and a self-critical reflection on its limits that moves to a general judgment of the heritage of Western Marxism which forms an appropriate conclusion to the volume.

New Left Review

Bibliographical Note

The essays in this volume were first published: Gareth Stedman-Jones, 'The Marxism of the Early Lukács', in *New Left Review* No. 70, November–December 1971; Michael Löwy, 'Lukács and Stalinism', in *New Left Review* No. 91, May–June 1975; Göran Therborn, 'The Frankfurt School', in *New Left Review* No. 63, September–October 1970, and *New Left Review* No. 67, May–June 1971; John Merrington, 'Theory and Practice in Gramsci's Marxism', in *The Socialist Register 1968*; André Gorz, 'Sartre and Marx', in *New Left Review* No. 37, May–June 1966; Ronald Aronson, 'The Social Theory of Jean-Paul Sartre', in *Telos* No. 1C, Summer 1973 (an earlier version); Norman Geras, 'Althusser's Marxism: An Assessment', in *New Left Review* No. 71, January–February 1972; André Glucksmann, 'A Ventriloquist Structuralism', in *New Left Review* No. 72, March–April 1972; Lucio Colletti, 'A Political and Philosophical Interview', in *New Left Review* No. 86, July–August 1974.

Biographical Note

Gareth Stedman Jones is a Fellow of King's College, Cambridge and author of *Outcast London*; a member of the editorial committee of *New Left Review*.

Michael Löwy is a Lecturer in Sociology at the University of Vincennes, and author of a forthcoming study of the political and intellectual development of Georg Lukács (NLB 1978).

Göran Therborn is Reader in Sociology at the University of Lund, and author of *Science, Class and Society* (NLB 1976) and *What Does the Ruling Class Do When it Rules?* (NLB 1978).

John Merrington is Lecturer in History, Middlesex Polytechnic; a member of the editorial committee of *New Left Review*.

André Gorz is author of *The Traitor* and *Reform and Revolution*; a member of the editorial committee of *Les Temps Modernes*.

Ronald Aronson is Professor of Philosophy at Wayne State University, Michigan, and author of a forthcoming study of the work of Jean-Paul Sartre, to be published by NLB in 1978.

Norman Geras is Lecturer in Government at the University of Manchester, and author of *The Legacy of Rosa Luxemburg*; a member of the editorial committee of *New Left Review*.

André Glucksmann is Lecturer in Sociology at the University of Vincennes, and author of *Le Discours de la Guerre*.

Lucio Colletti is Professor of Philosophy at the University of Rome, and author of *Fron Rousseau to Lenin* and *Marxism and Hegel* (NLB 1974).

The Marxism of the Early Lukács

Gareth Stedman Jones

Nearly half a century after its original publication in Germany, Georg Lukács's *History and Class Consciousness*[1] has at last become available in English. Those who now read the book for the first time may find its contents surprising. For the notoriety of this forbidden volume of the early Communist movement seems incommensurate at first sight with the familiarity of many of its themes. Despite the formal difficulty of Lukács's language, contemporary readers are likely to find themselves at home with most of the central leitmotifs in the book. For in one form or another, these have by now become part of the common intellectual universe of a large part of the left in the advanced capitalist world. But to say this is not to imply that the themes developed by Lukács some fifty years ago and today diffused so generally among socialist intellectuals, are self-explanatory truths or even manifest axioms of Marxism. If they are treated as such, it is because of a second surprising feature of *History and Class Consciousness* – the virtual absence in almost fifty years of any comprehensive or coherent critique of the book.

Not that it has always been greeted with unanimous acclaim. Far from it: it is well known that it was condemned by the

---

[1] Georg Lukács, *History and Class Consciousness*, tr. Rodney Livingstone, Merlin Press, London, 1971. This edition is excellently translated and contains some useful explanatory notes at the end of the book. One word of warning is necessary, however. Lukács's 1967 essay which is used as an introduction to the book, was designed for a volume of the German collected works which cover all his political writings in the 1920's and not solely *History and Class Consciousness* (hereinafter abbreviated to HCC). Thus, when on p. xiii Lukács refers to his essay on problems of organization, he is not referring to the essay on organization in HCC. It should also be noted that while Livingstone has translated the term '*zugerechnetes Klassenbewusstsein*' as 'imputed class consciousness', I have preferred the term, 'ascribed class consciousness'.

Comintern from the start, was subsequently renounced by Lukács himself, and when re-published in Western Europe after 1956, evoked local dissent. Even so, for all the Marxist literature that has appeared since *History and Class Consciousness* resurfaced it is impossible to discover any systematic or substantial criticism of the book as a whole.[2]

There is no doubt that in part the reason for this is the compelling scope and intensity of the work. Lukács's book has seemed to constitute a definitive statement, the locus classicus, of certain themes which have been repeated and re-echoed again and again since it was first written. This essay aims to provide at least the beginnings of such a criticism. It will first resume what is taken to be the *doctrinal core* of the book: secondly, provide the essential historico-cultural *background* to it, without which it cannot be adequately understood; thirdly, criticize the intellectual and political *consequences* of Lukács's theory; and finally, discuss the fundamental problem the book raises – but does not answer – for historical materialism.

1. Capitalism and Reification

Despite its complexity of logical sequence, the reading of Marxism to be found in Lukács's book represents a relatively systematic position.[3] The secret of capitalism is to be found in 'the solution to the riddle of commodity structure'.[4] Marx's chapter on the fetishism of commodities in *Capital* 'contains within itself the whole of historical materialism and the whole self-knowledge of the proletariat seen as the knowledge of capitalist society'.[5] The essential feature, then, of capitalism is commodity fetishism and the essential product of commodity fetishism for Lukács is

[2] An English work, entitled *Aspects of History and Class Consciousness*, ed. István Mészáros, London, 1971, does not contain any direct critique of the actual contents of the book.

[3] It is important to realize that *History and Class Consciousness* is a collection of essays written at different times, not arranged in chronological order, and not subsequently edited or significantly altered for book publication. The result is that quite apart from important changes of political position contained within it, the book also abounds with minor inconsistencies. This makes it extremely difficult to analyse the argument of the book as a coherent whole. All that can be claimed here is that an attempt is made to examine and criticize the main purport of the theses advanced.

[4] HCC p. 83.

[5] HCC p. 170.

reification. Lukács identifies reification as the process through which relations between men take on the appearance of relations between things; human society and human history, the products of man, appear not as the products of social activity, but as alien and impersonal forces, laws of nature which impose themselves on humanity from without. As capitalism advances, reification becomes progressively more extensive and intensive. Just as the transition from handicraft via co-operation to manufacture leads to greater and greater fragmentation of the object of production, so this fragmenting process progressively encroaches upon the consciousness of man, the subject of production. Man is no longer the authentic master of the process, 'he is a mechanical part incorporated into a mechanical system'.[6] Human activity becomes less active and more contemplative. Man must conform to the laws of the mechanical system. The activity of man in general becomes analogous to the 'behaviour of the worker *vis à vis* the machine he serves and observes, and whose functions he controls while he contemplates it'.[7]

The hallmark of this reification process is the application of the principle of 'rational mechanization' and 'calculability' to 'every aspect of life'. The process of rationalization develops with the division of labour. The result is a specialization of skills which 'leads to the destruction of every image of the Whole'.[8] Rational calculability, the essence of the capitalist enterprise, increasingly comes to permeate all other features of society. Following Weber, the modern state is viewed as 'a business concern'; 'the judge is more or less an automatic statute-dispensing machine', whose behaviour is 'predictable'; similarly, bureaucracy manifests the same principle of 'an inhuman standardized division of labour analagous to that . . . found in industry on the technological and mechanical plane'.[9] The process of reification is to be seen everywhere, whether it is in journalism where 'the journalist's lack of convictions, the prostitution of his experiences and beliefs is comprehensible only as the apogee of capitalist reification',[10] or in modern marriage where man's 'qualities and abilities are no longer

[6] HCC p. 89.
[7] HCC p. 98.
[8] HCC p. 103.
[9] HCC p. 99.
[10] HCC p. 100.

an organic part of his personality, they are things he can own or dispose of like the various objects of the external world'.[11]

But for Lukács the most consummate expression of capitalist reification is undoubtedly the method of natural science. 'There is something highly problematic in the fact that capitalist society is predisposed to harmonize with scientific method . . . when "science" maintains that the manner in which data immediately present themselves is an adequate foundation of scientific conceptualization and that the actual form of these data is the appropriate starting point for the formation of scientific concepts, it thereby takes its stand simply and dogmatically on the basis of capitalist society. It uncritically accepts the nature of the object as it is given and the laws of that society as the unalterable foundation of "science".'[12] When the ideal of scientific knowledge is applied to society 'it turns out to be an ideological weapon of the bourgeoisie . . . it must think of capitalism as being predestined to eternal survival by the eternal laws of nature and reason'.[13]

Scientific method is not merely a passive reflection of the onset of reification. For by its procedures it actively pulverizes any organic conception of totality not attained by a formal rational mode of cognition. It thus destroys metaphysics and creates a world of 'pure' facts divided up into specialized partial systems of laws unrelated to any meaningful totality.

The Search for an Identical Subject–Object

It was this reified and fragmented conception of the world that produced the distinctive problems of German critical philosophy and 18th-century materialism. Critical philosophy based itself on the idea that thought could only grasp what it itself had created and strove to master the world as a whole by seeing it as self-created. This attempt to establish a universal system on the premises of rationalism foundered on the problem of the thing-in-itself. The problem of the thing-in-itself symbolized the unpassable barrier erected by reification against any vision of the totality (i.e. 'the impossibility of apprehending the whole with the aid of the conceptual framework of rational partial systems and the irra-

[11] HCC p. 100.
[12] HCC p. 7.
[13] HCC pp. 10–11.

tionality of the contents of individual concepts').[14] Contemplative rationalism therefore found itself trapped in an irresoluble antinomy: the ever-fixed gulf between the phenomenal world of necessity and the noumenal world of freedom. In order to transcend this antinomy thought was forced to move from mere contemplation to praxis. Only in this new context would it be possible to conceive a subject of thought which could be theorised as producing existence. This attempt to discover 'an identical subject-object' can be seen foreshadowed in Kant's *Critique of Practical Reason* and in the attempts of Fichte, Schiller and Schelling to overcome the dualism of subject and object through art, where contemplative reason is replaced by an intuitive understanding which is seen as practical. Art is therefore seen as a resolution of the antinomy through its creation of a concrete totality. But in order for this solution to work, creation must be mythologized, and the world aestheticized. The real problem remains unsolved. The true location of the solution to the problem was discovered by Hegel, not in art but in history. 'Only if the true were understood not only as substance, but as subject, only if the subject (consciousness, thought) were both producer and product of the dialectical process, only if as a result the subject moved in a self-created world of which it is the conscious form and only if the world imposed itself upon it in full objectivity, only then can the problem of dialectics and with it the abolition of the antitheses of subject and object, thought and existence, freedom and necessity, be held to be solved.'[15] Hegel was, however, unable to discover the true subject-object of history and was forced to resort to conceptual mythology to arrive at a conclusion. This was not a personal limitation; it was the objective limitation of the bourgeois class outlook. Classical philosophy was paradoxically chasing a philosophy that would mean the end of bourgeois society.[16] For the identical subject-object was the proletariat.

It is only with the appearance of the proletariat that 'social reality can become fully conscious',[17] that man can become conscious of himself as a social being, as the subject-object of the historical process. Such an eventuality had been impossible under feudalism,

[14] HCC p. 116.
[15] HCC p. 142.
[16] see HCC p. 148.
[17] HCC p. 19.

since social relations had been interpreted as natural relations. It was the bourgeois class which had 'socialized' society, but it had performed this task unconsciously. It had pursued its immediate class interests and left the rest to the ruse of reason. The tragedy of the bourgeoisie was that class consciousness was incompatible with class interest (the antinomy between the progressive capitalist socialization of production and the interests of the individual entrepreneur). Bourgeois thought remained trapped, therefore, in the reified contemplative dualism of subject and object, which even Hegel was unable to transcend. The proletariat on the other hand must make history consciously. Since it is the most totally alienated class in capitalist society, it must abolish itself in order to achieve its own liberation, and to liberate itself it must liberate the whole of humanity. To understand itself, it must understand the whole, and to abolish itself, it must move from contemplation to praxis. 'Thus the unity of theory and practice is only the reverse side of the social and historical position of the proletariat, simultaneously subject and object of its own knowledge.'[18]

Ascribed Consciousness

This total standpoint of the proletariat, by its very nature shatters the reified consciousness of capitalism. In place of dualism and the fetishistic methods of science, it posits the unity of thought and being as aspects of a dialectical, concrete totality. In its thought the proletariat conceives reality not as empirical existence but as becoming – the mediation between past and future. In place of the reified concepts of the eternal, the natural, the empirical, it posits the social, the historical, the transitory. In place of a world of impersonal, inhuman facts, it sees the world as a product of the relations between men. Thus once fetishism is overcome, man becomes the measure of all things and history becomes the unceasing overthrow of objective forms.

Of course this total consciousness of the proletariat does not coincide with the actual empirical consciousness of that class. It is an 'ascribed' (*zugerechnet*) consciousness. 'By relating consciousness to the whole of society it becomes possible to infer the thoughts and feelings which men would have in a particular

---

[18] HCC p. 20.

situation if they were *able* to assess both it and the interests arising from it in their impact on immediate action and on the whole structure of society. That is to say, it would be possible to infer the thoughts and feelings appropriate to their objective situation'.[19] This 'ascribed' consciousness of the proletariat manifests itself in the period of revolutionary crisis. As individuals, proletarians remain subject to the reified world of appearance and the contemplative dualism of subject and object. It is only as a class oriented towards praxis that they are able to attain the viewpoint of the totality. Thus the attainment of this 'ascribed' consciousness is in effect synonymous with assuming the leadership of society, since an adequate consciousness is already a practice that alters its object. Lukács cites the young Marx to the effect that, 'it will then be seen that the world has long possessed a dream of things *which it has only to possess in consciousness in order to possess them in reality*'.[20] Economic evolution can only provide the proletariat with the abstract possibility of changing society. In the last resort however, 'the strength of every society is . . . a spiritual strength. And from this we can only be liberated by knowledge'.[21] Hence, the fate of revolution depends upon consciousness.

The status of historical materialism follows on logically from this analysis. It is the 'self-knowledge of capitalist society'.[22] It is the ideological expression of the proletariat's attempt to liberate itself. Its most important function is that of a 'weapon of war', which unmasks capitalist society.[23] The whole idea underlying Marx's *magnum opus* is 'the retranslation of economic objects from things back into processes, into the changing relations between men'.[24] Thus, to call historical materialism a science, at least as the word is usually understood, would be misleading since truth can 'only achieve an "objectivity" relative to the standpoint of the

---

[19] HCC p.51. It can be seen that the conception behind the idea of 'ascribed' consciousness is very closely related to the Weberian theory of ideal types. There is however a significant difference. For while the Weberian ideal type can never manifest itself in its pure form, since it is always overlaid by the complexity of interests in empirical reality, Lukácsian 'ascribed' consciousness appears in its pristine form or not at all.

[20] HCC p. 259. Italics in original.

[21] HCC p. 262.

[22] HCC p. 229.

[23] HCC p. 224.

[24] HCC p. 182.

individual classes'.[25] In effect historical materialism is identical with the 'ascribed' consciousness of the proletariat, and thus it is natural that for Lukács, Marxism is properly defined not by the 'primacy of economic motives in historical explanation' but by 'the viewpoint of the totality'.[26]

2. Nature and Science

In most writing on the nature and development of Marxism as a theory, the Lukács of *History and Class Consciousness* is grouped together with Korsch, Gramsci and other theoretical leftists of the Russian Revolutionary period. In this guise, he like the rest of the group is either praised or condemned for Hegelianism, historicism, humanism, voluntarism, spontaneism or ultra-leftism. At a certain level of theoretical generality, this type of characterization is perfectly appropriate and indeed illuminating. At this level the work of these writers can be seen as no more than individual variations on an invariant theme – the problematic of historicism. What this characterization is forced to ignore however, is precisely what is specific to Lukács's own theory: a problematic which differentiates him scarcely less radically from other theoretical leftists than from orthodox marxism. In Lukács's case this specific problematic is by no means a secondary question of local interest to the historian of ideas. For it has in fact cast a long shadow over the subsequent development of 'western marxism' and has recently permeated the attitudes and activities of radicals and revolutionaries who may never have read a line of Lukács's book and act under the banner of a Marx seen through the eyes of Marcuse, the Frankfurt School, Goldmann, Lefebvre or Debord.

This *differentia specifica* of Lukácsism has passed so naturally into the conceptual vocabulary and thought patterns of marxisant students and intellectuals and has been interiorized so completely into the corpus of western marxism, that it is at first sight difficult to comprehend its foreignness to historical materialism. If this is so, it is because it is part of a problematic much larger than itself: an invariant problematic which has been dominant in bourgeois thought ever since the period of the French Revolution and the

[25] HCC p. 189.
[26] HCC p. 27.

onset of industrial capitalism. It thus possesses all the deceptive obviousness of an ideology which fixates thought, and which in the course of its development and elaboration can only reproduce this fixation in different disguises. Like all such problematics, it constitutes a closed circle of thought, which confiscates from its subjects the possibility of thinking outside it. This problematic may be summed up in the opposition: nature versus science or industry.

Until the last years of the 18th century, the tension between these two poles was barely yet perceived.[27] Nature constituted a central category of Enlightenment thought. The path of human progress was in harmony with nature; only feudal contrivance and religious obscurantism withheld the blessings of nature's unseen hand. The demands of the bourgeoisie were the *natural* rights of man. Once the baleful influence of priests and kings was removed, nature's benevolent dominion would ensure social harmony, material prosperity, justice and peace. Man should refrain from unwarranted interference and allow nature to take her course. For nature and reason were in accord.

It was not until the aftermath of the French Revolution and the onset of industrialization that this unproblematic alliance between reason and nature was shattered, and replaced by an unbridgeable gulf between an ideology of scientistic and industrial progress on the one hand and a denunciation of its impoverishing and

---

[27] Some writers have attempted to read into Rousseau elements of a later romantic critique of reason, in the name of an idealized state of nature. This is a misreading of Rousseau, for whom the state of nature was not a prescription but a critical device. As Kant at least realized, Rousseau's 'writings did not propose indeed that man should go back to the state of nature, but that he should look back on it from the level he has now attained'. Rousseau never counterposed reason to intuition in the manner of the romantics since 'we arrive at the greatest ideas of divinity through reason alone'. (Emile was taught to govern his life by reason.) Nor did Rousseau present an idealized account of the state of nature: 'What progress could mankind achieve, when it was scattered in woods among animals . . .? So long as his existence is solitary, man is merely a stupid and limited animal. . . . It is within society that he acquires his intelligence.' Rousseau's disagreement with the *philosophes* had little or nothing in common with the later romantic critique of the Enlightenment. Both Rousseau and the *philosophes* agreed that it was reason that bore the torch of social betterment. Disagreement centred around whether man's moral progress inevitably accompanied this social betterment. For general accounts of the Enlightenment conception of nature, see Ernst Cassirer, *The Philosophy of the Enlightenment* (1932; tr. F. C. A. Koelln and J. P. Pettegrove, 1951); Peter Gay, *The Enlightenment: an interpretation*, 2 Vols, 1966 and 1969.

dehumanizing consequences on the other. It is impossible here to provide more than an extremely schematic account of the contrasting polarity henceforward contained within the couplet, nature/science-industry. In general terms, proponents of a scientistic-industrial viewpoint stressed man's ability to confront and overcome the unknown with the aid of intellectual weapons fashioned by himself. It was this ability which led to man's growing mastery over his natural environment: an environment which included both his natural surroundings and his own more primitive instincts. Thus history was viewed as the gradual assertion of man's power to reason (exemplified by science) over his animal nature whose blind emotions, baseless fears and dark superstitions testified to his original state. Scientific and technological progress was thus a wholly beneficial process which swept away a world of custom and ignorance by a world of calculation and control. This process would be immeasurably hastened by the application of the methods employed so successfully in the natural sciences to the study of man himself: to human behaviour in all its aspects. For this would make possible the formulation of analytic laws governing human behaviour as universal and as regular in their effect as those governing the physical and biological world. Mathematical manipulation of these laws would lead to the progressive elimination of the random and the arbitrary. Instrumental rationality would govern human affairs and social felicity would be predetermined and planned by exact calibration of utilities.

Seen from the viewpoint of the proponents of the 'natural' pole of the couplet, this account of the world was a panglossian hypocrisy. For, far from bringing man happiness and fulfilment, technological progress wrenched man away from nature and thus divorced him from his own essential being. Machinery, artifice, sophistication progressively turned man's achievements against himself. Men could no longer recognise themselves in the world of their own creation. Society became alienated from itself. For man is not just a machine whose motives and activities can be understood in terms of a model derived from mechanics or biology. Human society is not merely an aggregate of atoms subject to scientific laws. Nor are its members solely governed by rational self-interest. Man is also a passionate, feeling being. He does not merely work and feed himself; he also delights in art and play, and possesses a spirit whose freedom cannot possibly be contained within the narrow limits of natural scientific laws. People are not just cogs in a machine, but human beings who live in a community whose values and activities, when left undisturbed, are at one with the surrounding natural world. The real affinity between man and nature is not that of a being governed by the same soulless laws of science; it is, on the contrary a spiritual affinity with the rhythms and patterns of nature. Man should not merely plunder nature of her resources nor simply confront nature with his reason. For man's relation with nature is an 'organic' one. Nature is not only the source of his life, but also of his imagination, of his ideas of beauty and harmony. A triumphant industrial technology only subdued nature at the expense of violating man himself. Once the bonds uniting man and nature were sundered, man became a rootless, disoriented being whose outward material accomplishments were only attained at the expense of inward spiritual loss.

In one form or another, the attack on industrial technology, natural science and Enlightenment rationalism reflected a bitter rejection of the pretensions of the bourgeoisie. The form that it took varied from country to country. In France and Germany romanticism was born out of the reaction to the French Revolution. For Madame de Staël, Chateaubriand, De Maistre, the Schlegels, Novalis, Arnim, or Brentano reason was henceforth forever tainted by the excesses of the Terror. In place therefore of a 'mechanical' conception of existence, in Schlegel's words, romanticism stood for an 'organic' conception: in place of reason, intuition; in place of criticism, faith; in place of truth, beauty; in place of science, myth and folk-lore; in place of bourgeois values, the medieval world of fixed estates.[28] In England, on the other hand, the first generation of romantics (Wordsworth, Coleridge, Southey, Blake, Hazlitt) rapturously welcomed the French Revolution, and it was left to the Whig Edmund Burke and the political economist Thomas Malthus[29] to lead the tide of reaction against it. In England it was not so much the French

---

[28] For a discussion of romanticism as a European phenomenon, see A. Lovejoy, 'On the discrimination of Romanticisms', *Essays in the History of Ideas*, Baltimore, 1948, and René Wellek, 'The Concept of Romanticism in Literary History', and 'Romanticism Re-examined', *Concepts of Criticism*, Yale, 1963.

[29] Malthus's *Essay on the Principle of Population*, 1798, was originally conceived as an attack on Godwin's *Political Justice*, an anarchist utopia composed in the

Revolution as the visible effects of industrial capitalism justified by a bleakly utilitarian social philosophy that provided the main-spring of romantic protest. The organic ties of human community were being shattered by the triumph of 'industrialism'. Human relations were being replaced by a 'cash nexus'.

The Variations of Invariants

The reverberations of this polarity between nature and science/industry set in motion by the dual impact of the French Revolution and the advent of industrial capitalism have lasted down to the present day. The echoes of this problematic are to be found every-where in the habitual vocabulary of bourgeois thought: traditional-ism/modernism; status/contract; *gemeinschaft/gesellschaft*; *verste-hen/begreifen*; analysis/intuition; the dissociation of sensibility; *pensée sauvage*, etc. For the past 170 years it has remained an invariant problematic of bourgeois thought. Mill's juxtaposition of Bentham and Coleridge could be applied with equal justice to the gulf between Leavis and Snow or Leary and Eysenck.

Since all non-socialist culture and a large part of socialist culture has developed within the confines of this antinomy, the tendency to assimilate one or other of the poles of this couplet to a pro-gressive or reactionary standpoint has been overwhelming. In England, for instance, where the scientistic pole has been domi-nant and in general closely integrated with the viewpoint of the ruling class, the left has not surprisingly tended to endorse the essentially progressive nature of the romantic anti-scientistic tradition. This can clearly be seen in the work of the Leavisite school, and above all in Raymond Williams's book, *Culture and Society*. A simple equation between romanticism and progressive attitudes, however, can only be sustained by ignoring the rabidly racist and élitist character of many of the writings of the later exponents of the tradition: Carlyle's enthusiastic support of

---

Enlightenment tradition. By inserting the problem of population into nature, Malthus severely challenged the optimistic conceptions of nature prevalent in the 18th century. As Talcott Parsons has put it, 'Malthus introduced a very subtle serpent into the harmonious paradise of Locke. The whole theoretical structure threatened to crash.' (Talcott Parsons, *The Structure of Social Action*, Glencoe, 2nd ed. 1961, p. 104.) Henceforth, those who defended ideologies of technological progress, stressed not so much man's essential harmony with nature, as his ability to overcome it.

Governor Eyre's brutal suppression of the Jamaica revolt in 1865–66; Ruskin's advocacy of what amounted to a modified form of slavery as an alternative to 'industrialism'; the obsession with 'blood' and the proto-fascist anti-industrialism of D. H. Lawrence; T. S. Eliot's anti-semitism and flirtation with clerico-fascism, etc. At the same time the more progressive features of Ricardo, Hodgskin, J. S. Mill, Huxley, Spencer, Bradlaugh, Keynes and Russell are ignored or underplayed. The unpalatable fact remains that, depending on the prevailing political climate, romantic anti-capitalism is no less assimilable to right-wing extremism and variants of fascism than it is to socialism (exactly the same is also true in different political contexts of the scientistic-technological tradition).[30] The task which Williams sets out to perform is in fact impossible to accomplish. The Janus-faced character of this romantic tradition cannot be eradicated. The reasons for its ambivalence of political signification are to be found in the very nature of ideological discourse itself. As Althusser has put it, 'unlike a science, an ideology is both theoretically closed and politically supple and adaptable. It bends to the interests of the times, but without any apparent movement, being content to *reflect* the historical changes which it is its mission to assimilate and master by some imperceptible modification of its peculiar internal relations . . . Ideology changes therefore, but imperceptibly, conserving its ideological form; it moves, but with an immobile motion which maintains it *where it is*, in its place and its ideological role'.[31]

But the fact that the categories of ideological discourse are *labile* in their signification, in no sense implies that the polarity nature/science-industry, romanticism/positivism is a simple case of the identity of opposites indifferent in their political meaning. What it does mean is firstly that, because of its looseness of articulation,

---

[30] Writing of Romanticism as a European phenomenon, Eric Hobsbawm comes much nearer to an adequate conception of its political character: 'Whatever its content, it was an extremist creed. Romantic artists or thinkers in the narrower sense are found on the extreme left, like the poet Shelley, on the extreme right, like Chateaubriand and Novalis, leaping from left to right, like Wordsworth, Coleridge and numerous disappointed supporters of the French Revolution, leaping from royalism to the extreme left, like Victor Hugo, but hardly ever among the moderates or whig-liberals in the rationalist centre, which indeed was the stronghold of "classicism". "I have no respect for the Whigs", said the old Tory Wordsworth, "but I have a great deal of the Chartist in me".' (*The Age of Revolution*, 1962, p. 259.)
[31] Louis Althusser, *Reading Capital*, tr. Ben Brewster, London, 1970, p. 142.

a single ideological position is consistent with a variety of possible readings; and secondly that the precise *mélange* of 'progressive' and 'reactionary' sentiment clustered around one pole or the other will vary according to political circumstances. This can clearly be seen in the development of this problematic in the 19th century. In different contexts, Saint Simon could be claimed both as a father of socialism and as the founder of managerial big business ideology. The influence of Comte was extremely reactionary in Europe and in Mexico, where it was employed to legitimate the brutal dictatorship of Porfirio Diaz, but relatively progressive in Brazil, where Comte's slogans appeared on the banners of the republican revolution which abolished slavery, and in England where the leading Positivist E. S. Beesly was the only important intellectual to defend the Commune. A similar ambiguity surrounds the legacy of the German romantic idealist, Max Stirner, who has been claimed both as a father of anarchism and a direct ancestor of Nazism. A large section of the French working class movement could fall under the sway of the romantic anti-technological ideology of Proudhon, while in Germany a significant sector of the socialist movement fell for the positivist ideology of Eugen Dühring. At the end of the 19th century, while socialist working men in Britain avidly read the works of Ruskin, their French contemporaries followed with equal attention the works of Emile Zola (who believed that the novel must become a branch of science through the application of experimental method). The political ambiguity of either pole of the couplet is inherently irreducible.

The Weakness of German Positivism

In Germany, the positivistic pole of the nature/science antinomy remained extremely weak throughout the 19th century. In fact Germany was *par excellence* the country of romantic rancour, and the foremost breeding ground of anti-scientific and anti-rationalist philosophy. Even in the golden years of European positivism between the 1820s and the 1870s, Germany produced no positivistic thinker of major stature. Von Stein, Prince Smith and Dühring could scarcely compare with Comte or Mill. Certainly they presented a thin challenge to a tradition that included Novalis, Schleiermacher, Schelling, Schopenhauer, Nietzsche, and Stefan

Georg. Ultimately, no doubt, this general weakness of German positivism was related to the structural political weakness of the German bourgeoisie and the consequently chequered and half-hearted career of German liberalism.

Philosophically, the peculiarity of the German intellectual tradition was enormously reinforced by the Kantian division of human existence into a phenomenal and a noumenal realm. Man was both a physical body and a spiritual being. Nature, the phenomenal world of appearance, followed unalterable causal laws; as a phenomenal being, man was not only a knowing subject, but also an object wholly under the sway of the laws of nature. But man also possessed another aspect. He participated in a world of spirit and freedom. This moral life was free and self-determined. In this noumenal sphere, man was not subject to causal laws in the physical sense; hence, an understanding of man as a social being could only be achieved through the speculative methods of philosophy.

The effect of this Kantian distinction was to drive a firm wedge between science and ethics, fact and value, subject and object, being and thought, the natural and the social.[32] Thus, while in England and France social thought in the 19th century was dominated by a positivistic tradition which applied to society a general analytic theory derived from the model of natural science, in Germany the Kantian distinction set up a strong and permanent counter-positivist position. Since for the idealist philosopher, all that was significant about man, his social life, his culture, was radically excluded from the phenomenal realm, therefore an analytical atomistic approach to human society was forbidden. Thus, while a transitive mechanical causality was appropriate to the natural sciences, the realm of the human spirit could only be understood by the intuition of wholes. Society, history, art, religion and philosophy were manifestations of this human spirit (*geist*). In this realm the scholar could not ascribe cause, he could only intuit meaning. The effects of this bifurcation were pervasive throughout all branches of the human sciences (*geisteswissenschaften*). It meant that although Germany did experience a positivistic influence, particularly in the 1850s and 1860s, it made

---

[32] For an excellent account of the influence of Kant upon the 19th-century German intellectual tradition, see Parsons op. cit. pp. 473–99.

little lasting impact on official German culture[33] (with the exception of psychology). In the annals of official German culture, the positivistic interlude appears virtually as a void between the dissolution of the Hegelian system and the onset of the neo-Kantian revival.

In the last third of the 19th century, the anti-positivistic bias of German thought reasserted itself more strongly than ever, culminating in an irrationalist *lebensphilosophie* (philosophy of life) which began to exercise a strong influence on younger German intellectuals in the decade before the First World War. The origins of this tendency are to be found in the revival of Kantianism.

The neo-Kantian movement itself was in no sense uniform.[34] In its original and most orthodox manifestations, it remained close to the positivism which it attempted to supersede. The neo-Kantians of the Marburg school were primarily concerned to provide science with a rational epistemology and to combat metaphysics. Like Engels, they firmly restricted the scope of philosophy to logic and epistemology. The effect of their work was to stress a rigorous distinction between science and ethics, fact and value.

The neo-Kantians of the Heidelberg school were much more explicitly anti-positivistic. The chosen battleground of Windelband and Rickert, the most typical representatives of this current, was the status of history, a discipline which had been increasingly claimed by positivism in the middle years of the century. The dominant intellectual influence at Heidelberg was however Wilhelm Dilthey, an unorthodox neo-Kantian who in the later years of his life moved increasingly towards an unorthodox form of neo-Hegelianism.[35] Dilthey began with a position in many respects quite close to Anglo-French positivism. He turned increasingly against these positions in the course of his study of the

---

[33] See W. M. Simon, *European Positivism in the Nineteenth Century*, Cornell 1963, pp. 238–64, for an analysis of the influence of Comte in Germany; and Herbert Marcuse, *Reason and Revolution*, 2nd ed, NY. 1954, pp. 374–89, for a discussion of Lorenz Von Stein.

[34] The best account of the different schools of Neo-Kantianism to be found in English is Lewis White Beck, 'Neo-Kantianism', *Encyclopaedia of Philosophical Sciences*, 1966.

[35] The bulk of Dilthey's writings remain untranslated. A selection of excerpts from his major texts can however be found in H. A. Hodges, *Wilhelm Dilthey*, London, 1944. See also Carl Antoni, *From History to Sociology*, London, 1962; R. G. Collingwood, *The Idea of History*, Oxford, 1946; R. Aron, *Essai sur la théorie de l'histoire dans L'Allemagne contemporaine*, Paris, 1938.

romantic theologian, Schleiermacher. As a result of this work, Dilthey came to the conclusion that genuine historical knowlèdge is an inward experience (*erlebnis*) of its object, whereas scientific knowledge is an attempt to understand (*begreifen*) phenomena which are external. 'Mind understands only what it has created. Nature, the object of natural science, embraces that reality which is produced independently of the activity of the mind.'[36] History is comprehensible because it is essentially composed of 'objectifications' of the mind. These cultural totalities Dilthey called '*Weltanschauungen*' and were ultimately related by him back to three basic variations in an atemporal psychic structure. They were to be interpreted by the historian through a process which Dilthey, following Schleiermacher, termed hermeneutics; this process basically consisted of a projection of self into the other and this projection was ultimately not an intellectual but an imaginative act.

The Emergence of Lebensphilosophie

Dilthey himself retained positivistic residues until the end of his life, but the effect of his work was to give enormous impetus to the romantic anti-scientific and irrationalist philosophical trends which gathered strength in Germany from the beginning of the 20th century. His stress on intuition, as opposed to rationalist analytical modes of cognition, coincided with Bergson's intuitionist vitalism and a parallel intuitionist emphasis on non-empirical descriptive statements to be found in phenomenology. It was this combination of elements, together with the symbolist movement in literature, the diffused influence of Nietzsche and Dostoyevsky and the irrationalist political philosophy of Sorel which constituted the seedbed of *lebensphilosophie*. In particular, the stress on intuition fatally impaired the earlier neo-Kantian restriction of philosophy to the fields of logic and epistemology. It thus enabled the reintroduction of ontology back into philosophy already to be found in the work of Rickert's pupil, Lask, and subsequently to be resurrected on a far more grandiose scale in the works of Scheler and Heidegger.

This pessimistic anti-scientific tendency was also evident in German sociology during the same period. It informed many of

---

[36] Hodges, op. cit. p. 32.

the attitudes of Max Weber, although philosophically he clung to the more orthodox and positivistic variants of neo-Kantianism. It was he who first characterized capitalism as the bearer of a certain mode of scientific rationality. The triumphant progress of rationalization in the West was accompanied by a systematic elimination of magic, ritual and traditional corporate attitudes, and the progressive bureaucratization and standardization of everyday life. His attitude to this process was one of stoical resignation. 'It is horrible to think that the world could one day be filled with nothing but these little cogs, little men clinging to little jobs and striving towards bigger ones . . . This passion for bureaucracy is enough to drive one to despair . . . But what can we oppose to this machinery in order to keep a portion of mankind from this parcelling-out of the soul?'[37]

The full trappings of *lebensphilosophie* are even more apparent in the works of Weber's contemporary, George Simmel, an explicit anti-positivist much closer in spirit to the Heidelberg variant of neo-Kantianism.[38] Following Bergson, Simmel saw life as a perpetual force of creative movement. The opposite of life was form. But life could only become real in forms. The individual experience gave form to contents, and thereby created the objects of external reality. In certain respects, this idea had affinities with Dilthey's conception of culture as an objectification of the mind. But while in Dilthey this process appeared unproblematic, in Simmel it was loaded with tragic implication. The individual produced objects of culture to extend his life and potentialities. To do this, he had both to utilize the sum total of human products (objective spirit) and further to interiorize and reintegrate them into his own stream of life. But this reintegration of subject and object was unattainable. The objective spirit, in the shape of finished forms, became detached from the stream of life and took on its own dynamic, developing thereafter no longer as means but as ends. Thus man became progressively enslaved by his own products.

[37] Cited in J. P. Mayer, *Max Weber and German Politics*, Faber, 1943, pp. 127–8.
[38] Simmel is rather misleadingly known to the English speaking world as a pioneer in the sociology of small groups. His major work, however, was *Philosophie des Geldes* (Philosophy of Money), 1900. Some account of the main themes contained within this book can be found in S. P. Altmann, 'Simmel's Philosophy of Money', *American Journal of Sociology*, 1903; and Kurt Heinz Wolff, *George Simmel*, (ed), 1965.

The basic tendency of Dilthey, Simmel and the Heidelberg school – Windelband, Rickert, Lask – was not merely to maintain the traditional Kantian distinction between the human and natural sciences, but further to affirm that in some way historical knowledge was more real than scientific knowledge, and that hermeneutic intuition was more authentic than causal analysis. The problem that this assertion posed however was how the truth of historical knowledge could be guaranteed. For as Dilthey had stated: 'all thinking in the human sciences is axiological. They select their facts and formulate their questions from the standpoint of value'.[39] Dilthey himself sidestepped the relativistic implications of this statement by his optimistic belief in human progress and his anticipation of the creation of a master science of psychology. The lack of a satisfactory solution to the problem of relativism, however, remained for his followers a crucial unresolved dilemma from which irrationalistic and nihilistic conclusions could be drawn.

It was in these years of mounting reaction against the values incarnated by positivism, that the young Lukács served his intellectual apprenticeship.[40] He studied at Heidelberg, where he was a student of Simmel and a close colleague of Lask and Weber. He was influenced by Dilthey, Husserl, Bergson, Dostoyevsky and the symbolist movement. The themes that preoccupied him were typical of the spiritual flux into which European philosophy had begun to move. His first major work in German, *The Soul and Forms* (1910) raised from a Kantian position the question of the relation of human life to absolute values and posed the conditions under which human life could be 'authentic'. It rejected every form of compromise with everyday life as an evasion. The main effect of the book was to reintroduce Kierkegaard into philosophical discussion and the book has been claimed as a founding moment in modern Existentialism.[41] Between *The Soul and Forms* and his second major work, *The Theory of the Novel* (1916), Lukács devoted himself to a study of Kierkegaard's critique of Hegel. This

[39] Hodges, op. cit. p. 80.

[40] The best accounts of Lukács's early intellectual development are to be found in his autobiographical fragments, *Mein Weg zu Marx*, 1933; his 1962 introduction to *The Theory of the Novel*, and his 1967 introduction to *History and Class Consciousness*; accounts are also to be found in Lucien Goldmann, 'Introduction aux premiers écrits de Georges Lukács,' *Les Temps Modernes*, No. 195, August 1962, and George Lichtheim, *Lukács*, Fontana, 1970.

[41] Goldmann, op. cit.

study was never finished, but the influence of Kierkegaard was strongly apparent in *The Theory of the Novel*, in its depiction of time as a process of 'absolute degradation' – a screen that progressively interposed itself between man and the absolute. *The Theory of the Novel* moves from a Kantian to a Hegelian position, and a dialectical method is employed to contrast the epic of the ancient world where communal values were non-problematic, to forms of the novel (the product of modern individualism) where communal values can no longer be discovered. Whether as a Kantian or a Hegelian however, the dominant influence upon Lukács was that of *geistesgeschichte*, particularly as it had been developed by Dilthey. Writing of this period of his life Lukács stated in 1962, 'I was then in the course of passing from Kant to Hegel, but without in any way changing my relationship to the so-called human sciences; in this respect I remained essentially dependent on the impressions I had formed in my youth from the works of Dilthey, Simmel and Max Weber. *The Theory of the Novel* is essentially a typical product of the tendencies of *geistesgeschichte*.'[42]

Historicism and Social Democracy

It is important to realize that the tradition of historians and philosophers who culminated in the Heidelberg school – the anti-positivist tradition – was predominantly conservative, nationalist and romantic. In origin, the German historicist school was a conscious rebuttal of the French Revolution and the Enlightenment. The Hegelian attempt to fuse reason and history was answered by Ranke's assertion that every age was equal in the sight of God. The theory of natural law, a central weapon of the *philosophes*, was demolished by the historical school of Savigny. The economic liberalism of classical economics was dismissed by List, and later by Schmoller and the historical school of economics as *Smithismus* or *Manchestertum* – not the universally valid analytical laws of economic behaviour, but simply the peculiar manifestation of the English manufacturing bourgeoisie. In its final manifestations, this historicist anti-positivist tradition merged into *lebensphilosophie*. History was seen as a slow process of degradation. Capitalism meant the rule of the rational, the calculating, the bureaucratic mentality. It aroused in the Wilhelmine

[42] Georges Lukács, *The Theory of the Novel*, London 1971, pp. 12–13.

intelligentsia, not humanitarian horror, let alone socialist commitment, but rather a romantic aestheticist contempt. Capitalism increasingly narrowed the space in which an authentic life could be lived. The masses were supine or else driven by irrational passions, the bourgeoisie was complacent and philistine, the junkers were coarse and brutish. The only correct stance to adopt was that of the stoicism of the elect.

It is thus not surprising that Marxists and Social Democrats in the Second International and the German SPD should have had nothing to do with this tendency in German thought. As far as the revisionists possessed affinities with neo-Kantianism, it was not with the Heidelberg variant, but with the more liberal, progressivist and positivist Marburg current (Herman Cohen, Rudolf Stammler, Karl Vorländer). The German Social-Democratic movement absorbed from Marxism a firm belief in the value and beneficence of science. The inextricable alliance between natural science and historical materialism had been given the firm imprimatur of Engels. In the work of semi-official party philosophers like Dietzgen and Kautsky, historical materialism was interpreted as an extension of Darwinist evolutionism applied to human history. When the revisionist debate began, neither side questioned the value of a natural scientific approach. The revisionist use of Kant centred on the Kantian distinctions between science and ethics, fact and value. Neither side seriously doubted that Marxism was an empirical science. What was at stake in the eyes of the revisionists was the contamination of Marxism by a dialectical method which obscured the distinctions between thought and being, fact and value.[43] Orthodox Marxists defended against Kantian epistemology a simple materialist view whereby cognition was an emanation of matter and the objective world existed irrespective of perception. Kantianism was attacked, not for its positivist implications, but for its half-heartedness about science – its doctrine of the thing-in-itself, which Engels had labelled as a species of agnosticism.[44]

The sort of anti-capitalism which Lukács professed in the years

---

[43] On the connections between neo-Kantianism and revisionism, see Peter Gay, *The Dilemma of Democratic Socialism*, NY, 1952; and Karl Korsch, *Marxism and Philosophy*, London, 1970, passim.

[44] Engels, 'Ludwig Feuerbach and the end of Classical German Philosophy', *Selected Works*, Moscow, 1968, pp. 605–6.

before 1917 had nothing in common with this German social-democratic tradition. In his early writings, Lukács evinced a form of distaste for the values of bourgeois civilization similar to that found in the work of other Heidelberg thinkers of the period. Unlike Simmel and Weber, however, he did not combine this stoical pose with an unquestioning support for German imperialism; nor did he share with Dilthey or Thomas Mann a belief in the uniqueness and superiority of German culture. Lukács never accepted the cultural chauvinism of Wilhelmine Germany and could therefore take up no position in the First World War except that of absolute rejection and total despair. Perhaps it was because of the tension between world-sick *lebensphilosophie* and the national democratic aspirations of the Hungarian intelligentsia, which he fully shared, that Lukács could never surrender himself totally to romantic irrationalism. As he later explained his position, it was that of combining an ethical leftism with a right-wing epistemology.[45] While fully sharing the prevailing abhorrence of positivism, he sought to find some secure foothold which would prevent him from falling down the slope which led to the nihilism of Nietzsche. He was engaged in an attempt to discover what he was later to denounce as a 'third way'.[46] His elaboration of a 'tragic vision' in Pascal and Kant, his study of Kierkegaard and his move to Hegel can all be interpreted in this light. His anti-capitalism was not that of an orthodox socialist but that of a solitary romantic individual. Significantly he never felt any affinity with the Second International, and when he made his first serious study of Marx in 1908–1909, he saw him through the eyes of Simmel and Weber.[47] Politically he was much more strongly drawn to anarcho-syndicalism and the cataclysmic anti-capitalist phantasies of Sorel than to Hungarian Social-Democracy.[48] His rejection of capitalism in his

[45] Lukács, *The Theory of the Novel*, p. 22.
[46] Georges Lukács, *Existentialisme ou Marxisme?* Paris, 1948, p. 48.
[47] HCC p. ix.
[48] Lukács states that his interest in Sorel was aroused by Ervin Szabo, 'the spiritual mentor of the Hungarian left-wing opposition in Social Democracy' (HCC p. x). Lukács's distaste for Second International Social-Democracy is comprehensible not only in terms of his philosophical formation, but also in terms of the situation in Hungary before the breakup of the Habsburg empire. As a result of the legal repression of any form of explicitly political proletarian struggle, the Hungarian Social Democratic Party was dominated to an even greater extent than elsewhere by a timid and conservative trade-union leadership, whose power was permanently sustained by an organizational structure designed for industrial rather than political

early years was synonymous with his rejection of everyday life and his search for the authentic. In 1910, he wrote: 'the man who leads an ordinary life never knows where the rivers which carry him along will lead to, since where nothing is ever achieved everything remains possible . . . for men love everything which is hazy and uncertain in life, and adore the soothing monotony of the Grand Perhaps . . . When a miracle occurs then something real is achieved . . . a miracle forces itself into a man's life and makes it into a clear and unambiguous sum of things achieved . . . it strips the soul of all the deceitful veils woven from brilliant moments and vague feelings rich with meaning.'[49]

That 'miracle' occurred in 1917.

3. The Assault on Science

It is now possible to assess more clearly the specific place occupied by *History and Class Consciousness* in the history of Marxist thought. It represents the first major irruption of the romantic anti-scientific tradition of bourgeois thought into Marxist theory. It was not, as has sometimes been supposed, a simple return to a lost tradition of Hegel and the Young Marx, but a recovery of certain themes to be found in them, mediated by the thought of Dilthey, Simmel and the German romantic tradition. Precisely because this romantic anti-scientific tradition was *translated* into Marxism by a philosopher who, alone among his contemporaries in Central Europe, had read and studied *Capital* very deeply, the

purposes (voting for the party leadership was indirect and organized on the basis of shop stewards' conferences representing each craft and trade). The party leadership was deferential towards the government, unimaginative in strategy (especially towards the peasantry) and unflinchingly anti-intellectual. The result was that the discontent of the Hungarian intelligentsia could find no adequate expression within the party, and political education, which in other countries was generally regarded as part of the normal functions of the party, in Hungary was performed by parallel institutions outside it (particularly the Galileo Circle). Szabo came from a middle-class Jewish family (as did so many of the most prominent representatives of the Hungarian revolutionary intelligentsia) and became a Marxist under the influence of Russian exiles in Vienna. In the early 1900's he launched a major attack on the Hungarian SPD for 'timid parliamentarism' and for its establishment of an organizational structure designed to 'perpetuate the rule of a small trade-union oligarchy'. His general platform for the reform of the party was based on a model derived from French anarcho-syndicalism. For an interesting account of the character of the Hungarian socialist movement up to the revolutions of 1918–9, see Rudolf L. Tokes, *Bela Kun and the Hungarian Soviet Republic*, Stanford, 1967, pp. 1–49.

[49] Cited in Lucien Goldmann, *The Hidden God*, London, 1964, p. 39.

work it produced – *History and Class Consciousness* – was an extremely brilliant and persuasive one.

It is true, of course, that a certain relativization of science, dictated by the logic of the historicist problematic, is also to be found in the work of Gramsci and Korsch (who are generally assimilated to Lukács in latter-day discussions of theoretical leftism in the 1920s). But there is nowhere to be found in their work a comparably negative characterization of scientific progress as such. On the contrary, within the limits of their respective epistemological positions, both Korsch and Gramsci emphatically defended the emancipatory power of science and expressly defined Marxism itself as a scientific weapon of the working class. The very last page of Korsch's *Marxism and Philosophy* declares: 'Just as political action is not rendered unnecessary by the economic action of a revolutionary class, so intellectual action is not rendered unnecessary by either political or economic action. On the contrary, it must be carried through to the end in theory and practice, as revolutionary scientific criticism and agitational work before the seizure of state power by the working class, and as scientific organization and ideological dictatorship after the seizure of state power.'[50] Gramsci, for his part, went out of his way to stress the enormous secular importance of modern science and its indissoluble link with the emergence of Marxism itself. 'The rise of the experimental method separates two historical worlds, two epochs, and initiates the process of dissolution of theology and metaphysics and the process of development of modern thought whose consummation is in the philosophy of praxis. Scientific experiment is the first cell of the new method of production, of the new form of active union of man and nature.'[51]

In Lukács's book, by contrast, there is no suggestion of the liberating effects of industrialization and scientific discovery, let alone of Marx's belief that the theory of historical materialism was itself a real and responsible science. Indeed, Lukács actually goes so far as to castigate Engels for his assertion that industry and scientific experiment are forms of 'praxis'. For Lukács, on the contrary, they are 'contemplation at its purest'![52] In fact – and

50 Korsch, op. cit. p. 84.

51 *Selections from the Prison Notebooks of Antonio Gramsci*, ed. and tr. Quintin Hoare and Geoffrey Nowell Smith, London, 1971, p. 446.

52 HCC p. 132.

this is perhaps the strongest evidence of all *against* both Lukács and the whole romantic and post-romantic tradition from which he emerged – Marx himself is *strikingly and totally free from the tension between the two invariant poles of bourgeois social thought and sensibility*. Nowhere in his work is there even the sign of a serious 'temptation' by either romantic anti-industrialism or utilitarian positivism: he had equally scathing contempt for both Proudhon and Bentham. There is no mystique of *either* Nature *or* Industry in his writings. An optimistic and promethean imagery that is a far cry from either the 'felicific calculus' or the 'soul and its forms' permeates his work from start to finish. Moreover, Marx again and again insisted on the historically progressive role of the bourgeoisie and of the enormous material revolution it had wrought with the advent of modern machine industry, whatever the savage exploitation and suffering that had accompanied it in its train. There is a famous tirade against every variety of what is called 'feudal socialism' in the Communist Manifesto.[53] He was unshakeably convinced that his mature work itself represented the revolutionary foundation of a new science. *Capital* opens with the epigraph addressed to 'those readers who zealously seek the truth' and states: 'There is no royal road to science, and only those who do not dread the fatiguing climb of its steep paths have a chance of gaining its luminous summits.'[54] Furthermore, the metaphors of *Capital* are never those of the *Wasteland*: for all its immense brutality and oppression, capitalism was the absolute precondition and material foundation of the classless society of the future. Marx expressed this theme characteristically innumerable times, and nowhere more eloquently than in the famous passage where he declares: 'The ancient conception, in which man always appears (in however narrowly national, religious or political a definition) as the aim of production, seems very much more exalted than the modern world, in which production is the aim of man and wealth the aim of production. In fact, however, when the narrow bourgeois form has been peeled away, what is wealth, if not the universality of needs, productive powers, and so on, of individuals, produced in universal exchange? What, if not the full development of human

[53] Marx Engels, *Selected Works*, op. cit., pp. 53–55. For Marx's view on the Romantic Conception of Nature, see Alfred Schmidt, *Marx's Theory of Nature*, London, 1971.
[54] Karl Marx, *Capital*, Vol. 1, Moscow, 1961, p. 21.

control over the forces of nature – those of his own nature as well as those of so-called "nature"? What, if not the absolute elaboration of his creative dispositions, without any pre-conditions other than antecedent historical evolution which makes the totality of this evolution – i.e. the evolution of all human powers as such, unmeasured by any previously established yardstick – an end in itself?'.[55] Marx, in other words, had completely *superseded* the eternal bourgeois circle of romanticism/positivism by his theory of the proletarian revolution which by expropriating the expropriators would abolish the social formation which had given rise to it and produce a new order, beyond capital and its insuperable contradictions.

This supersession, which gives its ring to the whole *tone* of Marx's work, is completely absent from the version of historical materialism presented in *History and Class Consciousness*. Instead there is a wholly undialectical and unhistorical depiction of capitalism from its outset as a process of social decay and spiritual fragmentation. Capitalist development is not seen as a ruthless dynamism, liberating as well as destroying, but as an enveloping network of metaphysical passivity. Industry and scientific experiment become mere contemplation. There is nowhere any indication in the book that Lukács actually understood what Marx meant by the liberation of the forces of production from the social relations of production. Yet as Colletti has recently written: 'The self-government of the masses presupposes: a high productivity of labour, the possibility of a drastic reduction in the working-day, the progressive combination of intellectual and industrial work in the category of the worker-technician, masses conscious and capable of making society function at a higher historical level. In short, the self-government of the masses, the rule of the proletariat, presupposes the modern *collective worker*. These conditions can only arise on the basis of large-scale industry.'[56] In Lukács's book this dimension is wholly absent. The leap from the realm of necessity to that of freedom is given no material content. There is absolutely no vision of an advanced industrial *socialism*. The proletariat merely dominates that social totality to which it had always ascriptively aspired, and from which commodity fetishism

[55] Karl Marx, *Precapitalist Economic Formations*, tr. Jack Cohen, London, 1964, pp. 84–85.
[56] L. Colletti, 'The Question of Stalin', NLR 61, p. 79.

and reification had hitherto separated it. Therewith all objective forms are dissolved into processes.

The Triumph of Geistesgeschichte

This attack upon the role of science and technology is not simply a residual aberration carried over from Lukács's pre-Marxist past. It forms the *theoretical* core of the whole book and determines all the *political* errors and lacunae which thereafter derive from it. To start with, it is this central theme which accounts for the extraordinarily abstract and ethereal role assigned to the proletariat. Its role is not that of a concrete historical force, but that of a hitherto missing term in a geometrical proof. The proletariat is the *deus ex machina* whose timely appearance resolves the antinomies of *geistesgeschichte*. The problem that the German anti-positivistic school had been unable to resolve was how hermeneutic intuition was to arrive at a degree of objective certainty analogous, or if possible superior, to the analytic method of natural science. If thinking in the human sciences were really 'axiological', how could the spectre of cultural relativism be avoided? The achievement of *History and Class Consciousness* was the formulation of an elegant yet startling solution to this problem: all truth is relative to the standpoint of individual classes; the proletariat is by its essence a universal class; its subjectivity is universal; but a universal subjectivity can only be objective.

The consequence of this solution is that the traditional terms of debate about the nature of natural science are reversed. Science is subjectivized; value (in the case of the proletariat) is objectivized. Far from social-historical knowledge straining to attain a degree of certainty comparable to natural science, the methodology and findings of natural science are demoted to the status of being a particular form of expression of the world vision of the bourgeoisie. Like the rest of the bourgeois conception of the world, natural science is partial; it is a necessarily false consciousness which will be dialectically transcended by the totalizing standpoint of the proletariat, the last and only true claimant to the universal.

Moreover, just as the analytic rationality of modern science is merely a reflection of that capitalist reification which dominates the historical and social world, and hence can produce only 'partial' empirical findings, so conversely the proletariat's 'standpoint of the totality' is integrally valid even when it is incapable of producing *any* partial empirical truths at all. Thus Lukács seriously declares that: 'Let us assume for the sake of argument that recent research had disproved once and for all every one of Marx's individual theses. Even if this were to be proved, every serious "orthodox" Marxist would still be able to accept all such modern findings without reservation and hence dismiss all of Marx's theses *in toto* – without having to renounce his orthodoxy for a single moment . . . Orthodoxy refers exclusively to *method*.'[57] This famous dictum has been widely accepted and repeated on the Left, and indeed is proudly reaffirmed by Lukács in his 1967 introduction to *History and Class Consciousness*.[58] In fact, such a credo would simply be an intellectual suicide for Marxism: what scientific method in history has been able to survive the systematic disproof of every one of its findings? What possible charter could there be for it?

The Simplicity of History

The logical and necessary consequence of Lukács's contempt for those concrete facts which Marx spent so much of his life studying, is that *history* as such plays a purely spectral role in *History and Class Consciousness*. In actual fact, there is very little reference to, or awareness of the real history of either the capitalist mode of production or working-class struggle in the book.[59]

Messianic anti-scientism, indeed, inevitably finds itself in insoluble difficulties once it does attempt to discuss the central

[57] HCC p. 1.

[58] HCC pp. xxv–xxvi.

[59] Writing of the impact on him of Dilthey's *Das Erlebnis und die Dichtung* (Lived Experience and Literary Creation), Lukács later wrote, in his 1962 introduction to *The Theory of the Novel*: 'This new terrain appeared to us then as a mental universe of grandiose syntheses, both in the realm of theory and in the realm of history. We failed to see how little these new methods were based on facts. That great thinkers had achieved solid results, not so much because of this method, but in spite of it, was something that escaped us in our youthful enthusiasm. It became the fashion to start off from a few characteristic traits of a tendency or a period – traits usually grasped in a purely intuitive fashion – then to synthesize general concepts from them, and finally to return deductively to individual phenomena, in the conviction that this amounted to a grandiose view of the totality'. *The Theory of the Novel*, p. 13. This characterization of the hermeneutic method was designed by Lukács to explain his procedure in *The Theory of the Novel*. But it could be applied equally well to the method by which the concept of reification is established in *History and Class Consciousness*.

political and theoretical problems raised by Marx's work. Thus, in order to be squeezed into the straight-jacket that Lukács's philosophical position has prepared for it, historical development is pared down to a simple procession of economic-ideological totalities expressing the life conditions of successive class-subjects. Each class-subject possesses a conception of the world which dominates and totally permeates the historical totality which it inhabits. Moreover, since it is the class subject which bestows meaning upon its historical totality and not the mode of production which assigns social roles through the production process to classes which can transform them by struggle, the role of the economic is reduced to that of a shadowy substratum which only surfaces when called upon to explain the transition from one mode of production to another.

The necessary complexity of any given social formation, which may and usually does amalgamate *a number* of modes of production in a hierarchical set, is annulled from the outset by this imaginary parade. The Russian Revolution, which fused and *combined* a bourgeois and a proletarian revolution because of the intertwined co-existence of feudal and capitalist relations of production in the Tsarist social formation, is simply unthinkable within Lukács's scheme. No less so, of course, is the existence of petty commodity production in Western countries: the role of the peasantry in France is inexplicable within the terms of his book. *The Eighteenth Brumaire* might well never have been written for all its impact on Lukács's theory.

But it is not simply the economic history of modes of production – the 'base' – which is etherealized virtually out of existence by Lukács. The whole complexity of differential political and cultural systems in the *superstructure* is contracted into a few wooden leitmotifs. For Lukács, the thesis that the dominant ideology in any social formation is the ideology of the ruling class is interpreted as the saturation of the social totality by the ideological essence of a pure class subject. But it is important to notice that this domination has virtually no *institutional* apparatus whatever. It is simply 'pure ideology' – the unseen rays of a hidden centre of the universe: commodity fetishism. Thus in *History and Class Consciousness*, Lukács's whole account of bourgeois ideological domination is reduced to the invisible emanations of reification from commodities, which radiate out to bleach the consciousness of the inhabitants of capitalist society. What is strikingly and completely missing in Lukács's account is, of course, the whole institutional superstructure of bourgeois class power: parties, reformist trade unions, newspapers, schools, churches, families are scarcely mentioned. The actual cultural systems which in the real world constitute the foundations of bourgeois hegemony and which form the basis of what Lenin is talking about in *What is to be Done?* when he speaks of the 'massive and natural superiority of means'[60] enjoyed by bourgeois ideology over proletarian ideology, are wholly absent from the disembodied scenario of *History and Class Consciousness*. There, the bourgeoisie maintains its ideological rule, not through the corporeal communication of its political organizations, voluntary associations, press or educational systems but solely through the ghostly discourse of commodities. They alone speak.

Moreover, quite apart from the huge lacuna of any discussion of the *institutions* for the transmission of ruling class ideology in a capitalist society, there is also a drastic and crippling simplification of the nature of the *ideologies* transmitted. For Lukács, the dominant ideology in a social formation will be a pure manifestation of the ideology of the dominant class, and the ideology of the dominant class will be a pure reflection of the life conditions and conception of the world of that class. There are only two classes which can aspire to this form of domination – the bourgeoisie and the proletariat. Internal political or social differentiation within these classes are explained simply as contingent and adventitious failures to achieve full class awareness. The contamination of a pristine class ideological essence by elements derived from the ideologies of other classes is thus an automatic sign of political decline. In fact, Lukács's theory of ideology here is not merely 'schematic', it is incorrect in principle. For there has never existed the type of *pristine* ideological sway which he presupposes, because ideologies are not simply the subjective product of the 'will to power' of different classes: they are *objective* systems determined by the *whole field* of social struggle between contending classes. Thus, as Nicos Poulantzas has written: 'the dominant ideology does not simply reflect the life conditions of the dominant class-subject "pure and simple", but the political relationship in a

60 Lenin, *What is to be Done?* p. 131.

social formation between the dominant and dominated classes'[61] – to which need only be added the *extension* of this relationship into the total field of the *international* class struggle. There are innumerable examples in history of this phenomenon, all of them incompatible with Lukács's theory of class consciousness. Otherwise, what are we to make of the oft-cited incorporation of Jacobinism – a petty-bourgeois ideology of small producers – into the official doctrines of French capitalism? Or the so-called 'socialism' of the Indian big bourgeoisie and its Congress Party today, not to speak of innumerable other ex-colonial countries? Or the impact of imperialist ideology on the ruling establishments of non-capitalist countries?

Hegelian Collapse Theory

In the case of the dominated classes, Lukács's model leads to even more serious results and is mainly responsible for his inconsistent and uncomfortable handling of the notion of 'ascribed' proletarian class consciousness. There is no room in it for conceiving the possibility of a dominated class which does possess a consciousness which is neither 'ascribed', nor that of the ruling class, but is *uneven* and *impure*. Once again history is littered with examples of this impurity in which radical proletarian class instinct is often deeply overlaid by bourgeois ideological veneers of different sorts, or in which genuine proletarian ideology is mixed with contaminations from allied, rather than enemy, classes – peasants or urban petty producers for example. The Proudhonism of the early French working class is an example of the second type: the Lassalleanism of the early German working class, or the Fabianism of the British labour movement down to this day, are examples of the first. In Italy, Gramsci's distinction between 'corporate' and 'hegemonic' ideologies of the proletariat was, of course, precisely designed to grapple with just this problem of the co-existence of different ideological horizons and traditions within the ranks of the exploited. Lukács condemns all this to silence. Indeed, he literally has no other categorical option but to consign structurally 'impure' cases of class consciousness to non-existence. The peasantry or petty-bourgeoisie is thus *always* consigned to the dark void of complete unconsciousness: 'In all decisions crucial for

[61] Nicos Poulantzas, *Pouvoir Politique et Classes Sociales*, Paris, 1968, p. 219.

society its actions will be irrelevant and it will be forced to fight for both sides in turns but always without consciousness. We cannot really speak of class consciousness in the case of these classes (if, indeed, we can even speak of them as classes in the strict Marxist sense of the term) . . . Consciousness and self-interest are mutually incompatible in this instance. Since class consciousness was defined in terms of the problems of ascribing class interests, the failure of their class consciousness to develop in the immediately given historical reality becomes comprehensible philosophically.'[62]

The proletariat itself is necessarily always at one or the other of these extremes. Short of full 'ascribed' consciousness, it is condemned to no consciousness at all. This unconsciousness can only be surpassed by the proletariat as a class breaking through the reified structure of prevailing thought. The question then arises, what determines the proletariat's swing from one to the other of these two all-or-nothing poles in any particular historical case?

The answer is disconcertingly simple. For all its denunciations of the mechanical Marxism of the Second International, Lukács's model itself remains securely trapped within the problematic of the Second International belief in the final, cataclysmic economic collapse of capitalism that will usher in the socialist revolution – the *Zusammenbruch* theory. For the emergence of true proletarian consciousness is mechanically attributed by Lukács to the advent of a full-scale economic crisis. 'The active and practical side of class consciousness, its true essence, can only become visible in its authentic form when the historical process imperiously requires it to come into force, i.e. when an acute crisis in the economy drives it to action. At other times it remains theoretical and latent, corresponding to the latent and permanent crisis of capitalism.'[63] Here all Lukács achieves is a restatement of the old Luxemburgist and anarcho-syndicalist couplet, economism/spontaneism, in a new Hegelian terminology.

In the last two essays of *History and Class Consciousness*, an attempt is made to modify this extremely primitive economist/spontaneist model (which is much poorer than Luxemburg's more sophisticated version of it, from which it is derived) by suddenly

[62] HCC p. 61.
[63] HCC p. 40.

arguing that proletarian class consciousness *normally lags behind* the objective situation and therefore needs the party to bring it up to the mark of revolutionary Marxism. 'The class consciousness of the proletariat does not develop uniformly throughout the whole proletariat, parallel with the objective economic crisis. Large sections of the proletariat remain intellectually under the tutelage of the bourgeoisie; even the severest economic crisis fails to shake them in their attitude. With the result that *the standpoint of the proletariat and its reaction to the crisis is much less violent and intense than is the crisis itself* . . . Proletarian ideology lags behind the economic crisis.'[64] But Lukács is unable to show why the party should necessarily be able to compensate for this lag. In effect, he merely substitutes a mystical belief in the ideological efficacy of the party for that of the proletariat. Thus while the class languishes in the swamp of revisionism and menshevism, the party is assumed to be magically proof against this ideological crisis, and is endowed with the power to recall the class to its true historical vocation. The result is ultimately to exchange an economist spontaneism for an organizational voluntarism. Lukács comes little nearer to authentic Marxism, or to real history, with this shift. In fact, of course, it is often the masses who have to *educate the party*, and not just the party which organizes and guides the masses. The whole trajectory of the Russian Revolution is rich in episodes of this dialectical process. It was not the Bolshevik central committee which overthrew Tsarism in February; who invented the Soviets?

The Spiritualisation of Power

Lukács's conception of proletarian ideology and of the working-class party, moreover, does not merely prevent him from ever providing in *History and Class Consciousness* the elements of that 'concrete analysis of a concrete situation' which Lenin always said was the 'soul of Marxism'. It does not only situate the written book at a great remove from actual history. It also leads to an ultra-idealist form of *politics* proper. For Lukács's conception of class power is so totally confined to an etherealized ideology, that it not merely passes over the whole array of cultural apparatuses whereby the bourgeoisie *exercises* its ideological dominance in capitalist social formations, but it also largely neglects the political

[64] HCC pp. 304–5.

apparatus of capital *par excellence*: the State. There is very little in the main essays of *History and Class Consciousness* on the bourgeois State. Such passages as there are often betray a fundamental inability to comprehend its plain class role. Thus Lukács reproaches the judicial branch of the State apparatus for dispensing an impersonal justice like 'a ticket-machine' – as if it were merely the formal rationality and calculability of this justice which constituted its banefulness, and not the class oppression of its whole substantive content! Apart from this reference and a similar allusion to bureaucracy, there is no discussion of the army or the police. In other words there is no real mention of that State apparatus which Marx and Lenin taught had to be *broken physically* by the working class with material, insurrectionary struggle, to accomplish the socialist revolution. Lukács effectively ignores this crude coercive instrument of capitalist power.

The logical consequence is that he ends by affirming explicitly that the power of the ruling class is ultimately *spiritual* in character, and that therefore the emergence of true proletarian class consciousness is itself tantamount to the overthrow of the bourgeoisie. '*The strength of every society is in the last resort a spiritual strength. From this we can only be liberated by knowledge.*'[65] Lukács adds the logical rider to this axiom: '*To become conscious is synonymous with the possibility of taking over the leadership of society.*'[66] The conclusions are in fact inscribed in his whole initial epistemology. For according to the latter, the proletariat, when it accedes to true class consciousness, becomes the identical subject-object of history, and thereby the first class to acquire an adequate social comprehension of society and history. Because this consciousness is the self-knowledge of reality, and embodies the union of thought and being, the proletariat's very accession to its ascribed class consciousness *de facto* modifies its own class situation. *An adequate consciousness is already a practice which alters its object.* Lukács affirms this candidly idealist thesis black on white: 'An adequate, correct consciousness means a change in its own objects, and in the first instance, in itself.'[67] Thus when the consciousness of the proletariat as a class breaks through the reified laws of political

[65] HCC p. 262.
[66] HCC p. 268.
[67] HCC p. 199.

economy which condemn it to a commodity existence, it *thereby* decisively modifies its life-condition; 'When the worker knows himself as a commodity, his knowledge is practical. *That is to say, this knowledge brings about an objective structural change in the object of knowledge.'*[68]

Indeed, once the epistemological postulate of the 'identical subject-object' is established, it is inevitable that Lukács should have simply cancelled any distinction whatever between objectification and alienation, as he himself was later to admit. For if consciousness is itself a practice which alters its object, a subjective 'interiorization' of the object can not merely modify but *abolish it as an object altogether.* Again, Lukács has the courage to follow through the consequences of this surreal logic. He writes: 'For the proletariat, however, this ability to go beyond the immediate in search of the "remoter" factor means the *transformation of the objective nature of the objects of action.'*[69] Later, he adds that after the victory of the socialist revolution: 'The social significance of the dictatorship of the proletariat, socialization, means that . . . as far as *the proletariat* – regarded as a class – is concerned, *its own labour now ceases to confront it in an autonomous, objectified manner.'*[70] It is thus perfectly natural for Lukács to argue that for the proletariat to become class-conscious is 'synonymous' with the possibility of assuming the leadership of society. If social power is always ultimately spiritual in character, once the proletariat fulfils its vocation as the identical subject-object of history by acquiring an adequate consciousness of capitalist society, it abolishes this society in a final *interiorization* of it. The exact analogy of this procedure with the movement of Hegel's Spirit needs no emphasis. All that it omits is the brute, material struggle for power – strikes, demonstrations, lock-outs, riots, insurrections or civil wars – that is the stuff of terrestrial revolutions.

Marxist Lebensphilosophie

Lukács's basic schema, it should now be evident, is a rigorous form of idealism. Since class consciousness suffices to alter class situation and full class consciousness is equivalent to domination

---

[68] HCC p. 169.
[69] HCC p. 175.
[70] HCC p. 248.

of the social whole, power is ultimately ideological. A ruling class dominates and organizes its social totality by the impregnation of it by its own consciousness. It will be seen that if this syllogism is applied strictly, the Marxist party has no significant role to play in the socialist revolution. Lukács does, however, try to insert the party into his model in the later essays of his book, but the result is often an unhappy compromise between the philosophical millenialism which he was beginning to modify and Leninist theory, with which he was just beginning to become acquainted. Recalling the book in 1967, Lukács was to claim that his idea of 'ascribed class consciousness' was an attempt to make the same distinction as that developed by Lenin in *What is to be Done?* between 'spontaneously emerging trade-union consciousness' and 'socialist class consciousness' which is 'implanted in the workers from outside, i.e. from outside the economic struggle and the sphere of the relations between workers and employers.'[71] This retrospective justification is, however, not a convincing one. The Kautsky-Lenin schema, which stresses that bourgeois intellectuals are by definition the possessors of previous scientific accumulations, and must therefore be the *initial* bearers of Marxist theory 'to' the working class, is doubtless only a partial one (for it omits to stress that the historical preconditions and materials of this theory are the real struggles of the nascent working class itself, without which it would be impossible for historical materialism to have been forged). But it is at least, within its own self-declared limits, close to the historical facts, and moreover possesses the merit of posing sharply the question of what happens to the science of historical materialism when the masses adopt it in a revolutionary party. It thus confronts the central problem of the relation between the party and the masses by allowing for their *respective autonomy*. Lukács's formulations, however, tend to banish the problem altogether by collapsing science into consciousness, and class consciousness into (acute) class situation. Where Lenin had contrasted revolutionary Marxist science with spontaneous trade-unionism, Lukács juxtaposes a Weberian 'ascribed class consciousness' with non-consciousness trapped in the reified world of appearances. The transition from one to the other is presented at times as a moral ascesis, accomplished under the pressure of economic crisis: 'Class consciousness is the

71 HCC pp. xviii–xix.

"ethics" of the proletariat, the unity of its theory and its practice, the point at which the economic necessity of its struggle for liberation changes dialectically into freedom. . . . The moral strength conferred by the correct class consciousness will bear fruit in terms of practical politics.'[72] Here ethics expressly commands politics, in a philosophical moralization of class struggle. The role of the party is thus inevitably a supernumerary one, merely reduplicating the ethical bearing of the class. 'The true strength of the party is moral: it is fed by the trust of the spontaneously revolutionary masses whom economic conditions have forced into revolt.'[73] Thus when, in the later essays which end the book, the problem of the party is re-posed in more Leninist fashion, there is no epistemological basis for it. The parthenogenetic powers of the class are simply displaced onto the party, without there being any real effort to explain why the party is both distinct from the masses and yet a detachment of them, a vanguard which both teaches the masses and learns from them. These positions are formally affirmed in the closing pages of the volume, but there is no theoretical foundation for them within the book.

In effect the subordination of all political analysis in the main essays of *History and Class Consciousness* to the exigencies of a philippic against science render impossible any grasp of the complexity of the relations between party and class. By his refusal to concede that Marxism is not only a revolutionary political ideology, but also a materialist science of social formations, Lukács is disabled from discussing the relationship between science and politics, and hence of thinking problems of political strategy. The theoretical logic of the book, as we have seen, is highly idealist: the thaumaturgical powers of consciousness suffice to overthrow capital. But it would be wrong to think that it is *reformist*. Lukács's subjective revolutionary sincerity was unquestionable, and there are passages in the book – especially, of course, the later sections – where correct formulations about the character of the socialist revolution and other topics can certainly be found.[74] But these are necessarily unintegrated into the total

[72] HCC p. 42.
[73] HCC p. 42.
[74] For example, Lukács fleetingly admits the coexistence and hierarchy of different modes of production in a single social formation (HCC p. 242); once or twice speaks of historical materialism as a tiue science (HCC p. 224); or refers to workers' councils in the context of the dictatorship of the proletariat (HCC p. 80).

pattern of the work. In a sense, it is its very remove from concrete politics that saves it from the consequences of its most perilous arguments. The philosophical theory delineated in it can, by changes in the names of categories, co-exist equally genuinely and enthusiastically in different parts of the book with both Luxemburgist and Leninist political loyalties. There is no Lukácsian politics as such in *History and Class Consciousness*.[75] For the over-riding intention of the book lies elsewhere: its original hope, and ambition, is to arrange a marriage between romantic anti-scientific *lebensphilosophie* and historical materialism.[76]

The Path of Transition

However, having said all this, it is important to remember that Lukács himself characterized *History and Class Consciousness*, not as a Marxist essay, but as a transitional work in which elements of Marxism are blended with a pre-Marxist ideological problematic. This can clearly be perceived in the book itself. For there is a marked difference in quality between the last two essays – written in 1922 – and the rest. Lukács's essay on Luxemburg's critique of the Russian Revolution, despite utopian elements, marks a huge

[75] This point is correctly perceived, if perhaps over-enthusiastically pressed home in Jean-Paul Dollé, 'Du Gauchisme à l'Humanisme Socialiste', *Les Temps Modernes*, January 1966, where it is argued that an identical theoretical problematic could both provide the basis for ultra leftism in the 1920's and a flabby reformism after 1956.

[76] It is significant that only in two passages in the book does Lukács explicitly confront romanticism, in a passing discussion of the romantic conception of nature (pp. 135–40 & footnotes 47–53, pp. 214–5). Here he states that romantics from Schiller, Schlegel and Schelling to Ruskin and Carlyle, through their stress on intuition of the totality (derived from the model of artistic creation) have turned nature into a subjective mood. 'What would seem to be the high point of the interiorization of nature really implies the abandonment of true understanding of it.' (p. 214.) However Lukács's conversion of romantic 'Natural Philosophy' into merely a subjective 'mood' is an oversimplification which vastly exaggerates the irrationalist element in romantic thought. 'Natural Philosophy' was primarily a protest against the narrowness of classical mechanics rather than a rejection of science as such, and did actually result in important scientific discoveries (see Hobsbawm, *Age of Revolution*, pp. 294–6). Moreover, to reduce the romantic critique of science and 'reification' to a shapeless and fuzzy emphasis on intuition, is obviously tendentious. One need only think, in the case of England, of Blake's connection between Newtonianism and 'dark satanic mills', or Carlyle's analysis of the dehumanization of the 'cash nexus' or the link between capitalism and the 'dismal science' in *Past and Present*. This summary handling of early romantic anti-capitalism in *History and Class Consciousness* virtually seems to be designed to cover the author's own affinities with it.

step forward from the idealist abstractions of the preceding essays. For the first time in the book, the necessarily over-determined character of any revolutionary process is grasped. Lukács justly criticizes Luxemburg's exaggeration of the 'purity' of the proletarian character of the Russian Revolution, the consequent faults in her judgment of the critical tactical problems of land, nationalities and the constituent assembly. There is, moreover, an astonishingly perceptive discussion of the political results of the failure of the pre-1914 left inside the SPD to understand the importance of separate organization and their corresponding overestimation of the importance of ideological debate within an organically reformist party: the essentially *episodic* character of the pre-war revisionist-revolutionary debate itself. The main weakness of this essay is Lukács's failure to understand the gravamen of Luxemburg's charge that the Bolshevik leaders had under the duress of the civil war subordinated and devitalized the *Soviets* and Russian working-class institutions, and that this was certain to produce an ulterior degeneration of the USSR if a revolution in the West did not come to its aid. The necessity for autonomous proletarian institutions of political power escaped him. Nevertheless, given this major limitation, the essay is certainly the best appraisal of Luxemburg's critique written in Europe at that time, and is notable for its serene and warm tone at a time when Luxemburg's memory was already coming under sectarian attack.

The final essay on Organization reveals something of the same mixture of recurrent mistakes and very real advances. In a direct analysis of the structure and role of the revolutionary party, Lukács was still unable to provide any adequate theory of internal democracy and collective decision-making processes within it – not surprisingly, since only a firm grasp of the inseparability of these from a correct external relationship to the class could have helped him to produce one, and this was precluded by the terms of his initial philosophical model, as we have seen. However, there is clear acknowledgment now of the existence of a dialectical relationship between party and class, even if this is not theoretically founded – as can be seen by Lukács's solution to the problem of inner-party democracy, which simply proposes mechanical rotation and periodic purges to ward off the dangers of bureaucracy. At the same time, there is still idealist denial of the divisive effects of socio-economic stratifications within the proletariat on its ideological outlook, and hence an inability to see the party's function in overcoming these. But the essay does contain extremely intelligent sections on collective discipline and personal militancy, and an illuminating critique (much superior to the over-rated work of the renegade sociologist Michels) of the structural causes of reformism and passivity among the rank-and-file of the bureaucratized parties of social-democracy. Thus, right at the end of *History and Class Consciousness*, Lukács was clearly struggling to escape from the theoretical impasse in which the main problematic of his earlier philosophy had imprisoned him.

The Viewpoint of Historical Materialism

The success with which Lukács did break out of the historicist idealism of *History and Class Consciousness*, and the real and formidable power of his intelligence, can be seen in the short work which he published a year later – *Lenin*.[77] This remarkable book is in every respect superior to Lukács's earlier work: indeed, it inhabits an entirely different universe. Here, for the first time, were systematized and developed most of the lasting cornerstones of Leninist theory. The Hegelian terminology, the identical subject-object and ascribed class consciousness vanish completely. Hostility to science is no longer present; Marxism itself is conceded proper scientific status. Even the term 'reification' is abandoned (although the notion is still present). A certain confusion between Lenin's distinct concepts of the revolutionary situation and the revolutionary epoch is to be found in the initial chapter of the book; and an underlying unawareness of the significance of his final great struggle against bureaucracy, in the last chapter. But with these two exceptions, the main theses of Lenin's political theory and their *structural inter-connexions* have to this day never been better expounded and clarified than in this brief volume. This is not the place to discuss all its dimensions and insights. But it is necessary to stress that there are at least five or six *absolutely central questions* on which Lukács's *Lenin* represents a radical rupture with his *History and Class Consciousness*.

To begin with, in lieu of the formerly economist and spontaneist conception of a working-class revolution provoked by a straightforward depression and trade crisis, there is a singularly firm and

[77] Georg Lukács, *Lenin*, tr. Nicholas Jacobs, London, 1970.

lucid grasp of the basic Leninist thesis of the *combination* of different modes of production within single social formations and
historical epochs, and of the necessarily *overdetermined* character
of any revolutionary crisis: 'A particular mode of production does
not develop and play a historic role only when the mode superseded
by it has already everywhere completed the social transformations
appropriate to it. The modes of production and the corresponding
social forms and class stratifications which succeed and supersede
one another tend in fact to appear in history much more as *inter-
secting and opposing* forces.'[78] Lukács spells out the consequences
of these intersections very explicitly in reference to revolutionary
upsurges: 'The deeper the crisis, the better the prospects for the
revolution. But also, the deeper the crisis, the more strata of
society it involves, the more varied are the instinctive movements
which criss-cross in it, and the more confused and changeable will
be the relationship of forces between the two classes upon whose
struggle the whole outcome ultimately depends: the bourgeoisie
and the proletariat.'[79]

A Materialist Theory of Reformism

Lukács was thus now able to assimilate Lenin's strategic conception
of the *weakest link* in the ruling order of the class enemy, which had
to be seized and attacked if the working class were to wage its
struggle for emancipation victoriously: 'The need to take into
account all existing tendencies in every concrete situation by no
means implies that all are of equal weight when decisions are
taken. On the contrary, *every situation contains a central problem*
the solution of which determines both the answer to the other
questions raised simultaneously by it and the key to the further
development of all social tendencies in the future.'[80] At the same
time, the party whose function it is to lead the working class in the
socialist revolution is an altogether different entity from the
shadowy demiurge of *History and Class Consciousness*. Instead of a
Manichean alternation between party and class, Lukács now
develops a theory of the party that is authentically close to the
conceptions of Lenin, both in its stress on the need for maximum

[78] *Lenin* p. 45.
[79] *Lenin* p. 28.
[80] *Lenin* p. 84.

internal coherence and discipline and maximum *external* concern for the widest possible alliances of the exploited. Moreover, the party is no longer simply a vanguard that awakens the masses from a slumbering lethargy: it listens to the masses and learns from them, in a permanent dialectic between party and class. 'In no sense is it the party's role to impose any kind of abstract, cleverly devised tactics upon the masses. On the contrary, it must continuously *learn* from their struggle and their conduct of it. But it must remain active while it learns, preparing the next revolutionary undertaking. It must unite the spontaneous discoveries of the masses, which originate in their correct class instincts, with the totality of the revolutionary struggle, and bring them to consciousness.'[81]

Furthermore, Lukács now directly confronts the problem of a working-class consciousness that is *not* revolutionary, but reformist, and in doing so actually provides in some ways a more complex and subtle account of the roots of the phenomenon of reformism than Lenin himself. For, unlike Lenin, he does not confine his explanation simply to trade-unionist spontaneity and a labour aristocracy corrupted by imperialist superprofits. He stresses in addition to these forces, both the objective pressure of the socio-economic differentiation within the working class and – particularly strikingly – the subjective cultural advantages of a labour bureaucracy over its class, due to its relative monopoly of professional knowledge and administrative skills: 'Capitalist development, which began by forcibly levelling differences and uniting the working class, divided as it was by locality, guilds and so on, now creates a new form of division. This not only means that the proletariat no longer confronts the bourgeoisie in united hostility. The danger also arises that those very groups are in a position to exercise a reactionary influence over the whole class whose accession to a petty-bourgeois living standard and occupation of positions in the party or trade-union bureaucracy, and sometimes of municipal office, etc, gives them – despite, or rather because, of their increasingly bourgeois outlook and lack of mature proletarian class consciousness –a superiority in formal education and experience in administration over the rest of the proletariat; in other words, whose influence in proletarian organizations thus tends to obscure

[81] *Lenin* p. 36.

the class-consciousness of all workers and leads them towards a tacit alliance with the bourgeoisie.'[82]

Lukács's Theory of the State

Finally, Lukács in his *Lenin* supersedes his earlier preoccupation with an idealistically conceived 'ideology of reification', unanchored in institutional apparatuses, generally emanating from commodities, and virtually dispensing with the political coercion of the capitalist State itself. He shows in *Lenin*, how, on the contrary, it is precisely the whole *State apparatus* of bourgeois democracy in advanced capitalist countries that disintegrates and disorganizes the working class. 'The pure democracy of bourgeois society, connects the naked and abstract individual directly with the totality of the State, which in this context appears equally abstract. This fundamentally formal character of pure democracy is alone enough to *pulverize bourgeois society politically* – which is not merely an advantage for the bourgeoisie but is precisely the decisive condition of its class rule.'[83] However, the bourgeois State is surrounded by a large number of auxiliary apparatuses which in their own right contribute to and consolidate the class power of capital. The varied actors so prominently absent from *History and Class Consciousness* now step onto the scene: 'Political democracy of this kind is, of course, by no means enough to achieve this end by itself. It is, however, only the political culmination of a social system whose other elements include the ideological separation of economics and politics, the creation of a bureaucratic State apparatus which gives large sections of the petty bourgeoisie a material and moral interest in the stability of the State, a bourgeois party system, press, schools' system, religion and so on. With a more or less conscious division of labour, all these further the aim of preventing the formation of an independent ideology among the oppressed classes of the population which would correspond to their own class interests; of binding the individual members of these classes as single individuals, as mere 'citizens', to an abstract state reigning over and above all classes; *of disorganizing these classes as classes* and pulverizing them into atoms

[82] *Lenin* p. 28.
[83] *Lenin* p. 65.

easily manipulated by the bourgeoisie.'[84] Confronted with this serried institutional array of political domination, there is no longer any question of the working class winning power simply by acceding to its proper consciousness. Whereas Lukács had once asserted that 'the strength of every society is in the last resort a spiritual strength', he now had no doubts that class rule 'rests in the last analysis on force,'[85] and that therefore to *break* the capitalist State, the proletariat must create its own State apparatus, in the form of Soviets: 'Even in 1905, in their earliest and most undeveloped form, the workers' Soviets display this character: *they are an anti-government.*'[86] 'Workers' Soviets as a state apparatus: *that is the state as a weapon in the class struggle of the proletariat.*'[87] Thus here, too, Lukács decisively left behind the idealism of *History and Class Consciousness*: in his *Lenin* there is to be found, on the contrary, a classical expression of the materialist conception of the socialist revolution. This book, published in 1924 just as the tide of the international revolution was ebbing, shows that Lukács could possess an extremely clear and incisive grasp of the concrete, and that had his exceptional gifts been allowed to develop, he might well have emerged as one of the foremost *political* thinkers in the history of the revolutionary movement.

The Retreat from Politics

That this development was cut short must be accounted at once a major intellectual tragedy in Lukács's case, and a significant loss for the European labour movement in this century. For an extremely brief yet fertile period, Lukács was able to participate in the political life of both the Hungarian and German Communist Parties, although with very different perspectives in these two organizations. Under Zinoviev and Bukharin, the Comintern – for all its manipulative centralism – still possessed a certain plurality of factions and internal vitality. Lukács was a prominent and active member of the Landler tendency in the Hungarian Party, which consistently opposed Béla Kun's bureaucratic and

[84] *Lenin* p. 66.
[85] *Lenin* p. 65.
[86] *Lenin* p. 62.
[87] *Lenin* p. 64.

adventurist leadership. After Landler's death, Lukács briefly and ambiguously became General Secretary of the Party in 1928, when he drafted the celebrated Blum Theses which constituted a rejection of the Third Period line. The final *Gleichschaltung* of the Comintern, however, eliminated all diversity or dissent within it: under the notorious doctrine of 'social fascism', every party was ruthlessly purged and subordinated to Stalin. Lukács's theses were ferociously denounced, and he was silenced within the Hungarian Party.

Thus, in 1929, he had to choose between active oppositionism outside the Comintern, or retreat from active politics altogether within it. He opted without hesitation for the latter. The long history of his subsequent literary and philosophical career need not concern us here. It is well-known that after reading Marx's *1844 Manuscripts* in Moscow in the 1930s, he was to substitute the more optimistic concept of 'labour' for that of the 'commodity' as his starting point for historical materialism.[88] He was thereby enabled to abandon his anti-scientific past altogether, and to reinterpret the young Hegel in the light of this new position. Indeed, after the Second World War, Lukács was to write a massive and virulent indictment of the whole German idealist and irrationalist tradition from which he himself had sprung – the

---

[88] The substitution of the concept 'labour' for that of the 'commodity' enabled Lukács to arrive at a more internally consistent humanist interpretation of Marxism than had been possible in *History and Class Consciousness*. An identical subject-object implies a model of development similar to that elaborated by Hegel in the *Phenomenology*: an originally unitary subject becomes alienated from itself in the course of its development, poses its alienated essence in the form of an object, and finally recuperates it to become again an identical subject-object at the end of history. As József Révai pointed out in 1924, however, if the identical subject-object is posited to be the proletariat, then the original subject was not present at the beginning of the historical process, but only produced in the course of history by the development of commodity production. Thus the attempt to conceive the proletariat as the identical subject-object logically breaks down, and Lukács is as guilty of 'conceptual mythology' as Hegel himself. See József Révai, 'A Review of Georg Lukács's "History and Class Consciousness"', *Theoretical Practice*, No. 1, 1971, pp. 28–29. By substituting the concept of labour – the central notion of the *1844 Manuscripts* – Lukács was further enabled to substitute the concept of 'man' for that of the 'proletariat', and thus could arrive at a subject who would be present both at the beginning and at the end of the historical process. Moreover, once labour becomes the central unifying feature of man's development, the liberating as well as alienating role of science and industry can then be clearly perceived. For an illuminating comparison between Lukács's earlier and later philosophical positons, see Ben Brewster, 'Révai and Lukács', *Theoretical Practice*, op. cit. pp. 14–21.

Destruction of Reason.[89] In one sense, no one could have gone further in rejecting anti-scientific romanticism. But at a deeper level, Lukács seems to have re-assumed after 1928 the *structure* of his early *Weltanschauung*, even while repudiating its contents. For, in accommodating himself to Stalinism, Lukács rediscovered the distinctive posture of the tradition which had first formed him; stoical acceptance of the established powers of the external, political world, combined with an internal, aesthetic contempt for them. Indeed, except for a brief interlude in the twenties, Lukács doubtless maintained an attitude of silent, inward reserve and dissociation throughout his life, even when he appeared most closely involved in great political crises. Two examples of this may suffice. During the Hungarian Commune of 1919, Lukács furnished theoretical justification for the self-dissolution of the Communist Party which was later to be regarded as one of its gravest mistakes; he was *de facto* Commissar for Education and fought with the Red Army on the Tisza front. Yet his later comments reveal that Lukács all along probably regarded the Commune as a doomed and misguided affair. Then, during the second great revolutionary explosion in Hungary of this century, Lukács accepted a Cabinet post in the Imre Nagy government of 1956. But once again, he was to indicate afterwards that he did so only by way of formal solidarity: his tacit, private reservations about the Nagy government separated him from any positive conviction or participation in it. These were the two episodes of Lukács's career when he was directly involved in mass revolutionary upsurges: even then he kept an invisible distance from them. Most of his political life, however, was spent in the worst decades of Stalinist stagnation and repression. His attitude to this ruling environment seems to have been a faithful homologue of that of his earliest intellectual mentors. Just as Weber helped to provide an intellectual rationale for the practice and aims of Wilhelmine imperialism, while at the same time despising the coarse junkers and provincial bureaucrats who were its executors, so Lukács was to expound and defend the doctrines of Stalinism – from 'socialist realism' to 'peaceful coexistence' – while concealing an inward contempt for Stalin's scribes and policemen. Stoical

---

[89] Georg Lukács, *Die Zerstörung der Vernunft*, Berlin, 1954. This work is also available in Italian and French translation.

accommodation and secret disdain once again became his ruling code. From the viewpoint of revolutionary Marxism, the aristocratic *point d'honneur* of this outlook does not in either case save it from a humdrum conformism. The principles of socialist militancy are not those of aesthetic *lebensphilosophie*.

4. Science and Class Struggle

But in the capitalist world at least, little serious interest has been taken in Lukács's subsequent political and intellectual development. It is the romantic anti-scientific thematic of *History and Class Consciousness* that has remained the central focus of interest within western Marxism. Lukács's interpretation of the ideological battle between capitalism and socialism as a conflict between formal analytic rationality and the viewpoint of the totality is to be found again and again in the works of later thinkers, among them, Goldmann, Marcuse and Sartre. Moreover, in one form or another, this grandiose idea of an epic combat between methodologies has become an almost inseparable component of the spontaneous ideological baggage carried by radical student movements throughout the advanced capitalist world.

As has been shown, however, the pervasive appeal of this theme is no guarantee of its connection with Marxism. For it rests on a dual misunderstanding of the basic tenets of historical materialism. Historical materialism can theorise the significance of scientific activity as social practice and can formulate the specific social and historical conditions in which new sciences have emerged: but it does not thereby arbitrate their validity or their *scientificity*. To believe otherwise is to conflate the social bearers of a science with its substantive contents; the materialist history of a science with its epistemology. The laws of Newtonian Physics do not, in so far as they are scientific, depend for their scientificity upon the historical destiny of capitalism.[90] Seriously to believe that these 'partial' and 'reified' laws will be transcended by the triumphant totalizing praxis of the proletariat, is to fail to understand that the epistemology of a science is necessarily irreducible

---

[90] This is not to suggest, of course, that the scope and range of a science at a particular time, is not related to its historical condition of production, or that scientific theory at any particular point in time will not be blended with pre-scientific ideological elements generally indistinguishable to contemporaries.

to its historical conditions of production. There never will be a millenium in which the formal analytic procedures of natural sciences will cease to be applied to those objects for which they are the adequate instruments of appropriation. For every science employs a method and a conception of causality specific to the construction of its object.

The problematic area is not that of science but of ideology. For, historically, the opening up of new scientific continents has invariably been accompanied by the growth of philosophies parasitic upon them; philosophies which have wrenched methods and conceptions of causality specific to the construction of a certain scientific object away from their proper context and extended them into regions of knowledge where they may cease to have any adequacy: in other words the creation of scientistic ideologies whose modes of practice are the polar opposite of the sciences in whose names they seek to exercise dominion. Platonism, rationalism and positivism can each be seen as 'imperialistic' attempts to generalize the procedures of particular sciences and to impose them onto terrains of knowledge where they may be both obscurantist and obstructive.[91] The rational kernel of Lukács's long irrationalist crusade against 'science' in *History and Class Consciousness* was, in fact, an instinctive and passionate resistance to exactly this kind of philosophical scientism, which in its positivist form, has invaded wider and wider areas of bourgeois thought in the 19th and 20th centuries.

This project which the author of *History and Class Consciousness* set himself highlights the difficulties encountered by an infant

[91] Of course, such philosophical ideologies can play extremely important progressive roles in certain circumstances. The Platonic tradition, for example, played a crucial part in promoting the scientific revolution of the 17th century. Galileo's statement that 'the book of nature is written in geometrical characters' is explicitly Platonic in inspiration (see Alexandre Koyré, *Metaphysics and Measurement*, London, 1968, pp. 1–43). Similarly it can scarcely be doubted that Hobbes's transference of the Galilean law of uniform motion into the realm of political theory, if ultimately inappropriate, marked an enormous conceptual advance (see C. B. MacPherson, *The Political Theory of Possessive Individualism*, London, 1964, p. 77).

It should not be forgotten that as ideologies, such philosophies were profoundly inflected by class interests. Thus the progressive role of seventeenth and eighteenth century mechanical materialism was closely related to the progressive role of the bourgeoisie during this period. Conversely, the thoroughly reactionary character of positivism in advanced capitalist countries today is a reflection of the overwhelmingly reactionary position of the bourgeoisie in these countries.

science struggling for its autonomy. For it will be besieged, on the one hand, by those who deny its scientificity in the defence of its claim to autonomy, and on the other hand, by those who attempt to annex it to the domain of some pre-existing science – thereby denying its autonomy – in the defence of its claim to scientificity. In the case of historical materialism, these twin dangers are represented by romanticism and positivism. If the Lukács of *History and Class Consciousness* represents Scylla, Kautsky, Bukharin and a whole tradition of positivist Marxism represent Charybdis.

It is above all important for Marxists to realize, firstly that historical materialism is a science and not just a more universal form of consciousness; and secondly, that it is an autonomous science whose criteria of validity and conception of causality are specific to the construction of its object – and therefore cannot simply be borrowed from the methodological procedures of some pre-existing science. Paradoxically, this second point was extremely well put by Gramsci who wrote: 'Every research has its own specific method and constructs its own specific science, and the method has developed and been elaborated together with the development and elaboration of this specific research and science and forms with them a single whole. To think that one can advance the progress of a work of scientific research by applying to it a standard method, chosen because it has given good results in another field of research to which it was naturally suited, is a strange delusion which has little to do with science.'[92]

The scientific object which historical materialism is designed to construct is *history*. Historical materialism is the scientific theory of social formations and their transformation. Marxism is not simply this, however. For it is unified with a political practice, which it both seeks to explain and which in turn is based on it. This political practice is the mass struggle of the proletariat, itself the result of a dialectical relation between the revolutionary party and the working class. This special nexus between historical materialism and class struggle cannot be thought out on the basis of the relationships which govern other physical sciences, for it is dictated by the specificity of its scientific object: the transforma-

---

[92] *Selections from the Prison Notebooks*, op. cit. p. 439. Paradoxically, because at another stage in his career Gramsci hinted that history possessed an experimental structure, of which historical materialism was the moment of hypothesis.

tion of modes of production. It is clear that the relationship of science to politics, 'theory' to 'practice', in historical materialism bears no relation to that of hypothesis/experiment in physical sciences (whose practices anyway will differ among themselves). Is it necessary to say that the Marxist practice of proletarian class struggle, which aims to overthrow the capitalist state and relations of production, is not amenable to regulative models imported from physics and chemistry?

The reason for the dual threat to historical materialism from those of its supporters who in the name of 'scientific Marxism' import procedures derived from scientistic ideologies relating to pre-existing science, and those who reject all science in abhorrence at this prospect, is that the relation between science and politics, theory and practice, remains largely unsolved.[93] The fact of the non-solution of this problem leaves historical materialism prey to the inrush of alien ideologies (some of them, vast and tragic theoretical monuments of misguided ingenuity) which attempt to fill the conceptual void. Marx aimed and claimed to build a science, that would be the theory of the liberation of the working class. *History and Class Consciousness* remains the most powerful monument within the modern socialist tradition to the *difficulty* of this claim and the *novelty* of the task.

---

[93] This does not mean that historical materialism any more than any other science awaits some final post festum theoreticization divorced from the practice of the science itself.

Lukács and Stalinism

Michael Löwy

> We shall tell them that we do your bidding and
> rule in your name . . . That deception will be our
> suffering, for we shall be forced to lie
>
> Dostoyevsky, *The Brothers Karamazov*

From the early nineteen twenties, a process of bureaucratization began in the USSR, in the course of which the Bolshevik Old Guard was gradually replaced by a conservative layer, of which the most competent representative and unchallenged leader was Joseph Stalin. 1926 was one of the decisive moments in this historic turn. It was the year in which Stalin published *Questions of Leninism*, the first explicit formulation of the doctrine of socialism in one country, and Bukharin exhorted the kulaks to 'enrich themselves'. It was the year of the Fifteenth Congress of the CPSU, at which the Left Opposition (Trotsky, Zinoviev, Kamenev) were excluded from the Politburo. Lastly, it was in 1926 that Chiang Kai-shek was elected an 'Honorary Member' of the Praesidium of the Communist International and that the Soviet trade unions formed a joint committee with the right-wing leaders of the English trade unions who had just sabotaged the 1926 General Strike. Using the pretext of stabilization in Europe after the great revolutionary wave of 1917–23, the Stalinist leadership was gradually to replace revolutionary internationalism with a *Realpolitik* based on the State interests of the USSR.

In the 1967 preface to *History and Class Consciousness*, Lukács sums up his response to this transformation in the following terms: 'After 1924 the Third International correctly defined the position of the capitalist world as one of "relative stability". These facts meant that I had to rethink my theoretical position. In the debates of the Russian Party I agreed with Stalin about the necessity for socialism in one country and this shows very clearly the start of a new epoch in my thought.'[1] Indeed a decisive

---

[1] Georg Lukács (1967) in *History and Class Consciousness*, London 1971, pp. xxvii–xxviii.

re-orientation in the life and work of Lukács began in 1926; a profound theoretical and political break with all his former revolutionary ideas, and in particular with *History and Class Consciousness*. In a word, after 1926 his writings are characterized by an identification with Stalinism, albeit with many reservations and qualifications.

Hegel Reinterpreted

Just as Lukács's radicalization had initially been via aesthetics and morals, the new turn first took a cultural and philosophical form, before finding explicit political expression in 1928. In an article written in June 1926, *Art for Art's Sake and Proletarian Poetry*, Lukács criticized the *Tendenzkunst* (politically oriented art) of people like Ernst Toller, the poet and leader of the 1919 Soviet Republic of Bavaria, calling it an 'abstract and romantic Utopianism'. He gave a general warning about Utopian over-estimation in the cultural sphere: initially, the proletarian revolution can only contribute 'very little' to the development of art; cultural changes in the USSR were 'much less rapid than a superficial view might have led one to hope'. This Utopian superficiality 'explains the "disillusionment" with the Russian revolution felt by many of those intellectuals who had hoped it would provide an immediate solution to their own particular problems'.[2] For Lukács, this article represented a 'self-criticism' of his hopes of 1919 that a cultural revolution would appear in the wake of the socialist revolution.[3] His renunciation of the 'Utopia' of a new culture in the USSR meant for Lukács a return to the bourgeois cultural heritage.

Lukács also published in 1926 an article which is rightly acclaimed as one of his most stimulating and profound philosophical works: *Moses Hess and the Problems of Idealist Dialectics*. The essay is usually considered to be a direct extension of the Hegelian Marxism of *History and Class Consciousness*. In fact, the 'interpretation' of Hegel is not the same in the two works: in 1923 Lukács saw in Hegel the category of totality and the dialectic of subject/object; in 1926 he detected before all else the 'realistic'

[2] 'L'Art pour l'Art und proletarische Dichtung' in *Die Tat* 18/3, June 1926, pp. 220–23.
[3] Cf. the remarkable essay by Paul Breines, 'Notes on G. Lukács's "The Old Culture and the New Culture"', *Telos* no. 15, Spring 1970, pp. 16–18.

thinker. He now saw in Hegel's tendency to 'reconcile' himself with reality (e.g. the Prussian State) the proof of his 'grandiose realism' and his 'rejection of all Utopias'. He recognized that Hegel's tendency to stop at the present was politically reactionary, but from the methodological point of view he saw in it the expression of a profound dialectical realism.[4]

The starting-point for the ideological radicalization of the young Lukács in 1908–9 was opposition to Hegel's *Versöhnung* (reconciliation). Now at the end of his revolutionary period Lukács fell back into Hegel's 'reconciliation' with reality. The theme of *Versöhnung* was to reappear in many of Lukács's mature writings and indeed became one of the main axes of his thought.[5] Thirty years later, in a work published in 1958, he quoted a passage from Hegel on the *Bildungsroman* in Classical German Literature, which strikingly pin-pointed his own perspective: 'During his years of apprenticeship the hero is permitted to sow his wild oats; he learns to subordinate his wishes and views to the interests of the society; he then enters that society's hierarchic scheme and finds in it a comfortable niche.' Commenting on this passage, Lukács spoke of the 'youthful dreams' and the 'rebellion' of the heroes of the bourgeois novel, who are broken by the 'pressures of society'; reconciliation is thus 'forced' out of them by social pressures.[6] Described in such a way, is this evolution not similar to Lukács's own, his rebellion crushed at the end of what he was later to consider his 'years of apprenticeship'? Adorno, in a review of this work, stressed with some justification that Lukács's 'forced reconciliation' with the 'socialist' reality of the USSR can be compared with that described by Hegel: it was this reconciliation which 'blocked his road back to the Utopia of his youth'.[7]

In the 'Moses Hess' essay Lukács contrasted Hegel with the

---

[4] Georg Lukács, 'Moses Hess and the Problems of Idealist Dialectics', in *Political Writings 1919–29*, NLB 1972, pp. 181–223.

[5] See, for example, in the recently published Moscow Manuscripts, this remark written in about 1939–40: 'With Hegel, the all-embracing appropriation of reality, and the discovery and revelation of contradiction as its motive force, are inseparable from his particular type of idealism and his particular concept of "reconciliation".' Georg Lukács, *Ecrits de Moscou*, Paris 1974, p. 229. Also Georg Lukács, *Der junge Hegel und die Probleme der kapitalistischen Gesellschaft*, Berlin 1954, ch. 3, sect. 8.

[6] Georg Lukács, *The Meaning of Contemporary Realism*, London 1963, p. 112.

[7] Theodor Adorno, 'Erpresste Versöhnung', 1958, in *Noten zur Literatur*, II, Frankfurt 1965, pp. 186–7.

'revolutionary Utopianism' of Fichte, von Cieszowski and Moses Hess. In his opinion, the principle elaborated by Hegel in the Preface to the *Philosophy of Right* ('The task of Philosophy is to understand *what is*, because *what is*, is Reason') was closer to the materialist conception of history than all the moralistic dreams of Fichteanism. As a consequence, Marx's thought was not to be contrasted with Feuerbach, Hess and the 'left' Hegelians, who constituted what was essentially a neo-Fichtean current: 'methodologically, Marx took over *directly* from Hegel'.[8]

Obviously this argument contains a grain of truth. However, it is extremely one-sided. It leaves out that for Marx 'philosophers have only interpreted the world in different ways; the point is to change it'; and that, therefore, the 'philosophy of practice' of Fichte, von Cieszowski and Hess is *also* a foundation stone for Marxism, a *necessary* step in the evolution of the young Marx after his break with Hegel in 1842–43. The essence of Marx's revolutionary dialectic lies precisely in that it transcended and soared above both the conservative realism of Hegel and the revolutionary (moralistic) utopianism of the Fichtean type. Any attempt to trace Marx's thought back in a one-sided fashion to either of these sources alone produces a conservative, pseudo-realist 'Marxism' or an 'ethical' socialism with no objective basis.

Thus Lukács's essay on Moses Hess lacks balance. It tilts towards 'reconciliation' with reality and lacks even the dialectical revolutionary balance of *History and Class Consciousness*. After an ultra-left, idealist and utopian-revolutionary stage lasting from 1919 to 1921, and a short but monumental climax of revolutionary realism from 1922 to 1924, from 1926 Lukács drew nearer to realism pure and simple and, politically, closer to the non-revolutionary *Realpolitik* of Stalin. His 'Moses Hess' of 1926 had far-reaching political implications: it provided the methodological basis for his support for the Soviet 'Thermidor'.

'Hölderlin's Hyperion'

This hidden, implicit meaning, 'overlooked' by most of the critics, was further confirmed by an essay written in 1935, 'Hölderlin's Hyperion', in which Lukács dealt explicitly with Hegel's attitude to Thermidor itself: 'Hegel comes to terms with the post-

---

[8] 'Moses Hess' in *Political Writings*, op. cit. p. 203.

Thermidorian epoch and the close of the revolutionary period of bourgeois development, and he builds up his philosophy precisely on an understanding of this new turning-point in world history. Hölderlin makes no compromise with the post-Thermidorian reality; he remains faithful to the old revolutionary ideal of renovating "polis" democracy and is broken by a reality which had no place for his ideals, not even on the level of poetry and thought. While Hegel's intellectual accommodation to the post-Thermidorian reality . . . led him into the main current of the ideological development of his class . . . Hölderlin's intransigence ended in a tragic impasse. Unknown and unmourned, he fell like a solitary poetic Leonidas for the ideals of the Jacobin period at the Thermopylae of invading Thermidorianism. . . . The world-historical significance of Hegel's accommodation consists precisely in the fact that he grasped . . . the revolutionary development of the bourgeoisie as a unitary process, one in which the revolutionary Terror as well as Thermidor and Napoleon were necessary phases. The heroic period of the revolutionary bourgeoisie becomes in Hegel . . . something irretrievably past, but a past which was absolutely necessary for the emergence of the unheroic phase of the present considered to be progressive.'[9]

The significance of these remarks in relation to the USSR in 1935 is obvious. One has only to add that in February 1935 Trotsky had just published an essay in which, for the first time he used the term 'Thermidor' to characterize the evolution of the USSR since 1924.[10] Clearly, the passages quoted above are Lukács's reply to Trotsky, that intransigent Leonidas, tragic and solitary, who rejected Thermidor and was forced into an impasse. . . . Lukács, on the other hand, like Hegel, accepts the end of the revolutionary period and builds his philosophy on an understanding of the new turn in world history.[11] It can be noted in passing, however, that Lukács appears to accept implicitly Trotsky's characterization of Stalin's regime as Thermidorian.

[9] Georg Lukács, 'Hölderlin's Hyperion', in *Goethe and His Age*, London 1968, pp. 137–9.
[10] Leon Trotsky, *The Workers' State and the Question of Thermidor and Bonapartism*, London 1968.
[11] Cf. L. Stern, 'Lukács: An Intellectual Portrait', in *Dissent*, Spring 1958, p. 172; also the remarkable article on Lukács by Lucien Goldmann in the *Encyclopaedia Universalis*, Paris 1971.

'Hölderlin's Hyperion' is undoubtedly one of the most subtle and intelligent attempts to justify Stalinism as a 'necessary phase', 'prosaic' yet with a 'progressive character', in the revolutionary development of the proletariat seen as a unified whole. There is a certain 'rational kernel' in this argument – which was probably secretly held by many intellectuals and militants who had more or less rallied to Stalinism – but the events of the following years (the Moscow Trials, the German-Soviet Pact, etc.) were to demonstrate, even to Lukács, that this process was not exactly 'unified'. What Lukács failed to understand was that the Stalinist Thermidor was much more harmful for the proletarian revolution than the French Thermidor had been for the bourgeois revolution. The fundamental reason for this, as Lukács had earlier emphasized in *History and Class Consciousness*, was that, unlike the bourgeois revolution, the socialist revolution is not a blind, automatic process, but the conscious transformation of society by the workers themselves.[12]

Lukács's turn assumed a direct political form in 1928 with the 'Blum Theses'. Using the pseudonym 'Blum', Lukács drew up these draft theses for the Second Congress of the Hungarian Communist Party. Some writers attribute the political positions of this text to the influence of Bukharin or Otto Bauer.[13] In our opinion, all that lies behind them is an application to Hungary of the right turn of the Comintern; Lukács was only following the 'general line' of 1924–27. Hungary's tardiness stemmed from the unique precedent of the Béla Kun Republic, which made it difficult for the Communist Party to draw up a programme which retreated from the gains of 1919, i.e. from the socialist revolution. It was Lukács's misfortune that these Theses were to be the last echo of the right turn, coming as they did at the very beginning of the International's new 'left' turn.

The central argument of the 'Blum Theses' is that the aim of the Hungarian CP should no longer be the re-establishment of a Soviet Republic, but rather, simply, a 'democratic dictatorship of

[12] Cf. also Trotsky, op. cit. p. 57: 'In contrast to capitalism, socialism is not built automatically, but consciously. The march towards socialism cannot be separated from a state power wishing for socialism . . .' The anti-Stalinist Lukács of later years seems to have a more lucid and less vindicatory view than in 1935 as we shall see.

[13] G. Lichtheim, *Lukács*, London 1971, pp. 74–5; Y. Bourdet, *Figures de Lukács*, Paris 1972, pp. 92–3.

the proletariat and peasantry', whose 'immediate concrete content . . . does not go beyond bourgeois society'. The point was to replace the semi-fascist régime in Hungary by a bourgeois democracy, in which 'the bourgeois class . . . although it maintains its economic exploitation . . . has ceded at least part of its power to the broad masses of the workers'. Lukács thus gives the Hungarian CP the task of leading 'the true struggle for democratic reforms' and fighting the 'nihilism' prevalent among workers in relation to bourgeois democracy.[14]

We have purposely chosen the most 'right-wing' formulations from Lukács's text, by-passing some more 'leftish' passages which were no more than verbal concessions. The 'Blum Theses' as a whole were both a continuation of the line of the years 1924–27 and an augury of the Popular Front strategy of 1934–38. But they came both too late and too early: they ran totally counter to the ultra-sectarian turn of the Third Period (1926–33) which had just begun. As a result, Lukács was immediately given a formidable thrashing in the form of an 'Open Letter from the Executive Committee of the Communist International to the Members of the Hungarian Communist Party', which accused the 'liquidation-ist theses of comrade Blum' of having been written from the point of view of social-democracy, and of wanting to 'fight fascism on the battleground of bourgeois democracy'.[15]

Self-Criticism and Self-Justification

The Hungarian Communist Party continued to discuss the 'Blum Theses' throughout 1929, but after the intervention of the Executive Committee of the International, it was obvious that Lukács had lost the day. The Béla Kun faction rejected the Theses as totally opportunist, and even Lukács's faction (the old Landler tendency) was somewhat lukewarm.[16] Fearing he would be expelled from the Party, in 1929 Lukács published a self-criticism, which emphasized the 'opportunist, right-wing' character of his Theses. As Lukács later acknowledged on various occasions, this

[14] Georg Lukács, 'Blum Theses' (1928) in *Political Writing*, op. cit. pp. 243, 248, 250.

[15] 'Offener Brief des Exekutivkommittees der Kommunistischen Internationale an die Mitglieder der Kommunistischen Partei Ungarns' (1928) in Peter Ludz, *Georg Lukács, Schriften zur Ideologie und Politik*, Neuwied 1967, pp. 733–4.

[16] Lukács, 'Preface' (1967), op. cit. p. xxx.

self-criticism was totally *hypocritical*; in other words, he continued to be deeply and intrinsically convinced of the correctness of the 'Blum Theses', although publicly rejecting them with all the usual ritual attached to this sort of operation.

Why make such an unconditional capitulation? Because of a 'legitimate desire to stay alive', as certain critics suggest?[17] This does not seem a good explanation: in the USSR of 1929, Lukács ran no risks and nobody would have prevented him from going to Germany (as, incidentally, he did in 1931). The justification given by Lukács later on, in 1967, is more plausible: 'I was indeed firmly convinced that I was in the right, but I knew also – e.g. from the fate that had befallen Karl Korsch – that to be expelled from the Party meant that it would no longer be possible to participate actively in the struggle against Fascism. I wrote my self-criticism as an "entry ticket" to such activity.'[18] The trouble with this argument is that in 1929 the Communist Parties were far from leading any effective struggle against fascism. This was the time of the appearance of the infamous Stalinist doctrine which defined social democracy as 'social fascism' and which, obstinately rejecting the anti-fascist United Front of the workers' parties, proclaimed barely a year before Hitler's triumph, that 'the main blow should be aimed at the German Social-Democratic Party'.

Lukács obviously totally disagreed with this catrastrophic strategy. In 1967 he recalled that Stalin's theory of social democracy in 1928 as 'fascism's twin brother' had 'deeply repelled' him.[19] So why capitulation, self-criticism and passive acceptance of the Comintern's line? In our opinion, the evidence in Victor Serge's *Memoirs* provides some of the elements of an answer to this question, by illustrating Lukács's state of mind at that time: '"Above all", Georgy Lukács told me, as we roamed in the evening beneath the grey spires of the Votive Church, "don't be silly and get yourself deported for nothing, just for the pleasure of voting defiantly. Believe me, insults are not very important to us. Marxist revolutionaries need patience and courage; they do not need pride. The times are bad, and we are at a dark cross-roads. Let us reserve our strength: history will summon us in its time."'[20]

[17] Bourdet, op. cit. p. 170.
[18] Lukács, 'Preface' (1967), op. cit. p. xxx.
[19] Lukács, 'Preface' (1967), op. cit. p. xxviii.
[20] V. Serge, *Memoirs of a Revolutionary*, Oxford 1963, pp. 191–2.

Serge ascribes this conversation to 'Vienna, in or about 1926'. It may seem presumptuous of us to wish to correct Victor Serge's memoirs, but it seems much more likely that these words were spoken by Lukács in Moscow in 1929. First, no one was being deported in 1926 and, as Serge was in Vienna, it is hard to see how the Soviet government could have deported him to Russia. On the other hand, in 1929 Serge was one of the last oppositionists remaining in Moscow, under constant threat of deportation. Lukács's reference to the revolutionary lack of pride is incomprehensible in 1926; in 1929, at the time of his self-criticism, it is an accurate reflection of his attitude. Similarly, the expression 'the times are bad, and we are at a dark crossroads' conveys precisely Lukács's dilemma when faced with the sectarian turn of the Third Period. The (relative) complicity with Victor Serge which emerges from the conversation can also be understood in the light of the situation in 1929; to a certain extent, Lukács shared the criticisms which the Left Opposition (to which Serge belonged) made of the line of 'social-fascism'. But, unlike Serge, he did not dare lead the frontal attack within the Comintern. He was 'reserving his strength', hoping that 'history would summon him in its time'.

In other words, Lukács saw the 'left' turn of the Third Period as an isolated phenomenon, a temporary aberration, and he was deeply convinced that, sooner or later, the Comintern would return to a more realistic position, close to the one he was defending in the 'Blum Theses'. While he was waiting for this new turn, which would give first priority to the fight against fascism and so allow him to play an active role, he sacrificed his pride, through a self-imposed 'slight humiliation', the self-criticism of 1929. Lukács's forecast was not entirely incorrect: what he did not foresee was that the turn would only come when it was too late, after Hitler's victory and the establishment of fascism in the heart of Europe.

Lukács's Own Line

The 'Blum Theses' represent the fruition of a tortuous intellectual pilgrimage. They are the culmination of Lukács's political development and the ideological foundation for his intellectual output after 1928. Shocked by his failure, in 1929 Lukács was to abandon the sphere of political theory for the more 'neutral' and less controversial world of aesthetics and culture. However, as he emphasized in 1967, the basic positions of the 'Blum Theses' 'determined from then on all my theoretical and practical activities'. As further proof of this assertion, Lukács, with a certain irony, quotes the ex-pupil who became his main Stalinist critic, Joseph Révai. The latter wrote in 1950: 'Everyone familiar with the history of the Hungarian Communist Party knows that the *literary* views held by Comrade Lukács between 1945 and 1949 belong together with *political* views that he had formulated much earlier, in the context of political trends in Hungary and of the strategy of the Communist Party at the end of the twenties.'[21]

In fact, this applies not just to the period 1945–49, but, as Lukács himself suggests, to the *whole* of his literary and aesthetic output. Even in the Third Period he defended, with the necessary terminological precautions, the (bourgeois) cultural heritage against the 'proletarian literature' of writers in the German CP (such as Ernst Ottwalt and Willi Bredel).[22] But it was above all after the 'right' turn of the Comintern in 1934 that Lukács could freely express his literary theories. As Isaac Deutscher emphasizes : 'He elevated the Popular Front from the level of tactics to that of ideology; he projected its principle into philosophy, literary history and aesthetic criticism.'

Nothing illustrates this tendency more than Lukács's attitude respectively to Thomas Mann and Bertholt Brecht. For him, Mann represented rationalism, 'patrician dignity' and the respectability of the bourgeois tradition, as opposed to Nazism. Lukács's attempts to forge an ideological united front with Mann were the cultural equivalent of the Comintern's tactic of political coalitions with the non-fascist bourgeoisie (which entailed the renunciation

[21] Lukács, 'Preface' (1967), op. cit. p. xxx, and J. Révai, *Literarische Studien*, Berlin 1956, p. 235.

[22] Georg Lukács, 'Reportage oder Gestaltung', 'Kritische Bemerkungen anlässlich des Romans von Ottwalt' and 'Aus der Not eine Tugend' in *Die Linkskurve*, 1932. Nevertheless, this defence of the cultural heritage of the past, of Balzac and Goethe, against the sectarian divagations of Third Period neo-proletkult, did of course have a justifiable side to it; it was, moreover, related to the wing of the KPD that had most reservations about the Stalinist doctrine of 'social-fascism': Heinz Neumann and Willi Münzenberg. In this connection, see Helga Gallas, *Marxistische Literaturtheorie*, Neuwied 1971, p. 60. To a certain extent, this position of Lukács with respect to traditional culture had affinities with the theses defended by Trotsky in *Literature and Revolution*, when the latter was polemicizing against the Russian partisans of Proletkult.

of any class position). Brecht, on the other hand, was rejected outright because: 'Brecht's utter irreverence for the "bourgeois man", his provocatively plebeian sympathies, his extreme artistic unconventionality – so many dialectical counterpoints to Mann's outlook – implicitly conflicted with the mood of the Popular Front and were alien to Lukács.'[23]

We can now see why Lukács enjoys with some justification the reputation of an 'internal opponent' of Stalinism. Pure Stalinism implied uncritical and unconditional compliance with every twist and turn of the leadership and its international agencies. But Lukács did not automatically follow the 'general line' dictated by Moscow. *He had his own line*, which sometimes coincided with and sometimes clashed with the 'Centre'. While he accepted the fundamental premises of Stalinist politics (socialism in one country, the abandonment of revolutionary internationalism), Lukács was not a blind follower: whatever the circumstances, he refused to give up his own special popular-frontist ideology.

Therefore it is not surprising that Lukács should have been a figure of some standing in the political/cultural establishment of the official Communist movement in the years 1934–38 and 1944–48, while being in 'disgrace' in 1929–30, 1941 and 1949–50. It is no accident that, in the explicit criticisms he made of Stalinism after 1956, Lukács denounced in particular the aberrations of the Third Period, the theory of Social-Fascism and the 'grotesque' policy of the Comintern between 1939 and 1941 – when the struggle against Nazism and Fascism was simply swept under the carpet and replaced by a struggle against the Western democracies, accused of being instigators of the war.[24] What Lukács could not accept was Stalinist policy in the so-called 'left' periods, which considered bourgeois democracy (or social-democracy) to be the prime enemy rather than fascism; any implicit or open compromise with fascism was profoundly repugnant to him. More generally speaking, it might be said that Lukács was in opposition whenever Stalinism was in sharp conflict with Western (bourgeois) democracy and culture; which is why he was criticized as a right-

[23] Isaac Deutscher, 'Lukács as a Critic of Thomas Mann' in *Marxism in our Time*, London 1972, pp. 291 and 292.

[24] Cf. Lukács, 'Preface' (1967), op. cit. p. xxviii, and 'The Twin Crises', in NLR 60, 1970, pp. 39–40.

opportunist by the Comintern and the Hungarian CP in 1928–30 and why he was arrested in Moscow in 1941.

Lukács's Arrest

This arrest merits some comment. Lukács was held for a month or so and it appears that he was accused of having been a 'Trotskyist agent' since the beginning of the twenties.[25] According to Lukács's later reminiscences to his students in Budapest, he was ordered by the NKVD to write his political autobiography. Such a document usually served as a basis for police interrogation of prisoners, which is what happened in his case. In the Lukács Archive in Budapest, there is a three-page political autobiography in German, covering a period up to April 1941. More than likely this is a copy of a document given to the NKVD by Lukács. The text contains some detailed information about his life as a Communist militant, but includes a bizarre anomaly: there is absolutely no mention of what Lukács always presented as the central axis of his political activity and the reason why he remained loyal to the USSR and the official Communist movement – the struggle against fascism. The very words 'fascism' and 'Nazism' are nowhere to be found in the document, and there is only one fleeting, neutral reference to 'Hitler's rise to power' in 1933. The only possible explanation is that this text was written between April and 22 June 1941 (when the Nazis invaded Russia); i.e. during the time of the Molotov-Ribbentrop Pact and German-Soviet 'friendship'. If this is the case, Lukács may well have been arrested because he was considered a potential opponent of Stalin on the question of Nazi Germany – as, in fact, he was, although he took care to hide the fact in his autobiography for the NKVD – and he was released shortly after the German invasion (apparently after Dimitrov had made strong representations on his behalf), when his intellectual services to anti-fascism became useful once more.[26]

Lukács again found himself 'in opposition' in 1949–51, at the peak of the Cold War, and was denounced in Hungary (by Rudas, Révai, Horváth, etc.) as a 'revisionist', 'objectively aiding imperialism', etc. *Pravda* joined in the offensive with a violent attack by

[25] Cf. István Mészáros, *Lukács's Concept of Dialectics*, London 1971, p. 142.

[26] Evidence on this point is, however, contradictory: cf. Julius Hay, *Geboren 1900*, 1971, pp. 277–8.

Fadyeev and, for a time, Lukács believed he was in danger of being re-arrested. [27] This gives us a further insight into the spurious and profoundly insincere nature of his two most notorious self-criticisms of 1929 and 1949 – both, incidentally, rejected by his Stalinist censors as incomplete and unsatisfactory. For Lukács's political and intellectual career from 1928 onwards was coherent: it was a consistent attempt to 'reconcile' Stalinism with bourgeois-democratic culture.

Explaining the Turn

How can Lukács's great turn in 1926–28 and the break from his revolutionary past be explained? Running through his autobiographical writings and interviews of the last few years there is a recurrent theme: 'it was already clear by the nineteen twenties . . . that those very intense hopes with which we followed the Russian Revolution from 1917 on were not to be fulfilled: the wave of world revolution, in which we placed our confidence, did not come to pass.' [28] In 1919 Lukács had fostered a grand messianic vision of an international proletarian revolution which would be the dawn of a new world, the renaissance of humanist culture and the beginning of the age of freedom. This fervent hope runs through all his writings until 1924, albeit in a more subdued and realistic form. Lukács saw the revolutionary proletariat as the inheritor of all the best traditions of classical philosophy, rationalist humanism and revolutionary democracy, which had been betrayed, flouted and abandoned by the modern bourgeoisie. The new society and culture founded by the world-wide socialist revolution would be the dialectical *Aufhebung*, the conservation/negation/transcendence, of this political and cultural heritage.

The ebbing of the revolutionary tide, and the internal changes in the USSR after 1924, caused a profound and distressing disillusionment in Lukács, as in many intellectuals of that era. He refused to return to the fold of the bourgeoisie (as some of those 'disillusioned' intellectuals were to do); his support for the workers' movement was irrevocable. On the other hand, he thought the Left Opposition utopian and unrealistic; a return to the revolutionary principles of 1917–23 seemed impossible. What was he to

---

[27] Cf. Mészáros, op. cit. pp. 146–7. This was the time of Rajk's trial and execution.
[28] Lukács, 'The Twin Crises', NLR 60, op. cit. p. 37.

do? Confronted with the frustration of his great hopes in a new socialist world, the dialectical transcendence of bourgeois humanism, Lukács fell back on a less ambitious and more 'realistic' project: the reconciliation of bourgeois-democratic culture and the Communist movement. Because his ideas were too closely linked to the prospect of the imminent world revolution, he was left ideologically disarmed when faced with the relative stabilization of capitalism. Disoriented by the disappearance of the revolutionary upsurge, Lukács clung onto the only two pieces of 'solid' evidence which seemed to him to remain: the USSR and traditional culture. Seeing that the new, transcendent synthesis had failed, he would at least attempt a mediation, a compromise and an alliance between these two different worlds. Lukács's post-1926 writings, despite their intelligence, their undeniable interest and their theoretical depth, are rather like the glowing embers of a dying furnace.

Much later, in 1956, in common with many cadres, intellectuals and ordinary militants in the Communist movement, Lukács entered a period of open crisis, a period of questioning and criticism of Stalinism. Explicit criticism, let it be stressed, since veiled objections to Stalinist bureaucracy, expressed in 'Aesopian language', were to be found in some of Lukács's works written well before the Twentieth Congress. For example, in a 1952 essay Leo Kofler, using the pseudonym 'Jules Devérité', pointed out Lukács's criticism of Stalinist bureaucratic optimism in the essay 'People's Tribunal or Bureaucrat?', itself written in 1940.[29] However, in this particular text, not only is Lukács's criticism of bureaucracy in the USSR made in the name of Stalin himself (he claims that 'the elimination of bureaucracy in the USSR is part of the Stalinist programme of the liquidation of the ideological and economic remains of capitalist society'),[30] but, above all, his criticism remains very sketchy and superficial, confining itself to a denunciation of the rhetorical exhortations and feigned optimism of the bureaucrats and their literary spokesmen.

[29] Cf. L. Kofler, 'Das Wesen und die Rolle der Stalinistischen Bürokratie'(1952) in *Stalinismus und Bürokratie*, 1970, p. 63. In a 1969 text Lukács himself welcomed Kofler's essay as objective proof of his opposition to Stalinism before 1953. Cf. Georg Lukács, 'Lénine – Avant-propos', in *Nouvelles Etudes Hongroises*, Budapest 1973, p. 94.

[30] Georg Lukács, 'Volkstribun oder Bürokrat?' in *Probleme des Realismus* I, Werke Band 4, 1964. It might be argued that this is a precaution in 'Aesopian' style.

Settling Old Scores with Stalin

In 1956, Lukács began to 'settle old scores' with Stalinism – and, to a certain extent, with his own Stalinism. Of course, he welcomed the Twentieth Congress of the CPSU with enthusiasm, and was to consider it a sort of re-run of the Seventh Comintern Congress (1935), which had heralded the turn to the Popular Front.[31] His participation in the ephemeral government of Imre Nagy in 1956, as Minister for Culture, is well known. However, Lukács's post-1956 anti-Stalinism was of a particular type – both incomplete and (to use a convenient label) 'rightist'.

It was incomplete, in that Lukács refused to question some of the basic elements of Stalinist policy, such as socialism in one country; because he only condemned the Moscow Trials as 'politically superfluous, since the Opposition had already lost all power', thus implicitly accepting the 'correctness' of Stalin's policies, at the time.[32] A particularly striking example is the 1957 Preface to *The Meaning of Contemporary Realism*, in which Lukács ventures to compare Stalin's mistakes with those of Rosa Luxemburg.[33]

It was 'rightist', in that Lukács inclined towards defining Stalinism as essentially a 'leftist' deviation, a 'sectarian subject-ivism'.[34] From the time of his first anti-Stalinist text, the 28 June 1956 speech at the Political Academy of the Hungarian (Communist) Workers' Party, he put forward the argument that the main mistake of the past had been excessive loyalty to the 'truths of 1917'! According to Lukács, 'innumerable errors in strategy

---

[31] 'If we appear weak, if those forces wishing to show Leninism as Stalinism back to front are to succeed, then the Twentieth Congress will get bogged down, just as in the thirties the grand initiative of the Seventh Comintern Congress did not bear the fruits one might justifiably have expected in 1935' – Lukács, 'Discorso al dibattito filosofico del Circolo Petöfi' (15 June 1956), *Marxismo e Politica Culturale*, Milan 1972, p. 105.

[32] Georg Lukács, 'Brief an Alberto Carocci' (8 February 1962), in *Marxismus und Stalinismus*, Hamburg 1970. Cf. also the 1960 Preface to *Existentialisme ou Marxisme?*, Paris 1961, p. 7: 'Since Khruschev's speech in 1956, I know that the great trials of 1938 were unnecessary.' In the main part of the work, written in 1947, in a polemic with Simone de Beauvoir, Lukács was still defending the absurd argument that the Moscow Trials had 'increased the chances of a Russian victory at Stalingrad', ibid. p. 168.

[33] Lukács, 'Preface' (1957) in *The Meaning of Contemporary Realism*, op. cit. p. 10.

[34] In *The Meaning of Contemporary Realism*, written in September 1956, he sees Stalinism as a combination of 'economic subjectivism' and 'revolutionary romanticism'.

made by our Party can be traced to the fact that we simply carried over the truths of 1917 and of the revolutionary period immediately following 1917 . . . with no criticism at all, and without examining the new situation, into a period in which the main strategic problem was not the struggle for socialism, but a trial of strength between fascism and anti-fascism'.[35] It is not necessary to spell out the close links between this vision of the past and the problematic of the 'Blum Theses'. Unsurprisingly, the Stalinist period which he criticizes most vigorously is 1928–33. The orientation of the USSR between 1948 and 1953 seemed to him, in the last analysis, to be a relapse into the same basic errors.

Khruschevism

Lukács aims the same type of criticism at Stalin's domestic policy: he accuses him of having used 'methods of government from the Civil War period, in a situation of peaceful internal consolidation'; 'everything which is objectively inevitable in an intense revolutionary situation . . . was transformed by Stalin into the foundation of everyday Soviet life'.[36] In other words, not only does Lukács make no distinction between the USSR under Lenin (1917–20 was relatively the most democratic and 'pluralist' period in the history of Russia) and the USSR of Stalin, but his criticism of Stalinism is precisely that it 'artificially' maintained the politics, attitude and orientation of Lenin's time. This position is nothing more than a logical extension of Lukács's 'popular frontist' perspective, which dates back to the twenties.

Thus it is not surprising that Lukács totally supported 'Khruschevism', both in its internal aspects (partial criticism of Stalinism) and its external ones (peaceful co-existence as the international strategy of the Communist movement). He even went so far as to maintain for a time – even though he had always fought economism – that 'in the last analysis' economic competition between different systems 'determines . . . who will emerge victorious from co-existence in the international class struggle'. For 'it is clear that

[35] Georg Lukács, 'Der Kampf des Fortschritts und der Reaktion in der heutigen Kultur' (1956) in Marxismus und Stalinismus, op. cit. p. 139.

[36] Lukács, 'Brief an Alberto Carocci', in Marxismus und Stalinismus, op. cit. p. 183; and 'Zur Debatte zwischen China und der Sowjetunion, theoretische-philosophische Bemerkungen' (1963), ibid. p. 211.

economic competition between systems . . . is, in the last resort . . . the decisive ground on which to determine whether the people of one system will choose their own, or a rival system. . . . *Economic development itself is the most effective propaganda in this competition.*'[37] It is clear that because of these Khruschevist premises, Lukács was unable to foresee what, from 1963 onwards, was to become a major political phenomenon: the immense powers of attraction of the 'poor' revolutionary States (China, Vietnam, Cuba) for young people; these states are opposed to advanced capitalism, not by 'economic competition', but by a different *model of society* (economic, political, cultural and moral).

Lukács did, however, step outside the narrow confines of the Twentieth Congress and 'Khruschevism' in his criticism of the 'personality cult'. It seemed absurd to him that the problematic of a period of world-historic importance should be reduced to the individual qualities of one man: one must, he stressed, go beyond the 'person' to the organization, to the 'machine which produced the "personality cult" and then established it by an incessant, extended propagation . . . without the well-oiled operation of such a machine the personality cult would have been only a subjective dream, a product of abnormality'.[38] Around 1966 his views started to become more radical, and he criticized official 'de-Stalinization' as insufficient.[39] However, he never grasped the roots of the Stalinist phenomenon or sought to develop a Marxist analysis of the Soviet bureaucracy, but confined himself to denouncing its 'superstructural' aspects; brutal manipulation, predominance of tactics over theory, etc. At the beginning of 1968 he was still defining Stalinism as a type of 'sectarianism' which wished to 'perpetuate the *belle époque* of the Civil War'.[40]

---

[37] Lukács, *'Zur Debatte zwischen China und der Sowjetunion'* op. cit. pp. 208–9, and 'Probleme der Kulturellen Koexistenz' (1964), ibid. pp. 215–16 (Lukács's own emphasis). In fact this argument was too far removed from Lukács's basic position, too vulgarly economist for him to defend it for long. In 1966–7 he challenged it specifically: 'A rise in the standard of living alone will never be capable of acting as a real pole of attraction for Western countries (this was one of Khruschev's illusions)' – 'Le Grand Octobre 1917 et la littérature', in *L'homme et la Société* No. 5, July–September 1967, p. 14.

[38] Lukács, 'Brief an Alberto Carocci', op. cit. p. 172.

[39] Abendroth, Holz, Kofler, *'Conversations with Lukács'* (1966), Bari 1968, p. 189.

[40] Georg Lukács, 'Alle Dogmatiker sind Defaitisten', in *Forum*, May 1968.

The Final Return

In 1968, Lukács began to take a new turn towards the 'old Lukács'. At the risk of over-simplification of a contradictory development, this can be characterized as the beginnings of an orientation to the revolutionary left. In his last essays and interviews, elements can be found of a left criticism of Stalinism, which is qualitatively different from that of 1956–67, although there are points of continuity.[41] As in the past, the progress of his ideas is made up both of continuity and of change. The starting-point for this 'left turn' was of course that favoured world-historic year of the twentieth century, 1968 – which, in the space of a few months, experienced the Tet Offensive in Vietnam, student revolt on an international scale, the May Events in France, the Cultural Revolution in China, the Prague 'spring' and Soviet invasion. Lukács correctly grasped the crucial importance of these events: in an interview in 1969 he stated: 'Today this whole system is facing the initial stages of an extraordinarily profound crisis. . . . I mean by this the Vietnamese War, the radical crisis in the United States . . . the crises in France, in Germany, in Italy. . . . Looked at in a world-historical perspective, we are at the threshold of a world crisis.'[42] As for Czechoslovakia, in an informal conversation with one of his former Hungarian students, only weeks after the occupation of Prague by Warsaw Pact troops, Lukács clearly showed his anger and stressed the terrible historical implications of the event: 'This is the greatest disaster for the communist movement since the German social-democrats approved the Kaiser's war credits in 1914. That put an end to the first dream of the socialist fraternity of man. Need I say more?'[43] Some young revolutionary students from Western Europe, who visited Lukács in September 1968, were struck by the harshness of his criticism of the USSR and also by his great interest in the May events in

[41] On a series of issues – Stalin's 'realism' after the decline of the world revolution, self-criticism of the 'messianism' of History and Class Consciousness, etc. – Lukács did not totally abandon his former positions.

[42] Lukács, The Twin Crises, NLR 60, op. cit. p. 44.

[43] George Urban, 'A conversation with Lukács', in Encounter, October 1971, p. 35. We should add, in passing, that the vote on war credits in August 1914 was viewed by Lenin as the ultimate bankruptcy of the Second International, and thus the beginning of a realization of the need to set up a new international proletarian organization . . . However, we would be forcing the comparison a bit too far if we attributed such conclusions to Lukács!

France.[44] Lukács understood the dialectical relationship between the two crises, that of Stalinism and that of the bourgeois world, and constantly stressed their interdependence.

At the age of eighty-three, therefore, Lukács entered a new stage in his political/ideological development, which was, to a certain extent, a return to the revolutionary orientation of his youth. Obviously, history cannot be repeated, and the Lukács of 1969–71 can in no way be identified with what he was in 1919–24: the word 'return' is used metaphorically to point out a certain analogy between two distinct phenomena.

In this sense it is extremely significant that one of the first expressions of this return was a 're-appropriation' of Ady. At the beginning of 1969, Lukács wrote an article on Ady (following a long silence on his favourite poet of the past), which directly links the work of the great writer, who died in 1919, to the prospect of a deep-rooted change in contemporary Hungary: 'I believe that when Hungary has really passed beyond the Stalinist era and begun to construct a living socialism, founded on a new proletarian democracy, there will be many more people who find that Ady is their favourite poet.'[45] Lukács's strong praise for Ady as a consistently revolutionary poet was closely linked to a new opposition to Hegelian 'realism': 'I have never considered the Hegelian concept of reconciliation with reality (*Versöhnung mit der Wirklichkeit*) to be a valid one. Even during my Hegelian period my intellectual attitude was dominated by Ady's "veto by vocation"....'[46] By contrasting Ady's *Ugosca non coronat* with Hegel's *Versöhnung*, Lukács returned to the revolutionary problematic of his youth and challenged what, from 1926 to 1968, had formed – implicitly or explicitly – the 'philosophical' basis of his unstable and difficult compromise with Stalinism: the idea of reconciliation.

The Embers Flare

At the end of 1968, this challenge assumed a directly political form in an essay on Lenin and the transitional period, completed after the occupation of Czechoslovakia (only one chapter has been

[44] Report by C. Urjewicz to the author, September 1974.
[45] Lukács, 'The Importance and Significance of Ady', in *New Hungarian Quarterly*, No. 35, Vol. X, Autumn 1969, p. 60.
[46] Georg Lukács, 'My Road to Marx' (1969) in *Nouvelles Etudes Hongroises*, 1973, p. 78.

published, in Hungary in 1970). In this essay, Lukács contrasts the socialist democracy of Lenin with Stalinist bureaucratic manipulation. One example he mentions in this connection are the 'Communist Saturdays' of 1919, which were self-activity, freely chosen in the service of the community. It is no accident that, in this context, Lukács quotes his remarkable article of 1919, *The Moral Mission of the Communist Party*. Of course, he mentions its idealistic limitations; but the problematic of the 'reign of freedom' and the transition to Communism have once more begun to interest him.[47]

At the beginning of 1969, Lukács clarified his new position as a revolutionary left critic of Stalinism in an interview: 'So as not to conceal my personal ideas, by socialist democracy I understand democracy in ordinary life, as it appeared in the Workers' Soviets of 1871, 1905 and 1917, as it once existed in the socialist countries, and in which form it must be re-animated.'[48] Nearly all Lukács's interviews in the years 1969–71 contrast Workers' Soviets with both arbitrary bureaucracy and bourgeois democracy, as a true, authentic democratic system which arises each time the revolutionary proletariat appears on the stage of history.[49] For the first time, Lukács presented the Hungarian Soviet Republic of 1919, in spite of its weaknesses, as an example of socialist democracy – opposed, in every respect (particularly culturally), to the methods of the Stalinist era.[50] One of the most important political consequences of this new revolutionary perspective was Lukács's scepticism towards 'self-reform' by the bureaucracy. He had believed in this for a long while, and expressed himself prudently on so delicate a subject; but in his last interview, just before his death, he was clear and trenchant: 'I have never yet seen a reform carried out by bureaucrats ... I do not think there can be a bureaucratic change and, what is more, I do not really think there is any

[47] Lukács, 'Lenin und die Fragen der Übergangsperiode' (1968) in *Goethepreis, 1970*, pp. 84–5. Cf. on this point Mészáros, op. cit. p. 151.

[48] Lukács, 'Die Deutschen, eine Nation der Spätentwickler', in *Goethepreis, 1970*, p. 112. One significant detail: Trotsky is mentioned, together with Lenin, as a leader of the October revolution, both 'having led the movement of the Workers' Soviets'.

[49] Cf. for example, NLR 60, p. 41; NLR 68, p. 50; Y. Bourdet, *Figures de Lukács*, p. 187, etc.

[50] Lukács, 'La Politique Culturelle de la République des Conseils', interview of 1969 in *Action Poétique*, no. 49, 1972, p. 31.

such intention . . . they want to maintain the bureaucratic balance which we have today.'[51] Significantly, Lukács goes on to mention the events in Poland, the 'explosive strikes' of 1970, adding: 'what happened in Poland can happen today or tomorrow in every socialist country'.

His new orientation was also expressed in relation to the class struggle in the capitalist world, particularly in his attitude towards Vietnam. He emphasized the world-historical implications of the Vietnamese struggle in a striking analogy: 'The defeat of the USA in the Vietnam war is to the "American way of life" rather like what the Lisbon earthquake was to French feudalism. . . . Even if decades were to pass between the Lisbon earthquake and the fall of the Bastille, history can repeat itself, in the sense that out of movements which are at first ideologically completely immature and based solely on a legitimate feeling of revolt, real movements are formed.'[52] The Lisbon earthquake of 1755 triggered off an extraordinary ideological crisis in Europe, particularly in France. The deadly and absurd event (total destruction of the city and 20,000 deaths) challenged Leibniz's optimistic (and conformist) ideology 'We live in the best of all possible worlds', Alexander Pope's 'What is, is right', as well as the whole concept of divine Providence. Voltaire made his Doctor Pangloss, the philosopher of smug optimism, die in the Lisbon earthquake.[53] Thus, for Lukács, the consequence of the Vietnam war was, by analogy, as follows. Firstly, the end of optimistic illusions in an 'era of peace' on a world scale – illusions which he himself had harboured since 1956.[54] Secondly, the decline of what he called 'cybernetic religion': blind faith in machines, computers and electronic instruments, omnipotent and provident fetishes, substitutes for the God of the eighteenth century, which were all defeated by the NLF.[55] Last, and above all, the appearance of an enormous crisis of values, a radical challenge to imperialist ideology, which could,

---

[51] Lukács, Interview with Y. Bourdet in *Figures de Lukács*, op. cit. p. 186.

[52] *Goethepreis, 1970*, op. cit. p. 108.

[53] Voltaire also wrote a philosophical poem on the event. Cf. L. G. Crocker, 'The Problem of Evil', in J. F. Lively, *The Enlightenment*, London 1966, p. 159: 'The Lisbon earthquake, which occurred in that most Catholic of cities on All Saints' Day, 1 November 1755, was a *crise de conscience* for the eighteenth century.'

[54] 'We are now entering an era in which peace and co-existence have become possible.' Lukács, *Der Kampf des Fortschritts und der Reaktion* (1956), op. cit. p. 141.

[55] Interview with Lukács on ORTF, 1971.

in future, erupt in a massive revolutionary upsurge of international dimensions. This is no longer the messianic hope for immediate revolution that Lukács had in 1919; but, for the first time since the twenties, he was beginning to conceive of world revolution as a real historical prospect, in the present century.

Lukács began to criticize the reformist workers' parties: social-democracy, whose politics in Germany for fifty years had been just a 'series of capitulations', and the communist parties – 'In Germany, the parties, and unfortunately this includes the Communist Party itself, because of their exclusive orientation to tactical decisions and their loss of a grand historical perspective, no longer act as a pole of attraction for young people.'[56] He began to regard the student movement sympathetically, and with (critical) interest. He refused to label these radicalized youth currents 'leftist' – a convenient formula used far too frequently by the leadership of the traditional Communist parties. On the contrary he stated that: 'Anyone who thinks that he can apply a book written by Lenin in 1920 to American youth of 1969 or that Lenin's criticism of Roland Holst can be made to fit Dutschke would be terribly mistaken.'[57] In radical contrast to the bureaucratic line on the 'adventurist', 'manipulated', or even 'provocative' character of the young 'leftists', Lukács explicitly states: 'I think that this student movement which is springing up, not just in Germany, but all over the world, is an exceptionally positive phenomenon' which must be understood as the product of a simultaneous crisis in the two systems which triumphed in the Second World War: Stalinism and the 'American way of life'.[58]

On 4 June 1971 death cut short, at its outset, this astonishing 'return to first principles'; after half a century of 'reconciliation' and 'lost illusions', Lukács had, in the last three years of his life, begun to rediscover the intense hopes, the red flame of the People's Commissar of 1919.

[56] *Goethepreis, 1970*, op. cit. p. 110.
[57] Lukács, 'The Twin Crises', NLR 60, p. 43.
[58] Lukács, *Goethepreis, 1970*, op. cit. pp. 107–8.

The Frankfurt School

Göran Therborn

In France and Italy, the post-War period has seen the emergence of new schools of Marxist thought (Althusser, Della Volpe). In the German-speaking world, on the other hand, there is a complete continuity from the pre-War years. The veterans Lukács and Bloch are still active and influential, but the centre of the stage is firmly occupied by the group of theorists who have become known as the 'Frankfurt School'. Moreover, while the influence of recent French and Italian Marxism has been largely confined within its country of origin, the ideas of the Frankfurt School have spread, first, thanks to the emigration of the 1930's, to the USA, and in the last few years all over the world. Indeed, one of the most prominent of the members of the School, Herbert Marcuse, has become one of the bourgeoisie's latest bogey-men. Of course, Marcuse's influence is not so great as myth suggests. Nevertheless, in North America and Italy at least, the student movement has certainly been more affected by Marcuse's thought than by that of any other living Marxist, and the SDS in Germany has never emancipated itself intellectually from the Frankfurt tutelage, despite the fact that most of the members of the School teaching in Germany denounced it, often in the most violent terms. Moreover, in France, where the influence of the School was negligible until a spate of translations after the events of May 1968, student militants associated with these events have often spontaneously reproduced typical Frankfurt ideas in their own theory and ideology. This tenacity of the Frankfurt School, and the reflorescence of its ideas in a situation so unlike that of its origin (Germany in the 1930's) is remarkable. This article is an attempt to summarize and analyse the basis of these ideas,[1] and to provide some explanation for their reflorescence.

The School takes its name from the *Institut für Sozialforschung* (Institute for Social Research) set up in Frankfurt-am-Main in 1923.[2] A young left-wing philosopher, Max Horkheimer, became the Director of this Institute in 1930, and continued to direct it in exile after 1933, first in France and then in the USA, until it closed down in 1941. He was joined by the philosopher and musician, Theodor Wiesengrund-Adorno and an ex-student of Heidegger's, Herbert Marcuse.[3] Friedrich Pollock, Leo Löwenthal, Franz Neumann and Erich Fromm were closely associated with the Institute in the 1930's, as was Walter Benjamin, though more distantly. After the War, Marcuse remained in the USA, while Horkheimer and Adorno returned to West Germany, re-establishing the Institute in Frankfurt in 1950. Here it has found new adherents, most notably the philosophers Alfred Schmidt and Jürgen Habermas. The core members of the School are Horkheimer, Adorno and Marcuse. Some of the original members died during the War, others drifted away (e.g. Fromm), while the younger members have only been active for a few years. Hence this article is devoted almost exclusively to the work of these three

[1] There exists at least one full-length study of critical theory, G. E. Rusconi's *La teoria critica della società* (Bologna 1968, revised edition 1970). Rusconi's perspective is a broad history of ideas, focusing on Lukács and Marcuse, with rather limited attention to political and strictly theoretical analysis. For a major history of the School, see now Martin Jay, *The Dialectical Imagination*, London 1973.

[2] The original director was the Marxist labour historian Carl Grünberg, and the Institute continued to publish his journal, *Archiv für die Geschichte des Sozialismus und der Arbeiterbewegung*, usually known as the *Grünberg Archiv*. As well as scholarly research into the history of the labour movement, the *Grünberg Archiv* also published important works by Karl Korsch, Georg Lukács and David Riazanov, the director of the Moscow Marx-Engels Institute. The Frankfurt School journal *Zeitschrift für Sozialforschung* was a continuation of the *Grünberg Archiv*. The aims of the Institute before 1930 are reflected in the books produced under its aegis: e.g. Henryk Grossman: *Das Akkumulations- und Zusammenbruchsgesetz des kapitalistischen Systems* (The Law of Accumulation and the Breakdown of the Capitalist System); Friedrich Pollock: *Die planwirtschaftlichen Versuche in der Sowjetunion* (Experiments in Planned Economy in the Soviet Union); and a collective work, *Studien zur Geschichte der deutschen Sozialdemokratie* (Studies in the History of German Social-Democracy).

[3] The core members of the pre-War group were committed socialists, irreconcilably to the left of Social Democracy, but with an ambiguous relation to the Communist Party and no organizational affiliation. Only Marcuse had any practical political experience, in the USPD in 1917–18.

core members.[4]

Critical versus Traditional Theory

The denomination 'Frankfurt School' was not chosen by the members, but has been applied to them by others. Members of the group prefer their work to take its name from what they regard as their theoretical programme: *'critical theory'*. An examination of what they, and particularly Horkheimer, who coined the phrase, have meant by critical theory therefore serves as a convenient introduction to their work as a whole.

The term 'critical theory' does not appear in the early numbers of the Institute's journal, the *Zeitschrift für Sozialforschung*. 'Materialism' is used instead. 'Critical theory' was first discussed in an article by Horkheimer in the journal in 1937, entitled 'Traditional and Critical Theory'.[5] Adorno explains, thirty years later, that 'Horkheimer's phrasing, "critical theory", seeks not to make materialism acceptable, but to use it to make men theoretically conscious of what it is that distinguishes materialism',[6] and this is plausible, because the substitution of the vaguer term for historical materialism is accompanied by a considerable radicalization of Horkheimer's position. In fact, critical theory is Horkheimer's conception of Marxism, and the phrase derives from the conventional description of Marxism as the critique of political economy. I shall attempt to situate and systematize critical theory in three respects: its relationship to traditional theory, to science and to politics.

The basic dividing line between traditional and critical theory in Horkheimer's conception is determined by whether the theory assists in the process of social reproduction, or whether, on the contrary, it is subversive of it. Traditional theory is embedded in

---

[4] Both Horkheimer and Marcuse have republished their major essays from the 1930's. See Max Horkheimer: *Kritische Theorie I–II* (Frankfurt 1968) and Herbert Marcuse: *Kultur und Gesellschaft I–II* (Frankfurt 1965). Page-references to articles in these volumes will refer to them as KT and KG respectively. Some of the essays in KG have been translated into English as *Negations* (New York and London 1969). Hereafter referred to as N.

[5] Max Horkheimer: 'Traditionelle und Kritische Theorie', *Zeitschrift für Sozialforschung*, Heft 2, 1937 (hereafter referred to as ZfS);reprinted (with modifications – see notes 8 & 9 below) in KT 11, pp. 137–191.

[6] Theodor Adorno: *Negative Dialectic*, London 1973, p. 197.

the specialized work processes by which the existing society reproduces itself. It 'organizes experience on the basis of problems arising from the reproduction of life within present society'.[7] In the prevailing division of labour, the personal views of the individual scientist and his efforts for a free science have as little real significance as the individual entrepreneur's views of free enterprise. Both are allotted determinate roles in the process of social reproduction: 'The apparent independence of work processes which ought to derive their movement from the inner essence of their objects corresponds to the apparent freedom of the economic subjects, in bourgeois society. They think that they act according to their individual decisions, whereas, even in their most complex calculations, they are really only exponents of an obscure social mechanism' (KT II, p. 146).

Critical theory, on the other hand, was for Horkheimer an immanent critique of the existing society itself. For it was designed to bring the basic contradictions of capitalist society to consciousness, by placing itself outside the mechanisms of its reproduction and the limits of the prevailing division of labour. 'There now exists a human attitude which takes the society itself as its object. It is not merely oriented towards the removal of particular abuses, for the latter appear to it as necessarily bound to the whole arrangement of the social structure. Although this attitude has arisen out of social structure, it is no concern either of its conscious intention or of its objective significance that anything in this structure should function any better than it does' (KT II, pp. 155ff.). The intentions of this critical attitude 'go beyond the prevailing social praxis' (KT II, p. 158). Critical theory is primarily a *prise de position* (*Haltung*) and only secondarily a theory of a specific type. 'On the whole, its opposition to the traditional concept of theory derives from a difference of subjects rather than from one of objects. The facts as they arise from work in society are not so external to the bearers of this attitude as they are to the academic (*Gelehrte*), or to the members of the other professions, who all think as little academics' (ibid.). The critical theorist is 'the theoretician whose only concern is to accelerate a development which should lead to a

---

[7] Horkheimer: 'Philosophie und kritische Theorie', ZfS, 1937; reprinted in KT II, p. 192.

society without exploitation'.[8]

Hence the content of critical theory was essentially indeterminate: 'There are no general criteria for critical theory as a whole, for such criteria always depend on a repetition of events and thus on a self-reproducing totality. . . . Despite all its insights into individual steps and the congruence of its elements with those of the most advanced traditional theories, critical theory has no specific instance for itself other than its inherent interest in the supersession of class domination'.[9] The only properties of critical theory are a political position and a place in the history of philosophy seen as a reflection of social development: 'The categorical judgement is typical of pre-bourgeois society: that is how it is, man cannot change it at all. The hypothetical and disjunctive forms of judgement belong especially to the bourgeois world: this effect may occur under certain conditions, it is either like this or otherwise. Critical theory explains: it must not be like this, men could alter being, the conditions for doing so already exist' (KT II, p. 175n.).

The Inheritance of Classical Idealism

However, this sociological radicalism does have definite consequences for the logical structure of critical theory. For Horkheimer, the difference between traditional and critical theory was that they embody two different 'modes of cognition' (*Erkenntnisweisen*). Traditional theory's mode of cognition derives from and is applied in the specialized sciences, particularly the natural sciences. 'The axioms of traditional theory define general concepts within which all the facts in the field must be conceived. . . . In between, there is a hierarchy of genera and species, between which there are generally appropriate relations of subordination. The facts are individual cases, examples or embodiments of the genera. There are no temporal differences between the units of the

---

[8] Quoted from the original version in ZfS, Heft 3, 1937, p. 274. In the published version (KT 11, p. 170), 'injustice' (*Unrecht*) has been substituted for 'exploitation' (*Ausbeutung*), and the word 'only' (*einzig*) has been omitted.

[9] Quoted from the original version, op. cit., p. 292. In the republished version (KT 11, p. 190), 'social injustice' has been substituted for 'class domination' (*Klassenherrschaft*).

system. . . . Individual genera may be added to the system or other changes made, but this is not normally conceived in the sense that the determinations are necessarily too rigid and must prove inadequate where the relation to the object or the object itself changes without thereby losing its identity. Rather, changes are treated as omissions in our earlier knowledge or as the replacement of individual parts of the object. . . . Discursive logic, or the logic of the intellect (*Verstand*), even conceives living development in this way. It is unable to conceive the fact that man changes and yet remains identical with himself' (KT II, pp. 172ff.).

Critical theory, on the other hand, starts from a view of Man as the subject or creator of history, and compares the existing objectifications of human activity with Man's inherent possibilities. 'The critical theory of society, on the contrary, has as its object men as the producers of all their historical life forms' (KT II, p. 192). 'In the formation of its categories and in all phases of its procedure, critical theory quite consciously pursues an interest in a rational organization of human activity which it has set itself to elucidate and legitimize. For it is not just concerned with goals as they have been prescribed by the existing life forms, but with men and all their possibilities' (KT II, p. 193).

With this view of man and society, critical theory explicitly announces its concordance with German idealism from Kant onwards, and claims to represent the preservation not only of the heritage of German idealism, but also of philosophy *tout court*, with its roots in Plato and Aristotle. Indeed critical theory's conception of truth is also that of classical philosophy. Horkheimer asserted the objectivity of truth, in opposition to all the relativist currents of the 1930's: 'according to (critical theory), only one truth exists, and the positive predicates of honesty and consistency, of rationality, of the search for peace, freedom and happiness, are not to be discussed in the same sense as other theories and practices' (KT II, p. 171). Truth is objective in the metaphysical sense of being inherent in the essence of human reality, however dismal the latter may appear, 'for the goal of a rational society, which today, of course, only appears to arise in the imagination, is really invested in every man' (KT II, p. 199). In this way critical theory was able to present itself as an inherent part of the historical process and of the struggle for a free society. But this 'political' stand was no different from the ethical aims of the whole tradition of rational philosophy. As Horkheimer put it in *The Eclipse of Reason*, written during the War, 'the philosophical systems of objective reason implied the conviction that an all-embracing or fundamental structure of being could be discovered and a conception of human destination derived from it. They understood science, when worthy of this name, as an implementation of such reflection or speculation'.[10]

Thus, when examined from the epistemological point of view, the difference between critical theory and traditional theory turns out to be the difference between classical philosophy and modern science. Critical theory's epistemological basis is a *metaphysical humanism*.

What is the effect of this epistemology where the science of economics is concerned? What is critical theory's conception of the Marxist critique of political economy? The step from classical philosophical speculation to Marxism is simply to put idealism back 'on to its feet'. Classical idealism 'treats the activity which emerges in the given material as spiritual. . . . For the materialist conception, on the contrary, every fundamental activity is a matter of social labour' (KT II, p. 193). As an 'implementation' of humanist speculation, critical theory (i.e. for the Frankfurt School, Marxism) is a unique existential judgement on man's life in capitalist society. The Marxist critique is thus conceived as a negation of economic concepts, above all of the concept of just or equal exchange, which the Frankfurt School regards as the key concept of bourgeois economics, just as exchange is the central principle of the bourgeois economy. 'Unlike the operation of modern specialized science (*Fachwissenschaft*), the critical theory of society remains philosophical even as a critique of economics: its content is formed by the inversion of the concepts which govern the economy into their opposites: fair exchange into widening social injustice, the free economy into the domination of monopoly, productive labour into the consolidation of relations which restrict production, the maintenance of the life of the society into the immiseration of the people' (KT II, p. 195). But this radical philosophical critique has a paradoxical result. Since it is philo-

---

[10] Max Horkheimer: *The Eclipse of Reason*, New York 1947, p. 12. Cf. the chapters on one-dimensional thought in Herbert Marcuse: *One-Dimensional Man* (New York 1960). Hereafter, this book will be referred to as ODM. Page references are to the London paperback edition of 1968.

sophical and does not directly intervene in scientific discourse, it cannot create any new scientific concepts. It certainly 'transcends' bourgeois economics, but it leaves its system of concepts intact. Critical theory sees bourgeois economics as ahistorical, but not as incorrect or unscientific. 'The critical theory of society begins with an idea of simple commodity exchange defined by relatively general concepts; it then shows that, assuming all the available knowledge, and *without transgressing the principles of the exchange economy as represented by scientific political economy*, this exchange economy must, in the present state of men and things (which of course changes under its influence), necessarily lead to a sharpening of the social oppositions which drive towards wars and revolutions in the present epoch' (KT II, pp. 174ff. – my italics). The very radicalism of this interpretation of Marxism drastically limits its effects: the gaze of this philosophy on economics fulfils Wittgenstein's prescription. It leaves everything as it is.

The Reduction to Philosophy

In another sense, according to this programme text, critical theory is more the intellectual aspect of a political practice than a specific theory. The critical theorist's 'vocation is the struggle to which his thought belongs, not thought as something independent, to be divided from this struggle' (KT II, p. 165). Horkheimer's programmatic statement links critical theory, as a mode of cognition, to the proletariat. 'Those view-points which (critical theory) takes as the goal of human activity for historical analysis, and above all the idea of a rational social organization corresponding to the general will (*Allgemeinheit*), are immanent in human labour, without being present to individuals or in public opinion in a correct form. It is the property of a specific interest to experience and perceive these tendencies. Marx and Engels's theory claims that this will happen in the proletariat.' As the last sentence suggests, however, Horkheimer is not sure. 'But in this society, the situation of the proletariat does not provide any guarantee of correct knowledge, either. . . . The differentiation of its social structure which is fostered from above, and the opposition between personal and class interests which is only overcome at the best of times, prevent this consciousness from acquiring immediate validity' (KT II, p. 162).

Horkheimer then went on to explain the relationship between the critical theorist and the proletariat in the following terms: 'If we regard the theoretician and his specific activity alongside the oppressed class as a dynamic unity, such that his representation of the social contradictions appears not just as an expression of the concrete historical situation, but rather as a stimulating, transforming factor in it, then his function emerges clearly. The course of the conflict between the advanced parts of the class and the individuals who express the truth about them, and then the conflict between these most advanced parts together with their theoreticians and the rest of the class, should be understood as a process of mutual interaction in which consciousness unfolds with its liberating and propulsive, disciplinary and aggressive powers' (KT II, p. 164). Note that the relationship is not presented simply as one between the theoretician and the proletariat, but also as one between the theoretician and the 'most advanced parts' of the class on the one hand, and the rest of the class on the other. A few lines earlier, the expression 'advanced part' is equated with 'a party or its leadership'. In the main, however, Horkheimer's focus is on critical theory, not on a party. There is only one other reference to organization in Horkheimer's programme, and that is equally abstract. 'Something of the freedom and spontaneity of the future appears in the organization and community of those in struggle, despite all the discipline based on the need to prevail. Where the unity of discipline and spontaneity has vanished, the movement is transformed into a concern of its own bureaucracy, a drama which is already part of the repertory of recent history' (KT II, pp. 166ff.).

Thus critical theory's conception of politics also ends in a paradox. On the one hand, it presents itself as a mere component of a political practice; on the other, it lacks any specific political anchorage. This is not just a description of its historical situation after the victory of Nazism in Germany, but a rigorous consequence of Frankfurt School theory. The over-politicization of theory leads logically to the substitution of the theory as a surrogate for politics – an *Ersatzpolitik*.

So far our analysis has been confined almost exclusively to a single essay by Horkheimer outlining the differences between 'traditional' and 'critical' (Frankfurt School) theory. Nevertheless, two important conclusions have already emerged. Horkheimer argues that Marxism, or critical theory, is a completely new kind of theory; yet, on closer inspection, it becomes clear that the radical break is not with classical philosophy, whose heritage, on the contrary, it claims, but with science. Moreover, it does not propose to replace existing science with a new science, i.e., it refuses to enter the scientific arena, but denounces science from outside, from the realm of philosophy. The paradoxical result is that bourgeois science is retained, the only change being a philosophical (or even ethical) minus sign in front of its categories. Similarly, 'critical theory' associates itself with the struggle of the oppressed against capitalist class rule, but it is unable to situate this association in the political arena. It remains outside denouncing bourgeois class politics from the philosophical sphere. Horkheimer's critical theory involves *a double reduction of science and politics to philosophy*.

Backdrop: Rationalization and Reification

What was this philosophy which could thus be substituted for both science and politics in a revolutionary stance? In fact, the theory outlined in Horkheimer's programme and developed by the Frankfurt School from the 1930's to the present was by no means a completely original intellectual formation. It was rather an extreme development of the most philosophically self-conscious form of Marxism available to the Frankfurt theorists – the philosophy of the young Lukács and Korsch, which was itself a development of a whole trend of 19th- and 20th-century German sociological thought represented most completely by Max Weber's work. The central concern of this tradition was that of 'capitalist rationalization'.

The original conceptualization of this problem in Germany was made in 1887 when Ferdinand Tönnies published his book *Gemeinschaft und Gesellschaft* (Community and Society). The distinction which constituted the title was the contrast between the intimate personal relations of family and neighbourhood in rural pre-industrial and pre-capitalist society, and the impersonal contractual relations between men in urban, commercial and industrial society. The rationalization implied by *Gesellschaft* relations subsequently became the master concept of all Max Weber's work. For Weber, it was an inevitable destiny of Western society since the adoption of Judaeo-Christian religion in the West. It meant the *Entzauberung* (disenchantment) of the Western world, its liberation from magic, tradition and affectivity, and the development of instrumental rationality, calculation and control. Weber traced this development in religion – the Reformation; in the political sphere – bureaucracy; and in the economy – the capitalist firm and the 'spirit of capitalism'.

In his *History and Class Consciousness* (1923), the young Lukács linked Weber's 'rationalization' with Marx's conception of the 'fetishism of commodities', which he generalized into the concept of 'reification' – the reduction of human relations to relations between things. Reification was a feature not of modern society in general but of a particular type of modern society dominated by market exchange; capitalist society. The Vertex of reification was the labour market, where the free labourer, the proletarian, is forced to treat his living activity, his labour, as a thing. Hence the proletariat, the class most oppressed by capitalism, was the negation of capitalist society, and the force which could realise the philosophical critique of reification by a socialist revolution. The proletariat was the legitimate heir to German idealist philosophy, and revolutionary politics was the only means to make the divided and reified world whole and human.

This tradition, especially as represented by Lukács, had two important consequences for the subsequent development of the Frankfurt School. The first concerned its attitude to science, particularly the natural sciences; the second, its attitude to history and historical and social knowledge. The rise of the natural sciences was also part of the process Weber called rationalization, and one of the crucial problems of German idealism (using the term in the widest sense) during the latter half of the 19th century was therefore its relationship to science. In academic culture, the question concerned the relations between the natural and the cultural sciences. Historians, philosophers of history and sociologists in the idealist tradition, all insisted on a sharp distinction between them, both in the character of their object and in their method.

Paradoxically, however, the Marxism which developed in Western Europe after the First World War and the October Revolution faced the same problems, since it saw itself as the heir to classical German idealism. But these problems were also relevant to it for directly political reasons. Both classical Social-Democratic Marxism and revisionism had been permeated with a strong commitment to science, interpreted in a positivist and evolutionist sense, and with indifference and hostility, respectively, to Hegelian philosophy.

The revolutionary intellectuals of Western Europe in the 1920's, steeped in the Hegelian tradition, carried on the earlier fight of German historicism for a conception of social and historical theory different from the natural sciences. And just as Weber saw science as a moment in the process of rationalization, so Lukács regarded it as an aspect of reification, when applied to the human sphere. Immutable scientific laws of society were the expression of a world in which human relations had become things beyond human control, and the separation of different scientific disciplines revealed a specialization which destroyed the totality and historicity of human existence. For both Lukács and Korsch, the conception of Marxism as a strict science and the abandonment of the Hegelian dialectic were also directly connected with the political treachery of Social Democracy. They therefore regarded their re-introduction of Hegelianism into Marxist discourse as a re-affirmation of its revolutionary vocation.

In the early 1930's, the position on the natural sciences adopted by the Frankfurt School, and particularly by Horkheimer, was much the same as that outlined in Lukács's *History and Class Consciousness*. Lukács's critique of science was aimed at the contemplative position which he claimed it implied. To regard society as governed by scientific laws, was, according to Lukács, to take a reflective attitude to it, instead of intervening actively to change it and thereby transcend its laws. The Social-Democrats had oscillated between contemplation of an inevitable evolution to socialism and moralistic exhortation of the proletariat. In both, the unity of theory and practice had been broken. The Frankfurt School took up this critique, but as it was almost completely isolated from the working-class movement, the unification of theory and practice was broken *de facto* – especially, of course, after the victory of Fascism in 1933. Its critique of scientism therefore moves steadily away from the problem of its consequences for those who are to change capitalist society to the problem of its consequences for those who have to live in a still existing capitalist system. The emphasis is no longer on science as *contemplation* so much as on science as *domination*. In 1932, Horkheimer wrote: 'In the Marxist theory of society, science is numbered among the human forces of production. . . . Scientific knowledge shares the fate of productive forces and means of production of other kinds: the extent of their application is in grave contrast both to the level of their development and the real needs of men. . . . In so far as an attempt to found present society as eternity took over from the interest in a better society, which still dominated the Enlightenment, a restrictive and disorganizing moment entered science. A method oriented towards being and not towards becoming corresponded to the tendency to see the given form of society as a mechanism of equal and self-repeating processes.'[11] By 1944, however, Horkheimer and Adorno were arguing: 'Bacon's view was appropriate to the scientific attitude that prevailed after him. The concordance between the mind of man and the nature of things that he had in mind is patriarchal: the human mind, which overcomes superstition, is to hold sway over a disenchanted nature. Knowledge, which is power, knows no obstacles: neither in the enslavement of men nor in compliance with the world's rulers.'[12] The importance of this change for the political ideas of the Frankfurt School is discussed in the section on fascism below.

Theory as the Self-knowledge of the Object

A second influence of the historicist tradition on the Frankfurt School affected its view of history, and its characteristic form was that of a return to Hegel. Lukács had already stated this project in *History and Class Consciousness*. 'The fact that historical materialism is profoundly akin to Hegel's philosophy is clearly expressed in the function of the theory as the *self-knowledge of reality*.'[13]

[11] Max Horkheimer: 'Bemerkungen über Wissenschaft und Krise', KT 1, pp. 1–3.

[12] Max Horkheimer and Theodor W.-Adorno: *Dialectic of Enlightenment*, London 1973, p. 4. Hereafter, this book will be referred to as DE. This position produces the characteristic idea that nature is not something to be mastered by man, as it appears in most Western thought from the Greeks onward, but something that should be regarded as a 'garden', 'which can grow while making human beings grow' (see Marcuse: *Eros and Civilization*, Boston 1955). Some writers have argued that this idea is the defining feature of the School, but as we have seen, it was not present in Frankfurt thinking from the start. Moreover, it is shared by their arch-enemy, Heidegger (see *Brief über den 'Humanismus'* in *Platons Lehre von der Wahrheit*, Bern 1947).

[13] Georg Lukács: *History and Class Consciousness*, London 1971, p. 16. English modified.

Horkheimer's programme for critical theory states that this theory 'constructs the unfolding picture of the whole, the existential judgement contained in history' (KT II, p. 187). It is 'a struggle inherent in reality that by itself calls for a specific mode of behaviour'.[14] The basic conception of history which underlies this epistemology can be seen in a quotation from Marcuse: 'When historical content enters into the dialectical concept and determines methodologically its development and function, dialectical thought attains the concreteness which links the structure of thought to that of reality. Logical truth becomes historical truth. The ontological tension between essence and appearance, between "is" and "ought", becomes historical tension, and the inner negativity of the object-world is understood as the work of the historical subject – man in his struggle with nature and society' (ODM, p. 11).

History is viewed as one all-embracing process, in which an historical subject realizes itself. This subject is no longer Hegel's Idea, but Man. 'The goal of a rational society . . . is really invested in every man' (KT II, p. 199). This goal cannot be realized in the present society which is characterized, on the contrary, by its negation – the reification of human relations and the alienation of Man. But in spite of this, human beings still maintain a will and a struggle for a 'rational' organization of society, and it is through this will and this struggle, inherent in Man and human existence, that Man can discover the fact that human goals are negated in the prevailing conditions. Thus a knowledge of society becomes at the same time a judgement or evaluation of it. In this way, Man and social reality (created by Man) reach self-knowledge.

The reader will have noted that it is this historicist speculation which has in recent years constituted a primary target of Althusser and his followers. What effects does it have on the social theory of the Frankfurt School? The following list does not claim to be exhaustive, but it provides a starting-point for analysis.

1. It means that for humanist historicism, the term 'social totality' is something other than a scientific concept. In social science, the expression is used in a structural sense. To be able to explain a social fact, one must take into account the network of relationships of which it is a part, the structure which determines

14 *The Eclipse of Reason*, op. cit., p. 11.

the place of that social fact and its mode of functioning. Marxism is a social science in this sense, and it was by this procedure, for instance, that Marx showed that it is not the consumers and their needs and wishes which direct the capitalist economy.[15] In a historicist perspective, however, the totality becomes the totality of humanity's generically determined (*gattungsbestimmt*) history at a given moment. To grasp the totality then becomes to comprehend the existing reality from the standpoint of Man's goal, a rational society.

2. There is no room in the historicist conception of history for social totalities as structures of irreducible complexity, or for a discontinuous development of those complex structures. Society is always reducible to its creator-subject, and history is the continuous unfolding of this subject. At every given point in time, society is a unique manifestation of Man. This means that the concept of a mode of production, which in any classical reading of Marx is the central concept of historical materialism, plays at most a quite subordinate role. Capitalism is thus seen not as one mode of production among others, but as a completely unique moment in the history (or more strictly speaking, in the reified pre-history) of Man. Here the Frankfurt School appeals explicitly to the treatment of capitalism in classical German historicism, as expressed, for example, by Max Weber: 'Such an historical concept, however, since it refers to a phenomenon significant for its unique individuality, cannot be defined by the formula *genus proximum, differentia specifica*, but *it must be gradually put together out of the individual parts* which are taken from historical reality to make it up.'[16] Etienne Balibar has convincingly proved that the Marxist conception of capitalism is, on the contrary, constructed in precisely the way which Weber declares impossible.[17] Nevertheless, Weber's conception has been hailed by Adorno as a third alternative between positivism and idealism.[18] This historicist conception of the social totality has prevented the Frankfurt School from making the contribution to historical materialism

[15] Karl Marx: *Grundrisse*, London, Penguin/NLR library, 1973, p. 90ff.
[16] Max Weber: *The Protestant Ethic and the Spirit of Capitalism* (London 1967) p. 47.
[17] E. Balibar: 'The Basic Concepts of Historical Materialism' in Louis Althusser and Etienne Balibar, *Reading Capital*, London NLB, 1970.
[18] *Negative Dialectic*, p. 164ff.

which would seem to be implied in its programme of 'social research'.

3. Critical theory sees itself as humanity's self-knowledge. Therefore it cannot and must not have a structure which is (formally) logical and systematic. Such a systematization would mean that men systematized themselves, divided themselves up among the boxes of abstract categories. 'The formalization of reason is only the intellectual expression of mechanized production' (DE, p. 104). Formal logic is an expression of 'indifference to the individual' (DE, p. 202).

4. In a historicist interpretation, the scientific specificity of Marx's critique of political economy disappears. That critique is either regarded as a philosophical critique (Horkheimer), or as an examination of political economy from the standpoint of the totality of social being (Marcuse), but not as a scientific operation. This is quite clearly different from Marx's own conception of his work and of epistemology in general. In this context, Marx distinguished between four levels of thought: the economic subjects' immediate view of themselves and of the economy, special ideologies or speculative systems based on these immediate views, past science (above all, Ricardo's work, which Marx regarded as a science, but one which his own critique had superseded), and lastly positive science (Marx's own theory).[19]

5. However, the main effect of this historicist conception of knowledge is its view of capitalism, which is, of course, the present whose self-knowledge critical theory claims to represent. 'In the course of history, men attain a knowledge of their action and thereby grasp the contradiction in their existence' (KT II, p. 161). In capitalism, this contradiction is absolute; capitalism is a negation of humanity. Hence, for critical theory, all the institutions of capitalist society become expressions of a contradictory inner essence. Several options are then open to the historicist. The critical theorists could have taken as their starting-point Marx's treatment of the concept of the commodity in *Capital* and interpreted *reification* as the essential meaning of capitalism. This, of course, was Lukács's option: 'It might be claimed that

---

[19] Marx's most succinct formulation of this epistemology is perhaps to be found in *Theories of Surplus Value*, Vol. III, especially the chapter on vulgar economics. Cf. Marx-Engels: *Werke* (Berlin 1965), Bd. 26: 3, esp. p. 445.

the chapter on the fetish character of commodities . . . contains within itself the whole of historical materialism, the whole of the proletariat's knowledge of itself as knowledge of capitalist society.'[20] Or they could have started from the concept of labour and human activity, seeing capitalism above all in terms of *alienation.* This option is characteristic of all those who base themselves on Marx's *1844 Manuscripts.*[21] Horkheimer and Adorno have chosen a third path – to regard *exchange* as the 'fundamental relation' of capitalism. In this version, capitalism is the negation of just and equal exchange, producing increasing social injustice and the polarizations of power and oppression, wealth and poverty which go with it (KT II, pp. 173ff.). All these options say something true and important about capitalism, and they give an ideological judgement of it which can be used in the struggle to destroy it and replace it with a socialist society. But the tasks of Marxists are not confined to the ideological struggle, and from the point of view of science as a guide to political action, all these variants have to be refuted. They substitute for real history a construction derived from a philosophy of history, the 'history' of Man's alienation or reification or – in Frankfurt vocabulary – the dialectic of enlightenment. In the science of history, capitalism is a specific mode of production, characterized by a specific combination of forces and relations of production. This mode of production both sets the stage for the class struggle and is its object. Without a scientific analysis of the mode of production and social formation, no coherent class strategy can be developed by which to overthrow it. The Frankfurt School not only do not provide Marxism with any instruments to assist in the construction of this strategy, they denounce all such instruments *simply because they are instruments.*

Fascism as the Truth of Liberalism

As we have seen, a typical feature of the Frankfurt School's historicist ideology is the reduction of the complexity of the capitalist social formation to an essence which is then both

[20] Lukács. *History and Class Consciousness*, p. 170.
[21] Marcuse was among the first in the revolutionary camp to attach importance to the alienation of labour. See his 'Über die philosophischen Grundlagen des wirtschaftswissenschaftlichen Arbeitsbegriffs' (1933) in KG II.

expressed and masked by the different phenomenal forms which the essence takes in concrete historical existence. As history unfolds, the essence is more and more revealed. This ideological conception acquired great political importance when the Frankfurt School turned to the analysis of fascism.

Naturally enough, efforts to explain the roots of fascism were a major pre-occupation of all anti-fascist intellectuals in the 1930's and during the War. Many of these interpretations focused not on economic and political problems, but on ideological and cultural factors. It is remarkable that not only are these cultural explanations divided into two diametrically opposed camps where their interpretation of fascist culture is concerned, but also each of these camps contains both revolutionary and counter-revolutionary ideologists. To one of these camps, fascism was essentially an irrationalist phenomenon, a revolt against reason. To the other, on the contrary, it was the triumph of manipulative rationality. To the first camp belong both Karl Popper, with his *The Open Society and its Enemies*, and the later Georg Lukács in his *Die Zerstörung der Vernunft* (The Destruction of Reason). The Frankfurt School emphatically belong to the second group, where they find their reactionary counterpart in figures like Friedrich von Hayek. But within this basic framework, the Frankfurt School's theory of fascism has not remained static. The year 1939 provides a convenient divide between two distinct phases in this development.

In the first period, the Frankfurt School view of the roots of fascism contains two main themes with sources in Marxism and psycho-analysis[22] respectively. On the economic level, fascism is

---

[22] Freudian psycho-analysis and meta-psychology have been of great importance for Frankfurt theory. A psycho-analytic criticism of civilization as a repression of basic human instincts was thereby added to the Marxist critique of capitalist civilization. The core members of the group have refused to attenuate 'the uneasiness (*Unbehagen*) in culture', the conflict between society and human instinct, by sociologizing the latter, and Adorno and Marcuse have directly attacked the neo-Freudian revisionists, including their former colleague, Erich Fromm, for doing so (see Adorno: 'Sociology and Psychology', *New Left Review* 46 & 47, 1967–68, and above all Marcuse: *Eros and Civilization*, op. cit.). But they give Freudian theory an historical character by distinguishing a reality principle specific to capitalist society, the performance principle. This approach both sharpens the indictment of capitalist society and radicalizes its negation, which is associated with a realm 'beyond the reality principle', i.e. beyond the performance principle. The precondition for this is such a high level of the productive forces that labour can be abolished. Unlike Reich, sexual liberation in the genital sense is not the psycho-analytical aim of Frankfurt theory so much as the investment of all human activity with libidinous energy.

explained as the replacement of competitive capitalism by monopoly capitalism and as the seizure of power by the monopoly capitalists in order to deal with the economic and political crisis of capitalism. In a vivid essay on 'The Struggle against Liberalism in the Totalitarian View of the State', Marcuse shows that fascist attacks on liberalism notwithstanding, these two ideologies and political systems represent two different stages of the same type of society, to which both of them belong: respectively, monopoly capitalism, and competitive capitalism. Marcuse first points out that the attacks on the bourgeoisie, i.e. on the profit motive, in fascist ideology are directed against the capitalists of competitive capitalism. The 'merchant' (*Händler*) is reviled, while homage is paid to the 'gifted economic leader' (*Wirtschaftsführer*).[23] According-ing to Marcuse, fascism finds its most important spring-boards in 'the naturalistic interpretation of society and the liberalist rationalism that ends in irrationalism. Both believe in "natural", eternal laws of society. The liberal rationalization of the economy and society is essentially private, relating to the rational practice of the single individual; it lacks any rational determination of social goals. It therefore comes to an end when an economic crisis breaks through its supposed harmony of interests. At this point, liberal theory has to turn to irrational justifications of the existing system' (KG I, p. 31; N, pp. 17–18).

The second theme in the first phase of the Frankfurt School's explanation of fascism is the precedent for fascist moralism provided by anti-sensual bourgeois morality in general, with its condemnation of hedonism and happiness in favour of 'virtue'.[24] This hostility to pleasure emerges paradoxically in what Marcuse called 'affirmative culture', in which happiness and the spirit are split away from the material world into a separate, purely spiritual realm called *Kultur*. 'By affirmative culture is meant that culture of the bourgeois epoch which led in the course of its own develop-ment to the segregation from civilization of the mental and spiri-tual world as an independent realm of value that is also considered superior to civilization. Its decisive characteristic is the assertion of a universally obligatory, eternally better and more valuable

[23] Marcuse: 'Der Kampf gegen den Liberalismus in der totalitären Staatsauf-fassung', KG I, p. 25; *Negations*, pp. 11–12.

[24] See Marcuse, op. cit., and Horkheimer: 'Egoismus und Freiheitsbewegung', ZfS, 1936, etc.

world that must be unconditionally affirmed: a world essentially different from the factual world of the daily struggle for existence, yet realizable by every individual for himself "from within" without any transformation of the state of fact' (KG I, p. 63; N, p. 95). In the pre-fascist period, this culture could be characterized as an 'internalization' (*Verinnerlichung*), but 'during the most recent period of affirmative culture, this abstract internal community (abstract because it left the real antagonisms untouched) has turned into an equally abstract external community. The individual is inserted into a false collectivity (race, folk, blood, and soil)' (KG I, p. 93; N, p. 125).

Apart from culture in general, a crucial element in fascism, according to the Frankfurt School, was the psychology of the individual citizen which made fascist oppression possible, the so-called 'authoritarian personality'. The authoritarian personality, too, was for the Frankfurt School a creation of the classical bourgeois epoch. In the huge collective volume *Studien über Autorität und Familie* (Studies in Authority and the Family), whose principal contributions were written by Fromm, Horkheimer and Marcuse, the Frankfurt School examined the way in which the family functions as a mechanism to preserve the existing society, and, more specifically, the way in which the bourgeois family functions as an inculcator of authoritarianism.

In 1939, the Spanish Republic was defeated, Molotov and Ribbentrop signed the Nazi-Soviet pact and the Second World War broke out. This was the decisive crisis for the intellectual left of the 1930's. However, its effect on the Frankfurt School, was at first registered only in a practical retreat from politics, not a modification of theory. Hence the content of its theory of fascism changed very little, but its themes are more sharply expressed. This is well represented by Horkheimer's essay *The Jews and Europe*, which was completed in the first days of September of that year.[25] Horkheimer argues that the present crisis, far from bringing Marxism into question, vindicates its analyses of the power relations, monopolistic tendencies and eruption of crises in

---

[25] Horkheimer: 'Die Juden und Europa', ZfS, 1939 (hereafter referred to as JE). Characteristically, this resolute affirmation of the author's commitment to Marxism has been omitted from KT. However wild this article may be theoretically, it should be remembered that at this very time, renegades like James Burnham were beginning to concoct the idea of the 'managerial revolution'.

capitalist society. 'He who does not want to speak about capitalism should also be silent about fascism' (JE, p. 115). 'The (Marxist) theory destroyed the myth of a harmony of interests; it presented the liberal economic process as the reproduction of relations of domination by means of free contracts which are enforced by the inequality of property. The mediation has now been removed. Fascism is the truth of modern society, which this theory had grasped from the beginning' (JE, p. 116).

Logic as Domination

But the retreat from politics, even of the abstract type available to the Frankfurt School in the 1930's, eventually directly affected the theory, too, and as part of the theory, the theory of fascism. This is seen at its clearest in Horkheimer and Adorno's book *Dialektik der Aufklärung* (Dialectic of Enlightenment), written during the War. Horkheimer and Adorno ask 'why instead of entering into a truly human condition, does humanity sink into a new kind of barbarism?' Here a comparison can be made with Popper's *Open Society and its Enemies* and Von Hayek's *The Road to Serfdom*. These last two authors put the blame on socialism and the labour movement: Popper, because Marxism had allegedly substituted historicism and utopianism for 'piecemeal social engineering'; Hayek, because socialism had introduced the ideas of planning and State intervention into the paradise of competitive capitalism. Horkheimer and Adorno's answer to the question is, of course, quite different. For them, fascism is the self-destruction of the liberal Enlightenment. Fascism is not just the truth of liberalism in the sense that it nakedly reveals the real inequalities and oppression inherent in the apparently free exchange in the capitalist market. Fascism is the truth of the whole aim of the bourgeois Enlightenment from Bacon on to liberate man from the fetters of superstition. The main offender is not the market and the relations of production, but the natural sciences and their empiricist counterpart in epistemology. The whole meaning of science and logic is brought into question: 'Even though we had known for many years that the great discoveries of applied science are paid for with an increasing diminution of theoretical awareness, we still thought that in regard to scientific activity our contribution could be restricted to the criticism or extension of specialist axioms. Thematically, at any rate, we were to keep to the traditional disciplines: to sociology, psychology, and epistemology. However, the fragments united in this volume show that we were forced to abandon this conviction. If the assiduous maintenance and verification of the scientific heritage are an essential part of knowledge (especially where zealous positivists have treated it as useless ballast and consigned it to oblivion), in the present collapse of bourgeois civilization not only the pursuit but the meaning of science has become problematical in that regard.' (DE, p. xi.)

Horkheimer's programme for a critical theory still maintained the Lukácsian position on science: it was contemplative, as opposed to a commitment to fundamental social change. In *Dialectic of the Enlightenment*, however, the focus is wholly on science as an instrument of domination.[26] Now natural science and Bacon's empiricist theory of knowledge are the main targets. 'What men want to learn from nature is how to use it in order wholly to dominate it and men. Enlightenment behaves towards things as a dictator towards men. He knows them in so far as he can manipulate them' (DE, pp. 4 and 9). Logic as such is contaminated because of its indifference to the qualitative and to the individually unique. It is directly linked to the capitalist rationalisation of labour. 'The indifferent attitude to the individual expressed in logic draws the necessary conclusions from the economic process' (DE, p. 202). Fascism has granted science its full honours, freeing it from all moral considerations. 'The totalitarian order gives full rein to calculation and abides by science as such' (DE, p. 86).

Moreover, the form in which *Dialectic of Enlightenment* is written takes this critique of logic and science into account. It is a collection of philosophical fragments (Adorno's *Minima Moralia*, written at the same time, is similarly a collection of aphorisms). Its theme is the inner contradictions of the Enlightenment, defined as the 'disenchantment (*Entzauberung*) of the world', and the self-destruction these contradictions bring about.[27] An allegory for

---

[26] Cf. ODM, especially Ch. VI.

[27] This concept closely corresponds to Max Weber's notion of rationalization, whose initial manifestation was the absence or progressive elimination of magic from Western religion, starting with Mosaic Judaism, and from Western culture generally.

this dialectic can be found in the twelfth book of the *Odyssey*, where Ulysses' ship has to pass by the sirens, whose immensely beautiful song leads men to lose themselves in the past. Ulysses avoids this danger in two ways. He has one solution for his sailors: he blocks their ears with wax. 'The labourers must be fresh and concentrate as they look ahead, and must ignore whatever lies to one side.' The other solution is for himself, the landowner; he has himself bound to the mast. He can thus enjoy the sirens' song because he has made their temptation a merely contemplative object, an art, and the greater the temptation, the harder he makes his men bind him, like the later bourgeois who refuses himself happiness more and more obstinately, the nearer he comes to it through the growth in his power (DE, p. 54ff.). The theme is then pursued in Kant, de Sade and Nietzsche, in order to show that 'the submission of everything natural to the autocratic subject reaches its acme in the mastery of the blindly objective and natural' (DE, p. xvi). The authors also follow the development of the Enlightenment into commercial culture and mass communications: 'Enlightenment as mass deception'.

The most directly political analyses in the book are found in seven theses on anti-semitism. The seventh is the most remarkable. It was added after the War amidst the general democratic euphoria over the defeat of fascism. Precisely at this moment, Horkheimer and Adorno argue that fascism and anti-semitism have been preserved in the very structure of existing party politics. The tone of this thesis is set by the first sentences: 'But there are no more anti-semites. In their most recent form they were liberals who wanted to assert their anti-liberal opinions' (DE, p. 200). The preservation of anti-semitism is then illustrated by a reality of the US political system, the 'ticket' (e.g. the Nixon–Agnew ticket). 'Anti-semitic judgment has always born witness to stereotyped thought. Today this is all that remains. A choice is still made, but only between totalities. Anti-semitic psychology has been replaced by mere acceptance of the whole fascist ticket, the slogans of aggressive big business' (DE, p. 201). The ticket mentality is part of the all-pervasive process of the negation of individuality. Even progressive parties are directly attacked on these grounds. 'The basis of the development which leads to the acceptance of programmes and tickets is the universal reduction of all specific energy to a single, equal and abstract form of labour, from the battle-field to the film-studio. But the transition from these conditions to a more human state cannot occur because the good suffer the same fate as the evil. Freedom on the progressive ticket is just as external to the structures of political power on which progressive decisions are necessarily based, as anti-semitism is to a chemical cartel' (DE, p. 207).[28]

This treatment of fascism reveals very clearly the limits of historicism. An interpretation of fascism as the essence behind the phenomena, as the 'truth of' modern (capitalist) society, can never achieve the central aim of Marxist analysis, what Lenin called the 'concrete analysis of a concrete situation'. However deep its roots lay in the structure of monopoly capitalism, fascism was in fact a special type of monopoly capitalist State which arose in a specific historical conjuncture.[29] In failing to recognize this, the Frankfurt School in effect took up the positions adopted by the Comintern in the so-called Third Period, after the Sixth Congress of 1928: fascism was seen as an inevitable and culminating phase of capitalism. For all their virtuosity, the Frankfurt School explanations of fascism were thus ultimately an example of theoretical impotence. The theme of *Dialectic of Enlightenment* is the self-destruction of bourgeois reason: but this theory itself is a case of the self-destruction of intellectual radicalism. It is precisely the radicalism of the authors' rejection of bourgeois society and culture which wrests the weapons of socialist theory (science) from their hands, forcing them to retreat into speculative philosophical fragments.

The reduction of science to philosophy is thus revealed in this test case of Frankfurt School theory as doubly mystificatory. The direct condemnation of the logic of the sciences as responsible for fascism make it impossible to develop a conjunctural theory of fascism which would have helped to fight it more effectively. The retreat from Marxist scientific concepts into a philosophical (ideological) critique of capitalist society then covers up for the lack of a theory of it.

The Political Collapse of Horkheimer

The second reduction characteristic of the Frankfurt School, as we

[28] Hence it is possible to argue that all capitalist societies today are fascist still. This notion has pervaded much recent student thinking, especially in Germany, where it is embodied in the concept of '*Spätkapitalismus*' (late capitalism).

[29] See Quintin Hoare: 'What is Fascism?', *New Left Review* 20, Summer 1963.

have seen, is that of politics to philosophy. An examination of this entails an analysis of the attitude of the School to political practice. In this too there is an evolution, but it is further complicated by the political divergences of the School in the post-War years. As we have seen, their initial position, as represented in Hork-heimer's programmatic text of 1937, was similar to that of Lukács. The proletariat was still regarded as the agent of revolution, and the aim of politics was the unity of philosophy and the proletariat in a realized proletarian class consciousness. However, in the late 1930's it was impossible to sustain the young Lukács's belief in the immediacy of this revolutionary unification.[30]

After the signing of the Nazi-Soviet pact in 1939, this initial scepticism deepened. The bleak political situation induced a retreat from politics, but no immediate capitulation. 'Nothing is to be hoped for from the alliances of the great powers. No trust can be put in the collapse of the totalitarian economy. . . . It is completely naïve to call from the outside for the German workers to rise. He who can only play at politics should keep away from it. Confusion has become so general that truth has all the more practical value the less it meddles with any intended practice' (JE, p. 135). Horkheimer recalls the Jews' steadfast rejection of the worship of false gods: 'A lack of respect for an existing authority which extends even to God is the religion of those who, in the Europe of the Iron Heel, continue to devote their lives to the preparation for a better one' (JE, p. 136). Of anti-Communism, at this stage, there was not a word.

The post-War political position of Horkheimer and Adorno, by contrast, has had three aspects: the maintenance of critical theory as a pure theory; the retreat from politics into exclusive individual-ism; and academic integration. However, in none of their later works is either critical theory or its relationship to Marx and Engels repudiated.[31] In his *Negative Dialectic*, Adorno even openly scorns the idealist exploitation of the 'Young Marx' on the grounds that to centre critical theory on the concept of reification only serves to make it idealistically acceptable to the ruling con-sciousness.[32] They have also maintained a firm dividing line

[30] See above.

[31] See for example Max Horkheimer: 'Theismus-Atheismus', in *Zeugnisse* (a *Festschrift* for Adorno, Frankfurt 1963), hereafter referred to as TA; his preface to KT; and Adorno's *Negative Dialectic*.

[32] Op. cit., p. 190.

between their positions and those of conservative *Kulturkritik*.[33]

In Horkheimer's programme, critical theory was defined as part of the political practice of the oppressed classes. From the middle 1940's, critical theory was located elsewhere, in the individual mind. The whole tenor of Horkheimer and Adorno's works in this period is characterized by the conviction that the only place where anything is still possible in the totalitarian world is the 'individual sphere', where the task is to resist the intruding cruelty of the 'administered world'. This is well expressed by Adorno in the preface to *Minima Moralia* (1951): 'In face of the totalitarian unison with which the eradication of difference is proclaimed as a purpose in itself, even part of the social force of liberation may have temporarily withdrawn to the individual sphere. If critical theory lingers there, it is not only with bad conscience.'[34] Horkheimer added a decade later: 'Our hope rests in the work to ensure that in the beginning of a world period dominated by blocks of administered men, a few will be found who offer up some resistance, like the sacrifices of history, to whom belongs the founder of Christianity' (TA, p. 19). This religious solution has at times taken a Jewish form, too.[35]

The academic integration of the West German wing of the Frankfurt School is best represented by *The Authoritarian Personality*, published in 1950, with Adorno as its senior author and Horkheimer as director of the entire research project (entitled *Studies in Prejudice*). Here the stress on individual psychology becomes a complete capitulation to bourgeois social psychology in theory, method and political conclusions. Horkheimer says in his preface: 'It may strike the reader that we have placed undue stress upon the personal and the psychological rather than upon the social aspect of prejudice. That is not due to a personal preference for psychological analysis, nor to a failure to see that the cause of irrational hostility is in the last instance to be found in social frustration and injustice. Our aim is not merely to describe prejudice but to explain it in order to help its eradication. . . . *Eradication means re-education*, scientifically planned on the basis of understanding scientifically arrived at. And education in a

[33] See for instance Adorno's *Prisms* (London 1967).
[34] Theodor Adorno: *Minima Moralia*, London NLB, 1974, p. 18.
[35] See the interview with Horkheimer in *Der Spiegel*, January 5th, 1970.

strict sense is by its nature personal and psychological.'[36] In the last thesis on anti-semitism in *Dialectic of Enlightenment*, anti-semitism was embedded in the very core of the modern political system, both East and West. Here it has suddenly become something which can be done away with by personal education, presumably by the Adenauer government or the Western occupation authorities in Germany. It is profoundly symbolic that Adorno calls the consciously anti-authoritarian personality-type 'the genuine liberal'.[37] This is a long way from the thesis that fascism is the truth of liberalism and the anti-semite the liberal who wants to voice his anti-liberal opinion.

The effect of the combined factors of formal preservation of the theory, exclusive individualization and academic integration is a cumulative mystification. The formula here provides a legitimation for a purely ideological radicalism smugly installed in the cosy academic institution, without even an indirect relationship to politics as experienced by the masses, but still cultivating a critical theory going back to an interpretation of Marx.

This development has also been accompanied by a retreat from the resolute rejection of anti-communism in 1937 and even in 1939. *Dialectic of Enlightenment* already implies that the choice between the USSR and the USA is one between two equal evils, two totalitarian 'tickets', and in the Cold War period, Horkheimer and Adorno committed themselves further to the West against the East. Horkheimer has repeatedly declared his commitment to the 'most civilized' or 'European' States, against the threatening 'totalitarian world', in which are included not only the Communist States but the 'backward countries' with their 'exaggerated nationalisms' (TA, p. 23). According to the former director of *Studies in Prejudice*, not only should Kaiser Wilhelm II's warning of the 'menace of the yellow race . . . be taken very seriously today,' but 'it is perhaps more urgent than it appears', though, 'it is

---

[36] *The Authoritarian Personality* (New York 1950), p. VII. The reader may feel that, after criticizing the Frankfurt School for its rejection of science, I am ungrateful in rejecting this apparent appeal to a policy 'scientifically planned on the basis of understanding scientifically arrived at'. But an appeal to science does not ensure scientificity. Here it is the bourgeois ideology of social psychology which is meant. This is another case of the paradox of Frankfurt hyper-radicalism: the categories denounced philosophically have slipped back into academic discourse unscathed.

[37] Ibid., p. 781.

indeed not the only threat' to Europe.[38] In a recent interview, Horkheimer has gone over to the bourgeois camp in even more positive and ludicrous terms, no longer as the lesser of two evils (note also the motivation given for his philosophical works!): 'In my view, sociology today has still insufficiently noted the fact that the development of man is bound up with competition, that is, with the most important element of the liberal economy.' 'You see, I am thinking of my father [an industrial tycoon]. . . . The competitive struggle enabled him to exert himself practically, in a way not unlike that in which I myself developed my original philosophical interest according to the demands of an academic career, so as to be able to maintain my late beloved wife.'[39]

Marcuse: Integrity and Contradiction

Marcuse's political evolution has, of course, been a polar contrast. Not only did he survive the McCarthy period without compromising himself, like so many other left-wing intellectuals, but he has never rejected those students who have been inspired by his ideas to more practical forms of struggle, as Horkheimer and Adorno have done. Marcuse's political record is an exemplary one. But it does not necessarily imply a deep gulf between the theoretical structure of his thought and that of the other members of the school. An ideological problematic is characteristically labile and can be made to fit many political positions.[40] However, one important theoretical difference can be detected even in 1937. This concerned the relation between philosophy and Marxism as a theory of society. This difference is discernible in the discussion of Horkheimer's programme which followed its publication in the *Zeitschrift für Sozialforschung* under the title 'Philosophy and Critical Theory'. As we noted above, Horkheimer argued that 'the critical theory of society . . . remains philosophical even as a critique of economics'. This is because critical theory is something more than a specialized economic discipline, it is a theory and a judgement of the whole of human existence. For Marcuse, however, this transcendence of specialized economics is contained in a

---

[38] Max Horkheimer: 'On the Concept of Freedom', *Diogenes*, No. 53 (Paris 1966).

[39] *Der Spiegel*, op. cit.

[40] Habermas's suggestion that his political stand is due to an activism inherent in his Heideggerian formation need not be taken very seriously. Cf. J. Habermas (ed.): *Antworten auf Marcuse* (Frankfurt 1968), p. 12.

critical theory of society as such, which is the successor to classical philosophy. 'Philosophy thus appears within the economic concepts of materialist theory, each of which is more than an economic concept of the sort employed by the academic discipline of economics. It is more due to the theory's claim to explain the totality of man and his world in terms of his social being. Yet it would be false on that account to reduce these concepts to philosophical ones. To the contrary, the philosophical contents relevant to the theory are to be educed from the economic structure' (KG I, p. 102; N, pp. 134–5). This conception of the relationship between critical theory and philosophy explains the sub-title of *Reason and Revolution* – 'Hegel and the rise of social theory'. 'If there was to be any progress beyond this philosophy, it had to be an advance beyond philosophy itself and, at the same time, beyond the social and political order to which philosophy had tied its fate.'[41] In 1948, Marcuse re-affirmed this attachment to Marxism as a social theory which rejects philosophy in a critique of Sartre's *L'Etre et le Néant*. 'One step more (from Hegel's philosophy) toward concretization would have meant a transgression beyond philosophy itself. Such transgression occurred in the opposition to Hegel's philosophy. . . . But neither Kierkegaard nor Marx wrote existential philosophy. When they came to grips with concrete existence, they abandoned and repudiated philosophy. . . . For Marx, the conception of *"réalité humaine"* is the critique of political economy and the theory of socialist revolution' (KG II, p. 83; *Philosophy and Phenomenological Research*, VII, no. 3, March 1948, p. 335).

But these intellectual differences should not be taken too far. Marcuse's most famous work, *One-Dimensional Man*, is firmly in the Frankfurt tradition, and shares its theoretical faults, particularly the self-destructive intellectual hyper-radicalism which characterized *Dialectic of Enlightenment*. As Marcuse explains in the preface to the republication in 1965 of his essays from the 1930's, 'Thought in contradiction must become more negative and more utopian in opposition to the status quo. This seems to me to be the imperative of the current situation in relation to my theoretical essays of the 1930's' (KG I, p. 16; N, p. xx). But, as realized in *One-Dimensional Man*, this project reveals at its centre

---

[41] Herbert Marcuse: *Reason and Revolution* (Oxford 1941), p. 257.

a massive contradiction. The book is conceived as a picture of industrial society or 'the most highly developed contemporary societies', whereas in fact it is a highly conjunctural work, defined by the situation in the USA in the 1950's and early 1960's, before the internal effects of the Vietnamese War had made themselves felt, before the student movement and the rise of working-class resistance, and before the visible disintegration of US supremacy over Western Europe and Japan.[42] Marcuse's weakness is not his failure to see these future tendencies, but the fact that his analysis provides no concepts by means of which he might have discovered them. As Marcuse himself says, 'the critical theory of society possesses no concepts which could bridge the gap between the present and its future' (ODM, p. 14). Moreover, instead of using a Marxist analysis of modern monopoly capitalism, Marcuse relies on such works as Berle and Means: *The Modern Corporation and Private Property*, William H. Whyte: *The Organization Man*, and the writings of Vance Packard. The crucial argument about the integration of the working class is characteristically sustained by reference to academic American sociology. Once again, the radicalism of the critique has left its ideological object untouched.

In fact, *One-Dimensional Man* represents a step backwards for Marcuse *vis-à-vis* many of his attitudes to technology, to philosophy and to classical bourgeois culture. In *Soviet Marxism* he upheld the notion of the 'essentially neutral character' of technology and made it one of the corner-stones of his analysis of Soviet society; the change from a nationalized economy to a socialised one is a political revolution entailing the dismantling of the repressive State and the installation of control from below.[43] In *One-Dimensional Man*, the opposite view prevails: 'The traditional notion of the "neutrality" of technology can no longer be maintained. . . . The technological society is a system of domination which operates already in the concept and construction of techniques' (ODM, p. 14). Secondly, the conception of philosophy and its role in *One-Dimensional Man* contains a repudiation, though more implicit, of Marcuse's earlier positions. Instead of

[42] For the effects of the Vietnamese War, see my 'From Petrograd to Saigon', *New Left Review* 48, 1968; for the new tendencies of US capitalism, see Ernest Mandel: 'Where is America Going?', *New Left Review* 54, 1969, and 'The Laws of Uneven Development', *New Left Review* 59, 1970.

[43] *Soviet Marxism*, (New York 1958), pp. 160–191.

asserting the need to replace philosophy with a Marxist theory of society, *One-Dimensional Man* sets out to defend and maintain philosophy in the classical idealist sense, with concepts antagonistic to the prevailing discourse. This reversal is perhaps most clearly expressed in the following sentence, where instead of replacing philosophy with social theory and politics, he suggests that the problem is to replace politics with philosophy. 'In the totalitarian era, the therapeutic task of philosophy would be a political task. . . . Then politics would appear in philosophy, not as a special discipline or object of analysis, nor as a special political philosophy, but as the intent of its concepts to comprehend the unmutilated reality' (ODM, p. 159). Thirdly, the concept of 'affirmative culture' discussed in the 1937 article mentioned above, the sublimated bourgeois culture in which the values denied by bourgeois society in everyday life are affirmed in the sphere of high culture, is replaced by the concept of 'repressive desublimation'. Here we are basically dealing with a change in the object of analysis, from one type of bourgeois society to another, and in this sense the concept of repressive desublimation is an important and fruitful tool of analysis. But in another paradox of intellectual hyper-radicalism, what was once condemned as 'affirmative culture' is now hailed as a culture of negation, denouncing the poverty of society (ODM, p. 58ff.). In *One-Dimensional Man*, a critique which sets out to refute the very structure of logic and science bases its social analyses on pseudo-liberal journalism and academic sociology, and a critique which does not even find Marxism negative enough turns the affirmative bourgeois culture into a negative one.[44]

The Negation of the Negation

One-Dimensional Man is thus, of all Marcuse's works, the closest to the main-stream of the Frankfurt School. Yet it is also the book that has had the most political influence, more, probably, than anything else produced by the School in all its forty years of existence. Despite its pessimism, this book has become one of the standard texts of the student revolt of the late 1960's. But before

[44] These critical remarks should not, however, obliterate the differences between *One-Dimensional Man* and the post-War works of Horkheimer and Adorno. The former is still an attempt at a concrete social analysis with a direct bearing on politics.

examining the link between the views of the Frankfurt School and the recent student revolt, we must examine the concepts which underly these political positions. The most important one arises directly from the hyper-radicalism of the School's critique of capitalist society. Critical theory rejects any positive presence in capitalist society (such as the proletariat) and seeks the purest negation, *the negation of the negation*, as the essence of revolution. This Hegelian notion of revolutionary change has played a central and disastrous role in Frankfurt thought. In their search for the absolute negation of the prevailing theoretical and ideological discourse, the thinkers of the Frankfurt School feel forced to go outside both science, concrete social analysis, and formal logic. Horkheimer's 1937 programme for a critical theory tried to find an Archimedean point outside society in order to uproot itself from the process of social reproduction. In the 1940's, Horkheimer and Adorno considered it necessary to go even further, formulating their social critique only in philosophical fragments, because any continuous discourse was bound to lapse into positivity. The search for an absolute negation of the negation is also the rationale for Marcuse's retreat from Marxism in *One-Dimensional Man*: 'An attempt to recapture the critical intent of these categories (society, class, individual, etc), and to understand how the intent was cancelled by the social reality appears from the outset to be regression from a theory joined with historical practice to abstract, speculative thought; from the critique of political economy to philosophy. This ideological character of the critique results from the fact that the analysis is forced to proceed from a position "outside" the positive as well as the negative, the productive as well as the destructive tendencies in society' (ODM, pp. 12ff.).

This attempt by the theory to pull itself up by the hair does not make it more revolutionary, but rather more philosophical. The same attitude can be detected in the denial that the economic class struggle can play a revolutionary role in the developed capitalist countries.[45] The historical experience of revolutions shows that they have not been sustained by the absolute negativity of the

[45] Marcuse: *An Essay on Liberation* (1969), Chs. 3 & 4. This is still asserted despite the fact that the economic class struggle has been crucial to the militant working-class struggles of Italy and France in the last few years, and has also played a not insignificant role in the Scandinavian countries, which certainly cannot be dismissed as 'more backward capitalist countries'.

revolutionaries' demands, but by the determination with which concrete immediate demands have been urged in particular historical situations. Practical revolutionaries – Rosa Luxemburg as well as Lenin – have therefore always stressed the dialectical link between the various types of class struggle. None of them bothered to look for the absolute negation. On the contrary, Lenin's theory of revolution has two key moments. One is the building up of an organized revolutionary force and leadership. The other is the emergence of a revolutionary situation. This is characterized by a fusion of different contradictions such that the question of State power is put on the immediate agenda. The revolutionary situation can be ushered in by the most diverse, and apparently banal causes, including even a parliamentary crisis. The conception of the revolutionary situation as a fusion of different contradictions is not an *ad hoc* explanation, but follows logically from the analysis of society as a complex social formation with mutually irreducible elements.[46] Now we have already seen that, far from conceiving society as a complex structure, historicist theories of society look for an inner essence revealed in all its parts. If this essence is oppressive, the source for a transformation cannot be found inside society, for all its manifestations share the oppressive nature of the essence. The agent of transformation can only be an external Negating Subject. The first historicist versions of Marxism thought that this external negating subject was the proletariat, thrust out of capitalist society as the object of all its oppressions, incarnating the capitalist negation of humanity. Both Lukács's *History and Class Consciousness* and Horkheimer's *Traditional and Critical Theory* contain this conception of the working class. But the proletariat no longer seems 'absolutely' miserable and excluded in the so-called welfare state. The only groups who could still be so described are racial minorities and other outcasts. That is why, in his later works, Marcuse has tried to penetrate deeper into other human needs than economic ones, for he claims that the latter have now become means of integration and oppression. He has therefore turned his attention to the 'biological dimension', to vital instinctive drives, to 'erotic' needs in the broad sense of the

[46] Lenin's theory of revolution is most clearly elaborated in his *Letters from Afar* and *'Left-Wing' Communism, an Infantile Disorder*. The incompatibility of his theory with any kind of historicism has been demonstrated by Louis Althusser in his essay 'Contradiction and Overdetermination', *For Marx* (London 1969).

term. In doing so he has found a new Negating Subject in the student movement and its refusal of the performance principle, its rejection of an economy based on exchange and competition, and its practice of sexual liberation.

But was the role of the proletariat in Marx's theory ever that of an absolute negation of capitalist society? On the one hand, Marx says explicitly that the social polarization resulting from the immiseration of the working class is crucial to the proletarian revolution (though this need not necessarily take the form of a strictly literal economic pauperization). On the other hand, Marx characterizes the epochal crisis of capitalism by a structural rather than a simply political contradiction, a contradiction between the social character of the productive forces and the private character of the relations of production. In this context, the term 'productive forces' refers to the organizational/technical conditions under which production proceeds – handicrafts, manufacture, machine industry, and automated process industry are different levels of the productive forces. These productive forces, which come into contradiction with the private mode of their appropriation, include the increasing use of science, developed communications, a high educational level and an internalized discipline in the work force. Their effects on the working class are not immiseration but rather the provision of greater facilities for organization and a greater capacity to replace the capitalist regimentation of production by social appropriation and working-class control from below. There is always a social polarization between the working class and the bourgeoisie which arises directly from the fact of exploitation: this is intensified by economic crises induced by the contradiction between the productive forces and relations of production: a revolutionary situation then makes it explosive. Hence Marxist theory does not need a conception of the proletariat as the incarnation of the negation of human existence. A revolutionary situation is a function of the complex development of the social formation, whose different contradictions suddenly fuse in a 'ruptural unity', not of the simple degree of wealth or poverty of the proletariat.[47]

[47] The line of reasoning very summarily outlined here suggests that a careful analysis of the place and implications of the concepts of productive forces and revolutionary situation in Marxist–Leninist theory is a more promising way to tackle the problem than to rely textually on the *Grundrisse* drafts, comparing them with *Capital*, as in Martin Nicolaus's otherwise important essay, 'The Unknown

The Marxist concept of the contradiction between the social character of the productive forces and the private character of the relations of production has never been incorporated into historicist interpretations of Marx in a way which preserves the objective character of both aspects of this contradiction as structures of the capitalist mode of production. For the young Lukács, the 'decisive weight' is attached to whether ' "the greatest force of production" in the capitalist order of production, the proletariat, experiences the crisis as a mere object of the decision, or as its subject'.[48] Here the analysis of the structural pre-conditions for revolution has been spirited away, reducing the forces of production to the proletariat. In fact, this makes the concept itself superfluous: all that matters is the proletariat and its degree of insight into its historical mission, its relationship to class consciousness. The Frankfurt School, on the other hand, has used the concept of the productive forces in another way. They are seen as representing the objective possibility of a new and better society. 'This idea is distinguished from abstract utopia by the proof of its real possibility given by the present level of human productive forces' (KT II, p. 168). The productive forces are not part of a *structural* contradiction, a contradiction between social and private *systems*, which affects class relationships, but are seen as the stage of human evolution which now enables the Negating Subject to abolish poverty and misery from the human condition.[49] It is in this sense that the productive forces are 'neutral', a raw material of potentiality. This neutrality is later denied: from a raw material of potentiality, technology becomes a means of oppression. But in neither case are the forces of production seen in their Marxist structural context. Rather, the analysis slips away from any positive identification of the structures of the capitalist social formation, or of the forces within it capable of transforming that social formation; from Marxist science and politics to philosophy as *Ersatz* science and *Ersatz* politics. Even when apparently anchored in the social structure, the Negating Subject was a philosophical concept; as Révai long ago pointed out in a review of *History and Class Consciousness*, the 'assigned proletarian class consciousness' was

---

Marx', *New Left Review* 48, 1968.

[48] Lukács, op. cit., p. 421.

[49] See Horkheimer's essay, 'Geschichte und Psychologie', where the structural condition is replaced by 'the opposition between the growing powers of men and the social structure' (KT I, p. 17).

merely substituted by Lukács for the Hegelian *Geist.*[50] In the Frankfurt School, this reduction of politics to philosophy has come directly out into the open.

Anti-Capitalist Revulsion and Socialist Revolution

Before attempting a general historical assessment of the Frankfurt School, let us summarize the argument of this article hitherto. The thought of the School has evolved, and marked divergences between its members have appeared in the years since the War. Nevertheless, there is a persistent underlying structure. This takes the form of a *double reduction* of *science* and of *politics* to philosophy. The specificity of Marxism as a theory of social formations and its autonomy as a guide to political action are thereby simultaneously abolished. This first reduction is clearly revealed by the Frankfurt School's theory of fascism, in which a philosophical critique of capitalism replaces a scientific conjunctural analysis of the nature of the Fascist State. The second reduction appears in the conception of the revolutionary agent as a Negating Subject, which cannot be located in social reality, and therefore eventually has to be confined to philosophy, conceived as social reality's opposite.

Since its inception, the Frankfurt School has probably produced more work and covered a wider variety of subjects (many of which could not be dealt with in this short article) than any other comparable group of theorists. Their influence today is probably greater than it has ever been. Yet, as we have seen, the problematic underlying their thought has central and fatal weaknesses. What general verdict can we make of their historical achievement?

The theorists of the Frankfurt School were members of an academic intelligentsia with a high bourgeois background. They came to intellectual maturity in a period of international defeat for the working class, and were cut off from the proletariat of their own country by the Nazi counter-revolution. Like all members of the bourgeoisie, their initiation into a revolutionary position came about through a *revulsion* against capitalist oppression and capitalist ideology's hypocritical denial of that oppression. This

[50] József Révai: review of *Geschichte und Klassenbewusstsein, Archiv für die Geschichte des Sozialismus und der Arbeiterbewegung,* Vol. XI, 1925, pp. 227–236.

revulsion took the form of a direct denunciation of all the nostrums of bourgeois ideology, particularly the economic ideology of free and equal exchange. But just as they adopted these positions, the capitalist system in their country suddenly took on a political form of unparalleled monstrosity with the Nazi seizure of power. This political machine was also a direct threat to themselves and their families. Understandably, fascism became a Medusa's head for the Frankfurt School. The result was that the initial attitude of revulsion was *frozen*, instead of developing into a scientific analysis and participation in revolutionary political practice. Sober political analysis seemed morally impossible; an objective scientific description of Nazism seemed to condone it because it did not condemn it violently in every sentence: in the dark ages, 'A smooth forehead betokens/a hard heart' (Brecht).[51] When, to the surprise of most of the School, the monster was destroyed and Nazism was defeated, this attitude had become too fixed for them to make the step from philosophical revulsion to science and politics.

Hence to this day, Frankfurt School thought has never moved from a reflection on its theorists' revulsion from capitalism to a theory of the object of that revulsion and a political practice to transform it. It has therefore been able to develop a powerful and well-articulated anti-capitalist ideology, and this must be numbered among its achievements. It has helped to recapture that dimension of Marx's thought which deals with the qualitative aspects of work and human relations in capitalist society. As one of the School's severest critics, Lucio Colletti, has emphasized, neither the Second International nor the Comintern preserved this dimension. The decisive innovator here was Lukács, but the Frankfurt School has played an almost equally pioneering role, along with Wilhelm Reich, in enriching these ideas by adding a psycho-analytic dimension to them. It has also achieved a series of often brilliant and incisive critiques of bourgeois culture – Adorno's greatest contribution.[52]

Moreover, it is this function of Frankfurt theory as a developed reflection of anti-capitalist revulsion which explains the persistence

---

[51] *An die Nachgeborenen.*

[52] This essay has been mainly focused on the work of Horkheimer, chronologically and substantively the 'founder' of the Frankfurt School, with some discussion of the separate itinerary of Marcuse. Comparatively little space has been devoted to

of the School. The combination of institutional continuity and the freezing of a common attitude by the Nazi trauma has preserved it and its basic ideas despite all the changes of the last forty years. Hence it could suddenly re-emerge as something like a magical *anticipation* of the contemporary student movement, which spontaneously rediscovered the same themes in the 'sixties. Just as the Frankfurt School was formed when the revolution was taking place in Russia, but seemed to be absent from Germany, so today it can be seen in Vietnam, Cuba and China, but 'seems' absent from the metropolitan imperialist countries. Students in the West could thus feel cut off from it much as the Frankfurt School did in the 1920's and 1930's. At the same time, the student revolutionary today is a young bourgeois or petty-bourgeois recruit who has discovered the oppressive and murderous nature of imperialism. He or she is revolted. Because of their peculiar historical experience, because of the shock of Nazism, the Frankfurt School have preserved this attitude of revulsion in crystalline fragments, aphorisms and images. Hence the enormous attraction their work still exercises on those going through the same process. But we must hope that they will not suffer the same fate as the Frankfurt theorists. It is essential to move on from the discovery of the horrors of capitalism to an attempt to understand it scientifically and to unite with the masses in order to overthrow it. If this is not achieved, the Frankfurt School, or a new Anglo-Saxon, Italian, French or Scandinavian branch of it, may have another forty years of paralysed virtuosity ahead of it.

A Note on Habermas

Jürgen Habermas is at present the most celebrated of the successors of the Frankfurt School and the only one as yet well-known outside the Federal German Republic. In the essay above, I have

Adorno. It should be said, however, that while Adorno's contribution to the main methodological and philosophical themes of the School seems to have been secondary, his specific applications of them are often the most dazzling exercises within the collective oeuvre – perhaps because his chosen fields of music and literature more properly permit a strictly 'critical' analysis – criticism – than social formations or political systems.

discussed the work of Horkheimer, Adorno and Marcuse, the original nucleus of the Frankfurt School. The younger successors of the School were referred to, but not discussed, for two reasons. First, that the older three were of the same generation and had much the same historical experience in common, and second that, until the last few years at least, despite fundamental political differences, the original members remained true to their Marxist origins philosophically. This note will attempt to analyse Habermas's thought, and its development away from the Marxist positions of the founders of the School. It is important to analyse Habermas's ideas, because they are particularly attractive to reformist sociologists attempting to erect a 'critical' sociology in opposition to the conservative orthodoxy in that discipline.

Appropriately enough, Habermas's inaugural lecture as Professor of Philosophy and Sociology in Frankfurt is the key text in establishing the origins of his position in Horkheimer's ideas, but also the divergences which have supervened in the interval since Horkheimer originally formulated them. Entitled *Erkenntnis und Interesse* (Cognition and Interest),[1] this lecture invites comparison with the crucial statement of the classical Frankfurt School, Horkheimer's *Traditional and Critical Theory*,[2] for Habermas claims that the latter article 'underlies' his lecture (TWI, p. 147n.). However, classical critical theory is hardly discussed in the lecture, and it would be impossible to discern what the former was about from it. Horkheimer regarded critical theory as Marxism, albeit a very special interpretation of Marxism. In Habermas's text, Marx and Engels are not even hinted at (with the exception of a negative reference to Soviet Marxism). Instead, the points of reference are Greek philosophy, Schelling, Husserl and Adorno's critique of him, and contemporary hermeneutic philosophers such as Apel and Gadamer. With Horkheimer, critical theory was socially anchored in the revolutionary proletariat. In Habermas's

[1] This lecture should not be confused with the book *Erkenntnis und Interesse* (Frankfurt 1968). Hereafter the latter will be referred to as EI. The former is included in a collection of essays by Habermas entitled *Technik und Wissenschaft als 'Ideologie'* (Technique and Science as 'Ideology' – Frankfurt 1968), pp. 146–68. This volume is hereafter referred to as TWI. Three essays from TWI have been translated in Jürgen Habermas: *Towards a Rational Society* (London 1971), hereafter referred to as TRS.

[2] Max Horkheimer: 'Traditionelle und kritische Theorie', in *Zeitschrift für Sozialforschung*, Heft 2, 1937.

academic oration there is no room for any workers, still less for a revolutionary proletariat. The 'emancipatory interest' (to use a term of Habermas's) which guided Horkheimer and which he regarded as the 'only concern' of the critical theorist, was 'to accelerate a development which should lead to a society without exploitation'. It was clear from the context that this development was the proletarian socialist revolution. Habermas's interest in emancipation produces merely 'self-reflection' (TWI, p. 159).

Habermas's project is epistemology, *Erkenntnistheorie*, the theory of the conditions of possible knowledge. Habermas argues that since the middle of the 19th century, theories of knowledge have been replaced by theories of science. The frame of reference is no longer the knowing subject, but rather systems of scientific propositions and procedures. Habermas's aim is to bridge the gap between the traditions of *Erkenntnistheorie* and *Erkenntniskritik* (i.e. critique of knowledge).[3] He concludes that 'ultimately a radicalized critique of knowledge can only be carried out in the form of a reconstruction of the history of the species' (EI, pp. 84ff.). This argument is based on the Hegelian notion of the history of the species as a *Bildungsprozess*, a process of formation or education, in which the species constitutes itself. The link between the philosophy of history and the theory of knowledge is provided by the concept of 'interest', or to be exact 'knowledge-guiding interest' (*erkenntnisleitendes Interesse* – EI, p. 243). 'I call *interests* the basic orientations which are responsible for determinate fundamental conditions of the possible reproduction and self-constitution of the human species' (EI, p. 242). These interests determine the 'conditions of possible objectivity' for the various sciences (in the broad sense of the word *Wissenschaft* – TWI, p. 160).

Habermas distinguishes between three of these 'knowledge-guiding interests': 1. technical – 'adaptation to technical dispositions'; 2. practical – 'adaptation to the arrangements of practical life'; and 3. emancipatory – orientated to 'emancipation from naturalistic constraint'. They correspond to or guide three types of sciences: the empirical-analytical, the historical-hermeneutic and the critical sciences, respectively. These interests, and the

[3] See above all EI and his overview in 'Zur Logik der Sozialwissenschaften' (On the Logic of the Social Sciences), *Philosophische Rundschau* 1967, Beiheft 5. For a Marxist position on this issue in direct opposition to that of Habermas, see Louis Althusser: *For Marx*.

sciences they guide, develop in the three 'media' in which the social life of the human species unfolds: work, language and domination (*Herrschaft* – TWI, pp. 155ff.): 'This viewpoint (i.e., one from which we necessarily conceive reality as transcendental) derives from the complex of interests of a species, which is bound up from the beginning with determinate media of socialization: with labour, language and domination. The human species ensures its survival in systems of social labour and coercive self-assertion; by a traditionally mediated common life in colloquial linguistic communication; and finally with the assistance of ego-identities which reinforce the consciousness of the individuals in relation to the norms of the group at every stage of individualization. Thus the knowledge-guiding interests are responsible for the functions of an ego which adapts itself to its external life conditions in learning processes; which is trained by formative processes in the communications complex of a social environment; and which constructs an identity in the conflict between instinctual demands and social constraints' (TWI, pp. 162ff.).

The critical sciences naturally have a special place in this triple trinity of interests, media and sciences. Its medium anchorage, i.e. 'domination', is at first sight rather unclear. The term *Herrschaft* (surprisingly, perhaps) includes socio-psychological processes of role-learning and personality formation. In Hegel's 'dialectic of morality' (*Sittlichkeit*), these functions are fulfilled by the family. In later formulations, Habermas himself has subsumed them – together with the symbolic sphere – under the concept of 'interaction'.[4] He then conceptualizes Domination as 'distorted communication', deriving this concept from Freud.[5] In other words, critical sciences and emancipatory interest are linked to social action in the sense of Max Weber and Talcott Parsons, i.e. to conduct oriented to expectations of how *alter* will react to *ego's* action.[6] We can now understand the task of Habermas's critique:

---

[4] See the essay 'Arbeit und Interaktion: Bemerkungen zu Hegels Jenenser "Philosophie des Geistes"' (Labour and Interaction: Notes on Hegel's Jena 'Philosophy of Mind') in TWI, pp. 9–47.

[5] EI, pp. 341ff, and 'Towards a Theory of Communicative Competence', in Hans Peter Dreitzel, ed.,*Recent Sociology Number Two*, London 1970, pp. 144–148. The latter is referred to hereafter as TTCC.

[6] Cf. Max Weber: *Wirtschaft und Gesellschaft* (Tübingen 1925), Vol. 1 pp. 1ff., and Talcott Parsons *et al.*: *Towards a General Theory of Action* (Cambridge, Mass. 1951).

'The systematic *sciences of action*, i.e. economics, sociology and political science, have the aim of producing nomological knowledge, like the empirical sciences. Of course, critical social science has no complaints about this. However, it is concerned to see beyond this whether theoretical statements express invariant regularities of social action, or whether they express ideologically frozen, but in principle transformable relations of dependence.' Its basic assumption can be summed up like this: 'In so far as this is true, the *critique of ideology*, just like *psycho-analysis*, reckons with the fact that information about the complexes of laws governing consciousness can itself initiate a process of reflection in them; for this reason it is possible to transform the stages of unreflected consciousness which are part of the initial conditions of such laws. . . . The methodological framework which established the validity of this category of critical statements lacks the concept of *self-reflection*. The latter disengages the subject from dependence on hypostasized forces. Self-reflection is determined by an emancipatory knowledge-interest. The critically orientated sciences share it with philosophy' (TWI, pp. 158ff.). Habermas's chosen method is then immanent critique: 'The power of critical sociology lies in its remembrance of the original intentions behind the current goals of today and what has actually been established. It takes the pretensions of the existing arrangements at their word, for even where these words are utopian, they determine, realistically conceived, what the existing is *not*.'[7] Thus the psychoanalytic situation is supposed to exemplify the critical process (EI, chs. 10–12).

Horkheimer's ideas have clearly been drastically revised in this programme. Horkheimer saw the dividing line between traditional and critical theory essentially in sociological terms: his criterion was whether the theory assisted the reproduction of society or subverted it. Habermas's criterion is ontological, linked to a speculative conception of man derived from Hegel's Jena lectures (see TWI, pp. 9–47). Classical critical theory was sociologically determined in a second sense – however thin and fragile the actual bonds may have been, it was linked to a definite social force, the

---

[7] J. Habermas: 'Kritische und konservative Aufgaben der Soziologie' (Critical and Conservative Tasks of Sociology) in his collection of articles *Theorie und Praxis* (Theory and Praxis – Neuwied and Berlin, 2nd ed. 1967), pp. 215–30, especially p. 229. This book is hereafter referred to as TP.

working class. Habermas's theory is linked only to his own view of the 'functions' of the human ego. This is more clearly formulated in another article: "Reflection must go further back than any historically determined class interest and lay bare the complex of interests of a self-constituting species as such' (TWI, p. 91; TRS, p. 113). However, despite these fundamental changes, whose effects I shall analyse in more detail below, much in Habermas's thought derives from or is held in common with the ideas of the classical Frankfurt School. The hermeneutic orientation and emphasis on intersubjectivity which he shares with Horkheimer, Adorno, and even Marcuse, obliterates the line of demarcation between scientific theory and everyday intersubjective understanding within a linguistic-cultural community. This obliteration is a precondition for the contention that the criticism and supersession of a scientific theory or an allegedly scientific discourse can be reduced to a process of *Ideologiekritik* or criticism of ideology. Much as with the older generation of Frankfurt School theorists, the errors this gives rise to emerge most clearly in the consequent interpretation of Marx and Freud, and attempt to reconcile the two.

Marx and Freud

Many readings and interpretations have been made of Freud. Two are found in Habermas's work. One of these is hermeneutic; it starts from the clinical situation, the dialogue between the analyst and the analysand, and sees the therapy as a process of self-reflection both for analyst and analysand. The second is critical; it focuses on Freud's meta-psychological works, his books on culture, and the idea of human cultural development as the repression of human instincts.[8]

Whatever value these interpretations may have in a general cultural debate, they have no place in a discussion of the theory of science, but that is the context in which Habermas introduces them. They obscure all that makes Freud more than a conversational therapist and cultural philosopher, indeed, they obscure all that gives 'hermeneutic' or 'cultural' philosophers reason to turn to Freud for epistemological arguments. These interpretations

---

[8] Habermas's interpretation of Freud is keyed to the former interpretation, but contains both. See below and EI, chs. 10–12 and TTCC.

exemplify what the great French epistemologist Gaston Bachelard denounced as the parasitic utilization of science by philosophers for their own purposes.[9]

In Habermas's interpretation, the centre of psycho-analysis is a theory of linguistic failure, of systematically distorted communication – examples being dreams, everyday slips of the tongue, neurotic and psychotic symptoms, and also 'the hidden pathology of collective behaviour and entire social systems' (TTCC, pp. 117–18). As distorted communication, the neurotic symptom is characterized by the use of deviant linguistic rules, compulsive repetition, and discrepancy between levels of communication, all of which add up to the adoption of a private language on the part of the sufferer. This results from a childhood inability to resolve some conflict, the object of which the child and adult exclude from public communication by desymbolization and symptom formation. In the transference relationship between analyst and analysand, these primal scenes are recreated, and their re-enactment enables the analysand to reflect on the symptom, to understand its aetiology, and thus to restore the primal object of conflict to the status of a public utterance.

This might appear to be close to Lacan's reading of Freud, which shares its stress on the linguistic element of psycho-analysis, and sees the aim of the cure as the transformation of an 'empty speech' into a 'full speech'. But this apparent resemblance is only superficial. For Habermas, unconscious processes are only necessary to explain pathological pseudo-communication (significantly, he refers to Freud's later topography of id, ego and super-ego, rather than to the unconscious and conscious), whereas normal social communication is self-explanatory; inter-subjectivity is self-evident. Moreover, this normal and desirable transparency is extended to social systems as well, which are to be 'socio-analysed' by the critical social scientist. In Lacan's reading, on the contrary, the unconscious is precisely what the pathological and the normal have in common: it is omni-present (and omni-absent). Furthermore, the unconscious does not just underly the notions of everyday experience, conveniently explaining them. It is a scientific concept, and its discovery therefore entails the transformation of

[9] This theme is central to Bachelard's whole work. Cf. Dominique Lecourt: *L'epistémologie historique de Gaston Bachelard* (Paris 1969).

the notions of everyday life into concepts of the theory of psycho-analysis. Such is the case, for example, with one of the most central concepts of psycho-analysis, that of sexuality. A great step in the constitution of psycho-analysis as a science consisted precisely in the elaboration of a radically new definition of sexuality.[10]

Thus Habermas's recourse to Freud is an attempt to explain away phenomena like neurotic symptoms which do not fit into the schema of the transparency of inter-subjective communication, and then to use the notion of distorted communication to criticize and reform social systems so that their 'unconscious' aspects can be eradicated. Nothing could be further from a scientific reading of Freud.

The implications of Habermas's programme for the critical social sciences are perhaps even clearer when we turn to Marx. Habermas reduces Marx to a critic of ideology: 'According to Marx, the critique of political economy was simply a theory of bourgeois society as a critique of its ideology. But when the ideology of fair exchange collapses, the system of domination, too, can no longer be immediately criticized according to the relations of production' (TWI, p. 76; TRS, p. 101). Marx, however, did not content himself with 'criticizing' bourgeois ideology, i.e. with demonstrating the contrast between its assumptions and reality. *Capital* is not an immanent critique of liberalism – if it were it would be of little interest today. It is a work in which a new science is founded, a science of society and of history. In it Marx constructs a new concept of the economy, not as an effect of human 'propensi-ties' – whether Smith's 'propensity to trade, truck and barter' or Keynes's propensity to consume – but as a 'region' in a complex social structure, defined by the concepts of forces and relations of production.[11]

It is noteworthy that Marx in Habermas's interpretation, not to speak of Habermas's own brand of critical theory, represent basically the same type of critique of capitalism as those Marx and Engels found and attacked in the utopian socialists, Proudhon,

---

[10] See Sigmund Freud: 'Three Essays on the Theory of Sexuality', *Standard Edition* Vol. VII (London 1953), and Etienne Balibar: 'On the Basic Concepts of Historical Materialism' in Louis Althusser and Etienne Balibar: *Reading Capital* (London 1970), pp. 243–7.

[11] See Louis Althusser: 'The Object of *Capital*', in Louis Althusser and Etienne Balibar: *Reading Capital*, op. cit., pp. 182–93.

Saint-Simon, Fourier and Owen.[12] The latter had criticized bourgeois society from the point of view of its own ideals and had formed their utopias along the same lines. Marx and Engels showed that the bourgeois ideals – liberal conceptions of justice and freedom – were not fundamentally in contradiction with bourgeois society's real mode of functioning, but on the contrary were an expression of it. An immanent critique, like Fourier's, was capable of revealing the hypocrisy of most bourgeois ideologists. The scientific socialism of Marx and Engels, however, pointed to the necessity for another *goal* of socialism than that of the utopians – not Proudhon's society of fair exchange, but the transitional dictatorship of the proletariat and communism. It also showed other *preconditions* of socialism – structural conflicts between the forces and relations of production – in the capitalist economy. Thirdly, scientific socialism indicated new *means*: the class struggle, the revolutionary party, and the proletarian revolution.

Freud and Marx did not linger on the established terrains of psychological and economic discourse as 'critics'. They showed the sterility of those terrains, abandoned them and opened up new ones. So our task today is not to be the critical conscience of bourgeois social thought, but to *break* with it; it is not to construct 'critical social sciences' peacefully and parasitically co-existing with the traditional ideological output, but to reject the alleged scientificity of the latter and to set out upon the path of true science cleared by Marx.[13]

Labour and Interaction

Thus far my criticisms could be applied with equal force to the writings of Horkheimer or Adorno. But it is clear that Habermas's

---

[12] See Karl Marx: *The Poverty of Philosophy* and Friedrich Engels: *Anti-Dühring*.

[13] For example, the aim of the attack on bourgeois ideology is not to point out 'ideologically frozen but in principle transformable relations of dependence', but rather to reveal patterns of determinism beneath a voluntarist ideology. The bourgeois State is an objective structure of capitalist society which can be abolished only when class society is abolished, and it is neither a neutral tool in the hands of the parliamentary majority nor anything merely 'ideologically frozen'. The same is true of imperialism. It should perhaps be added that the necessary shift in terrain for Marxists concerns the basic theoretical problematic, not a simple disregard for what is produced by academic social research, much of which is valuable in one respect or another, and that the path of a scientific study of society will therefore be one of constant struggle with academic sociology.

departure from Marxism is far more radical than that of his fore-bears. The life-line to classical Marxism carefully maintained by the founders of the Frankfurt School, even in its wildest adventures, has been decisively cut by Habermas. I shall discuss the reasons for this break below. For the moment I shall concentrate on its result for his own position: Habermas has been forced to construct an alternative system of his own. I will now turn to this new system as such.

Habermas rejects the concepts of the productive forces and relations of production, substituting for them the notions of labour and interaction. The explicit motivation for this substitution is that the latter are more general, whereas the former are bound to assumptions about liberal capitalism which no longer hold (TWI, p. 92; TRS, p. 113). This explicit revision in fact stems from a more basic one which turns Marx's scientific innovation into a philosophy of history modelled on Hegel's dialectic of morality (*Sittlichkeit* – see EI, chs. 2–3).

For Marxism, which is an historical and social science of modes of production, the productive forces and relations of production denote objective economic structures. The level of the former constitutes the technical-organizational pattern of production as exemplified in handicrafts, machine industry, process industry, different facilities of communication, and so on. The relations of production refer neither to juridical property nor to actual disposal (in neither of these senses could capital be said to consti-tute a relation of production). They refer to the mode – specific to every mode of production – in which surplus-labour is extracted from the immediate producers. They determine the relation between the latter and those who expropriate their surplus-labour – between the slave and the slave-owner or between the wage-earner and the capitalist, for instance. They determine the aim of production – for consumption, for sale on a market, for profit. They determine the context of the immediate work situa-tion – whether independent, as in the tribute-duty village, or tightly controlled by the capitalist and his subordinates, and the relation between necessary and surplus-labour – separate or fused.[14]

---

[14] Among the key references for these concepts are *Capital* Vol. I, chs. 7 and 12–15, and Vol. III, chs. 47, 48 and 51. Two starting-points are provided by the distinctions in Vol. 1, ch. 7 between the labour process and the process of producing value, which

Such concepts are of little use to the philosopher of history bent on constructing a philosophy of the self-constitution of the human species.[15] Habermas clings to the concepts of Marx's early manuscripts and develops the notion of the self-realization of the human species in labour, and of labour as a materialist synthesis of man and nature.[16] In the language of modern sociology, the subsystem of labour covers all rational instrumental (*zweckrational*) action. It is within this general sub-system that factors of production (Habermas's notion of Marx's productive forces) have developed. But here a difficulty arises for such a philosophy of history. If, as Marx implies, the relations of production are also an economic concept, then all human activity is restricted to labour, i.e. to instrumental action. So Marx must be wrong. For while he included the relations of production within the mode of production, he also noted the existence of an *institutional framework* for the labour process, the role of one class over another, and a kind of *'communicative activity'* in the class struggle. These concepts arose in his material investigations. The contradiction thus implied between Marx's concepts and his theoretical conclusions Habermas attributes to his epistemological misconception of historical materialism as a natural science rather than as a *critique*. Habermas replaces the concept of the relations of production with a new term designating the 'institutional framework of society' – the notion of *'symbolically mediated interaction'*.[17]

It is obvious that this double revision – of a scientific theory

---

is spelt out in chs. 12–15; and by the definition of the *differentia specifica* of a mode of production in Vol. III, ch. 47, on the genesis of ground rent. The crucial text of interpretation is Etienne Balibar: 'On the Basic Concepts of Historical Materialism', op. cit. I have myself tried to elaborate this interpretation to some extent, but more particularly to apply it in a critique of various ideologies of economic systems: *Vetenskap och ideologi om ekonomiska system* (The Science and Ideology of Economic Systems – to be published). Marx's analysis showed that the industrial labour process, in contrast to handicraft production, entails an objective, technical subjugation of the labourer. Hence Marx did not believe in any 'neutrality' of technology. Neither Marcuse's recent existential judgement on the all-pervasive technological apparatus nor his prior belief in the neutrality of technology takes us very far as a social analysis.

[15] Hence Habermas's attack on Marx in EI. Habermas's philosophy of labour and interaction is developed in TWI, pp. 9–103.

[16] As it derives its concept of the economy from anthropological assumptions, this view is, of course, fundamentally akin to the 'propensity' philosophy of bourgeois economics from Adam Smith via the Marginalists to the Keynesians.

[17] Habermas has summarized his schema diagrammatically in TWI, p. 64; TRS, p. 93.

into a speculative 'species history', and of two key Marxist concepts – does considerable violence to the author of *Das Kapital*. What else can be said of it in a limited space?[18] A first result of Habermas's operation is to rob any serious analysis of society of important tools. As far as social analysis is concerned, Habermas's substitution of 'interaction' for the 'relations of production' simply emphasizes the importance of norms, cultural tradition and symbolic communication. These correspond to the ideological system every society contains, of which Marx was well aware, though he never wrote a counterpart to *Capital* on it. Marx was also aware of another non-economic structure, to the analysis of which he made an important though fragmentary contribution – the political-legal structure of the State. In Habermas's schema, by contrast, the State is divided between the sub-systems of labour on the one hand and interaction and relations of communication on the other.

The disappearance of the concept of the relations of production also abolishes relationships which determine human behaviour without being norms (or technical rules), although they may function *via* normative sanctions. No norm in our capitalist society says that the population should be divided into two basic classes, the bourgeoisie and the proletariat, but this is the most fundamental of all aspects of the institutional framework of life in capitalist society, patterning the 'free choice of occupation' and the mechanisms of distribution. Managerial ideologies ask us to believe that salaried managers are governed by other norms than the old entrepreneurs, and this may be true, but it naturally in no way proves that the capitalist economy has disappeared. The relations of production have not changed.[19]

Similarly, the concept of the productive forces highlights the complex material structure of the labour process – the relation between the labourer, the means and the object of labour – and its central importance for the variant forms of social domination.[20]

[18] See the more elaborate, but somewhat different criticism of Renate Damus: 'Habermas und der "heimliche Positivismus" bei Marx', in *Sozialistische Politik* no. 4, December 1969.

[19] There is a counterpart to this in ethnology where kinship is concerned. The norms of a society may say that A must marry B and C, D. But they do not present the network of kinship relations within a whole tribe or group of tribes which can be shown by ethnological analysis to govern those norms.

[20] Cf. *Capital* Vol. I, chs. 7, 14 and 15.

This is lost in the notion of labour as instrumental behaviour, as problem-solving. Whereas in a Marxist analysis the contradiction between the productive forces and the relations of production provides an important tool with which to reveal the functions of the State's economic intervention behind its screen of reformist ideology, Habermas gives us no tools of analysis – just two assertions: that State intervention is important and effective, and that science and technology help to legitimize domination.

In contrast to the relationship between the productive forces and the relations of production, the scheme of 'labour' and 'interaction' can circumscribe no structural contradictions. Habermas ignores the mode of extraction of surplus-labour as the *differentia specifica* of a mode of production and as what determines in the last instance the basic character and importance of the economic, political and ideological structures of society. In its place he puts . . . the type of legitimizing ideology! (TWI, pp. 65ff.; TRS, pp. 94ff.)

Hegel and Parsons

The schema Habermas has substituted for the Marxist theory of the social formation is a *mélange* derived essentially from two sources. The first of these is Hegel's Jena writings of 1803–1806 (see TWI, pp. 9–47). In these early writings, Hegel argued that the Spirit is an organization of three equally original means or instruments: languages, the tool and family property. Language refers not to linguistic communication, but to naming and memory, i.e. to the ego's distanciation from its surrounding world. With the tool, the ego submits to the laws of nature the better to master it. In the family, the ego achieves recognition in the struggle and reconciliation with other men by a process of education or socialization. For Habermas the last two are essential, and he has renamed them labour and interaction.[21] In labour, man confronts nature in instrumental action; in interaction, he confronts society in normative behaviour (*Sittlichkeit*). The later Hegel, according to Habermas, obscured this distinction by conceiving nature – the

---

[21] Language provides a faculty for the other two, and in Habermas's later writings it seems to be included in interaction. In TTCC, for instance, Chomsky is attacked for not acknowledging how much of language arises only in inter-subjective communication (TTCC, pp. 130–138).

Spirit's primary alienation – as another subject, thus assimilating the struggle of ego against nature with that of ego against alter. Marx, although as a young man he restored the distinction (in the *1844 Manuscripts*), then later assimilated ego's struggle against alter with its struggle against nature by asserting that the relations of production were a part of the mode of production, i.e. part of the material process of production, rather than a non-material instance in the social whole. He thereby rejoined the late Hegel.

The second source is modern bourgeois sociology, in particular the work of Talcott Parsons. As I remarked in my earlier essay printed above, one of classical sociology's main concerns was the distinction between traditional and industrial society, conceived in terms of some form of *Gemeinschaft/Gesellschaft* opposition. Habermas discusses this, and also Parsons' formalization of it into a general theory of social systems (the pairs of value-orientations: affectivity/affective neutrality, particularism/universalism, ascription/achievement and diffuseness/specificity). He attacks Parsons for de-historicizing these concepts, treating the features of a particular transition as universally valid (TWI, pp. 61–62; TRS, p. 91). But Habermas himself is still very close to Parsons, in two respects. First, Habermas's critique of Marx *vis-à-vis* the relation between instrumental activity and the normative institutional framework in which it is embedded is very similar to Parsons' critique of utilitarianism and his theory of action.[22] (Of course, Parsons was not simply concerned with instrumental activity, but with behaviour based on individual self-interest and the impossibility of deriving a satisfactory concept of society from such behaviour alone. Parsons pointed to the framework of social values and norms over and above individual self-interest and traced the emergence of a theory of action orientated towards these norms in the works of Marshall, Pareto, Durkheim and Weber.) Secondly, the labour/interaction couple, or put more formally, the opposition between the system of instrumental-teleological action and the institutional framework of symbolically mediated interaction (TWI, p. 64; TRS, p. 93), has only to be reduplicated to become very close to the four-functional pattern of Parsons' later work – with adaptation and goal-attainment in the first of Habermas's subsystems, and pattern-maintenance and integration in the second.

---

[22] Talcott Parsons: *The Structure of Social Action* (Cambridge Mass. 1937).

Habermas even largely allocates the modern State and economy to the first sub-system and the family and culture to the second, exactly as does Parsons, and his scheme of social development from primitive through traditional to modern industrial societies is essentially a differentiation process, as it is for Parsons.

The Aetiology of Habermas

We are now faced with the obvious paradox – the problem of the aetiology of Habermas's ideas. How did the Frankfurt School, which could at the very least lay claim to intellectual rigour and seriousness, give rise to this extraordinary amalgam of the Young Hegel and Talcott Parsons? In fact, on closer inspection, this paradox can be seen to disappear. Habermas's ideas are indeed what someone of his generation formed in the German Federal Republic might be expected to make of some of the more extreme ideas of the elder members of the School.

As I showed in the essay above, the classical Frankfurt School preserved Marx's critique of the evils of capitalist society, but grew increasingly sceptical about the remedies he proposed for those evils: the proletarian revolution and the release of the productive forces it would bring about. But this scepticism did not lead them to a renunciation of Marxist theory or to a reconciliation with capitalism, but rather to a hyper-radicalization of their ideological and political stance and a retreat from any political practice into philosophy and aesthetics. The most striking example of this pessimism-cum-radicalism appears in Horkheimer's and Adorno's discussion of science and technology, which had generally been treated as progressive and revolutionary in the Marxist tradition, but which the Frankfurt School increasingly saw as the direct cause and justification for social oppression. This position is outlined in *Dialectic of Enlightenment*, by Horkheimer and Adorno, and in Marcuse's *One-Dimensional Man*.[23]

It was this position of the older generation of the Frankfurt School that Habermas inherited. He ends his study of Marxism in the 1950's (1957) with a quotation from a lecture on Freud given by Marcuse in Frankfurt in 1956, a quotation which contains the germ of the thesis of *One-Dimensional Man* (TP, pp. 334ff.). A decade later, he was to formulate Marcuse's 'basic thesis' as

[23] See above for comments.

follows: 'In the advanced industrial countries, technology and science have not only become the primary productive force, laying the basis for a peaceful and satisfying existence, but also a new form of ideology, legitimizing an administrative coercion cut off from the masses'.[24] Marcuse's own political conclusion from these premisses was quoted in the essay above: 'Thought in contradiction must become more negative and more utopian in opposition to the status quo. This seems to me to be the imperative of the current situation in relation to my theoretical essays of the 1930's.'[25] Habermas draws very different conclusions. Since technology and science have become the 'primary productive force' and 'scientific-technical progress has become an autonomous source of surplus-value' (TWI, pp. 79ff.; TRS, pp. 104ff.; TP pp. 190ff.), the labour theory of value must be *revised*.[26] Because a technocratic ideology linked to State economic intervention has replaced the ideology of equal exchange as the legitimation of bourgeois society, the critique of political economy is no longer a sufficient *ideologiekritische* theory of society (TWI, pp. 74ff.; TRS pp. 100ff.). The technocratic system of economic regulation and political manipulation has substituted any clearly definable class rule and, on the basis of institutionalized scientific-technical progress, has created loyalties which cross social boundaries so that class contradictions have become latent. Marx's theory of class struggle is thus no longer unconditionally applicable in advanced capitalist societies, and must also be revised (TWI, pp. 84ff.; TRS, pp. 107ff.).[27] In a comment directed explicitly at Ernst Bloch, but clearly extendable to the older members of the

---

[24] J. Habermas, ed.: *Antworten auf Herbert Marcuse* (Frankfurt 1968), pp. 14ff.

[25] *Negations* (New York and London 1969), p. xx.

[26] TWI, pp. 79ff. and TP, pp. 190ff. Though related to a real problem – the importance of changes in productivity for the tendency of the rate of profit to fall – Habermas's critique merely echoes the Gotha programme. It is based on a naive, empiricist reading of the theory of value, allegedly calculated 'on the basis of the value of unskilled (simple) labour-power' (TWI, p. 80). See W. Müller: 'Habermas und die Anwendbarkeit der Arbeitswerttheorie' (Habermas and the Applicability of the Labour Theory of Value), *Sozialistische Politik* No. 1, April 1969. Cf. also Charles Bettelheim's critique of empiricist conceptions of the labour theory of value in the Eastern European price debate, *La transition vers l'économie socialiste* (Paris 1968) ch. 6.

[27] Cf. Habermas's arguments in his denunciation of the student movement in spring 1968: 'Die Scheinrevolution und ihre Kinder' (The Pseudo-Revolution and its Children) in *Die Linke antwortet Jürgen Habermas* (The Left Replies to Jürgen Habermas) (Frankfurt 1968), pp. 5–15.

Frankfurt School, Habermas attacks their 'tacit orthodoxy' in which 'a kind of long repressed echo of a critique of political economy still remains in the esoteric ghost of aesthetic reflection' (TP, p. 170).[28] *Horkheimer's and Adorno's post-war individualistic retreat from concrete political and economic problems preserved critical theory as a pure theory retaining a kind of philosophico-aesthetic shadow-life. Habermas has turned this relationship on to its head : the theory now has to be revised to restore its relevance to concrete social problems.*

It is hardly surprising that Habermas has taken this step. Born in 1929, he belongs to that generation of intellectuals who were formed politically by the Cold-War debates of the 1950's about 'stabilized capitalism', Stalinism and Marx's Early Works. Habermas intervened in this situation by defining Marxism as a 'critique' somewhere between a philosophy and a science: 'Marxist theory is distinguished by its position "between" philosophy and positive science' (TP, p. 179). From this standpoint, he verbally defended Marxism against the eclectic rapaciousness of the academic sociology of Mannheim, Friedmann and Dahrendorf. On the other hand, he accepted that it was, like a science, subject to empirical falsification: 'We can expressly state that its structure is that of a philosophy of history conceived for political purposes, and therefore scientifically falsifiable, without shunning the opportunity afforded a later generation to understand Marx better than he understood himself' (TP, p. 179). As a result, he was vulnerable to the then fashionable 'refutations' of the labour theory of value, of the theory of class struggle, of the theory of base and superstructure. 'Four facts' here speak against Marx, according to Habermas, '1. State intervention in the economy means that the latter is no longer autonomous, State and society can no longer be regarded as base and superstructure. 2. The rise in the standard of living even of "broad strata of the population" means that an interest in social emancipation can no longer be articulated in immediate economic forms. 3. In these conditions, the proletariat has dissolved as a proletariat (in the sense of critical theory): exclusion from disposal of the means of production is no longer

---

[28] Cf. TP, pp. 40ff, Habermas's introduction to *Antworte auf Herbert Marcuse*, op. cit., p. 12, and his contribution to the memorial volume on Adorno: 'Ein philosophierender Intellektueller' (A Philosophizing Intellectual), *Über Theodor W. Adorno* (Frankfurt 1968), pp. 35–43.

linked to such a loss of income, security and education that it must lead to class consciousness. 4. Marxism has come to play a role as the State ideology of the authoritarian régime in the Soviet Union' (TP, pp. 162–65; for other 'refutations', see TP, pp. 188–200 and TWI). These 'facts' are all familiar from the revisionism of the 1950's. Suffice it to note that Habermas goes so far as to rely on Strachey's *Contemporary Capitalism* and his purely Social-Democratic notion of bourgeois State intervention in the economy as an 'economic consequence of democracy' – an idea that belongs to a different universe from that of the Frankfurt School (TP, p. 197).

The Politics of Communication

So far, I have outlined Habermas's basic problematic and discussed its aetiology. Two things remain to be considered; two things which are in fact one and the same – the political position that follows from that problematic, and the vogue for Habermas among young academics in the fields of sociology and social philosophy.

Habermas's stress on the moment of 'interaction' in the social totality, and its separation from the world of economic production, lead him to locate political problems in a world of ideas far from the class struggle and its brutal materiality (though the latter can be invoked as a warning against too militant positions and actions). Habermas reformulates the goal of social emancipation in terms of communication, as 'communication free of domination' and 'a general and unforced consensus' (TWI, pp. 64, 163; TRS, p. 93). The result is an extreme idealistic vagueness; Habermas's ideas are very different from those of the classical Frankfurt School, where emancipation was viewed in more substantial economico-political and erotic terms (later also in terms of a distinctive mystique of nature). But communicative relations are also the object of a large-scale historical study by Habermas of the changes in bourgeois *Öffentlichkeit* (an untranslatable German term meaning something between 'public opinion' and the 'public domain').[29] Characteristically, there is no discussion of a proletarian *Öffentlichkeit*, and even the Paris Commune and the councils movement are related

[29] *Strukturwandel der Öffentlichkeit* (Neuwied and Berlin 1962).

only to a physiocratic insight into the natural order![30] The study's conclusion is a conception of liberal pluralism emphasizing free communication within the dominant organizations as the solution to modern problems of public opinion. Thus the book is an excellent illustration of the political effects of an immanent critique of bourgeois ideology. In Habermas's conception, the State appears primarily as the effective stabilizer of the capitalist economy. As we have seen, this is a central feature of his view of advanced capitalism. He has no *political* concept of the State, however. In his theory of *Öffentlichkeit*, the State is thus subsumed under the concept of *Herrschaft* or domination, idealistically interpreted. Domination is reduced to the ideologies by which it is legitimized (TWI, p. 163). Habermas also discusses domination in terms of 'distorted communication' (EI, pp. 341ff. and TTCC). On the other hand, in a different context Habermas freely warns against the potential violence of the State – in order to advise student activists to refrain from violence of their own.[31]

The 'conflict zone' is no longer that of class antagonisms. It has become that of *Öffentlichkeit*, and turns on the masking or unmasking of the difference between progress or rationalization in the instrumental sphere and emancipation in the institutional framework. Protest in this sense originates from groups of students, and in the future Habermas sees a 'system problem' which, if sensitized, would make this protest into a political force: the quantity of social wealth produced under automated conditions will make it increasingly difficult to tie status assignment convincingly to individual prestation (TWI, pp. 100–103; TRS, pp. 120–22). This 'system problem' is, of course, a faint idealist and individualist echo of the contradiction between the social character of the productive forces and the private character of the relations of

[30] Ibid., p. 156. This shows how little Habermas has understood the Marxist theory of the State.

[31] 'Die Scheinrevolution und ihre Kinder', op. cit. Habermas has twice denounced the militancy of the student movement on crucial occasions. The one I have referred to was on June 1st 1968, after the violent anti-Springer demonstrations and the occupation of the University of Frankfurt. A year earlier, at the beginning of the massive wave of student struggles in connection with the anti-Shah demonstrations in West Berlin when the police killed an on-looking student, Habermas had warned of the dangers of a 'left fascism'! He has also been careful to distance himself from the views of Marcuse; see his introduction to *Antworten auf Herbert Marcuse*, op. cit.

production. But where for Marx this contradiction was to be overcome by a class struggle which transforms capitalist productive forces and relations of production into socialism by means of a revolutionary seizure of State power, Habermas's reduction of Marxism to the mere critique of ideology leads directly to the suggestion that it will be harmoniously settled through criticism of the structures of public opinion by the enlightened efforts of critical students and scholars.[32]

Hence Habermas's popularity among young Anglo-Saxon reformist academics. He combines an apparently left-wing pedigree, conventional humanism and a notion that the basic political problems are problems of communication. The blandness of these ideas is evident. Since, however, it is a law of ideological gravitation that eclecticism attracts empiricism, British and Scandinavian sociology incipiently feels strongly drawn towards him. A vogue for Habermas is a predictable product of its own horizons.

---

[32] Habermas is now generally regarded as a conventional revisionist on the German left. Cf. the critiques of the 'Habermas School' in the West Berlin journal *Sozialistische Politik* No. 4, December 1969. These are a far cry from the confusion in several of the contributions to the volume defending the student movement against Habermas's attack of June 1968. The editor of this volume, the young Frankfurt philosopher Oskar Negt, even reproached Habermas with having Leninist views! *Die Linke antwortet Jürgen Habermas*, op. cit., p. 31.

Theory and Practice in Gramsci's Marxism

John Merrington

During the past decade there has been a growing interest among European socialists in those Marxist writers and activists of the period immediately preceding and following the October Revolution, whose theories grew out of the collapse of the Second International and the failure of the revolutionary wave which swept Europe in 1917–20. The emergence of reformist tendencies in the socialist parties in the pre-war period, the subsequent capitulation of the German SPD, the failure of the socialist leaderships to combat factional tendencies within their parties and their fatal inaction in the face of events immediately following the war, created a situation in which only radical new departures could create new theoretical solutions and hence new practical possibilities. Both Lukács and Gramsci responded in different ways to this need, moving beyond the terms of the earlier 'revisionist debate' – both 'revolutionaries' and 'reformists' had remained locked within the same basic problematic – carrying out a new diagnosis and prognosis from their experience of the postwar defeat, placing a renewed stress on the active, voluntary component of historical change, on the problem of agency in the making of a revolution.

For the increasing incapacity of European social-democrat leaderships, nakedly revealed in the postwar crisis, was itself the outward manifestation of a more profound malaise; the ossification of bureaucratic structures of organization went hand in hand with an 'official Marxism' based on a rigid set of categorical doctrines, 'laws of social development' of the natural-scientific type. The need for a renewal of Marxism in these circumstances was urgent. Both Lukács and Gramsci reacted energetically against these positivistic inroads into Marxism, the positivist-scientism which was the theoretical basis of the Second International's orthodoxy. With the imposition of the new orthodoxy of Stalinism during the 1930's, however, these theories became, and have largely remained, a subordinate current within the international socialist movement, and it was only after the 20th Congress of the CPSU in 1956 that their rediscovery became widely possible. The recurring tendency of Marxism to become petrified into a schematic system of fixed categories, eternally valid, invoking concepts rather than rediscovering them in relation to each new conjuncture, has made the work of Gramsci particularly relevant to the problems of postwar socialism in the west. The 2,800 pages of the *Prison Notebooks*, which began to be published after the war and the collapse of Italian fascism,[1] constitute the most wide-ranging and sustained attempt to renew Marxism, reformulating old categories and inventing new concepts through the confrontation of contemporary social and cultural developments, to have come from the pen of a twentieth-century western Marxist. Gramsci's work represents above all a model of that type of critical-development, as opposed to blind exegesis, of Marxism, which 'actualizes' theory in relation to each specific conjuncture, locating the changing centres of contradiction in the capitalist world and elaborating the appropriate strategy. At every point, new insights produce new theoretical solutions as a means, not of rejecting all existing reality, myopically intent on retaining the purity of the original formulations, but of coming to grips with reality, revealing its contradictions, locating the focal points of change as a means to guiding and directing action towards revolutionary socialist goals. The need for an integral 'rethinking' of Marxism in the post-Stalinist period, not only in economic terms but in relation to the totality of social and cultural developments in the capitalist west; the continued dependence on traditional forms of organization in the socialist movement, as well as the increasing passivity of strategic options on the Left have made incumbent a confrontation with 'the genius', as Eugene Genovese has aptly remarked, 'who posed and faced western socialism's most difficult problems'.[2]

---

[1] All references to the *Prison Notebooks* in this article are to the English edition edited by Quintin Hoare and Geoffrey Nowell-Smith, *Selections from the Prison Notebooks*, London 1971 (henceforward SPN), except for texts not included in the above, where references are given to the 1948–51 Italian edition of the *Opere di Antonio Gramsci*.

[2] In Britain, Gramsci's work was first drawn on in a number of articles in the *New Left Review*. For commentaries in English, see Gwyn Williams: 'Gramsci's

I

What were the general features of Gramsci's renewal of Marxism? A precondition for such a renewal was for Gramsci, as for Lenin or Lukács, the rejection of 'economism' in all its forms, the tendency to reduce the various levels of superstructure to the status of 'appearance' or 'phenomenon'. In the hands of the 'professorial' Marxists of the Second International, this tendency had produced an evolutionary-determinist conception of history, governed by objective laws whose unfolding lay beyond the scope of active human intervention. The practical result was a catastrophic fatalism in the face of events, sustained by a blind belief in the 'forces of history', in the inevitable collapse of capitalism due to its internal contradictions. It was in relation to this deviation of Marxism that Gramsci entitled an early article of November 1917 'The Revolution against "Das Kapital"', in which he hailed the Bolsheviks for having broken the iron timetable of the stages of history.[3] In the prison notes, fatalism is characterized as 'a direct ideological "aroma"' of Marxism, 'rather like religion or drugs (in their stupefying effect). It has been made necessary and justified historically by the "subaltern" character of certain social strata', maintaining perseverence in periods of defeat and adversity: '"I have been defeated for the moment, but the tide of history is working for me in the long term."' But in periods of organic crisis, when the subordinate becomes potentially 'directive', it becomes a substitute for taking real initiatives; the result is vacillation, passivity and 'idiotic self-sufficiency'. For this reason, 'the claim, presented as an essential postulate of historical materialism, that every fluctuation of politics and ideology can be presented and expounded as an immediate expression of the structure, must

---

Concept of "Egemonia"', *Journal of the History of Ideas* Vol. XXI, No. 4, October/ December 1960, pp. 586ff. See also the important recent study *Antonio Gramsci and the Origins of Italian Communism* by John M. Cammett, Stanford University Press, 1967, which, while somewhat unbalanced and subject to limitations of approach, provides much useful information especially for the immediate postwar period of the Turinese factory councils, and a good bibliography. *Cf.* Review of Cammett's book by Eugene Genovese, *Studies on the Left* Vol. 7, No. 2 (1967) p. 83ff. For a good recent biography see G. Fiori, *Antonio Gramsci – Life of a Revolutionary*, London 1970.

[3] 'The Revolution against "Capital"', *Political Writings 1910–1920*, pp. 34–37. Henceforward PW.

be contested in theory as primitive infantilism.'⁴ Citing Engels' remark in his correspondence, that 'only in the last analysis is the economy the determining force in history', he goes on to dismiss the possibility that 'immediate economic crises of themselves produce fundamental historical events. . . . The specific question of economic hardship or well-being as a cause of new historical realities is a partial aspect of the question of the relations of force, at the various levels'.⁵

This rejection of economism was coupled with a rejection of the positivist tendency to objectify the discrete atomistic data of immediate actuality, dissolving the totality of social processes into the fragmentary 'facts' of contingent reality, thereby declaring its categories universal. In his critique of Bukharin's *Theory of Historical Materialism* (1921) Gramsci rejected the crude material-ism and 'false objectivity' of Bukharin's method, in which Marxism was conceived as a means of predicting future events with the exactitude of the natural sciences. Echoing an earlier critique by Lukács, Gramsci insisted on the impossibility of prediction which diverted attention from the possibilities of active political intervention; Marxism's 'laws of social development' were 'laws of tendency' only. Vulgar materialism and technologism merely reproduced the categories of bourgeois science and ignored the dialectical nature of the Marxist totality.⁶ Gramsci's critical effort was directed towards the restoration of the dialectic and hence the possibility of conscious praxis, the interplay between sub-jective and objective in the historical process, within which the specific forms of superstructure, cultural, political and ideological, have a relatively autonomous existence, irreducible to the status of 'emanations' of the economic structure, conceived of as an

---

⁴ SPN pp. 336–37, 407.

⁵ SPN pp. 162, 184.

⁶ SPN pp. 434–35, 169–72. 'But if the question is framed in this way, one can no longer understand the importance and significance of the dialectic, which is relegated from its position as a doctrine of knowledge and the very marrow of historiography and the science of politics, to the level of a sub-species of formal logic and elementary scholastics.' SPN p. 435. *Cf.* The informative article by Aldo Zanardo: 'Il Manuale di Bukharin vista dai comunisti tedeschi e da Gramsci', *Studi Gramsciani*, Rome, 1958, pp. 337–68; in which Gramsci's position is compared to that of Lukács, who similarly pointed out 'the closeness of Bukharin's theory to bourgeois, natural-scientific materialism' derived 'from his use of "science" (in the French sense) as a model'. See the translation of Lukács' 'Technology and Social Relations', *New Left Review* 39, pp. 27–34.

idealist 'essence'. In his unwavering opposition to that deformation of Marxism represented by a long arc of official theory from
Plekhanov[7] to Kautsky and Bukharin, encrusted with evolutionist
determinism, Gramsci clearly prefigures more recent theoretical
developments of the post-Stalin period, the recognition of the
need for a more integrated and total Marxism as opposed to the
eclecticism of recent tendencies, with an emphasis on the specific
role of the superstructures, of historical conjuncture and the
complexity of the Marxist totality, determined only in the last
instance by the economic. As Althusser has put it: 'From the
first moment to the last, the lonely hour of the last instance never
comes'.[8]

It is therefore the range, the all-inclusive scope of Gramsci's
Marxism which is its distinctive feature. Economism was not
merely unable to explain crucial aspects of contemporary social
and political reality, the role of Catholicism or the rise of Musso-
lini; not only were its theoretical insights mediocre, but it was also
a partial vision of the socialist future limited to the alteration of
the economic structure. In place of this it was imperative to affirm
a total vision based on a total critique. Private ownership of the
means of production is a *necessary* but not a *sufficient* basis of
capitalist domination; similarly, because socialism reorganizes the
economic structure, this does not mean that 'superstructural
factors should be left to themselves, to develop spontaneously to a
haphazard and sporadic germination.'[9] Gramsci's Marxism was
not limited to the material conditions of existence but included
also the content of existence, the integral development of human
potentialities over the whole field of experience and the vast
expansion of creative possibilities which socialism would make
possible. This widening of focus required a new emphasis on the
role of consciousness and ideas in the transformation of society,
which Gramsci developed through a life-long confrontation with
the neo-idealists, represented in Italy pre-eminently by the
philosopher-historian Benedetto Croce, the most influential
spokesman of speculative liberalism throughout the period. Just
as the theory of Lukács was the result of a synthesis with the anti-

[7] SPN p. 387.
[8] Louis Althusser, *For Marx*, London 1969, p. 113.
[9] SPN p. 247.

positivist sociology of Weber and Simmel, Gramsci's Marxism developed out of his critique of Croce. The European-wide reaction against positivism from the 1880's onwards thus found its dialectical response within the Marxist tradition itself. Gramsci's concept of Marxist orthodoxy is 'not based on this or that follower, or this or that tendency linked to currents outside the original formulation . . . but on the fundamental conception of Marxism as "sufficient to itself", sufficient to create an entire civilization, total and integrated'.[10]

This integral Marxism was in turn made concrete by the enormous project Gramsci set himself during his long imprisonment: to rework, to actualize theory in relation to a specific national experience and culture in order to present a global critique and challenge to existing social reality. It was his refusal to apply schematic solutions to a particular 'effectual reality' that made him underline the specificity of the conjuncture of forces, national and international, which determine the form a crisis will take in any particular case and hence the strategy of the revolutionary movement. In the prison notes he attacked 'closed and definitive systems' and added that 'the unity and systematic quality of a theory is to be found not in its external and architectonic structure but in its intimate coherence and fertile comprehension of each particular solution'.[11] In his note *Against Byzantinism* we read: 'Identity in concrete reality determines identity of thought, and not vice versa. It can further be deduced that every truth, even if it is universal, and even if it can be expressed by an abstract formula of a mathematical kind (for the sake of the theoreticians), owes its effectiveness to its being expressed in the language appropriate to specific concrete situations. If it cannot be expressed in such specific terms, it is a byzantine and scholastic abstraction, good only for phrase-mongers to toy with. [1932].'[12] The particular requirements corresponding to each situation cannot be fixed in advance: 'But reality produces a wealth of the most bizarre combinations. It is up to the theoretician to unravel these in order to discover fresh

---

[10] *Il Materialismo storico e La Filosofia di Benedetto Croce* (henceforward MS): p. 157. *Cf.* Lukács in 1923: 'It is not the primacy of economic motives in historical explanation which decisively distinguishes Marxism from bourgeois science, it is the view-point of the totality.' *History and Class Consciousness*, London 1971, p. 27.

[11] MS: p. 180.

[12] SPN p. 201.

proof of his theory, to "translate" into theoretical language the elements of historical life. It is not reality which should be expected to conform to the abstract schema. This will never happen, and hence this conception is nothing but an expression of passivity.'[13] Each national conjuncture is 'the result of a combination which is "original" and (in a certain sense) unique: these relations must be understood and conceived in their originality and uniqueness if one wishes to dominate them and direct them.' There is no one road to socialism applicable for all cases: 'The line of development is towards internationalism, but the point of departure is "national" – and it is from this point of departure that one must begin.'[14] It was this overriding concern for national conjuncture, in contrast to the formal internationalism of Trotsky and of Rosa Luxemburg,[15] that enabled Gramsci to discern the specificity of the problematic in the case of western countries and to adapt the experience of Leninism and the Russian Revolution to the different conditions of the West.

It is all the more essential to emphasize this close link between theory and actual movements within society since the tendency to interpret Gramsci's theories as an 'idealist Marxism' overlooks the unity of theory and practice, linked indissolubly with the needs of concrete struggle, which underlay his work. Gramsci's weapon against both materialism and idealism was 'the energetic affirmation of unity between theory and practice'.[16] The underlying thematic of his philosophical, historical and cultural studies was a response to an essentially political problem. The traditional organizations and leadership of the working class had proved unable to surmount the dilemma which faces every socialist movement, working at once within bourgeois society and utilizing its institutions, while at the same time working for its overthrow. The result was generally a defensive and corporatist posture coupled with declamatory and utopian appeals for mass-action from the Left (syndicalism and spontaneism). This was particularly true in the case of the 'Maximalist' leadership of the Italian Socialist Party (PSI), which, in spite of its nominal allegiance to the

[13] SPN p. 250.
[14] SPN p. 240.
[15] See Nicolas Krassó: 'Trotsky's Marxism', New Left Review 44, p. 81, and for Gramsci's comments on Trotsky's internationalism, SPN pp. 236, 240–41.
[16] MS: p. 232.

Third International at the Congress of Bologna (1919), proved incapable of moving beyond the twin polarities of opportunist participation in society or isolationist withdrawal from society. It therefore failed to come to grips with the situation of the postwar crisis, or to provide an active revolutionary leadership; the result was a fatal kind of inaction, barricaded behind old-established positions and empty rhetoric. The same tendency towards isolationism was reproduced by the dominant faction of the Italian Communist Party (PCI) in the early period from its foundation at the Congress of Livorno in 1921. The sectarian 'abstentionism' of the group led by Bordiga represented the same inability to intervene actively in the political arena, based on the same mechanistic assumptions that underlay the inaction of the PSI and in glaring contrast to the policies laid down by the Comintern. Lenin had already condemned this 'Left-Wing Communism' in 1920: 'Comrade Bordiga and his "Left" friends draw from their correct criticism of Turati and Co. (the reformists) the wrong conclusion. . . . Not only in the parliamentary field, but in *all* fields of activity, communism *must introduce* (and without long, persistent and stubborn effort it will be *unable* to introduce) something new in principle that will represent a radical break with the traditions of the Second International.'[17] Gramsci's early opposition to the PSI leadership, culminating in the experience of the factory councils movement in Turin, became after 1921 a struggle against the sectarianism of the early PCI, only won with his rise to leadership of the party in 1924. This position was again accentuated by the change of Comintern policy in 1929–30. During a series of political discussions with fellow prisoners in late 1930, he is reported to have strongly criticized the recrudescence of 'the old maximalist phraseology' and the failure of the party to confront fascism: 'they do not know how to adjust the means to different historical situations'.[18]

Against this political background, the defeat of Italian socialism

[17] Lenin: *Left-wing communism, an infantile disorder*, Progress Publishers, Moscow; Addenda pp. 92–93 (original italics).

[18] Athos Lisa: 'Discussione politica con Gramsci in carcere', *Rinascita* XXI, 49, 12. XII. 64, pp. 17–21; a report by one of Gramsci's fellow prisoners at Turi. For the early history of the PCI, see the recent and competent history by Paolo Spriano: *Storia del Partito comunista italiano*, Vol. I: *Da Bordiga a Gramsci*, Turin, 1967. *Cf.* also Cammett, *op. cit.*, Chapter 8.

and the triumph of fascism, Gramsci's lasting achievement remains that of having overcome, both in theory and in his political practice, the sterile alternatives of participation and abstention, through a radical redefinition of the essential problem, the nature of power in western society; underlining the active work of politicization and mobilization of the masses, restoring the possibility of revolutionary initiative by a conscious political agency based on an ideological and political unity between the 'intellectuals' and the 'masses' making up the revolutionary bloc. The problem was to elaborate the specific character of a 'collective will' which would make possible the passage from a sectoral, corporate and hence subaltern role of purely negative opposition, to a *hegemonic* role of conscious action towards revolutionary goals; not seeking a partial adjustment within the system, but posing the question of the state in its entirety.[19] For this to be possible, the partial, determined character of opposition must become a universally-oriented challenge over the whole range of social relations, so that 'structure ceases to be an external force which crushes man, assimilates him to itself and makes him passive; and is transformed into a means of freedom, an instrument to create a new ethico-political form and a source of new initiatives.' The passage to the hegemonic moment represents the transformation of the 'objective' into the 'subjective', from 'the purely economic (or egoistic-passional) to the ethico-political moment that is the superior elaboration of the structure into superstructure in the minds of men'.[20] This transition from the purely economic struggle required a new conception of the role of ideology, of the 'intellectuals' (in a broad sense, of all those who have an organizing and educative role), an emphasis on the voluntary character of the revolutionary organization as an agency bringing about the transformation of consciousness and cultural renewal at all levels of society.

It was Gramsci's great strength that he posed these problems in terms which admitted of practical solutions. The disjunction of theory and practice was seen as the root cause of the debility of strategic options on the Left. This signified that socialism was still passing through 'a relatively primitive historical phase, one which

[19] SPN p. 182.
[20] SPN pp. 366–67.

is still economic–corporate, in which the general "structural" framework is being quantitatively transformed and the appropriate quality–superstructure is in the process of emerging, but is not yet organically formed.'[21] The divorce of theory from concrete struggle, from the specific possibilities contained within society, produced 'arbitrary' schema in the place of that 'organic' unity which alone could restore a creative dialectical relationship between objective situation and revolutionary initiatives. Gramsci's long isolation in prison, far from leading to disinterested contemplation, was compensated by an enormous effort of political engagement. His 'intellectual' and 'political' roles were inextricably linked and the tendency to separate them – particularly tempting in his case, since the division corresponds to the two periods, of political activity (including political journalism) 1916–26 and imprisonment 1926–37 – can only lead to a disjunction between his theories and his intentions, which gives at best a partial view. Such schematic and unilinear interpretations do less than justice to the originality and underlying coherence of the prison notes, despite their fragmentary character. Gramsci was saved from any idealist or formal solution by his close grounding in political reality. 'But the most important observation to be made about any concrete analysis of the relations of force is the following: that such analyses cannot and must not be ends in themselves (unless the intention is merely to write a chapter of past history), but acquire significance only if they serve to justify a particular practical activity, or initiative of will.'[22] His analyses are never limited to the adumbration of purely conceptual alternatives; their unity and coherence lie in the theoretical-practical framework which constituted his field of research. This involved taking into account the limits present and possibilities open; 'a research into the conditions necessary for freedom of action towards certain ends. . . . It is not a question of establishing a *hierarchy of ends* but a *graduation of ends* to be attained'.[23] This cannot be 'the result of a rationalistic, deductive, abstract process – i.e. one typical of pure intellectuals (or pure asses),' but an organic process in which

---

[21] SPN p. 335.

. [22] SPN p. 185.

[23] MS: p. 98. Williams, in the article quoted above, appears to make this disjunction, as a result concluding with the suggestion that Gramsci represented a purely 'moral socialism'. *Op. cit.*, pp. 598–99.

theory finds its authenticity in practice, in which analysis is guided towards strategy, in which analysis is 'active' rather than 'descriptive.'[24] The final test of any analysis was its 'practical efficacy' in terms of 'effective reality'.

To understand better the nature of this 'collective will' in Gramsci, it is necessary to turn to the crucial role of ideology and the superstructures in his analysis of the power structure in western societies.

II

Gramsci's polemic against economism was based on the need to reformulate the 'problem of the relations between structure and superstructure which must be accurately posed and resolved if the forces which are active in the history of a particular period are to be correctly analysed, and the relation between them determined.'[25] The 'economist' hypothesis affirms an 'immediate element of strength' directly produced by the determinism of the structure. The result is the identification of 'state' with 'government' or repressive-coercive apparatus only, proper to a 'fraction of the ruling class which wishes to modify not the structure of the State, but merely government policy,' for whom it is a question merely of 'a rotation in governmental office of the ruling-class parties, not the foundation and organization of a new political society and even less of a new type of civil society'.[26] The conception of an unmediated element of force is not enough. In this case 'an analysis of the balance of forces – at all levels – can only culminate in the sphere of hegemony and ethico-political relations'.[27]

The concept of hegemony is thus linked to Gramsci's aim to re-define the nature of power in modern societies in more comprehensive terms, allowing for the articulations of the various levels or instances of a given social formation, political, cultural or ideological, in the determination of a specific power structure. In a letter from prison in 1931 he outlines the place occupied by the

[24] SPN pp. 189, 197. *Cf.* Gramsci's distinction between a purely 'literary' theory, the monopoly of isolated thinkers, and that of Machiavelli, who represents a 'man of action', a 'politico in atto'. SPN pp. 135, 172.

[25] SPN p. 177.

[26] SPN p. 160.

[27] SPN p. 167.

problem of intellectuals in his programme of research, which entailed the 'further elaboration of the concept of the State as the equilibrium between political society (either dictatorship or coercive apparatus to conform the popular masses according to the type of production and economy of a given moment) and civil society (or the hegemony of a social group over the entire national society by way of the so-called private organizations, such as the Church, the unions, the schools, etc.)'.[28] The concept of state thus assumes 'a wider and more organic sense' which includes 'elements which need to be referred back to the notion of civil society (in the sense that one might say that state = political + civil society, in other words hegemony protected by the armour of coercion).'[29] The state becomes, in this wider sense, 'the state proper and civil society' or 'the entire complex of practical and theoretical activities with which the ruling class not only justifies and maintains its dominance, but manages to win the active consent of those over whom it rules.'[30] The conception of power is thus extended to include the whole complex of institutions through which power relations are mediated in society, ensuring the 'political and cultural hegemony of a social group over the entire society, as the ethical content of the state'.[31] The function of 'dominio' (coercion) is complemented by that of 'direzione' (leadership by consent) as the two modalities or 'moments' of power relations. The significance of Machiavelli in Gramsci's research lay, not only in his political realism, but in the 'double nature' of his Centaur, both beast and human, containing both 'degrees' of force and consent, of authority and hegemony.[32] Gramsci's conceptual approach transcends the categories of political science and sociology; the state is no longer a mere apparatus of coercion but itself has a retroactive influence in the sphere of civil society through 'this multiplicity of private associations (which are of two kinds: natural, and contractual or voluntary)', which

---

[28] Letter to Tatania (7.9.1931). *Lettere dal Carcere*, pp. 479–83.

[29] SPN p. 263.

[30] SPN p. 244.

[31] *Passato e Presente* (henceforward P), pp. 164–65.

[32] SPN p. 170. 'Russo in his *Prolegomeni* makes *The Prince* into Machiavelli's treatise on dictatorship (moment of authority and of the individual), and *The Discourses* into his treatise on hegemony (moment of the universal . . .). Russo's observation is correct, although there are allusions to the moment of hegemony or consent in *The Prince* too, beside those to authority or force.' SPN p. 125.

constitute the 'hegemonic apparatus of one social group over the rest of the population (or civil society): the basis for the State in the narrow sense of the governmental-coercive apparatus.'[33]

In advanced capitalist countries the autonomous role of the superstructures is fully developed; the superstructures are 'an effective and operating reality'.[34] While the various political and ideological formations correspond to the interests of the dominant class, they cannot be reduced to mere emanations or epipheno-mena of the structure, and are susceptible to different historical forms and combinations which in turn react upon the structure. It is through this 'unity in multiplicity' that it becomes possible, by the analysis of relations in forces within a determined historical situation, to establish the objective co-ordinates of the political struggle as a whole, taking account of the possibility of error or unforeseen results of actions on the part of the agent.[35] Gramsci makes a distinction between 'organic' movements of the structure which reveal its 'incurable contradictions', giving rise to relatively permanent groupings, whole classes within society, and potentially challenging the very existence of the superstructure; and 'occasional, immediate, almost accidental' movements of 'con-juncture', which are limited to adjustments within the existing power structure. The failure to establish the precise dialectical relationship between these two 'leads to presenting causes as immediately operative which in fact only operate indirectly, or to asserting that the immediate causes are the only effective ones' and on the one hand to economism; on the other hand to ideolog-ism, 'an exaggeration of the voluntarist and individual element'.[36] On the basis of this general principle, he analyses the various 'moments' of the dialectic of structure and superstructure, from the basic social relations of production to political and organiza-tional groupings. These depend on different degrees of homo-geneity, organization and political consciousness, from the 'elementary' solidarity of the economic-corporative phase to the wider solidarity of the class 'for itself', but still acting within the existing political-juridical framework of society; finally the most distinctly 'political' moment, 'which marks the decisive passage

[33] SPN pp. 244, 259, 264–265.
[34] MS: pp. 236, 237.
[35] SPN pp. 166–67.
[36] SPN pp. 177–78.

from the structure to the sphere of the complex superstructures', in which a group surpasses the limits of its corporate interests. These become the interests of other allied and subordinate groups; the sectional interest is superseded and comes to 'propagate itself throughout society – bringing about not only a unison of economic and political aims, but also intellectual and moral unity, posing all the questions around which the struggle rages not on a corporate but on a "universal" plane, and thus creating the hegemony of a fundamental social group over a series of subordinate groups.'[37] The political moment, in order to become universal must move beyond 'interest', surpassing the economic categories of existing society, to constitute an integral challenge, political, cultural, ideological, a qualitative affirmation of the new social order.

Hence the crucial role of ideology and the means by which consciousness is mediated in capitalist society, preserved and protected behind the whole complex of institutions, private and public, which legitimize bourgeois dominance, rendering its values and definitions universal because accepted as the definitive values of society as such. Developing his analysis from Marx's *Preface* of 1859 – that 'it is in the sphere of ideology that men become conscious of this conflict and fight it out'[38] – Gramsci developed, through the Sorelian concept of *historical bloc*, a theory of the role of intellectuals as 'experts in legitimation', in mediating the ideological and political unity of the existing hegemonic structure, rendering it acceptable to allied and subordinate groups, universalizing its dominance. The establishment of this intellectual and political hegemony in the nineteenth century occupies a large part of Gramsci's historical analysis, particularly in the case of post-Risorgimento Italy. Thus he dwells on the process of 'molecular absorption', through which the national 'revolutionary' forces, represented by the Party of Action, were cut off by their failure to mobilize a mass support among the peasants of the south and without any organic class basis, failed to challenge the dominant historical bloc formed by the northern bourgeoisie in alliance with the southern landowners. In this way the Moderates were able to build up the hegemony of a coalition of agrarian and industrial

[37] SPN pp. 181–82.
[38] Marx: Preface, *Selected Works*, Moscow, 1958, Vol. 1, p. 363.

interest-groups and their clientele, exercising a 'spontaneous attraction' on the southern intellectuals and functionaries.[39] This process of 'trasformismo' represented the gradual widening of the social base of the Italian ruling class bloc, the absorption of opposition and allied groups by 'private' individual initiatives, in which, as in the case of republican France from 1870, corruption and bribery played a significant role 'characteristic of certain situations when it is hard to exercise the hegemonic function, and when the use of force is too risky.'[40] Only in periods of organic crisis was naked coercion rendered necessary, since the ruling class stood isolated and hence vulnerable, the exercise of hegemony becoming impossible. The resolution of such a crisis would depend on the forces available; the arbitration by a charismatic mediator claiming to represent the 'national interest', the Caesarist solution, was the result of a static stalemate.[41]

This resort to the 'moment of force' is a sign of great weakness; normally the hegemonic equilibrium is characterized by a 'combination of force and consent, which balance each other reciprocally, without force predominating excessively over consent. Indeed, the attempt is always made to ensure that force will appear to be based on the consent of the majority, expressed by the so-called organs of public opinion – newspapers and associations – which, therefore, in certain situations, are artificially multiplied.'[42] In western democracy the degree of institutionalization has made the superstructures peculiarly 'dense' and '"civil society" has become a very complex structure and one which is resistant to the catastrophic "incursions" of the immediate economic element (crises, depressions, etc.).'[43] In his last report to the party on the general situation, before his arrest in 1926, Gramsci observed that in the countries of 'advanced capitalism', which are the 'key stones of the bourgeois edifice', 'the dominant class possesses political and organizational reserves, which it did

[39] SPN pp. 55, 108–109.

[40] SPN p. 80. The point is made in reference to the Third Republic in France. It equally applies to the Reform League in the 1868 election in England; see Royden Harrison: *Before the Socialists*, 1965, Chapter 4.

[41] SPN pp. 219–20. Gramsci distinguishes between 'progressive' and 'regressive' Caesarism. He also refers to a 'degree' of Caesarism within parliamentary régimes, the MacDonald coalition of 1931 being a solution of this kind.

[42] SPN p. 80.

[43] SPN pp. 235–38.

not possess, for example, in Russia. Even the gravest economic crises do not have an immediate repercussion in the political field. Politics always lag considerably behind economic development'. In the more peripheral countries like Italy the existence of 'large intermediate strata' between capital and labour, with their own political and ideological influence, especially on the peasantry, creates further superstructural peculiarities.[44] In the case of democratic forms of government the principle of the division of powers, of 'impartial arbitration' by the executive 'who reigns but does not govern', helps to ensure the consent of the governed, masking the real nature of power relations in capitalist society behind a façade of formal and abstract, juridical, notions of citizenship. Under these conditions consciousness is mediated and fragmentary, refracted through the existing hegemonic apparatus of bourgeois 'direction', while conflict is regulated to ensure that disputes are kept within the narrow bounds of procedural compromise, registered by the election vote.[45]

These considerations imply, in terms of strategy, that the 'war of manoeuvre' becomes progressively the 'war of position'. Borrowing the military terminology of the first world war, Gramsci wrote: 'Before 1870 ... society was still, so to speak, in a state of fluidity . . . (there was) a relatively rudimentary state apparatus, and greater autonomy of civil society from state activity'. With increasing bureaucratization, 'the massive structures of the modern democracies, both as State organizations, and as complexes of associations in civil society . . . constitute "trenches" and the permanent fortifications of the front in the war of position', against which an artillery attack only destroys 'the outer perimeter', leaving the defence lines still effective. This is a problem specific to modern states, not to backward countries or colonies, in which 'the structures of national life are embryonic and loose, and incapable of becoming "trench or fortress."'' This in turn meant that the 'Forty-Eightist formula of the "Permanent Revolution" is expanded and transcended in political science by the formula of

[44] 'Un rapporto inedito al partito, 1926', ed. Franco Ferri, *Rinascita* – Il Contemporaneo, 14 April 1967, p. 23. The report is entitled 'Situazione interna italiana; elementi per la linea politica del partito'. Political Writings 1921–26 (forthcoming). Henceforward PW(f).

[45] SPN pp. 148, 192–93, 245–46.

"civil hegemony"'.[46] Whereas in Russia for instance, 'the State was everything, civil society was primordial . . . in the West the State was only an outer ditch, behind which there stood a powerful system of fortresses and earthworks.' The 'accurate reconnaissance of each individual country' made it necessary to 'translate' Lenin's practice into the terms appropriate for a 'war of position', the only possible one in the west, a strategy of siege to challenge and breach the hegemonic apparatus of the bourgeoisie.[47]

The passage to the 'war of position' becomes increasingly the key to western strategy in Gramsci's analysis; the 'war of reciprocal siege' represents the most difficult, but the most decisive phase of the struggle, which requires an 'unprecedented concentration of hegemony', a mobilization on the part of the dominant groups of 'all the hegemonic resources of the state' through controls of every kind, to 'organize permanently the "impossibility" of internal disintegration'.[48] In his notes on *Americanism and Fordism*, Gramsci analysed the corresponding trend towards the rationalization of the work force and the internalization of control over the whole area of the worker's life in the most advanced sectors of capitalist production, which represented 'the ultimate stage in the process of progressive attempts by industry to overcome the law of the tendency of the rate of profit to fall.'[49] Such developments of hegemony in the productive processes themselves, the adaptation to new forms of psychic discipline, together with the existence of a 'working class aristocracy with its bureaucratic . . . and social-

---

[46] SPN pp. 235–38, 243. Trotsky's theory of 'permanent revolution' is related to the 'war of manoeuvre', appropriate to an earlier period. 'In this case one might say that "Bronstein" (Trotsky), apparently "Western", was in fact a cosmopolitan – i.e. superficially national and superficially Western or European. Ilitch (Lenin) on the other hand was profoundly national and profoundly European.' SPN p. 237. Trotsky's theory 'of frontal attack in a period in which it only leads to defeats' is thus a 'typical manifestation of sectarian thought. . . . The belief in the capacity to always do the same thing even when the "politico-military situation" has changed.' SPN p. 238.

[47] SPN pp. 237–38.

[48] SPN pp. 238–39.

[49] SPN p. 286. The special conditions of American life, which make this degree of rationalization possible, mean that 'hegemony here is born in the factory and requires for its exercise only a minute quantity of professional, political and ideological intermediaries.' The elaboration of the new type of man 'suited to the new type of work and productive process' was still (before the crisis of 1929) at its initial phase 'of adaptation . . . through high wages; . . . the fundamental question of hegemony has not yet been posed'. SPN pp. 285–86.

democratic connections' demanded 'a more complex and long term strategy and tactics than were necessary to the Bolsheviks in . . . 1917', he wrote in a letter of 1924.[50] Under these circumstances the reliance on 'conditions', on the principal contradiction of capitalism, to 'produce' an opposition was a vain delusion, for the 'determination which in Russia launched the masses on the revolutionary path was complicated in western and central Europe by all the political superstructures created by the greater development of capitalism'.[51] An integral opposition could only come about by the properly political work of organizing and mobilizing the masses, not in terms of corporate interest, but in terms of the hegemonic leadership of the working class organized in a revolutionary party with an active mass basis. Only in this way could that transformation of consciousness take place, which would make possible a transcendence of the existing categories of society, both in theory and in revolutionary practice, transforming both workers and intellectuals into intellectuals of a new type through the active educative and political work of the revolutionary organization. 'But the existence of objective conditions, of possibilities or of freedom is not yet enough: it is necessary to "know" them, and know how to use them. And to want to use them.'[52] Both the sectarian and the syndicalist positions underestimated this active work of mass organization in the formation of a 'collective will'. Gramsci's authentic Leninism lay in his rejection of all forms of spontaneism and syndicalism, which he criticized in Sorel and Rosa Luxemburg,[53] the tendency among the critics of the Second International to assume the existence of a revolutionary agency in society and to appeal to the 'direct action' of the masses, without the necessary intervention of political organization. Neither was political organization in itself sufficient; the sectarian resort to the opposite extreme reproduced the same result in practice, the divorce between the party, the intellectuals

[50] Letter to Togliatti of 9 February 1924, marking Gramsci's decisive break with the Bordigan faction. Ferrata and Gallo, ed., *op. cit.*, I p. 673. PW(f).

[51] Ibid.

[52] SPN p. 360.

[53] For Gramsci's critique of syndicalism, which is addressed to 'a subaltern group, which is prevented by this theory from ever becoming dominant, or from developing beyond the economic-corporate stage and rising to the phase of ethical-political hegemony in civil society' see SPN p. 160. For the critique of Luxemburg's theory of 'mass strike' see SPN pp. 127, 233.

and the masses, the failure to create that 'organic' relationship which alone could establish a revolutionary hegemony, overcoming the fragmentation created and sustained by the dominant bloc and building a new coherence, capable of responding to the needs and aspirations of all exploited groups on a national scale.

The politicizing of the worker meant the transcendence of his corporate interests as a wage-earner, which are themselves determined by the capitalist wage-relation. 'The proletariat, in order to be capable of governing . . . must rid itself of every corporatist residue, of every syndicalist prejudice or incrustation.'[54] The Trade Union, Gramsci wrote in *L'Ordine Nuovo* in 1919, is a 'form of capitalist society, not a potential successor to that society. It organizes workers, not as producers, but as wage earners, i.e. as creatures of the capitalist, private property regime, selling the commodity labour'.[55] The problem was therefore to develop institutions which would allow the worker to develop his autonomous initiative as a producer. In the conditions of postwar Italy the means of mobilizing the working class in Turin as a revolutionary force was through the factory council movement, which represented the direct democratic control of the productive process by all the producers in the factory; the introduction of direct democracy of producers organized as an autonomous force, in the area of production itself, the one area where democracy was crucially denied in capitalist society, at work, was seen by Gramsci as the key to the future society, in which the producers become, 'instead of simple executors, agents of the process; from being cogwheels in the mechanism of capitalist production, become subjects'.[56] Cammett shows in his study how the factory council represented a means by which the 'workers could educate themselves as producers'; it could not therefore be subjected to the trade union and PSI bureaucracy, but had to be organized on an autonomous basis. The tendency to see the factory councils movement as a form of syndicalism ignored their role as a politically educative institution.[57] 'The proletarian dictatorship can

---

[54] 'La questione meridionale', 1926, Ferrata and Gallo, *op. cit.* I, p. 805. *Cf.* 'Lettera di Gramsci al comitato centrale del PCUS nel 1926', *Rinascita* 22, 1964; reprinted in Ferrata and Gallo ed., *op. cit.*, vol. I, pp. 824–25. PW(f).

[55] 'Syndicalism and the Councils', PW pp. 109–13.

[56] PW pp. 142–46, 260–64.

[57] Cammett, *op. cit.*, pp. 79–88. Sorel expressed his admiration of the movement. For a 'syndicalist' interpretation see N. Matteucci, 'Partito e consiglio di fabbrica nel

only be embodied in a type of organization that is specific to the activity of producers, not wage-earners, the slaves of capital. The factory council is the nucleus of this organization',[58] the means by which the proletariat can 'educate itself, gather experience and acquire a responsible awareness of the duties incumbent upon classes that hold the power of the state'.[59] In his report of July 1920 to the Comintern, Gramsci described the Turin councils as 'shift(ing) trade union struggle out of its narrowly reformist and corporatist framework up to the level of revolutionary struggle, control over production and proletarian dictatorship.' This meant the direct control of the councils by the producers themselves, 'not by the upper echelons of the trades-union bureaucracy'.[60] In this way, the 'Turinese communists posed concretely . . . the question of the "hegemony of the proletariat", in other words of the social basis of the proletarian dictatorship and the workers' state'.[61] The factory council was the means by which the party, as the conscious vanguard of the struggle, could be directly linked to the active mass participation of the working class as producers, conscious of their responsible and liberated role. The factory council was 'the model of the proletarian state', in which political society itself would progressively be 'organically' absorbed by civil society.[62]

It was essential that this transition from a corporate to a directing function take place before the actual conquest of power; instead of a mechanical symmetry between base and superstructure a dialectical relation enables the revolutionary movement to exercise a *de facto* leadership in civil society this side of power. 'A social group can, and indeed must, already exercise "leadership" before winning governmental power (this indeed is one of

---

pensiero di Gramsci, *Il Mulino* IV, 4 April 1955, pp. 350–59. Gramsci traced the defeat of the German revolutionary movement to the failure to move outside the traditional institutions of the working class, imposing external controls on the workers; hence the revolution was 'shackled and domesticated': 'The Party and the Revolution', PW p. 143.

[58] 'Union and Councils', PWI pp. 98–102.
[59] 'Syndicalism and the Councils', PW p. 109–113.
[60] 'The Turin Factory Councils Movement', PW p. 316. The dispute between Gramsci and Angelo Tasca was over this issue, of the autonomous role of the councils. See PW pp. 239–99 for the relevant texts.
[61] 'Alcuni temi della questione meridionale' (1926) Ferrata and Gallo ed., *op. cit.*, I, p. 799. PW(f).
[62] 'Unions and Councils', 'The Turin Factory Council Movement', PWI pp. 98–102, 310–20; SPN p. 260.

the principal conditions for the winning of such power); it subsequently becomes dominant when it exercises power, but even if it holds it firmly in its grasp, it must continue to "lead" as well.'[63] This meant that the working class could not establish its hegemony 'without some sacrifice of its immediate interests' to the interests of all its potential allies in society; in particular, in Italy, it would have to ally itself with the rural masses of the south. The 'southern question' has been rightly described as the 'primordial problem' of Italian socialism; to Gramsci the Turin movement had 'one undeniable merit', that of having 'brought the southern question to the attention of the vanguard of the working class, formulating it as one of the essential problems of the national policy of the Italian proletariat'.[64] The future of the workers' movement in the north and the peasants movement in the south were indissolubly linked; the workers had an immediate interest in not allowing 'southern Italy and the islands to become a capitalist counter-revolutionary base'. At the same time in the establishment of the workers' state lay the salvation of the peasantry.[65] If this alliance is not created 'the proletariat cannot become the "directing" class and those strata, which in Italy represent the majority of the population will remain under bourgeois direction, enabling the state to defeat and resist the proletarian impetus'.[66] The mechanical formulae of both the PSI leadership and the Bordigan group towards any autonomous initiative, either of the workers or towards the peasants,[67] was one of the major factors in the defeat of socialism in the postwar crisis.

[63] SPN pp. 57–58, 253.

[64] PW(f).

[65] 'The Northern bourgeoisie has subjugated the South of Italy and the Islands, and reduced them to exploitable colonies; by emancipating itself from capitalist slavery, the Northern proletariat will emancipate the Southern peasant masses enslaved to the banks and the parasitic industry of the North'.

[66] '*La questione meridionale*'. *op. cit.* I, p. 805 PW(f). *Cf. L'Ordine Nuovo* I, p. 90: 'In Germany and Hungary the proletarian movement was not accompanied by any movement of the poorer peasant strata; the city in revolt was isolated, surrounded by the incomprehension and indifference of the countryside.'

[67] Cammett, *op. cit.*, pp. 91, 132. Bordiga regarded the factory councils as founded on the 'error that the proletariat can emancipate itself by gaining ground in economic relations, while capitalism still holds political power . . .' Serrati expressed the maximalist position on the peasants' movement: 'Everybody knows that the movement for the occupation of lands . . . was a demagogic and petty bourgeois movement aimed at *entrancing the agricultural masses*.' (My italics.)

The problem of alliance raised the whole question of the cultural and ideological preparation of the socialist movement. 'But from the moment in which a subaltern group becomes really autonomous and hegemonic, thus bringing into being a new form of State, we experience the concrete birth of a need to construct a new intellectual and moral order, that is, a new type of society, and hence the need to develop more universal concepts and more refined and decisive ideological weapons.'[68] The creation of this new intellectual and cultural unity was itself a condition for the 'directing' function: the integration of culture was a vital complementary task of socialism. Hence the crucial role of the intellectuals in the 'cementing' of the revolutionary bloc: 'Critical self-consciousness means, historically and politically, the creation of an *élite* of intellectuals. A human mass does not "distinguish" itself, does not become independent in its own right without, in the widest sense, organising itself; and there is no organization without intellectuals, that is without organisers and leaders (*dirigenti*), in other words, without the theoretical aspect of the theory-practice nexus being distinguished concretely by the existence of a group of people "specialised" in conceptual and philosophical elaboration of ideas.'[69] The theoretical-practical relation necessitated in practice a new relation between the 'intellectuals' and the 'mass', a new unity of consciousness through a unified political practice. In this sense the discovery by Lenin, 'in the field of political organization and practice, of the concept of hegemony as complementary to that of "state-as-force"' represented 'a great philosophical advance as well as a politico-practical one. For it necessarily supposes an intellectual unity and an ethic in conformity with a conception of reality that has gone beyond common sense and has become . . . a critical conception.'[70] The political unity of the revolutionary alliance requires a corresponding ideological coherence, and a new 'total' conception of culture, in which the party, the intellectuals and the masses are brought into an 'organic' relationship, qualitatively projecting an integral vision of the new civilization in all spheres of life.

[68] SPN p. 388.
[69] SPN p. 334.
[70] SPN p. 333.

III

The work of cultural renovation, of 'intellectual and moral reform' was therefore a crucial correlate of socialist hegemony;
'the unity based on traditional ideology is broken; until this
happens, it is impossible for the new forces to arrive at a consciousness of their own independent personality.'[71] Through his
confrontation with Croce, Gramsci derived 'the importance of the
"cultural aspect" even in practical (collective) activity. An
historical act can only be performed by "collective man", and
this presupposes the attainment of a "cultural-social" unity
through which a multiplicity of dispersed wills with heterogeneous aims, are welded together with a single aim, on the basis
of an equal and common conception of the world.'[72] Through the
existing ideological and cultural forms, the bourgeoisie is able to
'universalize' its 'direction' of society, to hold together disparate
and even opposition groups on the basis of a consensus. The
consciousness of subordinate groups is thus mediated and partial;
theory is often in contradiction with actions. This is not due to
'self-deception', an explanation which would apply to individuals, but to the uncritical 'borrowing of conceptions' which
'holds together a specific social group, it influences . . . the direction of will, with varying efficacity but often powerfully enough to
produce a situation in which the contradictory state of consciousness does not permit of any action, any decision or any choice, and
produces a condition of moral and political passivity'.[73] Hence
the vital importance of the critique of existing culture and ideology, not in the sense of negation, but revealing its partial nature,
the universality of which, now distorted in metaphysical terms,
will be realized in the passage to socialism.[74] Through this process of demystification on the intellectual level, the fragmentary
state of 'common sense' gives way to 'critical self-consciousness'
and the 'old collective will becomes dissolved into its contradictory elements', giving rise to a new cohesion.[75]

[71] SPN p. 136.
[72] SPN p. 349.
[73] SPN pp. 327, 333.
[74] SPN pp. 405, 407. 'Many idealist conceptions, or at least certain aspects of
them which are utopian during the reign of necessity, could become "truth" after
the passage, etc.'
[75] SPN pp. 195, 323–25.

Gramsci's emphasis on the educative aspect of socialism, achieving through the mass transformation of consciousness the 'creation of a new civilization', a universal and integrated culture, is developed from the earliest of his articles in the Turinese socialist weekly *Il Grido del Popolo*, which he edited from 1917 to 1918. In contrast to the anti-intellectualism of Bordiga ('One does not become a socialist through education, but through the real necessities of the class to which one belongs') or the traditional socialist populism of the previous editor, Maria Giudice ('When the masses feel in a socialist way . . . they will act in a socialist way'),[76] Gramsci's lucid and Socratic articles were aimed at educating the worker to his role in the leadership of the revolutionary struggle. Journalism became in his hands a means of 'elaborating, making to think concretely, transforming, homogenizing according to an organic process which leads from simple common sense to systematic and coherent thought'.[77] In part this emphasis was a product of his own experience as a scholar from Sardinia, one of the most backward provinces in Italy, and the enormous intellectual effort it had required 'to overcome a backward way of life and thought, such as that of a Sardinian at the beginning of this century, to reach a way of life . . . that is no longer restricted to the region and the village, but is national'.[78] Even more important, however, was the fact that he was well placed, as a provincial newcomer in the most industrialized city in Italy, to observe the 'borrowing of conceptions' in the corporatist and exclusive socialism of the PSI leadership, which looked upon the south as the 'backland', an obstacle to economic progress and source of cheap labour.[79] Italian socialism had 'suffered the sad fate of being approximated to the most arid, sterile thought of the nineteenth century, to positivism'.[80] In the hands of Marxists like Loria, for whom 'Facts' were 'divine, principles human', or Colajanni ('In the hedonistic principle alone and exclusively lies the justification of the class struggle')[81] Marxism had become a

---

[76] Fiori, *Antonio Gramsci*, p. 103.

[77] *Gli intellettuali e l'Organizzazione della cultura*, p. 142.

[78] P: p. 3.

[79] Cf. Fiori, *op. cit.*, pp. 93–95.

[80] 'Bergsoniano!' *L'Ordine Nuovo*, 3 January 1921.

[81] Santarelli, E., *La Revisione del Marxismo in Italia*, Milan 1964, pp. 34, 36. The astute prime minister, Giolitti, in a speech to the Chamber of Deputies (18 April 1911) declared that the Socialist Party had 'so moderated its principles that Karl

drab evolutionism in the dress then *à la mode*; to Gramsci this
tendency was especially dangerous since it sanctified the corporat-
ism of the socialist movement. 'Every revolution,' he wrote in
1916, 'has been preceded by an intense labour of criticism, by the
diffusion of culture and the spread of ideas' and he added: 'We
need to free ourselves from the habit of seeing culture as encyclopaedic knowledge, and men as mere receptacles to be stuffed full
of empirical data and a mass of unconnected raw facts, which have
to be filed in the brain as in the columns of a dictionary, enabling
their owner to respond to the various stimuli from the outside
world. This form of culture is really dangerous, particularly *for
the proletariat*.'[82] Gramsci's struggle against positivism was at the
same time a struggle for the unity of the revolutionary bloc. 'The
first task of the Turinese communists was that of changing the
political orientation and general ideology of the proletariat itself,
as a national element, which lives inside the complex life of the
state and undergoes unconsciously the influence of the schools, the
newspapers, of the bourgeois tradition.' The Socialist Party had
'given its blessing' to the 'whole "southernist" literature of the
clique of so-called positivist writers. . . . Once again, "science"
had turned to crushing the wretched and exploited, but this time
it was cloaked in socialist colours'.[83]

The development of a revolutionary consciousness required a
new emphasis on the role of ideas in changing the objective
reality of external phenomena. While Gramsci's early intellectual
formation took place under the aegis of neo-idealism, he underlined his 'complete break' with this tradition, in terms of a radical
historicism, shorn of transcendental and ahistorical categories.
To confront Croce's speculative historicism, in which 'history
becomes a formal history, a history of concepts and in the last
analysis an autobiographical history of the thought of Croce', it
was necessary to 'reduce it to its real significance as an immediate
ideology, divesting it of the brilliance with which it is accredited as
a manifestation . . . of serene and impartial thought, situated far

Marx has been relgated to the attic'. *Ibid.*, p. 33 n. For the influence of positivism on
the Reformists, especially Turati, see Lelio Basso: 'Turati, il riformismo e la via
democratica', *Problemi del socialismo*, February 1958.
[82] PW pp. 10, 12. My italics.
[83] 'La questione meridionale', ibid, p. 800. PW(f). On the positivist literature,
sustaining the belief in 'southern backwardness' and 'inferiority' see SPN p. 71.

above the miseries and contingencies of daily life, in disinterested contemplation'.[84] Croce represented the 'lay Pope' of bourgeois hegemony, comparable to the position of Erasmus in relation to the Reformation. The failure of the idealists lay in the exclusiveness of their ideas, in 'not having known how to create an ideological unity between the élite and the masses, between the intellectuals and the masses'. Their conception of education lacked any 'organic character'; it resembled 'the first contacts of English merchants and the negroes of Africa'.[85] The ultimate failure of idealism was the divorce of theory from the real struggles of history, through which history became reduced to an arbitrary and abstract schema; Gramsci's method, in combating both idealism and 'crude materialism', was 'the "logical" point at which every conception of the world makes the passage to the morality appropriate to it, when contemplation becomes action and every philosophy becomes the political action dependent on it. In other words, it is the point at which the conception of the world, contemplation, philosophy become "real" since they now aim to modify the world and to revolutionise praxis. One could say therefore that this is the central nexus of the philosophy of praxis, the point at which it becomes actual and lives historically (that is socially and no longer just in the brains of individuals), when it ceases to be arbitrary and becomes necessary – rational – real'.[86] This emphasis on the practicity of theory, the intentionality of 'philosophy', is directed above all to the practical problem of the mass diffusion of Marxism as a world conception; the many references to 'philosophy' passing into 'real history' have this polemical-indicative sense. Althusser has recently suggested, on the grounds of the 'latent' tendency of every historicist proble-

---

[84] For Gramsci's early idealism see the article of 1918, 'Misteri della cultura e della poesia', *Scritti giovanili*, pp. 325ff., in which 'the essentials' of Marxism are traced to 'philosophical idealism' and history appears as the teleological 'becoming' of a proletarian consciousness-subject. This is possibly the closest Gramsci came to the idealist position of Lukács in *History and Class Consciousness. Cf.* N. Poulantzas, 'Marxism in Great Britain', *New Left Review* 43, pp. 60–61. For the critique of Croce, see MS pp. 174, 189, 191, 217, 221. While Croce's 'instrumental value' is recognized for having drawn attention to the 'cultural front as essential', 'it is necessary to carry out with regard to Croce's conception the same reduction that (Marx) carried out for the Hegelian conception'. p. 199. See also Bobbio, N., 'Nota sulla dialettica in Gramsci', *Studi Gramsciani*, Rome, 1958, p. 81.

[85] SPN pp. 330–31, 392–94.

[86] SPN p. 369.

matic, that this results in an underestimation of 'theoretical practice' itself, a confusion between theory and ideology, in which 'philosophy' becomes reduced to an expression of a historical 'essence' in a Hegelian-type 'expressive unity'. Theory thus becomes a reflection of history, a 'historically-determined abstraction', resulting in an empiricist approach on the one hand or an idealist voluntarism on the other.[87] Without entering into the general sense of Althusser's discussion, it may however be questioned that Gramsci represents this historicist tendency; Althusser overlooks the theoretical-practical field of Gramsci's research, in which theory is not a passive 'reflection' of history, but an essential moment in the overcoming and surpassing of existing structures, reacting against them in terms of conscious praxis. Gramsci's historicism represents the means by which both theory and practice are 'actualized', within the determined context. He therefore avoids both spontaneism and voluntarism; the relationship between 'philosophy' and 'history' is a *critical* one, and by no means precludes the theoretical dimension as such.[88]

Gramsci's critique of idealism was not only a confrontation with the most significant philosophy of the time, of abstract man divorced from his social environment; it was also above all part of his critique of 'pure intellectuals', of the 'cosmopolitan' tradition in Italian culture, expressed in the supra-national institutions of Empire and Papacy, which in turn had determined that fundamental Italian problem, of a country whose history had long been marked by a severe disproportion between social and economic backwardness and pre-eminence in the artistic and cultural field, by the wide gap between the enlightened lay culture of a small minority and the religious superstition of the masses. In Italy, he noted, the term 'national' had a restricted sense, not coinciding with that of 'popular', 'since . . . the intellectuals are removed from the people, that is from the "nation", and are on the contrary

---

[87] Althusser and Balibar: *Reading Capital*, London 1970, pp. 126–35.

[88] For discussions of Gramsci's 'historicism', see N. Badaloni 'Gramsci storicista', *Critica Marxista* Quaderni n. 3, 1967 and Cesare Luporim: 'Realta e storicita: economia e dialettica nel marxismo', *Critica Marxista* n. 1, 1966. 'The identification of theory and practice is a critical act, through which practice is demonstrated rational and necessary, and theory realistic and rational.' SPN p. 365. It remains true however, that at times Gramsci comes close to a pan-ideologism, reminiscent of Mannheim. See for example SPN p. 328, on the 'lay-faith' derived from the Crocean conception of religion.

linked to a tradition of caste . . . the tradition is "bookish" and abstract . . . and the typical intellectual feels more linked to Hannibal Caro or Hippolitus . . . than to the peasant of Apulia or Sicily'. In relation to the people the intellectuals were 'a caste and not an element organically linked to the people themselves'.[89] It was the absence of any 'national-popular' culture which constituted the primordial weakness of Italian society, which in turn had made the achievement of national unity a 'passive revolution' governed by external forces, rather than developing its own internal dynamic.[90] Gramsci uses the term 'Jacobin' in two distinct senses: first, to refer to the intellectualist and abstract divorce of theory from the concrete possibilities contained within society, in the sense that Trotsky 'had the Jacobin temperament without an adequate political content', while in Lenin there was 'Jacobin temperament and content derived . . . not from a literary and intellectualistic label'.[91] His criticism of the sectarian position was thus linked to that of idealism: 'The position of "pure intellectual" becomes either a really deteriorated form of "Jacobinism" – and in this sense "Amadeo" (Bordiga) can, on a different intellectual level, be compared to Croce – or a disdainful Pontius-Pilatism, or even both simultaneously'.[92] In the second sense, Jacobinism refers to active intervention in the creation of a 'national-popular collective will', the 'protagonist of a real historical drama'; in this sense, the 'precocious Jacobinism' of Machiavelli is traced to his proposed reorganization of the Florentine militia, bringing the peasants 'simultaneously' into political life.[93]

These considerations govern Gramsci's redefinition of the role of intellectuals and that of the hegemonic party as a 'collective intellectual'. There exists 'no independent class of intellectuals, but every social group has its own stratum of intellectuals, or tends to form one', to give it 'homogeneity and an awareness of its own function not only in the economic but also in the social and

[89] *Letteratura e vita nazionale*, pp. 105–106; P, p. 15. *Cf.* Gramsci's linguistic studies *Gli Intellettuali*, pp. 21–29.

[90] SPN pp. 86–90, 97–102, 109–110.

[91] SPN pp. 84–85.

[92] MS: pp. 174–75.

[93] SPN pp. 130–31, 141, 143. *Cf.* The failure of the intellectuals of the Party of Action to develop an 'organic' rural base, 'to be "Jacobin", not only in external "form", in temperament, but most particularly in socio-economic content'. SPN p. 74.

political fields. The capitalist entrepreneur creates alongside himself the industrial technician, the specialist in political economy, the organisers of a new culture, of a new legal system.'[94] These 'organic' intellectuals, who usually represent '"specialisations" of partial aspects of the primitive activity of the new social type which the new class has brought into prominence' are distinguished from the category of 'traditional' intellectuals, which are 'already in existence' and which appear as 'representatives of an historical continuity uninterrupted even by the most complicated and radical changes in political and social forms'.[95] The relation between intellectuals and the world of production is not as direct as it is with the fundamental social groups but is, in varying degrees, '"mediated" by the whole fabric of society and by the complex of superstructures, of which the intellectuals are, precisely, the "functionaries"'.[96] To the intellectuals, in this broad sense, in terms of their function which is 'directive and organisational, i.e. educative, i.e. intellectual', falls the role of mediating the hegemony of the dominant group, ensuring that '"spontaneous" consent given by the great masses of the population to the general direction imposed on social life by the dominant fundamental group', carrying out the work of 'organization and connection' as 'the dominant group's "deputies" exercising the subaltern functions of social hegemony and political government'.[97] It becomes imperative therefore for the revolutionary movement not only to win over elements of the 'traditional' intellectuals, but above all to develop its own 'organic' intellectuals to create 'favourable conditions' for the expansion of its own class from a subordinate to a directing capacity. The restoration of the theory-practice nexus required 'cultural stability and an organic quality of thought' which can only be realised 'if there had existed the same unity between the intellectuals and the simple as there should be between theory and practice. That is, if the intellectuals had been organically the intellectuals of those masses, and if they

---

94 SPN pp. 60–65. *Cf.* SPN p. 170, where the failure of the medieval Italian communes is traced to their not having developed their own organic intellectuals. 'Religion was consent and the Church was civil society, the hegemonic apparatus of the ruling group, for the latter did not have its own apparatus, did not have its own cultural and intellectual organization.' *Cf. Lettere dal carcere*, pp. 479–83.

95 SPN pp. 6–7.

96 SPN p. 12.

97 SPN pp. 12, 16.

had worked out and made coherent the principles and the problems raised by the masses in their practical activity, thus constituting a cultural and social bloc'.[98] This involved the development of a new type of revolutionary intellectual, who would arise 'directly out of the masses, but remain in contact with them to become, as it were, the whalebone in the corset'.[99]

The essentially educative relation implied by the term 'organic' becomes the basis of the hegemony of the revolutionary bloc; the dialectical relation between the 'intellectuals' and the 'masses', the party and the active participation of its social base. This relationship is active and reciprocal in which 'every teacher is always a pupil and every pupil a teacher'.[100] In contrast with previous 'world-conceptions', Marxism 'does not tend to leave the "simple" in their primitive philosophy of common sense, but rather to lead them to a higher conception of life', making possible 'the intellectual progress of the mass and not only of small intellectual groups.'[101] All men are to a certain degree intellectuals, in that they participate in a world-conception; in this wider sense of 'intellectual', Gramsci writes of changing the relationship between intellectual and muscular effort to create a 'new equilibrium', and a new type of intellectual, who is 'actively involved in practical life', combining specialist technique with science and humanism, thus becoming '"directive" (specialised and political)'.[102] Society itself becomes a system of educative relationships 'throughout society as a whole and for every individual relative to other individuals. It exists between intellectual and non-intellectual sections of the population, between the rulers and the ruled. . . . Every relationship of "hegemony" is necessarily an educational relationship. . . .'[103] One is reminded of Che Guevara's writing of the need for 'the development of a consciousness in which all the old categories of evaluation become changed. Society in its

[98] SPN p. 330. 'This cannot come about unless there is a continually felt need for cultural contact with the non-intellectuals (semplici).' See also the need for an 'organic rupture' among the intellectuals 'to break up the intellectual bloc, which forms the flexible but resistent armour of the Southern agrarian bloc'. 'La questione meridionale', Ferrata and Gallo, *op. cit.*, I, p. 819. PW(f).

[99] SPN p. 340.

[100] SPN p. 350.

[101] SPN p. 332.

[102] SPN p. 10.

[103] SPN p. 350.

complexity must become a gigantic school'.[104]

In 1919 Gramsci had developed, in the factory councils programme, the means through which such a relation could be expressed, which 'corresponded to latent aspirations and con-
formed to the development of the real forms of life' among the
Turin workers. 'At that time,' he later recalled, 'no initiative was
taken that was not tested in reality . . . if the opinions of the
workers were not taken fully into account. For this reason, our
initiatives appeared as the interpretation of a felt need, never as the
cold application of intellectual schema'.[105] The task was always,
for Gramsci, to find the 'present form of the struggle', the form
that would activate a response, since it corresponded to the
'revolutionary thread' in the real historical situation; in this way
making possible the passage from science to action, 'not the pure
act', the Bergsonian abandonment to the irrational, which Gramsci
criticized in Sorel, but the 'real "impure" act, in the most profane
and worldly sense of the world.'[106] While the problem of hegemony was posed in this way by the *Ordine Nuovo* group in 1919–21,
they had few illusions about the likelihood of failure. The
'optimism of will' was always tempered by a 'pessimism of awareness', to use a phrase characteristic of Gramsci. In the absence of
political leadership at the national level, the Turinese movement
was isolated. 'Abandoned on all sides, the Turin proletariat was
forced to confront the nation's capitalists and the power of the
State entirely on its own.'[107] The Socialist Party had become a
mere spectator of the unfolding of events, had failed 'to lay down
a general line and unify or concentrate revolutionary action'.
The Party had shown itself to be a 'mere bureaucratic institution,
with no soul or will', with the result that 'the working class will
instinctively move to form another party and shift its allegiance
to the anarchist tendencies'.[108] The factory councils could not in
themselves provide a solution; as Togliatti put it in 1920: 'The

[104] Che Guevara: 'Socialism and Man'.
[105] Letter to Togliatti (27.3.1924). Ferrata and Gallo, *op. cit.*, Vol. I, p. 677.
PW(f). SPN pp. 9–10.
[106] PW pp. 146, 293.
[107] 'The Turin Factory Council Movement', PW pp. 310–20.
[108] 'Towards a Renewal of the Socialist Party', PW pp. 190–96. *Cf.* 'The Communist Party', PW pp. 330–339. The Socialist Party 'which proclaims itself to be the
head of the working class, is nothing but the baggage train of the proletarian army'.
p. 338.

constitution of councils only has value if it is viewed as a conscious beginning of a revolutionary process. . . . Control of production has meaning only as an act . . . in this process.'[109] To Gramsci, the existence of a coherent leadership was 'the fundamental and indispensable condition for attempting any experiment with Soviets. In the absence of such a condition, every experiment proposed should be rejected as absurd'.[110] The need for a new conception of political leadership was the lesson to be drawn from the defeat of the Italian revolution. Gramsci's concern was to develop a leadership that would 'move ahead' of events, with a coherent strategy, 'so that it may win their (the masses) permanent trust and thus become their guide and intellect'.[111]

Gramsci's conception of the party follows closely the general framework of his ideas on the intellectuals, hegemony and the specificity of the superstructures. The party is not reducible to an epiphenomenon of 'class'; it is the political agency of the working class responsible for developing and organizing the political conditions for the foundation of the workers' state. Gramsci developed his notion of the hegemonic party through his opposition to the sectarian tendencies of the early PCI, but already by 1921, he wrote: 'An association can be called a "political party" only in so far as it has succeeded in making concrete . . . its own notion . . . of the State, in concretizing and diffusing among the masses its own programme of government, organizing in terms of practice, that is within determined conditions, in relation to real men and not abstract phantasma . . . a State'.[112] His long struggle against sectarianism was due to the fact that the party was not conceived 'as the result of a dialectical process, in which the spontaneous movement of the revolutionary masses and the organized and directive will at the centre converge, but only as something nourished on air, which develops in itself and by itself . . .'.[113] The result was passivity and inaction, the failure to intervene actively in the work of building up the ideological and political unity of the revolutionary class and its allies. 'In the modern world, a party is such – integrally, and not, as happens, a fraction

[109] Cammett, *op. cit.*, p. 82.
[110] PW p. 195.
[111] PW p. 191–92.
[112] 'Lo Stato operaio', *L'Ordine Nuovo* II, p. 3. PW(f).
[113] Letter to Togliatti (9.2.1924), Ferrata and Gallo, *op. cit.* I, p. 672. PW(f).

of a larger party – when it is conceived, organised and led in ways and in forms such that it will develop integrally into a State (an integral State, and not into a government technically understood) and into a conception of the world'.[114] The hegemonic party is based on a continually progressing dialectic between the proletariat and its conscious vanguard, an active, reciprocal relationship, that by far surpasses the categories of the Nennian 'democratic' and the 'totalitarian' interpretations of many commentators, vitiated by the language of Cold War ideology. Lichtheim, for example, in his summary treatment, claims that 'his (Gramsci's) own approach was quite consistent with the totalitarian assumption that revolutions are made by élites'.[115] Yet no reading of Gramsci, however casual, could support such an assertion. All his opposition to sectarianism was precisely directed *against* any tendency in the party towards authoritarianism or 'party vanity', against the error of regarding as self-sufficient the organization itself, 'which meant only to create an apparatus of functionaries who would be "orthodox" towards the official conceptions'.[116] In the face of Stalinism, his strictures against party bureaucracy in the *Prison Notebooks* have an unambiguous ring; the bureaucratic tendency represents a 'most dangerously hidebound and conservative force; if it ends up by constituting a compact body . . . and feels itself independent of the mass of members, the party ends by becoming anachronist and at moments of acute crisis it is voided of its social content. . . .'[117] And writing of 'the unhealthy manifestations of bureaucratic centralism . . .

---

[114] SPN p. 267.

[115] *Cf.* also: Gramsci developed 'a doctrine more totalitarian than that of his gaolers' [*sic*]: George Lichtheim, *Marxism, a historical and critical study* (1961), pp. 368–69. Or H. Stuart Hughes in *Consciousness and Society*, 1959, who writes: 'As so often in Gramsci's writings, a totalitarian thought was clothed in liberal guise', p. 101; a slightly more subtle variant. For a typically 'Nennian' interpretation see G. Tamburrano: *Antonio Gramsci, la vita, il pensiero, l'azione,* Bari, 1963.

[116] Ferrata and Gallo, *op. cit.* I, p. 671.

[117] SPN p. 211. For Gramsci's political position in prison in the early 1930's, see the testimony of his brother Gennaro Gramsci in Fiori, pp. 252–53; Athos Lisa's report, published in *Rinascita* 12.xii. 1964; and Giuseppe Cereas's testimony, in which Gramsci is described as 'combating those abstract mechanical, antimarxist positions, which were based on the "misery" factor'. In Lisa's report, Gramsci puts forward the need for a hegemonic alliance against fascism: 'without winning over these allies, the proletariat is precluded from any serious revolutionary movement'. Fiori, p. 256. See also his report to the central committee of the CPSU on the eve of his arrest in 1926, in which he criticized the way in which party disputes were being

because of a lack of initiative and responsibility at the bottom', he described the resultant 'unity' as that of a 'stagnant swamp, on the surface calm and "mute"'.[118]

In contrast, Gramsci's conception of the party was based on the premise that 'a party cannot exist by virtue of an internal necessity' but through an organic relationship with the class it represents, expressed by his formula of 'spontaneity and conscious direction'. Defending the factory councils' experience against the accusation of voluntarism, he wrote: 'This leadership was not "abstract"; it neither consisted in mechanically repeating scientific or theoretical formulae, nor did it confuse politics, real action, with theoretical disquisition. It applied itself to real men, formed in specific historical relations, with specific feelings, outlooks, fragmentary conceptions of the world, etc., which were the result of "spontaneous" combinations of a given situation of material production with the "fortuitous" agglomeration within it of disparate social elements. This element of "spontaneity" was not neglected and even less despised. It was *educated*, directed. . . . It gave the masses a "theoretical" consciousness of being creators of *historical* and institutional *values*, of being founders of a State. This unity between "spontaneity" and "conscious leadership" . . . is precisely the real political action of the subaltern classes, in so far as this is mass politics and not merely an adventure by groups claiming to represent the masses.'[119] 'Conscious direction' must be applied if spontaneous movements are to become a positive political factor; from the postwar experience, Gramsci learned that 'the decisive element in every situation is the permanently organised and long-prepared force which can be put into the field when it is judged that a situation is favourable (and it can be favourable only in so far as such a force exists, and is full of fighting spirit)'.[120] But this 'force', the political party, was not to be organized on rigid lines, nor on the basis of a doctrine, 'artificial and mechanically super-imposed' but rather 'organically

---

handled, while not taking the side of the 'opposition'. Ferrata and Gallo I, pp. 820–26. 'Unity and discipline cannot be mechanical and coercive', he wrote. The Soviet party was 'running the risk of annulling the directing function which the Communist Party of the USSR had conquered through the work of Lenin', pp. 823, 825. PW(f).

[118] SPN pp. 189–190.
[119] SPN p. 198.
[120] SPN p. 185.

produced . . . historically . . . in the struggle'.[121] The party could only successfully move beyond the existing political framework and actively promote the surpassing of existing society and politics, if it became the elaborator 'of new integral and totalitarian intelligentsias and the crucibles where the unification of theory and practice, understood as a real historical process, takes place'. It was therefore necessary that the party 'should be formed by individual memberships and not on the pattern of the British Labour Party, because, if it is a question of providing an organic leadership for the entire economically active mass, this leadership should not follow old schemes but should innovate'. Hence the need for a leadership, but organized on the principles of 'democratic centralism', a 'centralism in movement'; when the party is progressive, it 'functions "democratically" (democratic centralism); when the party is regressive it functions "bureaucratically" (bureaucratic centralism)'.[122] Only as an organism in perpetual movement, rather than a rigid structure, 'a continual adaptation of the organisation to the real movement, a matching of thrusts from below with orders from above, which ensures continuity and the regular accumulation of experience', could the party, while it 'juridically neither rules nor governs', represent nevertheless a '"de facto power"', and exercise the hegemonic function and hence that of holding the balance between the various interests in "civil society"; the latter, however, is in fact intertwined with political society to such an extent that all the citizens feel that the party on the contrary both rules and governs'.[123] Finally, parties come into existence within a historical context; since they represent the 'nomenclature' of social classes, the ultimate goal of a party which aims progressively to educate the masses to self-management, to widen vastly the sphere of the 'political' in civil society, is its own disappearance.[124]

The underlying thematic of Gramsci's Marxism thus finds its unity and coherence in his creative confrontation of the social and historical realities of his world. His renewal of Marxism was never the detached work of a 'scientist' but rather the product of a lifetime of political struggle. In one of his earliest articles he wrote:

[121] *Note sul Machiavelli*, p. 296.
[122] SPN pp. 155, 335, 188.
[123] SPN pp. 188, 253.
[124] SPN p. 152.

'To live means to take sides'[125] and in a letter from prison: 'My whole intellectual formation was of a polemical kind and to think "disinterestedly", that is to study for study's sake, is difficult for me. Only occasionally, I manage to forget myself . . . and find, so to speak, the interest in things in themselves to apply myself to their analysis. Normally I have to move from a . . . dialectical standpoint; otherwise I feel no intellectual stimulus.'[126] The result was a Marxism adapted to the actual problems and needs of the Italian struggle. The conception of socialism as concerned above all with the qualitative, rather than quantitative, transformation of society was never confined to an abstract level but directed towards its concrete realization, in terms of the fundamental political task, which was to bring the 'objective' into relation with a programme to be realized; to apply the will to the creation of a new equilibrium of existing and operating forces, based on the force considered to be progressive, thereby moving 'on the terrain of effective reality, but . . . in order to dominate and transcend it (or to contribute to this). What "ought to be" is therefore concrete.'[127] In spite of imprisonment and appalling conditions, illness and isolation, Gramsci remained in a real sense a 'political activist'; like that other exile from political life, Machiavelli, his armies were 'only armies of words' and he was reduced to 'showing concretely how the historical forces ought to have acted in order to be effective'.[128]

Gramsci has recently been called 'the theoretician of revolution in the west'.[129] Certainly it is true that no Marxist has confronted with such lucidity the problem of organizing and sustaining a socialist movement in the conditions of advanced capitalism. While it would clearly be against his whole spirit to adopt his ideas uncritically in a new and different context, the unity and range of his Marxism, the absence of fixed categories in his work, its practical and active rather than passive approach, still constitute a vital source for the corresponding development of an authentic *British* or *American* Marxism and the renewal of the socialist movement in the Anglo Saxon world.

[125] *Scritti giovanili*, p. 78. See also the article 'Indifference', PW pp. 17–18.

[126] *Lettere dal Carcere*, p. 390.

[127] SPN pp. 171–72.

[128] SPN p. 173. Eugenio Garin 'Antonio Gramsci nella cultura italiana', *Studi Gramsciani*, Rome, 1958.

[129] Achille Occhetto, 'Un teorico della rivoluzione in occidente', *Rinascita*, 14 April, 1967, pp. 25–27.

Sartre and Marx

André Gorz

A Marxist can approach the *Critique of Dialectical Reason*, the most recent of Sartre's works, in a number of ways. It would be possible to write a historico-critical essay on the complex dialectical relationship between Sartre and Marxism as a movement. Equally it would be possible to write an essay on the history of philosophy which discussed Sartre's place in contemporary thought, showing the internal logic which led a philosopher whose starting point was the 'cogito' of Husserl to move beyond this towards dialectical materialism, and studying the validity of this development and its compatibility with Marx's method itself.[1] Finally, and best of all, it would be possible to do both at the same time – using the regressive-progressive method which Sartre himself recommends. In this case, one would start from Sartre's work as the singular enterprise of an individual, and then proceed to situate it in the historical context which conditioned it, showing how Sartre grappled with the problems of his time in general and Marxism in particular. This would provide a critical reconstruction of his own particular way of surpassing his problems and of being surpassed by them.

So far, none of these three possible approaches has been attempted by Marxist scholars. Whether in France, in Italy or elsewhere, most of them have postulated from the outset that Sartre *must be* an idealist since he has not repudiated his early work and its phenomenological method. And some have tried to prove this postulate by taking issue with the Sartrean vocabulary.

[1] In spite of its embryonic character and limited scope, Nicos Poulantzas's *La 'Critique de la Raison Dialectique' et le Droit* (Archives de Philosophie du droit, tome X, Sirey, Paris 1965) is a very interesting attempt of this kind.

Let us, therefore, define the aim and method of Sartre's work, before examining how it is related and what it adds to contemporary Marxist thought.

The aim of the *Critique* is to found dialectical materialism as a method and to define the sector of being to which it is applicable. It is not as such an attempt to apply it practically in a specific field of inquiry. Put another way, the structures, notions and categories which are brought into play in the *Critique* are not yet *operational*, but pertain to the critique of a method which has been applied empirically by Marxists with success, without becoming conscious of itself and its own possibilities.

The attempt to *found* dialectical materialism is indubitably related in all sorts of ways to the work of the later Husserl. Husserl said of science in his time: 'It has become unable to account for itself.' The judgment is valid *a fortiori* for the human sciences and for dialectical materialism. Scientific praxis, by failing to question its own status, and by claiming to put lived experience in parentheses, has become opaque to its own practitioners. Man absents himself from the science he produces and it sheds no light on him. The sciences which study man take him for their object, ignoring the fact that the object is itself the subject (as a man of science) inquiring into it. They thereby prevent themselves from ever giving an account of their own potentialities. Finally, just as the man of science cannot understand himself from the point of view of the sciences which study man, so Marxism has been unable to explain Marxists. In other words, Marxists become unable to explain themselves.

Husserl, writing in *La Crise des Sciences Européennes*, remarked: 'We lack the real awareness by which the cognitive subject could account for itself – not only in its effective actions and innovations, but also in the dimensions whose meaning is obscure and sedimented, the underlying presuppositions of its instruments, notions, propositions and theories. Do not science and the scientific method today resemble a precision machine – a machine which is obviously rendering useful service, and which anyone can learn to manipulate correctly, without having the least idea of its basis and necessity? Thus scientific method, having developed into the progressive accomplishment of a job, is a *technique* which can be transmitted, but which does not thereby necessarily transmit its true meaning. Thereafter theoretical work can only dominate the infinity of its themes by an infinity of methods, and an infinity of methods only by meaninglessly technical thought and activity. It is for this reason that theory can only remain genuinely and pristinely meaningful *if* the man of science has developed the capacity to return to the original meaning of all his ideas and methods: to their *basis in history* . . .'. In order to provide a basis for the possibility of authentic knowledge, Husserl sought to rid scientific thought of objectivism – and the psychologism, epiphenomenalism, dogmatism and scepticism which resulted from it – by restoring to it our original experience of the world as we live it. Sartre's efforts to provide a basis for dialectical reason are close to those of Husserl, at least at first sight: the dialectic has no basis unless it first has experience of itself 'as a double movement in knowledge and in being'.[2]

Man and Nature

Unless it is irrefutably confirmed in the unity of experience as deriving from individuals, as 'the logic of action', we can only speculate or make dogmatic assertions about the existence of a sector of dialectical intelligibility. The kind of dogmatism which asserts the *a priori* existence of a Dialectic of Nature and wishes to make human history into no more than a specific variant of natural history inevitably ends in scepticism. If human history is only one section of a much vaster and enveloping totalization and is ruled by the supposed finality of developments in nature, then its truth lies outside itself and there can be no authentic knowledge. As Kojève remarked, if Nature is creative in the same way as man, then truth or science in the true sense are only possible at the end of time. The upholders of the Dialectic of Nature imagine that they can get out of this difficulty by allowing to man the privileged faculty of understanding the total meaning of developments in nature, while remaining immanent within it. But this metaphysical postulate – also to be found in religious systems, where man is supposed capable of knowing God and his Purposes (necessarily impenetrable) – makes authentic knowledge dependent on a *postulate* and on the *faith* which one has in it. This is why transcendental materialism can only avoid scepticism by refusing to question its own method, out of sheer dogmatism. By making the

[2] *La Crise des Sciences Européennes.*

meaning of human history depend on that of Natural History, human history is subjected to a dialectic outside itself, in a way which Marx seems to reject when he writes, in the 1844 *Manuscripts*, that 'man is his own origin'.[3] Sartre continues: 'If we do not wish the dialectic to become a divine law again, a metaphysical fate, it must proceed *from individuals* and not from some kind of supra-individual ensemble.'[4] In other words, the dialectic can have no basis unless the individual – not, of course, conceived as a monad, but grasped in the totality of his conditions and relations as a totalization in process of retotalization – can experience it in terms of himself and his own praxis. But why this 'privileged' position of the individual? The answer is quite simple and leads us back to Marx. It is that there is no certainty, no meaning, no comprehension except *for* somebody. For example, to establish if History has a dialectical intelligibility (or more simply if it is intelligible at all) there is no other way than to seek to understand it. But as to understand means for everyone 'I understand', this means to see if History can be reconstructed from a multiplicity of individual praxes, which as partial and conscious totalizations, are capable of understanding themselves. History is intelligible to dialectical knowledge if it can be understood as a totalization of totalizations. But the criterion of intelligibility cannot be that God, or Nature, or my father, or the leader claim to have understood: it is that I understand (and therefore that everyone can understand). The criterion of intelligibility is self-evidence.

Is this a privilege granted to the subject? Certainly, as the demand to understand – and particularly the demand to understand

---

[3] 'This external materialism lays down the dialectic as exteriority. The Nature of man lies outside him in an *a priori* law, in an extra-human nature, in a history that begins with the nebulae. For this universal dialectic, partial totalizations do not have even a provisional value; they do not exist. Everything must always be referred to the totality of *natural history*. . . . Thus History is held to be a complete distortion of its object. . . . But when everything has apparently culminated in sceptical objectivism, we suddenly realize that it has been imposed on us dogmatically, that it is the Truth of Being as it appears to universal consciousness. Spirit *sees* dialectic as the law of the world. Consequently we fall back into complete dogmatic idealism. . . . However one looks at it, transcendental materialism leads to the irrational, either by ignoring the thought of empirical man, *or* by creating a noumenal consciousness which imposes its law as a whim, *or again*, by discovering in Nature "without alien addition" the laws of dialectical Reason in the form of contingent facts.' *Critique of Dialectical Reason*, NLB London, 1976, pp. 27–28, 32.

[4] *Critique*, p. 36.

History, which is made 'by individuals pursuing their own ends' and which makes individuals and turns back on them as necessity insofar as *others* make it – is a demand of the 'subject' and not of the 'object'. If I pose in advance that there is an intelligibility or a dialectic or a History, but that we cannot understand it, I find myself in the same kind of relation to it as the believer is with God – faith. More seriously, I deny in advance the possibility of communism – what Marx called in *The German Ideology* the possibility for 'united individuals' to 'submit to their power' and to 'make impossible all that exists independently of them', the possibility of their becoming the 'subjects of History' and of recognizing themselves in it as in the product of their own voluntary and conscious collaboration.

The fact is that any discourse on Being that tries to abstract from the speaker and to grasp Being beyond the cognitive situation (i.e. the practical relations) of the speaker, is implicitly a metaphysical discourse: it claims to pronounce on Being in the absence of men. Any certainty that lacks the criterion of being certain for me (of being evidence) on the basis of lived experience, is an act of faith that sooner or later leads to dogmatism. Conversely, the only way to eliminate metaphysics is always to refer the affirmation or the investigation to the praxis – historically situated, methodologically defined, oriented towards determinate goals – of the investigator. In other words, any research or affirmation must have its critical counterpart: must take responsibility for itself as a project in progress, producing its own goals, its own tools and its own principles. Any other course is to grant a metaphysical privilege to the inhuman.

The Dialectic

To return to the dialectic: if it is to appear with complete transparency, if it is not to be a fact of nature or an empirical and unintelligible law such as the law of falling bodies, it must itself be intelligible. It must be one with the knowledge it has of itself; in other words, totalizing knowledge must be homogeneous with the totalization it knows, and the known totalization must include a knowledge of itself (or the permanent possibility of that knowledge) as its own structure.[5] The dialectic, then, for the individual

5 *Critique*, pp. 44–47.

who understands it, is the living logic of his own praxis insofar as this operates the totalization of diversity and is totalized by the praxis of others. In brief, until the contrary is proved, dialectical reason is only of transparent and certain value in that sector of being which is the practical totalization by men of inorganic matter and the totalization of praxis by worked matter: human history. It is of value for this sector on condition that it is possible to reconstruct from the individual praxis collective realities and practical ensembles* which are fully intelligible.

For Marxists, the theoretical and practical issues at stake in this attempt at reconstruction are obviously immense. It is obviously not, as many of them believe (even Poulantzas) a question of starting from the *solitary* individual. In the section entitled 'Critique of Critical Investigation', on the contrary, Sartre points out that 'only a man living inside a sector of totalization can grasp the ties of interiority that unite him with the totalizing movement'. He goes on: 'The epistemological starting point must always be *consciousness* as apodictic certainty (of) itself and as consciousness *of* such and such an object. But we are not concerned at this point with interrogating consciousness about itself: the object it must give itself is precisely the *life*, the objective being, of the investigator, in the world of Others, insofar as this being totalises itself from birth and will continue to totalise itself until death. On this basis, the individual disappears from historical categories: alienation, the practico-inert, series, groups, classes, the components of History, labour, individual and communal *praxis* – the individual has lived, and he still lives, all of these in interiority. But if there is a movement of dialectical Reason, it is this movement which produces his life, this membership of a particular class, of certain milieux and of certain groups; it is the totalisation itself which brought about his successes and failures, through the vicissitudes of his community, and his personal joys and sorrows, through his love or family relations, through his friendships and through the "relations of production" that have marked his life, the dialectical bonds reveal themselves. *For this reason, his understanding of his own life must go so far as to deny its distinctiveness so as to seek its dialectical intelligibility within human development as a whole.'*[6]

---

* Practical ensembles: general term for human multiplicities.
[6] *Critique*, p. 51. My emphasis.

The endeavour to reconstruct from individual praxes the dialectical intelligibility of the material mediations whereby, at various levels, praxis inverts into the passive anti-dialectical unity of materially structured economic and social processes, possessing their own laws of evolution, does not of course prevent these processes from being the object of a specific scientific study regulated by analytic reason. This type of reason can be applied, for example, to monetary circulation or capital accumulation precisely insofar as these are praxis made passive in the exteriority of the inert, turning against agents and governing them from the outside according to inflexible, insurmountable laws. However, analytic reason is by its nature incapable of dealing with the foundation of these processes, considered in themselves – the multiplicity of the praxes that sustain them, and make them insurmountable for each agent. In other words, although it is legitimate to a certain level of investigation, it is incapable of rendering intelligible laws which it presents as quasi-natural.

The aim of Sartre's enterprise, by which it stands or falls, is to establish the dialectical intelligibility of historical processes (this is not the same as the study of these processes themselves), and by the same stroke to provide a reciprocity of perspective that permits an understanding of the individual as the alienated agent of history. The following observations will serve to stress the importance of this undertaking.

If, as certain sociologists – both Marxist and non-Marxist – maintain, the individual is to be explained by materially structured social wholes without these being intelligible through individuals, then society cannot be known except as an external object and from an external (non-dialectical) point of view. The individuals, similarly, can only be known from outside as a purely passive product. The subjectivity that was to have been eliminated now returns through the back door: it is now the sociologist himself who poses as sole subject, absolute subjectivity, the solipsistic witness from the beyond, in his claim to know individuals as pure objects through a society that he alone recognizes as their truth.

If the individual is explicable through the society, but the society is not intelligible through individuals – that is, if the 'forces' that act in history are impermeable and radically heterogeneous to organic praxis – then socialism as the socialization of man can never coincide with socialism as the humanization of the social. It cannot come *from* individuals as their reappropriation by collective praxis of the resultant of their individual praxes. It can only come *to* individuals by the evolution of their society according to its inner logic. The positivist (or transcendental materialist) hypothesis is that the historical process is impermeable to dialectical intelligibility. If so, then socialism, born of an external logic, will also remain external to individuals and will not be a submission of Society and History to individuals and their demands, but a submission of individuals to Society and its demands on them; not the 'full development' but the negation of individuals, not the transparency of the social for individual praxis, but the opacity of the individual for himself, insofar as his being and his truth have become completely external to him. Thus the social individual is not the individual recognizing himself and achieving himself in the community, but the individual radically denying himself – his needs, his interests, his certainties – for the profit of the society experienced as the absolute Other, to the point of regarding it as false to see it as Other.[7] We know that this conception of socialism prevailed for a long period, that it still has its adherents, that it profoundly affected Marxist philosophy, and that it must therefore be liquidated on this terrain as well.

Sartre clearly indicates that this was one of his aims and that, on the other hand, his work was inserted within Marxism and had the strictly limited object of testing out the possibility of a dialectical intellection.

Scope and Aims

Sartre's attempted reconstruction could not, in fact, yet bear on History itself. His aim was to establish beforehand the dialectical intelligibility of the elementary and formal structures of which History is the 'totalization without a totalizer'. He was concerned

---

[7] A very good description of this conception, in its subjective aspect, can be found in Kazimierz Brandys' *Defence of Granada.* It is neatly resumed by Czech popular humour in the following joke. The director of the State Plan confided in a militant from the base well-known for his intelligence, that the national economy was in a lamentable state, and asked him his advice. The militant advised the rigorous application of the official line, expounding this with eloquence. 'I know all that', said the director. 'It's your personal opinion I'm after. Have you got one?' 'Oh yes,' replied the militant, 'but I'm wrong'.

to forge from regressive experience the instruments for a dialectical understanding of History, to discover 'the intelligibility of practical structures and the dialectical relation which interconnects various forms of active multiplicities.'[8]

I must now show by some rather long quotations how the circularity of certain Sartrean arguments is the object of an express warning from Sartre himself. He very precisely delimits the scope and aims of his work. 'The experience of the dialectic is itself dialectical: this means that it develops and organizes itself on all levels. At the same time, it is the very experience of living, since to live is to act and be acted on, and since the dialectic is the rationality of *praxis*. It must be *regressive* because it will set out from lived experience (*le vécu*) in order gradually to discover all the structures of *praxis*. However, we must give notice that the investigation we are undertaking, though in itself historical, like any other undertaking, does not attempt to discover the movement of history, the evolution of labour, or of the relations of production, or class conflicts. Its goal is simply to reveal and to establish dialectical rationality, that is to say, the complex play of praxis and totalization.

'When we have arrived at the most general conditionings, that is to say, at materiality, it will then be time to reconstruct, on the basis of the investigation, the schema of intelligibility proper to the totalization. . . . Thus our task cannot *in any way* be to reconstruct real History in its development, any more than it can consist in a concrete study of forms of production or of the groups studied by the sociologist and the ethnographer. Our problem is *critical*. Doubtless this problem is itself raised by History. But it is precisely a matter of testing, criticizing and establishing, *within History* and at this particular moment in the development of human societies, the instruments of thought by means of which History thinks itself, in so far as they are also the practical instruments by means of which it is made. It can be formulated in the following terms: on what conditions is the knowledge of *a History* possible? To what extent can the connections brought to light be necessary?'[9]

From the fact that Sartre shows how the group can arise from the series and how the series can be reborn from the group, it

[8] *Critique*, p. 817.
[9] *Critique*, pp. 39–40.

should not be concluded that Sartre poses – consciously or other-wise – any *a priori* impossibility of disalienation, and withdraws desperately into solipsism. Sartre himself writes: 'But it will never be sufficient to show the production of ensembles by individuals or by one another, nor, conversely, to show how individuals are produced by the ensembles which they compose. It will be necessary to show the dialectical intelligibility of these transforma-tions in every case. Of course, this is a matter of *formal* intelli-gibility. By this I mean that we must understand the bonds between praxis, as self-conscious, and all the complex multiplicities which are organized through it and in which it loses itself as *praxis* in order to become *praxis-process.* However – and I shall have occasion to repeat this still more emphatically – it is no part of my intention to determine the concrete history of these incarnations of *praxis.* In particular, as we shall see later, the practical indivi-dual enters into ensembles of very different kinds, for example, into what are called *groups* and what I shall call *series.* It is no part of our project to determine whether series precede groups or vice versa, either originally or in a particular moment of History. On the contrary: as we shall see, groups are born of series and often end up by realizing themselves in their turn. So the *only* thing which matters to us is to display the transition from series to groups and from groups to series as constant incarnations of our practical multiplicity, and to test the dialectical intelligibility of these reversible processes. . . . Every moment of the regress will seem more complex and general than the isolated, superficial moment of our individual *praxis*, yet from another point of view, it remains completely abstract, that is, it is still no more than a *possibility.* Indeed, whether we consider the relations between group and series formally, in so far as each of these ensembles may produce the other, or whether we grasp the individual, within our investigation, as the practical ground of an ensemble and the ensemble as producing the individual in his reality as historical agent, this formal procedure will lead us to a dialectical circularity. This circularity exists; it is even (for Engels as much as for Hegel) characteristic of the dialectical order and of its intelligibility. But the fact remains that reversible circularity is in contradiction with the irreversibility of History, as it appears to investigation. Though it is true in the abstract that groups and series can in-differently produce each other, it is also true that historically a particular group, through its serialisation, produces a given serial ensemble (or conversely) and that, if a new group originated in the serial ensemble, then, whatever it might be, it would be irreducible to the serial ensemble.'[10]

Sartre's Development

Before proceeding further and posing the question of the relevance of the *Critique* for Marxist inquiry, I should like to suggest certain reflections on the relationship of the *Critique* with *Being and Nothingness*, on the vicissitudes of the Sartrean cogito and on the problem of alienation.

One of the aims of *Being and Nothingness* was to give a foundation to psychology and, more especially, to psychoanalysis – by ridding them of mechanist explanations and by giving a theoretical basis to a method which, in practice, implied the possibility for the individual to rework himself and to make himself master of his existential choice. Sartre begins by expelling from consciousness the objects which psychologists have placed there in their attempt to 'explain psychic life': images, sensations, feelings, emotions. Psychologists portray these as flowing through consciousness, conceived of as a passive milieu. Sartre expels the motives, drives, motivations, instincts which are held to govern conscious behaviour from behind the scenes and to explain it, without themselves being intelligible. He wanted to restore consciousness to itself as freedom, translucidity, activity through and through, total and undifferentiated comprehension of its own behaviour, and its own foundation. It is only if this restitution is possible that morality has a meaning. If it is not possible, if the individual is governed from outside or from behind by external and unconscious determinisms, he does not belong to himself and there is no sense in asking him to account for his actions, to answer for the world to the degree to which he makes it, or to humanize it.

The purifying reflexion which was the cogito of *Being and Nothingness* remains, however, purely abstract. Making freedom once again the ground of all action – including flight from and refusal of freedom, that is to say bad faith – Sartre demonstrated the possibility in principle of a reconquest over alienation in its subjective dimension, while founding the *formal* possibility of

[10] *Critique*, pp. 65, 67–68.

this alienation. He did not, on the other hand, make *real* existence intelligible: the reasons why bad faith is infinitely more wide-spread than authenticity were a matter, in *Being and Nothingness*, of pure contingency. That work only indicated the ontological reasons why human reality may – or is given to – be misled about itself. If you prefer, *Being and Nothingness* allows one to under-stand how *it is possible* that a being who is free praxis may take himself for a statue, a machine or a thing, how it is possible that he may not gain an explicit and thematic awareness of his nature as praxis. In the *Critique* Sartre is concerned, on the contrary, to analyse the reality of alienation as necessity – *practical* necessity in *this* world, which cannot be transcended by a simple subjective conversion, and which becomes intelligible only if one goes beyond the framework of the reflexive cogito, not in order to abandon it forever, it is true, but rather to return to it constantly.

The cogito, in the *Critique*, no longer concerns in fact the formal (ontological) structures of interiority of the relation of the for-itself to the in-itself and to the Other. It is constantly transcended by the attempt to grasp the material mediations by which this relation, in its practical, objective reality, is deviated, degraded, alienated in a world of inorganic inertia, sealed – that is to say rendered practically impossible to transcend – by other praxes. The cogito of the *Critique* thus no longer refers to the for-itself in its relation to the in-itself, but to the for-itself in so far as – being a reworking of the material field towards an end, that is to say being praxis and being work – it extends outside itself, into the materiality and the time of things, in which its totalizing action (that is to say the action of reorganizing the diversity of the given towards an end) *is acted* by the quasi-totalization of its praxis in exteriority, in the world of the inert, as one praxis among others exercised at the same time.

This being-acted, this collapse of praxis into the sealed inertia of matter which gives back to me my action as that of another, remote-controlled towards other ends (which may be those of nobody), and turning against my own ends, this is one of the forms of alienation, and presents itself immediately to experience. The necessity of alienation has, however, no longer this character of immediate evidence. The necessity of alienation is not the same, for Sartre, as the necessity of objectification, but as that of objectifi-cation in a world of scarcity and of sociality as series and as *passive* being.[11] Sartre writes most notably: 'From the moment in which impotence becomes the meaning of practical power, and counter-finality the deep meaning of the aim pursued, when *praxis* discovers that *its* freedom is the means chosen elsewhere to reduce it to slavery, the individual suddenly finds himself back in a world where free action is the fundamental mystification; he no longer knows it except as a reality . . . as the propaganda of the oppressors against the oppressed. But it is important to see that this experience is no longer that of the action, but that of the materialised result; it is no longer the positive moment in which one *does*, but the negative moment in which one is produced in passivity by what the practico-inert ensemble makes out of what one has just made.'[12]

Necessity 'is the moment where, through the very freedom which produces it, the Thing, transformed by other freedoms, presents, *through its own characteristics*, the objectification of the agent as a strictly predictable but completely unforeseen alteration* of the ends pursued. . . . Necessity manifests itself neither in the action of the isolated organism, nor in the succession of the physico-chemical facts: the reign of necessity is the domain – the real, but still abstract domain of History – in which inorganic materiality envelops human multiplicity and transforms the producers into its product. Necessity, as a limit within freedom . . . is the shifting ensemble of unlucky materiality in so far as it is simultaneously affirmed and stolen away, for everyone and in any free act, by all free acts as Others; that is to say, as forging our chains.'[13]

While, in *Being and Nothingness*, there were the formal couples for-itself – in-itself, freedom – contingency, transcendence – facticity, in the *Critique* one finds: praxis – practico-inert, dialectic – anti-dialectic (that is to say passive totalization of a multiplicity of praxes by the inert), constituent dialectic – constituted dialectic. Sartre explicitly excludes from the notion of alienation the objectification of solitary praxis in a passive matter which this praxis has produced or transformed in accordance with its original ends, and even if it fails to achieve these ends. He shows on the

---

[11] *Critique*, pp. 318–41.
[12] *Critique*, pp. 336–37.
* Alteration: *Altération* has the sense of deterioration as well as modification. Sartre employs it and *alterity* because they imply theft of my praxis by the Other.
[13] *Critique*, p. 339.

contrary that failure[14] can in no way be assimilated to an alienation (or to an experience of necessity as alienation): the failure of a
solitary act exercised in a field in which it is acting alone, where the
failure is due to the opacity of matter, is foreseen-unforeseeable:
unforeseeable because matter is opaque, but foreseen because its
opacity gives us the certainty that the unforeseen may happen.
You split wood with an axe, the handle gives and the blade flies
off and strikes you on the head, or the axe slips and you split your
shin: this type of accident was foreseen. Far from presenting
itself as a counter-finality or a necessity, it appears to you as the
consequence, prepared by yourself, of your foolishness, of your
clumsiness ('I could have expected it, I was a fool'), in short as
your own act. The experience of alienation, on the other hand, is,
among other things, the experience of a curse of matter which
turns my actions or their result against me, to the advantage of the
ends of another, or which makes it impossible for me not to give
reality freely to the prefabricated being which comes towards me
like a sentence pronounced over me and engraved in things. Now,
things do not dominate man and are not *insurmountable* for him
except in so far as they have absorbed other activities come from
elsewhere – in so far as they are not purely passive, but are like a
passive activity, a materialized practice, the practico-inert,
sustained and sealed by other praxes.

It should also be stressed that alienation does not present itself
as necessity except *in the world of serial dispersion and of scarcity*,
that is to say in a world in which each is for himself and for others
an Other than himself. The use by Sartre of the terms 'Other' and
alterity seems to have made some inattentive readers believe that
for him there was an alienation inherent in the coexistence of a
multiplicity of individuals: it is inherent in the coexistence of a
multiplicity of *dispersed* individuals acting *separately* in a common
situation of *scarcity*, that is to say in a world in which 'life is
improbable', in which 'there is not enough for everyone' and in
which the others are therefore for every man and every man for
the others a supernumerary or an 'anti-man', that is to say 'one
more', an Other than himself and other than man.

The Intelligibility of Alienation

The wager which the *Critique* makes (and fufils) is that *the reason*

[14] *Critique*, pp. 222–25, 811–12.

of alienation is intelligible. In other words, that this 'curse of matter', which makes man into the Other or the anti-man for man, is neither a natural fatality, nor an inherent characteristic of 'human nature', but a destiny which comes to men from men, on the basis of determined material circumstances (certain of which, most notably scarcity, have a natural origin) and through the mediation of worked matter. To show that the reason of alienation is intelligible, is to show at the same time that this reason, born of human praxis, is capable of being suppressed by that praxis. This is the profound meaning of history.

Sartre therefore starts off from the abstract individual in order to rediscover the reason of his concrete objective reality in as much as that reality cannot come to him from *his own* isolated practical determinations but from the dialectical connections which unify his praxis — taken in the first instance at its most abstract or immediate level — with the praxis of others by the mediation of worked matter. But these connections (whose concrete characteristics must of course *also* be studied from the point of view of analytic reason, in as much as they carry the mark of natural exteriority — but this is not the object of the *Critique*) must be capable of being the object of experience since they are precisely the objective reality of praxis, the *life* of the individual which in producing itself is produced. The interrogation of the individual — and no other interrogation is possible — to discover the rationale of his socio-historical reality is aimed at rediscovering his insertion into the practical fields which he totalizes, which totalize him and which are totalized by History in process, and whose mediation alone allows a comprehension of his concrete characteristics.

I do not intend to discuss the different practical ensembles or modes of totalization that Sartre discusses.[15] I will simply mention that he distinguishes 'practico-inert ensembles'[16] from 'groups',[17] which enables him in the last section to study the relationship between groups and series, and to introduce certain schemas which already have a diachronic dimension.

Practico-inert ensembles — series and collectives — are the passive unity of a multiplicity of *discrete* praxes. They are forms

[15] There are some good partial summaries, notably Marco Maggió's in *Aut Aut*, no. 82, pp. 58–92.

[16] *Critique*, pp. 79–341.

[17] *Critique*, pp. 345–663.

of social existence which are characterized by their *external* cohesion: unity is bestowed on the praxis of molecular individuals by the material world which binds each into the *recurring* praxis of all, the unity of all being defined as the unity of *Others* expressed as a negation of each. The class, a serial unity of series, appears as a collective among others. Membership of the class is a prefabricated and insurmountable future which awaits the individual at birth, and which he cannot surpass, since he is – in the case of the worker, for instance – surpassed by others in the attainment of their ends when he uses instruments by which he will, in fact, realize *their* ends whilst pursuing (or believing himself to be pursuing) his own.

Groups on the other hand are characterized by a common praxis, by an *internal* cohesion which is based on the reciprocity of its members, who undertake together to transform the situation which is shared by them in the direction of a common end. The unity is not imposed on the group from without, like a seal which is affixed upon a plurality of praxes by inorganic materiality. On the contrary, it is produced as a means to the common end, or as an end in itself, whose pursuit is the condition of realizing the common end. Groups are moments of a constituent dialectic (not a constituted dialectic) in social existence: they are organized specifically with a view to social and historical action.

Scarcity

I will now confine myself to two remarks. One concerns the significance attached by Sartre to *scarcity*; the other concerns the reversible transformations from the series to the group. Sartre stresses that scarcity is the 'passive motor of history', the material precondition of historicity, the foundation of all possibility of history. It is the *negative* synthesis of human plurality, a negation imposed on man externally by nature, which is repeated as a negation of man by man. In other words, scarcity is the *ultimate* foundation of history as the struggle of classes. As such, history *cannot* be natural history, but is rather an anti-physis: that is, a negation in practice of an original negation in fact. This is not true merely of undeveloped countries. Both the theory and the reality of relative immiseration in capitalist societies can only be understood if the fact of scarcity is taken into account. A Marxist starting from the analyses of the *Critique* could show that industrial development reproduces scarcity at other levels – scarcity of time, of men, of primary resources, of energy, etc. – and that all new scarcities, including those which have become apparent in socialist countries, stemmed precisely from basic scarcity.

For a Marxist today must refuse to isolate developed countries from others; he must, on the contrary, situate them in a global context in which every *local* and partial victory over scarcity brings with it a *displacement* of scarcity into other areas. This alone enables one to understand the aggravation of imperialist wars, inter-imperialist struggles and even, lately, rifts within the socialist camp. This obviously does not mean that struggle against scarcity should be considered hopeless. It simply means that in a world where three quarters of mankind are still under-nourished, and two thirds are actually starving, in a world where the fore-seeable growth of world population is greatly outstripping production of food (even locally, given the present growth of population) human life remains precarious. The industrial zones are enclaves in a world which lacks the minimum necessary for survival. Famine and the struggle against famine remain the defin-ing truth of this century and probably of the century to come. Victory over scarcity – abundance – remains *for us* inconceivable.

Sartre thus ranges himself against those Marxists – there are fewer and fewer of them it is true – who consider scarcity as a circumstance and product of the capitalist phase of development. Furthermore, since Sartre considers that *violence* is *internalized scarcity* – that is, the negation of man in exteriority becomes the negation of the Other by each Other acting in a situation of scarcity – it is understandable that for Sartre socialism cannot yet suppress violence in human relations, nor alienation as the sealed inorganic negation of human praxis. Socialism cannot yet abolish 'the reign of necessity'.

Yet the *suppressibility* of the reign of necessity is clearly shown by Sartre when he describes the group as the reassumption of necessity as a necessity of freedom, as the dissolution of seriality, through common praxis – although this can only be a *provisional* suppression in present material and historical circumstances. It should be remembered that necessity has revealed itself to dialec-tical understanding as 'a strictly foreseeable and utterly unfore-seen alteration' of the objectified praxis of each by the praxes of all as others, passively unified in matter. It follows that necessity can reconvert itself into liberty. For it must be possible in determinate circumstances for the activity of all to be no longer the negative destiny of each. In this case, the unity of multiplicity, instead of being exterior and *endured* is interiorized and created in all by each and in each by all, through the *production* of a common end by common action. This is the recovery of necessity as freedom. Sartre takes great care to define the circumstances of the emergence of a *fused group*. Among the conditions he emphasizes are: vital urgency (danger of death, for instance), geographical proximity, previous objective unification (in the face of the common enemy) of the multiplicity into a 'collective' which will be the 'matrix' of the group. When the threat which weighs upon each as other among others cannot be removed except by the common action of all, and the *physical and historical circumstances are propitious*, each totalizes all in the same way as they totalize him, in the movement towards a shared goal. The interiorization of number and the accompanying communalization of the object of praxis are not just subjectivist sleight of hand. They describe the more or less daily experience of each of 'us': the factory worker who feels himself one of five thousand or ten thousand other workers is powerless when he is separated from all the others by seriality, by the reign of terror. He naturally asks himself: 'Why fight back if nobody else does?' The serial behaviour of each worker, as Other in the passive unity of the collective, will take the form of putting himself first. But when, in certain definite situations, the repression which is directed against one or more of these separate Others becomes seen as an external threat to the vital interests of each, then each becomes five thousand or ten thousand as himself, in the demand that everywhere each worker 'interiorize' their number, and so experience it as the shared force of the shared being of all in shared activity. Each man, by liquidating in and about him seriality and impotent alterity, behaves as he would wish all and each to behave. Each becomes the way by which all become themselves and all become the way by which each becomes himself. The necessity of freedom is this praxis of the common individual who recognizes and reflects himself in the common praxis and common object of all. He both effects the ongoing totalization and, at the same time, feels himself required as part of the totalization effected about him. 'The group is both

the most effective *means* of controlling the surrounding materiality
in the context of scarcity and *the absolute end* as pure freedom
liberating men from alterity.'[18]

Violence

Much could be said about the group seen as sovereignty and as the
original source of juridical power.[19] This raises the question of
the *pledge*, which is both the affirmation of the power of each
individual over all as each becomes guarantor of the unity of the
group, and demands of all that they should forbid the relapse of
each into serial alterity. This right exercised by each over all and
all over each tends to replace fear of the enemy or of common
danger – temporarily past – by fear which has been produced as
the free product of the group: by Fraternity-Terror.[20] It is
astonishing to find Marxists rejecting the notion of Terror, of
violence both against the Other and against the 'selves' as structures of the revolutionary group, and dismissing these concepts as
the product of Sartre's 'aesthetic romanticism'. The real romantics
– bourgeois romantics – are those wistful dreamers who think that
groups constitute themselves not out of revolt against the necessity
of the practico-inert, as a violent refusal to be subjected to violence,
but as the result of some sort of social contract or convergence of
individual interests. Again, Sartre cannot be accused of voluntarism; he insists that groups and common action can only be
produced *in struggle*, directly counter to the common threat and
imposition of violence. The real voluntarists are those who go on
dreaming of a non-violent transformation of society, carried out by
decree, in accordance with rules established and accepted in
advance by some kind of popular 'consensus'.

It may seem difficult to accept Hope, Terror, Violence and
sovereign Freedom as structures of this kind of group formation if
we view these things simply from a tactical point of view in a
given situation. But we need only have experienced a strike – even
a small strike – or a mass demonstration to realize that these are
indeed the 'essential structures'[21] of the fused group and hence of
the pledged (or statutory) group. A strike is always waged against

[18] *Critique*, p. 673.
[19] See N. Poulantzas, *op. cit.*
[20] *Critique*, p. 405f.
[21] *Critique*, p. 407.

both the class enemy *and* against fear, which gives birth to betrayal, to the serialised Other, to the scab. Violence against scabs need not necessarily be physical; violence is nonetheless the climate of a mass strike. Non-violent revolution (or even non-violent strikes) are not made possible just because our particular situation rules out the opportunity for armed insurrection. For any transition to socialism, however effected, by whatever kind of mass action, will be a violent rejection of violence – the violence of the class enemy, real or threatened. Hence there will be 'sacred unity' and 'Terror' in the sense defined above. This violence can perfectly well also be exercised against those within the revolutionary group who advocate armed force. Every militant is well aware that 'moral' violence ('moral pressure') against advocates of physical violence is a kind of violence in its turn.

Two thirds of the second book of the *Critique*[22] are an attempt to describe the formal laws of the dialectic which will enable us to understand the metamorphoses of the group: the gradual degradation of the fused group into the statutory group and thence into the institutionalized group, which by exercising a monopoly, is able to manipulate serial ensembles from without and thus, eventually, relapse into seriality in its own turn. At this point, we are back where we first started, the cycle is completed. 'This enables us to reach the concrete at last, that is to say, to complete our dialectical investigation.' This does not mean that Sartre is trying to show the circularity of History and the eternal re-emergence of the same structures. His aim is rather to reconstruct and render dialectically intelligible 'the set of formal contexts, curves, structures and conditionings which constitute the *formal milieu* in which the historical concrete must necessarily occur.'[23]

In other words, dialectical experience has made intelligible the emergence from individual praxes of all practical ensembles, and their transformation into each other, given that no single one of them has any *historical* priority *vis-à-vis* the others. The series, collective, fused group, statutory group, institutionalized group, etc., are not successive *stages* of historical development but coexist, clash and coalesce as the elementary formal structures (partial totalities and totalizations) of which History is the totalization.

[22] *Critique*, pp. 345–673.
[23] *Critique*, p. 671.

The Revolutionary State

Sartre's descriptions of the metamorphoses of the group have, nevertheless, a very particular contemporary interest. For they schematize the modern historical experience of the formation of States and bureaucracies after periods of revolutionary élan. Sartre refers implicitly (and sometimes explicitly) to the French, Russian, Cuban and Algerian revolutions. It is quite clear that for Sartre the 'formal laws of the dialectic' have inevitably led the fused group – a community which is active and sovereign through and through – to the point where it is dissipated, clouded and serialized. The Marxist movement has not yet fully eliminated its heritage of Stalinism; this is no reason for seeing Stalinism as a more or less accidental deviation, or for refusing to try to understand the process by which all past revolutions have ended up in more or less petrified bureaucratic forms, even when – as in Yugoslavia – they have made efforts to fight against this. Nor must we dismiss as Stalinists those who do try to understand the dialectical laws of this kind of process.

It is true that for Sartre the fused group represents the elimination of serial alienation, but this cannot be a lasting elimination in a world of scarcity and struggle. The fused group exists as the instant of the revolutionary apocalypse, of full freedom, when totalization is produced everywhere and in everyone, under everyone's sovereignty, when there are no leaders, no hierarchies, no functions. Every slogan and initiative is immediately recognized by each individual as a common slogan and initiative, in the service of a common goal.

The fused group, in which all men are brothers, is produced as an ongoing unity by a multiplicity of individual syntheses, all of which share a common goal and in doing so demand and sustain this unity. 'The unity of the group is immanent in the multiplicity of syntheses', it 'is never that of a created totality, but rather that of a totalization which is carried on by everyone everywhere.' 'The intelligibility of the group as *praxis* depends on the intelligibility of individual *praxis*.'[24]

Now, in order to realize its goal, the group must necessarily endow itself with inertia. It must safeguard itself against breakdown by the *pledge*, by exercising juridical power over each of its members. It must differentiate itself in order to cope with a diversity of tasks and hence reorganize itself by creating *functions* and *specialized sub-groups*, with their own inertia, discipline and a hierarchy. It passes from constituent reason (or dialectic) – that of living organic individual praxis – to constituted reason, to the praxis-process of the *organization*. The unity of group praxis is no longer assured by the synthesis of each individual action but by the inertia of an organization and an apparatus or, in other words, by a dead mechanism. 'The group is *constructed* on the model of free individual action', 'it produces an organic action without itself being an organism', 'it is a machine for producing non-mechanical reactions' and 'inertia – like every human product – constitutes both its being and its *raison d'être*'.[25] The specialized sub-groups, capable of coping with tasks of increasing complexity and scope, fall into a permanent danger of being out of step with every other sub-group, of being separated and serialized. Hence it is necessary to co-ordinate and integrate their activity – to incarnate the unity of the group – by means of a supreme organism, a *sovereign* (for example, the State or the Leader) who controls and monopolizes group function, guaranteeing and reflecting the practical unity of the group, even while it is being serialized and petrified. Thus we arrive at the institutionalized group, which is created when 'under the pressure of exterior circumstances, the common individual tries to become a thing which is held against other things by the unity of a seal; the model for the institutional group is *the forged tool*'.[26] This is the moment, in other words, of the reification of praxis. A special study would be needed to show the rich contribution this part of the *Critique* could make to a Marxist theory of law and of the State.[27] I will restrict myself to a few brief remarks:

Sartre explicitly rejects 'the optimistic notion, constructed too hastily' of the dictatorship of the proletariat, 'the very idea (of which) is absurd, being a bastard compromise between the active, sovereign group and passive seriality'.[28] He denounces as a mystification 'the idea of a diffuse popular sovereignty becoming

[25] *Critique*, p. 553.
[26] *Critique*, p. 606.
[27] *Critique*, pp. 600–70. In this connection, see also N. Poulantzas, 'Préliminaires à l'étude de l'hégémonie dans l'Etat', *Les Temps Modernes*, November and December, 1965.
[28] *Critique*, pp. 661–62.

embodied in a sovereign'. Sovereignty can only belong to organic praxis, whether of the individual or the group. 'What is known as the State can never be regarded as the product or expression of the totality of social individuals or even of the majority of them.'[29] On the contrary it appears as a specific group produced by the ruling class to defend its general interests against the conflict of particular interests within the ruling class itself, and to render this general interest acceptable to other classes. In other words, the State is the sovereign group by which the serialized ruling class is guaranteed in its unity *but maintained in its serial dispersion*, manipulated and thwarted in its efforts at regroupment.

The group thus undergoes an inevitable degradation, as it becomes increasingly differentiated, and a serialization, as each specialized sub-group becomes ignorant of the actions of the other sub-groups and divided from them by menacing conflicts of interest. This in turn creates the demand for a retotalization of the unity of partial praxes by a 'sovereign'. But immediately, with the sovereign, the unity of the group falls into radical exteriority, for its sovereignty becomes incarnated in a Third Party (who is the only Third that cannot be transcended, the only totalizer of the group), and its members have no more than serial relations between them. Each of them is for the other an Other, they are the *same* only by the mediation of the sovereign Third. This degradation perhaps evokes Stalinist Russia – or China today, where the unity and truth of the society reside for each member in the political thought of Mao, source of all rights and duties. Now the following thesis is defended by certain Marxists: namely, that the root of alienation is the *natural* division of labour, hence it can be suppressed by a *voluntary* division of labour (or co-operation). But the problem here is to know under just what conditions there can be genuine 'voluntary co-operation' and what one means by this term. In a large country, under present material conditions, the rational unity of social praxis can only be forged by organized voluntary co-operation, by the formation of sub-groups whose common task is linked to that of other sub-groups which are themselves inter-linked by the centralizing group or sovereign. It is evident that this is a society whose praxis-process is organized with rigorous rationality on the model of petrified individual

[29] *Critique*, p. 635.

praxis, and cannot be totalized by any of the group's individuals. 'Volunteer work' – in the Chinese model for example – is the product of internalized constraints which the individuals impose on themselves and on others (with all the persuasive mildness in which Fraternity-Terror can be clad) in the name of the sovereign. The belief that this generalized rational organization – with the failures and wastages which are the inevitable product of bureaucrats fearing the central authority and distrusting their equals – *is* communism, or the end of alienation, was held in honour in China in 1958, in the heroic epoch of the Communes.

The Fused Group in History

The *Critique*, by contrast, suggests that the only true model of 'voluntary co-operation' is the fused group. That the fused group cannot have a durable basis is due to several factors: (1) to scarcity and to the multiplicity of antagonistic processes in the world; (2) to the nature of tools (or means of production), that is to say, the resistance, the inertia, and the complexity of the practical field structured as it is by the available techniques. This inertia and complexity obliges the group to make itself inert and complex in order to be effective and determines within it both specialization and scarcity of productive forces. It should at this point be remembered that, for Marx in Books II and III of *Capital*, communism is distinguished by the end of scarcity, by polytechnicism (the opposite of specialization) which will permit the indefinite permutation of tasks between individuals, and by the abolition of work as 'an obligation imposed by poverty and by external goals'. The realization of these three conditions still remains difficult for us to imagine, more difficult perhaps than a hundred years ago.

Marxists should therefore not be astonished that the *Critique* suggests that, in the world of scarcity and of class struggle, any group which raises itself above alienation and the practico-inert finishes by falling back into it. Can one be a Marxist and believe, even for an instant, that in this hunger-ridden world, ravaged by imperialist wars, by inter-imperialist antagonisms, by the conflicts between the oppressed peoples themselves, a revolutionary group – even supposing that it embraced the totality of the class or people grouped for its liberation – could locally triumph over alienation? Such a belief derives, properly speaking, from the spirit of optimistic utopianism that one finds in communities like the Quakers. Sartre has provided us with a devastating criticism of just this spirit in *Le Diable et le Bon Dieu*.

Of course, the revolutionary Marxist movement can and even must work to limit the ravages caused by the objective tendency towards petrification and serialization in society and in parties, towards the centralization and sclerosis of every apparatus. But this corrective work is necessary just because this objective tendency is a 'formal law of the dialectic', and it is possible only if one starts by recognizing the existence of this tendency and the impossibility of suppressing it once and for all in present circumstances.

The work of the philosopher is to raise problems, to show their existence, not to pretend presumptuously to solve them. To turn against him the problems which he poses, and on the pretext that he does not know the answers, to accuse him of nihilism or despairing solipsism is to dispose of problems cheaply and to outlaw philosophy. In fact, most of the criticisms so far addressed by Marxists to Sartre start with *petitio principii* unverified by historical experience. He has been accused of not showing that alienation, scarcity, violence, bureaucracy, the State and so on can be abolished. Under cover of Marxist 'science', these critics abandon science and above all the effort to understand history. By contrast, Sartre's enterprise is to give himself (and us) the instruments of dialectical understanding, and thereby the means to pose the question of the possibility of suppressing the inhuman in human history, and of the eventual conditions of its suppressibility. To anticipate the answer to these questions by giving them in advance in the guise of Marxist 'science' or to refuse them by announcing that they stem from idealist speculation, is the best way to learn nothing. Such an attitude reveals a singular lack of confidence in Marxism: a fear that the discoveries we might make will shatter our convictions and the depth of our commitment.

The Individualist Social Theory of Jean-Paul Sartre

Ronald Aronson

Searching, radical and encyclopaedic, Jean-Paul Sartre has been a major intellectual force of our generation. The list of Sartre's interests, of topics on which he has spoken with authority, could go on for pages. Writer of stories, novels and plays, Sartre has also given us volumes of essays about art and politics, philosophical works, biographies of Genet and Flaubert, as well as his auto-biography. For almost forty years he has been man for all seasons: existentialist author in the thirties, philosopher and playright of individual rebellion in the early forties, engaged intellectual moving towards Marxism immediately after the war, independent Marxist activist, essayist and philosopher in the fifties, disillu-sioned activist intellectual searching for self-understanding in the early sixties, biographer seeking to bring all his wisdom to bear in grasping how the individual becomes who he is, and radical activist seeking new directions to the left of the Communist Party, in the late sixties and the seventies.

At least two things about this process stand out: the steady deepening of Sartre's political commitment and his willingness to change directions. His political activity, beginning with work on resistance writers' committees, has never been casual. Sartre was nearly assassinated as his apartment was bombed twice during the struggle over Algerian independence in the early 1960s. He turned down the Nobel Prize for literature in 1964 in part because of the political uses the Swedish Academy had made of the award during the Cold War. More recently he was arrested for allegedly libelling the French police. He has taken over editorship of banned leftist newspapers and challenged the government to act against him. Pictures appearing in *The New York Times Magazine* of October 17, 1971, show Sartre selling one such paper on the streets of

Paris. At sixty-five the revolutionary intellectual refused to rest on his laurels, but rather continued to take stock, to listen to those younger than himself, to take personal and intellectual risks, to change in accordance with his personal development and the historical situation.

Sartre's development raises basic questions. How did the philosopher of 'Hell is other people' transform his basic terms to become one of the major recent theoretical spokesmen for Marxist socialism? How did the author of 'Man is a useless passion' change his ideas to square with the deep optimism of Marxism?

Sartre's early theoretical writings, culminating in *Being and Nothingness* (1943), laid down an oppressive, gloomy vision of reality beside a totalistic argument for our freedom. The totally free person *had to* blunder into hells of other people, *had to* be a useless passion. Much as Sartre condemned it in *Psychology of Imagination* (1940) and mocked it in *Nausea* (1938), his own thought reserved effective freedom for art. Whatever Sartre's hesitation, his peculiar vision of freedom fitted quite well with his peculiar vision of the world's oppressiveness; one implied the other. The individual was wholly disconnected, the world's weight was all its own. This was not a mere 'position' taken because of its internal coherence: Sartre's vision revealed a distancing from the world which simultaneously made the world overwhelming and us free insofar as we withdraw from it. Sartre's early freedom is one which looks at the world from the outside, fearful of being totally crushed by it. It then sets up the perpetual project of getting *to* the world. True of *Nausea*, this also describes the 'activist' *Being and Nothingness*, which claims that the slave in chains is free to break them – and appeared under the German occupation. In the end we are responsible for our life, and life is hell. [1]

The second chapter of the brilliant but neglected *What is Literature?* completed this theoretical picture by presenting a vision of art as a 'successful passion'. [2] Its third chapter, along with 'Materialism and Revolution' [3] challenged it. In 1947 Sartre's key

[1] For this interpretation of Sartre's early thought see my essay, 'Interpreting Husserl and Heidegger: The Root of Sartre's Thought', *Telos*, Number 13, Fall 1972.

[2] See *What is Literature?*, London 1947, translated by Bernard Frechtman.

[3] See 'Materialism and Revolution', in *Literary and Philosophical Essays*, London 1955, translated by Annette Michelson.

new idea was that all the human processes he had earlier described as ontological (the self-other conflict, man's alienation from the world) were social and historical products. Thus he now pointed towards a society in which both hells would be overcome – by collective human action. This implied a reversal of the sharp separation of people from the world. He now argued that we in fact *create* the world we live in. In his postwar writings Sartre also conceded that our freedom is drastically conditioned, that meaningful talk of freedom points towards social and political change and not towards a dialectic common to everyone or some unconditioned process of individual consciousness. He also implied that human relations, the basic structures of which he sought to grasp in *Being and Nothingness*, inevitably take place in historically defined class societies.[4] Sartre's vision thus started to become less ontological, less self-enclosed as his terms became more charged with historical reality. At the same time, he set out to create a politically engaged theatre and launched a steady stream of political essays.

Both during and after this period of great ferment Sartre looked back on his earlier writings with a critical eye. He was later, for example, to comment on *Nausea*: 'What I lacked was a sense of reality. I have changed since. I have slowly learned to experience reality. I have seen children dying of hunger. Over against a dying child *La Nausée* cannot act as a counterweight.'[5]

Profound as they may be, however, in terms of Sartre's basic conceptual framework, these changes were only tendencies, initial explorations, strivings of Sartre's thought *en route* to Marxism. He had thoroughly to transform the basic terms of his outlook if his individualism was to give way to a sense of society; if his conception of a given world was to yield to a notion of the world as made by human beings; if his sense of irreducible ontological problems was to give way to a belief in historical change. Our question is: what was the result when Sartre came to articulate his Marxist vision – his view of reality underlying and demanding radical political commitment? In other words, when he wrote the *Critique of Dialectical Reason* (1960), what happened

---

[4] See Sartre's stirring '*Presentation of Les Temps Modernes*', translated in Eugen Weber, *Paths to the Present*, New York, 1960.

[5] Interview with Jacqueline Piatier, 'Jean-Paul Sartre s'explique sur *Les Mots*', *Le Monde*, April 18, 1964.

to the structure and key terms of his earlier philosophical thought? In this essay, I will try to show that in effect Sartre integrated Marxism into *his* philosophy rather than transforming it. I will focus on those decisive points where no shift occurs. What is there about this world view that, for all its political radicalism, dwells on problems that are absolutely beyond human social control? What is this world view, even when it calls itself Marxist, that makes art always seem like a likely place to take refuge?

In Appreciation of the Critique

Georges Gurvitch says that Sartre creates in the *Critique* an 'artificial, unreal and quasi-imaginary world'. Yet he misses the great adventure of the *Critique*, which, be it a success or a failure, makes it one of the monumental works of twentieth-century thought. In the *Critique*, in fact, Sartre is very much in touch with reality. It is a basically false, upside down vision that he presents. But he raises many of *the* questions, with incredible energy and intellectual radicalism. The world can be understood, Sartre is saying: it is possible to get to the root of things. Human beings *can* articulate the underlying principles of such an understanding and describe the basic forms of human ensembles, or groupings, which act in the world. There is not the slightest cynicism here, not even a glimpse of surrender before the world's enormous complexity. Sartre's goal is to render all social structures nearly translucent, to describe them as accretions of intentional human energy, even if turned against itself.

Sartre begins by showing individuals alone, labouring on the world in isolation from each other. The dialectic of the group begins with his depiction of how, in an insurrectionary situation such as the storming of the Bastille, separate individuals combine to form a *groupe en fusion*. They cease being passive and isolated and become instead participating members of a group acting towards a common goal. After overcoming the external threat the group turns inward to guard against possible defection of its members, who are always free to leave. They swear an oath to remain loyal, and so impose inertia on themselves and try to limit their own freedom. The pressure the group's members impose on each other leads to a state of terror, threatening anyone who

6 Georges Gurvitch, *Dialectique et Sociologie*, Paris 1962, p. 225.

defects and cementing the loyalty of everyone else. As it seeks to stabilize itself the group assigns specific functions to individuals. The group becomes an organization, supervising a distribution of tasks to meet the common interest, common danger, and common need. Each individual now controls a small corner of the world, but does so for the benefit of the organization and not himself.

The group still exists to meet the common needs of its members, who still freely decide to join and remain within it; but to preserve itself it has taken on considerable inertia. Created when its members entrust their freedom to the group, the apparatus for preserving the group becomes a power over them and begins to resist change and solidify into an institution. An authority begins to set itself over the group's members, and then narrow its own base. Individuals relate to the authority by obedience. Those in positions of authority, fearful lest the individuals organize themselves, keep people separated from each other in order to guarantee their obedience and powerlessness. So we move, inevitably, from the revolution to Stalin, from the collective act of individuals altering history to the collective submission of individuals to their product.

One concept is the key to Sartre's project: *praxis*. Human beings labour on the world in order to transform it to meet their needs. In the process they take on a more or less coherent view of the world before them. See what it lacks, set projects, go beyond the given world to transform it so that the need is met. This is dialectics, the logic of *praxis*. In the argument that runs through the book Sartre sets himself against two distortions: the urge of Engels and Soviet Marxists to raise the dialectic beyond human beings and put it out of our hands, and the conviction of proponents of 'analytical reason' that reality is merely an agglomeration of discrete units whose interrelations are external and secondary. To the second Sartre says that the world is indeed an internally connected whole in-the-making; to the first he argues that the dialectic exists only because men and women create the world.

This twofold vision stands behind much of what is best in the *Critique*. Struggling through it the reader will have the sense again and again of seeing behind such social facts as dictatorship, bureaucracy and terror, of grasping them as being produced in a process, of seeing that process as rooted in human goals and human activity to meet those goals. As the dead weight of a terror-based bureaucratic institution increases, Sartre never lets us forget for a moment that it is all the result of intentional human activity.

The *Critique* also gives us a series of particular keys for understanding our world which stand up even after we fault some of Sartre's basic concepts. For example, Sartre's description of *seriality* in its many forms: waiting for a bus, reading the newspaper on the bus, listening to the radio or the 'top ten' records, accepting public opinion and conformity. Each form reveals me as mass man: I alienate myself from my own purposes and, separated from but alongside other people, adopt the conduct I expect the others to adopt. Each serial individual acts by himself but as *others* would want him to. Standing alongside each other, we only appear to act together: each of us is dominated and radically isolated. The book abounds in sharply drawn and insightful descriptions of such phenomena.

Scarcity and Human Relations

Scarcity and the practico-inert are two terms which, together with *praxis*, lie at the base of Sartre's explorations. The terms inform his analysis, drive it forward, and impart to it its tone. In studying them one after the other we can assess Sartre's success in the *Critique* in transforming his original ideas and in adequately conveying social reality. Sartre argues very early on in the *Critique* that scarcity is a central fact of human history. This is because, very simply, '*there is not enough for everybody*'.[7] To a person living among others this fact means that 'the consumption of a certain product elsewhere, by others deprives him *here* of an opportunity of getting and consuming something of the same kind'.[8] Where there is not enough food there are too many people. Under conditions of scarcity 'each person is the inhuman man for all the Others'.

The Other is my perpetual enemy as long as there are too many of us for the available means of sustenance. He may lay claim to what we both need, marking me as expendable in his eyes. Man's inhumanity to man does not proceed from any such abstraction as 'human nature', but is rather scarcity interiorized in each of

[7] *Critique of Dialectical Reason, I, Theory of Practical Ensembles*, London NLB, 1976, translated by Alan Sheridan-Smith and edited by Jonathan Rée. See p. 128.
[8] *Critique*, p. 128.

us: 'Nothing – not even wild beasts or microbes – could be more terrifying for man than a species that is intelligent, carnivorous and cruel, which can understand and outwit human intelligence, and whose aim is precisely the destruction of man. This, however, is obviously our own species as perceived in others by each of its members in the context of scarcity.'[9]

It is important to note that scarcity may not even directly be involved for the Other to become a terrifying enemy. In a general environment of scarcity there is always someone who does not have enough, someone who is treated as, and therefore becomes, an anti-man. In such a situation, any freedom is a hostile force because it can be my own undoing. 'In other words, it is undeniable that what I attack is man as man, that is, as the free *praxis* of an organic being. It is man, and nothing else, that I hate in the enemy, that is, in myself as Other; and it is myself that I try to destroy in him, so as to prevent him destroying me in my own body.'[10]

For scarcity to have its terrible effect, direct violence need not be necessary. 'It merely means that the relations of production are established and pursued in a climate of fear and mutual mistrust by individuals who are always ready to believe that the Other is an anti-human member of an alien species.'[11] Apportioned out among members of society, scarcity becomes institutionalized in societies divided into classes. Historical materialism correctly describes this environment: all the structures of social life are determined by the society's mode of production. Even socialism has not known how to abolish this fundamental determination of human life, 'except possibly through a long dialectical process of which we cannot yet know the outcome'.[12] Scarcity, in short, is the principle of negativity in history. 'This provides a foundation for the intelligibility of that cursed aspect of human history, both in its origins and today, in which man constantly sees his action being stolen from him and totally distorted by the milieu in which he inscribes it. It is *primarily* this tension which, by inflicting profound dangers on everyone in society, by creating diffused violence in everyone, and by producing the possibility for everyone of seeing his best friend approaching him as an alien wild

[9] *Critique*, p. 132.
[10] *Critique*, p. 133.
[11] *Critique*, p. 149.
[12] *Critique*, p. 139.

beast, imposes a perpetual state of extreme urgency on every *praxis*, at the simplest level, and, whatever its real aim, makes the *praxis* into an act of aggression against other individuals or groups.'[13]

At first sight these passages seem to fulfill Sartre's postwar evolution, discernible for example in *What is Literature?* Sartre's earlier sense of an ontological – and inevitable – basis for human struggle has become material and contingent. The Other continues to be my enemy, but now for intelligible – and ultimately suppressible – historical reasons. As André Gorz argues, Sartre seems to have given us keys for developing a realistic understanding of the human miseries of human history. Gorz's excellent defence of the *Critique* argues that an activist Marxist thinker might build on it to show how an underlying scarcity, for example, reproduces itself at other social levels and becomes displaced from one society to another. He emphasizes that Sartre's grim analyses point to facts of life which Marxists cannot wish away: famine, violence, 'the reign of necessity'. It is now possible to untangle a history filled with violence, slavery, war, massacres and genocide, by pointing to the ultimate and objective threat every human being holds for every other human being.[14] Yet if we look at the actual use scarcity receives throughout the *Critique*, we encounter a strange paradox. So far Sartre has given us only a statement of first principles: individual *praxis*, scarcity, the practico-inert. Brilliant insights, perhaps, but their true place can only emerge throughout the whole *Critique*. In the subsequent 500 pages, focused on the formal structures and development of social groupings, we should expect scarcity to play a decisive and recurring role. How, for example, does scarcity enter into social formations, become 'interiorized', as Sartre would put it, and then reappear in the very tissue of human groupings and collective action?

It doesn't. Sartre *refers* to it again and again. In a world conditioned by scarcity, individual *praxis* solidifies into the menacing practico-inert. The anti-dialectic of the practico-inert depends 'on the multiplicity of individuals coexisting in the field of scarcity'.[15] In the stage of scarcity I 'see the menace of death in

---

[13] *Critique*, p. 150.
[14] André Gorz, 'Sartre and Marx', *New Left Review*, No. 37, May–June 1966. See above, pp. 176–200.
[15] *Critique*, p. 320.

the man' coming towards me.[16] Economic exploitation 'establishes itself against a background of scarcity'.[17] In a world conditioned by scarcity, no fused group, no union of free individuals can *stay* that way. But each of these arguments is no more than a throw-away reference to a first principle which in fact stays external to the real adventure of the book from beginning to end. In fact, most of the *Critique* pursues the dynamic which leads to the formation and ossification of the fused group as an internal process of the group itself. Sartre sets out his basic ideas on classes without making scarcity one of these central conditions and he does the same with revolutions, the division of labour, social organization, dictatorship and bureaucracy. Then, the circle completed, Sartre turns back to his original terms, acting as if they had been present all the time: 'the contingency of scarcity . . . is reinteriorized in the contingency of human reality'.[18] As if to emphasize what has been missing all along, Sartre now relates scarcity to classes by arguing that 'given a scarcity of food and of labour, certain groups will decide to constitute, with other individuals or groups, a community defined both by the obligation to do surplus labour and by the need to reduce themselves to a controlled under-consumption'.[19]

But it is too little and too late: this is the closest Sartre comes to explaining *how* classes form, whether in relation to scarcity or not. For the rest he is concerned with their ontological status or how they operate against each other. Put differently, Sartre's basic terms everywhere claim to be material, claim to base themselves, as Marxist terms should, on labour and the human struggle for survival. But most of the *Critique* deals with developments which seem to have their *own* logic, which are never connected back to that basic material level.

As Sartre presents it *scarcity* is a sophisticated, alluringly 'Marxized' restatement of the original ontology. Scarcity does not enter into Sartre's studies because it is *prior* to human action, a 'formal condition of history', an ultimate given which human beings can *only* interiorize. History is built *on* it; it lies prior to and conditions what gets built. As André Gorz notes 'scarcity is the *ultimate* foundation of history as the struggle of classes'.[20]

[16] *Critique*, p. 197.
[17] *Critique*, p. 739.
[18] *Critique*, p. 735.
[19] *Critique*, p. 737.
[20] 'Sartre and Marx', p. 191 above.

To see what is at stake in this approach we need only look at the social vision presented in the quotation assembled above. We see separate individuals, each engaged in his or her own *praxis* out of his or her own need, but doing so in a material field where there is not enough for all: resulting in fear, violence and classes. Scarcity and its effect on human relations is Sartre's key. Yes, Sartre agrees, human societies form to combat scarcity, and yes, much of history is a progressive struggle against it. But these facts clearly are not of the same rank as the curse of scarcity.

Yet this odd, terrifying picture is simply wrong. For on the most fundamental level we do not encounter each other primarily as threat and mainly because there is not enough. Sartre de-emphasizes, to the point of ignoring it, the manifest fact that societies would not last a single day were they not also co-operative. Above all a society must feed, clothe and house its members. The society may indeed be unable to produce enough, but its scarcity – and how to distribute it – can only be determined in a context which includes existing social ways of arranging the common struggle for survival and an existing level of productive capacity. These existing facts are already social and have required co-operation at every step of their history.

At their root the most exploitative societies are contradictory, not merely negative, as Sartre's emphasis might lead us to conclude. In one fashion or another we organize to do the work needed to get our collective living. We may not produce enough, and we may fight over our product. I may impose on you a form of antagonistic co-operation so that I benefit relatively and you suffer relatively from the scarcity. We then co-operate while I exploit you and you accept your lot or wait to resume the struggle. Helper *and* threat, you are both the key to my life and the prospect of my death. Our relationship must be contradictory, at least until the end of scarcity – or its more or less equal sharing – and the end of class society.

Like any fact, scarcity has no meaning prior to social life in history. Drawn into the texture of a genuinely social analysis, scarcity would cease to be Sartre's ultimate term. Scarcity, today and always, is a political fact, perpetuated and aggravated by certain societal forms and international dynamics, combated and overcome by others. There is no reason for scarcity today. The sheer technical means have been created by a history of antagonistic co-operation to 'cure' it in a generation – if the decision could be made to do so. Such a 'decision', however, would mean completely revolutionizing social structures which have a vested interest in limiting or wasting production; transforming people's attitudes towards their lot and their social life; destroying the current system of international relations; attacking 'backwardness' at all levels. It would mean, in short, revolutionizing the entire world.

Whether or not this is to happen is, above all, a political question. Gorz's grim Sartrean vision is false insofar as it tends to render these political facts as quasi-natural ones – 'in a world where the foreseeable growth of world population is greatly outstripping production of food' – and presents a worldwide political situation as the continuous displacement of a given fact – 'every local and partial victory over scarcity brings with it a displacement of scarcity into other areas'.[21]

To call scarcity a political fact is simply to assert that no single fact 'stands behind' or 'conditions' historical development. Scarcity appears as one decisive factor of a matrix which contains, in the most intimate interconnection, other decisive factors. Co-operative human *praxis* to create the means of subsistence is one of them and it implies that there is a fundamentally social nature to all individual activity. Another is the way in which the means of production are controlled. A class society is necessarily divided into owners of the means of production and those labouring in a subservient position to the owners, with an inevitably uneven social distribution of the fruits of labour. Another is the historically attained level of productivity and skills – how far any society has advanced in the struggle to create an apparatus for meeting needs and combating scarcity.

These are only some of the determinants of the basic socio-historical matrix in which facts become what they are. The point is that the extent and prospects of need fulfilment in any society cannot be grasped outside of that matrix. Sartre may indeed be profoundly right in his insistence on seeing scarcity as the under-lying source of negativity in the dialectic and history, 'scarcity as the negation in man of man by matter'. But by isolating 'matter' – lack of adequate foodstuffs, clothing, shelter, productive apparatus,

---

[21] *Ibid.*, p. 192.

and technique – from the social relations in which alone it appears, he presents it as an over-powering *external* force rather than a decisive factor *within* social life. He reifies it – makes it into a given rather than a product of human activity.

It is not enough to say there is not enough. Famine itself is a 'decision' of the social apparatus: a certain social organization with its own history and inertia prohibits the development of productive capacities beyond a certain subsistence level, arresting *praxis*, perpetuating scarcity. In this context, calamities of nature become defined as particular human calamities.

This context, this matrix – and not any single abstracted and isolated factor produced in it such as 'scarcity' – is, after all, the 'formal condition of history'. What Sartre has done, by contrast, is to lay down a formal condition, an ultimate term which – in the style of *Being and Nothingness* – is virtually beyond our grasp and dooms all our efforts to get behind it. Because of it the Other will threaten us, no matter what. Having paid due respect to Marxism and to the contingency of his 'ultimate' fact, Sartre has returned to his old bogeys. He lifts out a single factor from a complex process and uses it as a limiting term of the human adventure before it even begins. In the philosopher of scarcity can be discerned our old friend, the philosopher of 'hell is other people'. Sartre's project of social ontology seeks to grasp the underlying conditions and relations which form the basis for all historical development. But it willy-nilly becomes a philosophy of history as Sartre unfolds various laws and inevitabilities of human life. Sartre is trying to deduce conclusions which should have no place in his study of 'formal conditions of history'. In this respect, Sartre's fault is not that he probes behind history for its formal conditions, but rather that he wants to use those conditions to explain too much about history before it begins.

Marx, as does Sartre, sees human social activity lying behind its finished and frozen products: his ontological starting point is that human beings create the human world and that its 'laws' and necessities spring from and express the forms of their activity. Marx's starting point sketched in *The German Ideology*, leaves everything to be investigated. It points to a fluidity, a structured intentional activity behind all the apparent givens. Marx wants to reveal, in all their specificity, the forces whose interaction is history. His *German Ideology* is the abandoned preface to a lifetime of study. Sartre, on the other hand, wants 'to settle, outside concrete history itself, the incarnations of individual *praxis*, the formal structural conditions of its alienation and the abstract conditions which encourage the constitution of a common *praxis*'.[22] Any point of departure outside history will yield us timeless problems – problems which cannot be solved within history. Sartre takes the starting point for the explanation: scarcity leads to the hell of other people. In our world, at least, it is inevitable.

The Practico-Inert

A second key term of the *Critique* is the *practico-inert*. Sartre's discussion of the 'hell of the practico-inert' takes up most of the book and, like his discussion of scarcity, is noteworthy for its gloominess. Human *praxis* is activity which transforms the material field around it. The concept of the practico-inert refers to the fact that alongside its intended positive results our *praxis*, our work on the world, usually backfires. We become dominated by unintended features of our produce or our tools. Sometimes our *praxis* backfires because our activity itself gets out of hand, as that of the Chinese peasants who, each clearing the trees from their own land, together caused massive floods over the countryside. Sometimes the practico-inert is the négative power of our tools: 'in the most adequate and satisfactory tool, there is a hidden violence which is the reverse of its docility'.[23] The primitive understands that an arrow or a hatchet is to be feared and revered, seeing in them his 'own power become malignant and turned against him'.[24] He grasps the 'hidden hostility' in his tool's beneficial and menacing power.

In modern times our tools come to make demands on us and, indeed, to dominate us. The late eighteenth and early nineteenth centuries saw the creation of large-scale machinery for mass production. Unfortunately such machinery is not merely a tool for human purposes; it also shapes the human beings who are to operate it. A 'new being' is created by a type of worked matter which is in turn created by humans struggling against scarcity.

[22] *Critique*, p. 66. Translation modified.
[23] *Critique*, p. 183.
[24] *Critique*, p. 249, n 58.

The practico-inert is 'the domination of man by worked matter' in such a way that man becomes 'a product of his product'.[25] A positive fact – the use of coal on a grand scale, the development of social wealth through industrialization – has a negative result. It creates a working class which must submit to the new means of production in order to survive.

The practico-inert is the book's 'first dialectical experience of necessity',[26] for it is the inevitable outcome of human *praxis*. Sartre claims that 'every object, in so far as it exists within a given economic, technical and social complex, will in its turn become exigency through the mode and relations of production, and give rise to other exigencies, in other objects'.[27] This is so because all societies finally rest on dispersed individuals, each transforming nature by himself through his own *praxis*. In other words, the practico-inert finds 'its fundamental intelligibility in the serial action of men'.[28]

This points, by way of explanation, to a picture of individuals at work alone, perhaps even side by side, each grasping the world and transforming it from his or her particular point of view. It indicates that I am dominated not by the results of my *praxis*, but by the entire material field which has been created by everyone at work. Isolated, 'men realize unwittingly their own unity in the form of antagonistic alterity through the material field where they are dispersed and through the multiplicity of unifying actions which they perform on this field'.[29] Our 'unity' is imposed by the material system we separated individuals have created – and so it is beyond any individual control from the outset.

This is not, Sartre insists, the power of society over the individual: the practico-inert dominates me as matter which has escaped human control. Out there is a material field which remains exterior to me because I did not create it, because it emerged from within a hundred or a thousand other individual *praxes*. Thus it threatens and dominates us all. It is out of my control and out of anyone's control. We all bear the same relationship to it. Hence, alongside each other but separated, we wind up facing 'a magical field of

[25] *Critique*, p. 184.
[26] *Critique*, p. 222.
[27] *Critique*, p. 189.
[28] *Loc. cit.* Translation modified.
[29] *Critique*, pp. 220–21.

quasi-dialectical counter-finality'.[30] It is magical not because I control it through arcane devices, but because it comes to have a life of its own.

Human Society and the Practico-Inert

Sartre's example of Chinese peasants deforesting their land sums up and starts to reveal some of the weaknesses of his account: 'uprooting a tree in a field of sorghum becomes *deforestation* from the point of view of a large plain and of terraces of loess, united by the work of separate men; and *deforestation* as the real meaning of the individual action of uprooting is simply the negative union of all those who are isolated by the material totality which they have produced'.[31]

Sartre's description is too general and timeless. The Chinese peasants were not the victims of human *praxis* as such, but of a society which they did not rule and whose rulers refused to exercise social foresight, of a low level of material and technical development. Their activity escaped them because no one acknowledged it as social and needing social control: it was a problem which social struggle and historical development could overcome. In this example, however, Sartre gives us a 'pure' practico-inert, just as he earlier gave us a 'pure' scarcity: facts are abstracted from a complex socio-historical matrix and then injected back as independent and awesome forces.

Moreover, Sartre's account of the practico-inert rests on a view of individuals working separately but side by side, as if this is a natural work relation. Why this *series* should be the basic form of collectivity Sartre does not say. Nor, for that matter, does he tell us how people got side by side in the first place. He gives us no sense of the socio-historical process leading to their separation. Furthermore, Sartre never considers that other social groupings might differently organize their relations to the material field.

Certainly under some conditions the fruits of human labour become terrifying weapons. But under other conditions they can remain useful tools and paths of liberation. The conditions are, very simply, social. The 'worked matter' of which Sartre speaks is never at bottom an independent or quasi-natural force: it is a

[30] *Critique*, p. 224.
[31] *Critique*, p. 225.

social reality from the outset. In other words, there is no 'worked matter' as such: there is only this apparatus as part of the life of this society. A productive apparatus democratically operated towards the goal of meeting social needs would weigh on us very differently from one whose components are controlled separately by a few for their own profit. A socialist factory of the future in which the workers truly controlled their activity and products, as part of a wider social apparatus in which they had decision-making powers would have a different look. It might, for example, be designed so the workers would be allowed maximum familiarity with all of its processes – as a necessary concomitant of routine rotation from one job to another, and of workers' planning. It might be spacious, light, and clean.

Certainly even in the best situation workers would have to be on the job; they would have to perform these tasks, at this moment. Even breaking the assembly line into work crews would not abolish those social and technological necessities whose purpose remains to transform nature in order to meet our material needs. But if workers control the work itself, if they labour reduced hours and freely exchange functions, if they are assured of a secure level of subsistence and co-operate with each other in socially meaningful work – at some point the grim rule of necessity can end, quantity can change into quality and the practico-inert can come under human control. It would be humanized, shot through with human vitality and freedom and power, so that our very sense of work would change.

Do such objections merely resuscitate the 'simplistic Marxism' against which Sartre polemicizes throughout the *Critique*? In fact, the more simplistic analysis is Sartre's. Matter, or the simple fact that it is transformed by men and women, does not determine the fact or degree of its dominance over us. We are not subjected to 'every object, in so far as it exists within a given economic, technical and social complex'. The character and degree of its dominance over us is decided by the social-historical matrix in which objects are created and used. Abstracted from their social matrix – and thus their origin in a process which could conceivably be reoriented – things may, of course, indeed often appear overwhelming.

It is not surprising, then, that Sartre makes direct reference to *Being and Nothingness* at the end of the section in the *Critique* dealing with the practico-inert. Suddenly, seventeen years and supposed worlds of thought later, he suddenly conjures up the vision of the 'in-itself-for-itself' again. For, after all, it is 'this fundamental relation', the necessity of creating the practico-inert, 'which explains why, as I have said, man *projects himself* in the milieu of the In-Itself-For-Itself'.[32] Although Sartre shifts from his account in *Being and Nothingness* when he now writes that 'the foundation of necessity is practice', his key terms actually show no shift: man, the for-itself, 'revealing itself initially as inert or, at best, practico-inert in the milieu of the in-itself'.[33] Whether man creates it or it is given, the world remains for Sartre what it always was – a power over us, a force beyond our control.

Separate individuals labour side by side to create a world that overwhelms them. Sartre's vision raises specific features of advanced capitalist society to the status of universal structures. Recent discussions of the issue of pollution in America are a relevant example here of how a problem stemming from the specific priorities of a particular social structure, can be mystified in this way into a more generalized and remote case of human activity getting out of hand. 'We' are told that we should all help to control our waste – private citizens, government bodies, corporations. But pollution is, of course, a political problem. Firstly, it is the very nature of a capitalist enterprise to be concerned with its own profits at whatever social cost, rather than with social well-being. Secondly, capitalism is generally so structured that there can be no social control over society's productive processes – the economy. Thirdly, capitalist society anyway develops an ethic and rationale of economic activity in which *no one* is responsible. The magical work of the 'invisible hand' theoretically co-ordinates the dispersed activities of millions. So each capitalist does what he wants. To this extent, the social vision of capitalist society is that there is no society. Sartre's description of the hell of the practico-inert aptly conveys it. But this description fits the world of *today*, for specific social and historical reasons, not because of the very nature of human praxis. The separate and unco-ordinated work controlled by each capitalist becomes an enormous anti-human social power, beyond anyone's control, even that of any bourgeois government.

[32] *Critique*, p. 228, n. 68.
[33] *Loc. cit.*

The Historical Versus the Isolated Individual

Society – and particularly the alienated and contradictory social life of all class societies – is the missing term of Sartre's social thought. He ignores it in explaining the dominance worked matter comes to have over us, just as he ignores it in explaining the force of scarcity. What in his thought makes him unwilling – or unable – to use this key? The question brings us to the basic problem of the *Critique*. For Sartre's work of social theory is ultimately constructed in ways that make it impossible to understand social realities. It is built not on a sense of society at all, but on abstract, isolated individuals.

Sartre protests the opposite. He writes, for example: 'To consider *an individual* at work is a complete abstraction since in reality labour is as much a relation between men as a relation between man and the material world'.[34] He repeats this half a dozen times in the course of the *Critique*, even emphasizing that the very solitude of the isolated worker can only be produced by a specific historical and social reality.[35] He proclaims his intention not to stop the *Critique* at the level of abstract individuality – it would be 'false and idealist' to do so. 'But since our starting point is individual *praxis*, we must carefully follow up every one of those threads of Ariadne which lead from this *praxis*, to the various forms of human ensembles; and in each case we shall have to determine the structures of these ensembles, their real mode of formation out of their elements, and finally their totalising action upon the elements which have formed them.'[36] Individual *praxis* and the isolated person who performs it are abstractions which Sartre will take as heuristic devices – the immediate and given starting points of an enquiry which will penetrate far beneath the individual's apparent isolation. Thereby, Sartre will 'rediscover through deeper and deeper conditionings, the totality of his practical bonds with others and, thereby, the structures of the various practical multiplicities and, through their contradictions and struggles, the absolute concrete: historical man'.[37]

After our examination of his conceptions of scarcity and the

---

34 *Critique*, p. 91.
35 *Critique*, p. 95.
36 *Critique*, p. 65.
37 *Critique*, p. 52.

practico-inert, such assertions of intention pose a difficult intellectual problem. How can we disentangle Sartre's clearly unhistorical, unsocial explanation of historical and social phenomena from his seeming commitment to portray the 'concrete absolute', historical man? A look at how the *Critique* is constructed will help us.

Following two introductory chapters ('The Dogmatic Dialectic and the Critical Dialectic', and 'Critique of Critical Investigation') Book I of the *Critique* begins: 'From Individual Praxis to the Practico-Inert'. In these pages the *Critique* progresses from 'abstract' individual *praxis* to the most primary human ensembles: here is where Sartre locates the individual's basic social relations, from which all others spring and to which all others return. The first step is to describe individual *praxis*. Then, in no less than four separate headings, we see our isolated individual encountering others. These sections reveal Sartre's peculiarly unsocial social individual.

It is quite fitting that Sartre's first move beyond isolated individual *praxis* should be a leap, not a step at all. We began with the isolated individual at work on the material field around him. How then do we get to social groupings? Does Sartre look more deeply at this individual, to see the historical and social imprint on everything he does? This would be an internal way of uncovering sociality within every apparent individuality. Instead, Sartre simply adds on other individuals. 'From my window I can see a road-mender on the road and a gardener working in a garden. Between them there is a wall with bits of broken glass on top protecting the bourgeois property where the gardener is working. Thus they have no knowledge at all of each other's presence; absorbed as they are in their work, neither of them even bothers to wonder whether there is anybody on the other side. Meanwhile, I can see them without being seen, and my position and this passive view of them at work situates me in relation to them: I am "taking a holiday" in a hotel.'[38]

From one individual at work we move to three individuals at work, separately. But to build social relations simply by multiplying individuals is not to build social relations at all. Three or a dozen or a thousand individuals are not social unless links between

---

[38] *Critique*, p. 100.

them can be shown whose nature and logic binds them in a shared, common activity, linking them in a reality which is qualitatively different from the sum of its isolated parts. Instead of discovering others by revealing their actual implication in any single person's *praxis*, Sartre simply places them there beside the latter. We are already familiar enough with our abstract individual's next two social encounters ('Scarcity and Mode of Production', and 'Worked Matter as the Alienated Objectification of Individual and Collective "Praxis"') to see that they, too cast others and the social life that develops with them in an arbitrary, external light.

Which Comes First, Individual or Social Praxis?

In other words, Sartre aims at social and historical being from premises that can never get us there. The *Critique*'s goal, 'historical man', contradicts its basic premise, the isolated individual. This contradiction explains much of the book's obscurity. Side by side with Sartre's repeated throwaway references to the abstractness of individual *praxis* and his proclaimed intention to move to a more socially and historically concrete level, we find a quite different idea. Individual *praxis*, Sartre makes clear, is the book's fundamental principle. It is the source of all dialectic, the only ontological reality. The heuristic device turns out to be the core of the book, from beginning to end.

Sartre claims that his approach is based on the very nature of the dialectic itself. 'The dialectic, if it exists, can only be the totalization of concrete totalizations effected by a multiplicity of totalizing individualities.'[39] Sartre's argument is that no collectivity of individuals can possibly grasp its surrounding material field as a whole, perform an action on it, alter it and so meet human needs – unless *each* individual can do it. 'The entire *historical dialectic rests on individual praxis in so far as it is already dialectical.*'[40] This is why Sartre first studies the logic of individual labour. Acknowledging that separated individuals appear as such only 'in a given society, and given a certain level of technical development'[41] he explains to us why he will not now advance to the level of society, but must instead consider our vacationing

[39] *Critique*, p. 37.
[40] *Critique*, p. 80.
[41] *Critique*, p. 45.

writer, our gardener and road-mender.

There is no question, he repeats, that any relations we study are always specific and historical, so that under diverse systems of oppression, such as feudalism and capitalism, social relations in the work process will differ sharply. Here, as we reach the core of the issue, I shall quote at length from Sartre. 'History itself does not cause there to be human relations in general. The relations which have established themselves between those *initially separate* objects, men, were not products of problems of the organisation and division of labour. On the contrary, the very possibility of a group or society being constituted – around a set of technical problems and a given collection of instruments – depends on the permanent actuality of the human relation (whatever its content) at every moment of History, even between two separate individuals belonging to societies with different systems and entirely ignorant of one another. This is why the habit of skipping the abstract discussion of the human relation and immediately locating ourselves in the world of productive forces, of the mode and relations of production, so dear to Marxism, is in danger of giving unwitting support to the atomism of liberalism and of analytical rationality. This error has been made by several Marxists: individuals, according to them, are *a priori* neither isolated particles nor directly related activities; it is always up to society to determine which they are through the totality of the movement and the particularity of the conjuncture. But this reply, which is supposed to avoid our "formalism", involves complete formal acceptance of the *liberal* position; the individualistic bourgeoisie requires just one concession: that individuals passively submit to their relations and that these are conditioned in exteriority by all kinds of other forces; and this leaves them free to apply the principle of inertia and positivistic laws of exteriority to human relations. From this point of view it hardly matters whether the individual really lives in isolation, like a cultivator at certain periods, or whether he lives in highly integrated groups: *absolute separation* consists in the fact that individuals are subject to the historical statute of their relations to others in radical exteriority. In other words – and this amounts to the same thing, though it misleads certain undemanding Marxists – absolute separation is when individuals as products of their own product (and therefore as passive and alienated) *institute* relations among themselves (on the basis of relations established by earlier generations, of their own constitution and of the forces and requirements of the time).'[42]

Sartre's thesis is that the moment we postulate 'society' as an *a priori* term we set up an overwhelming conditioning force over us – an abstraction that makes our life appear to be suffered, undergone and submitted to. The *Critique* argues, by contrast, that the activity of 'abstract', isolated individuals, the sole possible *praxis*, is the root of social theory. Thus Sartre's constant references to our historical and social reality do not keep him from seeing a *more essential dimension* within whatever social or historical situation we dwell in, a dimension which must be studied first: 'the abstract stage of human relations'. The curious result is that, in his account, the individualist bourgeoisie becomes the proponent of the priority of a social-historical dimension, while Sartre the Marxist becomes a proponent of individual separation.

Let us follow Sartre as he continues to try to dissolve false abstraction to reach a more basic dimension: 'This brings us back to our problem in the first part of this book: what does it mean to *make* History on the basis of earlier conditions? I then said: if we do not distinguish the project, as transcendence, from circumstances, as conditions, we are left with nothing but inert objects, and History vanishes. Similarly, if human relations are a mere product, they are in essence reified and it becomes impossible to understand what their reification really consists in. My formalism, which is inspired by that of Marx, consists simply in recognizing that men make History to precisely the extent that it makes them. This means that relations between men are always the dialectical consequence of *their activity* to precisely the extent that they arise as a transcendence of dominating and institutionalised human relations. Man exists for man only in given circumstances and social conditions, so every human relation is historical. But historical relations are human in so far as they are *always* given as the immediate dialectical consequence of *praxis*, that is to say, of the plurality of *activities* within a single practical field.'[43]

But Sartre is mistaken. To believe that human activity is fundamentally dialectical and therefore capable of rising up and transforming the conditions in which it occurs, we need not believe

---

[42] *Critique*, pp. 96–97.
[43] *Critique*, pp. 98–99.

that we must speak of individual activity. *Praxis* is, first of all, social. Free, transforming, totalizing activity which remakes the world is possible only as social activity. Work is not an individual activity that happens, in some circumstances, to be performed alongside other people, but a social activity which members of any society perform from their place, according to their skills, according to arrangements which are only – and always – social and historical.

Long before there can be any epistemological encounter between our vacationing intellectual, our gardener and road-mender, there must be a process of antagonistic co-operation in which they share. The intellectual can gaze out of his window only because there are people to mend the road, tend gardens, plant and grow food, make beds, build hotels, transport food, build trucks, supply fuel, make kitchen utensils, cut vegetables, cook food. Whatever their 'formal' relations the activity of each in this society implies the activity of all others. Any vacationing intellectual depends on their labour. The labour of each is thus mystified if it is seen primarily as individual *praxis*. Individuals carry it out, to be sure, but as social individuals carrying out aspects of a complex and highly organized social *praxis*. No step of the activity is not social.

My tools, my place of work, the materials I work on, my very patterns of work – all these dimensions of individual *praxis* develop only in and for a society at a certain point in history. This is true of what seems to be the most idiosyncratic individual activity. For example, our vacationer who establishes relations between individuals does so as part of a certain philosophical tradition. His leisure depends on a social division of labour which deems it important that certain groups of people are permitted the time to do such things. Strictly speaking there can no more be a purely individual *praxis* than there can be an individual reason. Social individuals work with social tools, using social skills on a social field, to accomplish socially-defined purposes. This is so of all labour, even if executed over here, by this individual. The very formula 'the individual' means one particular social being – conditioned by and living in history, possessing skills, speaking a language.

To be sure, Sartre claims to acknowledge all this, which makes the *Critique* in many ways so puzzling a work. Gorz even argues that the book is 'obviously' not built on the *solitary* individual but rather shows the individual's internal links with each of his creations, each of the social realities shaping him. Gorz italicizes Sartre here: 'Starting from this, his own life, *his understanding of his own life must lead to the denial of its singular determination in favour of a search for its dialectical intelligibility in the whole human adventure.*'[44] We have seen that the *Critique* does this without inner necessity, only by leaps and bounds. But even as formulated the project is mistaken: Sartre would *seek out* the links between individual *and* society, rather than seeing the individual as social *from the outset*. Thus when the decisive intellectual decisions are to be taken, Sartre returns to this point: social *praxis* is the combined activity of individuals who happen to be at work on the same field.

Social Individuals

Sartre would retort to the criticisms developed here that they make dialectical activity – free activity, *praxis* – unintelligible, by refusing to cast the individual as prior to society. He would argue that they serve an ideology that is bourgeois, by making the individual appear determined but not equally determining. What, he would ask, is this strange entity, society, if it is somehow before and beyond individual activity? How is it possible ever to hope to control it or transform it if we don't create it? André Gorz raises these questions in his sharp defence of Sartre's focus: 'If the individual is explicable through the society, but the society is not intelligible through individuals – that is, if the "forces" that act in history are impermeable and radically heterogeneous to organic *praxis* – then socialism as the socialization of man can never coincide with socialism as the humanization of the social. It cannot come *from* individuals as their reappropriation by collective *praxis* of the resultant of individual *praxes*. It can only come *to* individuals by the evolution of their society according to its inner logic. The positivist (or transcendental materialist) hypothesis is that the historical process is impermeable to dialectical intelligibility. If so, then socialism, born of an external logic, will also remain external to individuals and will not be a submission of society and history to individuals and their demands, but a submission of individuals to society and its demands on them; not the "full development" but the negation of individuals, not the transparency of the social for individual *praxis*, but the opacity of the individual for himself, in so far as his being and his truth have become completely external to him. Thus the social individual is not the individual recognizing himself and achieving himself in the community, but the individual radically denying himself – his needs, his interests, his certainties – for the profit of the society experienced as the absolute Other, to the point of regarding it as false to see it as Other. We know that this conception of socialism prevailed for a long period, that it still has its adherents, that it profoundly affected Marxist philosophy, and that it must therefore be liquidated on this terrain as well.'[45]

The argument is clear: unless individual *praxis* is seen as the basis of society, society must be seen as independent of individuals and unchangeable by them. But the argument runs into trouble when we ask what it means to anticipate a society controlled by individuals. What does it mean to speak of 'the humanization of the social' coming 'from individuals'? Neither Sartre nor Gorz can possibly have in mind isolated, separated individuals each controlling his or her own sphere of activity. A vision of 'collective *praxis*' can mean only one thing: individuals collectively controlling the society they create. 'Collectively' means acting together in social groups, making group decisions about group goals, with the group controlling the product of its labour. No individual can conceivably submit society or history to his demands unless he is a social individual.

The vision of a society controlled 'by individuals' makes sense only if those individuals see themselves as social from the outset and move together to take control of their *common* product. We must, in short, reverse the Sartre-Gorz argument: for socialism to be possible as the collective control of collective activity, it is necessary for the individuals involved first to be living a – however alienated – collective life. Socialism makes no sense as the 'reappropriation by collective *praxis* of the resultant of individual *praxis*', but only as the reappropriation of the resultant of heretofore alienated collective *praxis*. It means bringing under social control an *already* socialized process of production rather than transforming individual production *into* social production.

Gorz and Sartre are obviously struggling with an important problem: the tendency, within socialist as well as bourgeois thought, to make individuals the passive objects of abstract forces beyond their control. However, we can restore the intellectual possibility of human beings making history and controlling their society, without basing their social life on imaginary presocial individuals. Certainly Sartre is right in arguing that there can be no society that exists independently of the individuals who make it up. Yet everything hinges on whether individuals are seen as fundamentally social beings, whose basic activity and possibilities for liberation are alike seen as social.

In spite of Sartre's attack on organicist views of the individual's relation to the society and in spite of his refusal to give the group an ontological status, it remains indisputable that any society is always more than the sum of its individuals. Society is produced by individuals, but collectively. It contains the supra-individual conditions for our common survival and well-being. At whatever point in history, society is our collective power, our collective ways of arranging life, our collective agencies for preparing individuals to live that life. Product of those individuals though it may be, society is also the *source* of our activity, and is both our very deepest identity and a power over us – like it or not. It is a power, Sartre begins to agree in his subsequent biography of Gustave Flaubert, which makes us ourselves.

Back To the Roots

Why was Sartre unwilling to see this for another dozen years? What in Sartre's thought makes it so difficult for him to see the social determinations at the core of each individual? The question sends us back to the roots of Sartre's thought. For in the end we find the same account of the world in the *Critique* as in Sartre's early writings. He still tries to explain social phenomena with analyses drawn from a perspective based on isolated individuals. He still regards the world – now the world men and women have created – from the view-point of an isolated individual confronting an overwhelming reality. He still labours strenuously to defend that individual's freedom – now *praxis* – against that reality, rather than studying its social sources and prospects of transformation.

We find in the *Critique*, as in his early writings, that Sartre's probing radicalism is constantly compromised by his tendency to take what he sees at face value: our separation and isolation, our mutual hostility, the weight of the world. For all his hostility to positivism, he continues to take as his standard of evidence and basis of study these immediately apparent givens of social experience. But the testimony of immediate consciousness – 'as apodictic certainty (of) itself and as consciousness *of* such or such an object'[46] – can hardly serve as the basis of social theory, if indeed it were adequate in any other area. Wilfred Desan, speaking of this approach, has commented accurately: 'Sartre has a method, but a method which only emphasizes his Cartesian seclusion.'[47]

Sartre holds doggedly to this 'epistemological point of departure'. The result, as we might expect, is that his attempt to impose an approach proper to some areas of study, on other regions quite distant and foreign to them, shapes his facts before he looks at them. It shapes the facts by making this or that individual's immediate activity decisive, at the cost of forgetting that such 'immediacy' can only be the mediated product of a social and historical process. It shapes the facts by relegating the more theoretical forms of awareness – of our historical and social being – to a secondary position. It shapes the facts by passing over such realities of our lives as society, or depriving them of ontological status, simply because individual consciousness does not immediately perceive them.

Thus it is no wonder that we return, in the *Critique*, to the familiar and depressing ground of *Being and Nothingness*. The same sweeping human conclusions are drawn from the same individualist epistemology. Our alienation is our freedom: such was the message at the core of *Being and Nothingness*. At the core of the *Critique of Dialectical Reason* we now find that only the abstract individual guarantees human freedom. The concept of the abstract individual, we have also seen, guarantees our hostility to each other. It ensures our domination by scarcity, our alienation from our creations, our subjugation by the practico-inert. These key terms of Sartre's thought remain unchanged through all his changes.[48]

[46] *Critique*, p. 51.

[47] Wilfred Desan, 'Sartre the Individualist', in *Patterns of the Life-World: Essays in Honor of John Wild*, ed. by James M. Edie, Francis H. Parker, and Calvin Q. Schrag (Evanston, 1970), p. 247.

[48] Gorz's political optimism here is his own, not Sartre's. It is accompanied by certain implicit conceptual shifts from the *Critique*, such as when he claims: 'To show that the reason of alienation is intelligible, is to show at the same time that this reason, born of human *praxis*, is capable of being suppressed by that *praxis*'. ('Sartre and Marx', p. 190.)

Sartre and Marxism

We find then in Sartre a profound mistrust of social being, an inability to see it as both our basic dimension and our only hope of liberation. What becomes of a Marxist commitment in such a theoretical framework? Obviously Sartre's Marxism can have none of the deep optimism of a Marx, Engels or Lenin. Indeed, Sartre's Marxism must be, ultimately, a philosophy of despair. The revolution may succeed, but so will Stalin. The individual will be overwhelmed by the practico-inert and isolated from and threatened by others, except for that brief moment when the group comes together. For the rest we are fated to make a world side by side with one another, which remains beyond our control.

Individualism is a logic of despair. So is Sartre's unhistorical ontological thinking. Problems inscribed in *being*, be it individual or social, are problems for all time. If history enters the analysis thereafter, it is already too late: all the traps have already been set. We are enmeshed in the laws of the dialectic, stuck in its 'necessary' circularity. Determined at the outset to show how the world we live in springs from our own hands, Sartre ends up by lodging it in isolated individuals. In so doing he takes it out of our hands.

It is no wonder that Sartre's Marxism becomes, in the final analysis, academic. Marxism has classically sought to be intellectually rigorous and yet inseparably wedded to political action. This basic posture informs all its theoretical projects, as a demand to ground study on the social bases of human activity. In *Search for a Method*, the lengthy preface to the *Critique*, Sartre poses quite a different goal: to explain the individual. Sartre sets as his goal to 'reconquer man within Marxism'[49] by trying to 'see the original dialectical movement in the individual and in his enterprise of producing his life, of objectifying himself'.[50]

On this scholarly level Sartre is hardly pessimistic. Interviewed in 1971, he said that 'the underlying plan in my Flaubert is to show that, eventually, everything can be communicated, and that without being God, being a man like any other – one can arrive at a perfect understanding of another man as long as one has all the information necessary'.[51] No stronger intellectual energy is con-

[49] *The Problem of Method*, London 1963, p. 83.
[50] *The Problem of Method*, p. 161.
[51] 'Interview with Jean-Paul Sartre', Michel Contat and Michel Rybalka, *Le Monde Weekly*, June 17–23, 1971, p. 6.

ceivable. This energy – visible all the way back in his earliest writings – springs from a belief that reality can indeed be understood. Understood, yes, but decisively changed, no. There is the optimism, there is the pessimism. They indicate well the directions Sartre takes in his absorption of Marxism.

His is, after all, a formidable *scholarly* project. Sartre wants to use a reshaped Marxism in order to *understand the individual*. Indeed, from 1950 to 1972, most of Sartre's intellectual energy has been devoted to just this task: studying himself, Tintoretto, Genet and Flaubert – well over 3400 pages worth, the great bulk of it on Flaubert. These works are studies of individuals, artists struggling alone with their overwhelming world – and taking flight in imagination. Now that we see what kind of a world Sartre describes as a Marxist, we can understand why he occupies himself with artists who both escaped it and transformed it in their imagination.

Sartre's basic early theoretical direction still holds: the individual isolated in an impossible world escapes into imagination. By 1960, however, Sartre was too politically committed and intellectually sophisticated to make this an explicit position, as he came close to doing in *Nausea*, *Psychology of Imagination* and *Being and Nothingness*. By the 1970's and the appearance of Sartre's third *magnum opus*, *L'Idiot de la famille* (1971–72), his theoretical retreat into imagination had come to rest side by side with his strong activist bent. In this sense, politically committed though the later Sartre may be, his intellectual work is hardly Marxist.

Nowhere is this split seen better than in the interview Sartre gave to the then Italian Communist Party journal, *Il Manifesto* in September 1969. The editor, Rossana Rossanda, was struggling with the dilemma that some sort of organized party seems absolutely necessary to carry out a revolution, yet at the same time such a party always seems to develop a stake in its own survival as an organization. In response, Sartre freely stated this to be a necessary contradiction, and using his concepts of seriality and institutionalization, perceptively analyzed the role of the French Communist Party in May 1968.

Throughout the interview Rossanda, while operating within Sartre's conceptual framework, refused to accept the contradiction as inevitable. She again and again pressed Sartre to see a way out of the dilemma, or posed her own solution to him. Again and again, Sartre returned to the *Critique*'s position: 'While I recognize the need of an organization, I must confess that I don't see how the problems which confront any stabilized structure could be resolved.'[52] Rossanda, a Marxist and an activist, could hardly submit to these ontological limits on her political work. So, as Sartre's thought brought her to a dead end, she sketched a way out: an open-ended relationship of the party to the working-class in which the party puts itself at the service of the struggle of the class. Let us follow his reply: 'I agree, on condition that this dialectic manifests itself as a dual power, and that one does not claim to solve it within a purely political schema. Even then, there are many problems which remain. You speak of a methodological or a theoretical "grid", provided as it were in advance and through which experience may be interpreted. But is it not the case that the concept of *capital* remains a thin and abstract notion if one does not constantly elaborate anew the analysis of modern capitalism, by research and by the permanent critique of the results of research and of struggle? *True* thought is certainly *one*: but its unity is dialectical – it is a living reality in the process of formation. What is required is the construction of a relationship between men which guarantees not only freedom, but *revolutionary* freedom of thought –a relationship which enables men to appropriate knowledge completely and to criticize it. This, in any case, is how knowledge has always proceeded, but it is never how the "Marxism" of Communist parties has proceeded. So that the creative culture of its members may grow and in order to enable them to acquire a maximum of true knowledge, the party – the political organization of the class – must make it possible for them to innovate and to engage in mutual argument, instead of presenting itself as the administrator of acquired knowledge. If one looks outside the party, the debate on Marxism has never been richer than it is now because, particularly since the break-up of monolithism and the posing of the problem of the diversity of socialism, there exists a plurality of Marxist inquiries and open disagreements between them.'[53]

The disconcertingly complicated character of this statement is due to the fact that the basic movement of Sartre's thought has re-asserted itself. Sartre has shifted the level of discourse, so that

[52] 'France: Masses, Spontaneity, Party', in *Between Existentialism and Marxism* London NLB, 1974, p. 132.
[53] *Ibid.*, pp. 133–34.

Rossanda's urgent political problem – pronounced to be irresoluble by Sartre, who had supplied the very terms in which it was conceptualized – becomes for Sartre an intellectual issue. What are the 'many problems (which) would remain unresolved'? Certainly not political problems, but questions of 'investigation', 'true thought', and 'culture and truth'. Unable to deal with the practical issue of how a party is to seize power yet avoid ossification, Sartre sidesteps it to ask how to guarantee 'the revolutionary freedom of thought – a relationship which enables men to appropriate knowledge completely and to criticize it'. Therewith Sartre's Marxism steps into an academic refuge. Presenting the external world's problems as overwhelming, he retreats into a rich and free inner world of culture. Never fully a political way of thinking, Sartre's Marxism falls back into its existentialist dynamic when political questions press against its pessimism.

Althusser's Marxism: An Assessment

Norman Geras

In a body of work which has received considerable attention in France and elsewhere and become one of the focal points of contemporary Marxist controversy, Louis Althusser has registered the necessity for a reading of Marx at once critical and rigorous. *Critical*: the assimilation of Marx's important discoveries can only be the product of a major theoretical effort which, so far from taking for granted that the whole of Marx forms a coherent and valid unity, attempts to distinguish *in* Marx between theoretical deficiencies, terminological ambiguities and ideological 'survivals' on the one hand, and truly scientific concepts on the other. *Rigorous*: the condition for the fruitful application and further elaboration of these concepts is a strict and scrupulous regard for their definitions, their implications, their scope and their boundaries, for what they exclude as much as for what they include. Only by dint of this will Marxist research escape the pitfalls of taking these concepts for what they are not and of remaining satisfied with the inadequate substitutes which can masquerade in their place.

The insistence on this double requirement bears witness to the self-conscious intention of a Communist philosopher to avoid both the shackles of uncritical orthodoxy and the temptations of conceptual imprecision. At the same time, the exercise should not be regarded as a purely academic one in which the only stake is the scholarly interpretation and assessment of Marx. For, if Althusser has thought it necessary to challenge those tendencies (humanism, historicism, Hegelianism) which have haunted Western Marxism since Lukács's early work and become powerfully influential in the last two decades, it is because he believes that, being theoretically deficient, they cannot but produce serious negative effects in the political practice of the class struggle. Unable to provide an adequate scientific knowledge of the real political problems thrown up by this struggle, and offering instead the imaginary comforts of merely ideological formulae, such tendencies cannot contribute to the solution of these problems and may indeed be impediments to their solution. The stakes, ultimately, are political. The precise counts on which the humanist and historicist themes of Hegelian Marxism are found to be theoretically deficient will be elaborated in due course. Here it is sufficient to observe that Althusser defines his work as an intervention against these tendencies within Marxism and that it is only by situating it in this context that its significance is properly understood.

The first part of this article is an exposition of the theoretical positions of *For Marx* (1965) and *Reading Capital* (1965), Althusser's major, and most systematic, works to date despite the reservations he has since expressed about them. In the second part, I attempt a critical assessment of these positions, and conclude with some remarks on the texts Althusser has written since 1965 – texts which are collected in *Lenin and Philosophy and other essays*. All these works are now available to the English reader in Ben Brewster's excellent translations.[1]

I Exposition

The Althusserian project receives its unity from one central and overriding concern: 'the *investigation* of Marx's *philosophical* thought.'[2] Behind the diverse problems considered and the solutions proposed, there is always one question at issue, for Althusser the essential question, namely, '*What is Marxist philosophy? Has it any theoretical right to existence? And if it does exist in principle, how can its specificity be defined?*'[3] The approach to Marx's *Capital* too is informed by this question. For all that it is primarily a work of political economy, it is seen by Althusser and his collaborators as the basic site of the philosophy which is the object of their

[1] Louis Althusser, *For Marx* (Now newly in print again – NLB, London, 1977); Louis Althusser and Etienne Balibar, *Reading Capital* (NLB, London, 1970); Louis Althusser, *Lenin and Philosophy and other essays* (NLB, London, 1971). Referred to hereinafter as FM, RC and LP respectively.

[2] FM p. 21. All italics in the original except where otherwise stated.

[3] FM p. 31.

search.[4] Thus their reading of that work is an explicitly philosophical one undertaken by philosophers[5] in order to be able to
respond to one of the exigencies confronting contemporary
Marxist theory: the need for 'a more rigorous and richer definition
of *Marxist philosophy*'.[6]

What is the source of this exigency? In the first place, the nature
of Marx's own achievement: 'By founding the theory of history
(historical materialism), Marx simultaneously broke with his
erstwhile ideological philosophy and established a new philosophy
(dialectical materialism). I am deliberately using the traditionally
accepted terminology (historical materialism, dialectical materialism) to designate this double foundation.'[7] It is an achievement
involving two distinct disciplines, but it is marked by a certain
unevenness, for historical materialism and dialectical materialism
have received different degrees of theoretical elaboration. The
former, the Marxist science of social formations and their history,
was mapped out and developed in Marx's mature works, to be
enriched subsequently by theoreticians such as Lenin engaged in
the practice of the class struggle. On the other hand, 'Marxist
philosophy, founded by Marx in the very act of founding his
theory of history, has still largely to be constituted, since, as Lenin
said, only the corner-stones have been laid down'.[8] Dialectical
materialism, that is to say, represents a philosophical revolution
'carried in' Marx's scientific discoveries;[9] at work in them, it
exists in an untheorized practical state;[10] its mode of existence is
merely 'implicit'.[11] Whence the need to give it proper theoretical
articulation, resisting the temptation offered by its implicitness
simply to confuse it with historical materialism.

For if the latter has been able to develop up to a point in the
absence of an explicit and thorough formulation of the principles
of Marxist philosophy, this absence has not been without serious
consequences and to continue to tolerate it would be to incur
further risks. Anticipating somewhat the further course of this

[4] RC pp. 30–1, 74.
[5] RC pp. 14–5.
[6] RC p. 77.
[7] FM p. 33.
[8] FM pp. 30–1.
[9] RC pp. 75–6.
[10] FM pp. 173–5; RC p. 185.
[11] FM pp. 33, 229.

exposition, I will simply indicate here that, for Althusser, Marxist philosophy is a 'theory of the differential nature of theoretical formations and their history, that is, a theory of epistemological history',[12] or, what comes to the same thing, 'the theory of the history of the production of knowledge'.[13] It is, in short, 'the theory of science and of the history of science.'[14] As such, a well-founded Marxist philosophy is indispensable to the science of historical materialism, in order to identify its fragile points, to pose clearly its problems so that they may be capable of solution, to give it the concepts adequate to its tasks, and to facilitate its path in those areas of study where it has only just begun, or has yet to begin, to make its way. As the vigilant guardian of its scientificity, dialectical materialism can assist in consolidating and defending historical materialism against the ideologies which threaten it both at its weak points and at its frontiers. But without this philosophical attention, the scientific activity, left to develop spontaneously, will be helpless in the face of these threats and open to the invasions of ideology. This has happened in the past and will continue to happen so long as the science lacks the explicit theory of its own practice.[15] This is why 'the theoretical future of historical materialism depends today on deepening dialectical materialism'.[16]

Enough has been said, then, to establish that what we can expect to find in Althusser's work is primarily an elaboration of this Marxist philosophy, dialectical materialism, a provisional specification of its precise character and content. In aiming for a clear presentation of this Althusserian construction, I shall avail myself of the following distinction. As theory of science and of its history, Althusser's dialectical materialism contains a series of concepts pertaining to the nature and process of theoretical knowledge, in other words, a set of *epistemological* concepts. In

[12] FM p. 38.

[13] RC pp. 56, 44, 75, 89, 157.

[14] RC pp. 145, 86, 153. Cf. Macherey who gives this conception of philosophy its most acute formulation: 'La philosophie n'est rien d'autre alors que la connaissance de l'histoire des sciences. Philosophes sont aujourd'hui ceux qui font l'histoire des théories, et *en même temps* la théorie de cette histoire . . . philosopher c'est étudier *dans quelles conditions*, et à *quelles conditions* sont posés des problèmes scientifiques.' L. Althusser, J. Rancière, P. Macherey, E. Balibar and R. Establet, *Lire le Capital*, 2 vols. (François Maspero, Paris, 1965), vol. I, p. 216.

[15] FM pp. 169–73; RC pp. 29–30, 89–90 n.5, 145–6.

[16] RC p. 77.

addition, to the extent that it functions as the theory of the particular science of historical materialism by reflecting on its concepts and problems, it incorporates a set of *historical* concepts. The two areas defined by this distinction (which is merely an expository convenience: as will be seen, the epistemological and historical concepts are integrally related) are, however, founded on one and the same first principle, which is principle of intelligibility for both. This principle is the central Althusserian concept of *practice* or *production*. The exposition will therefore proceed as follows: from i) a preliminary discussion of the concept of practice/production, to a consideration of ii) the epistemological concepts and iii) the historical concepts which are based upon it.

1. Practice/Production

The '*primacy of practice*' is established for Althusser 'by showing that all the levels of social existence are the sites of distinct practices',[17] and Marx's double achievement, scientific and philosophical, can be summed up precisely in this, that, in breaking with the inadequate, ideological concepts which governed the thinking of his youth, he founded 'a historico-dialectical materialism of *praxis*: that is, . . . a theory of the different specific *levels of human practice* (economic practice, political practice, ideological practice, scientific practice)'.[18] This concern to emphasize that each level (or instance)[19] of the social totality is a practice must not be permitted to obscure Althusser's insistence, equally forceful, that the various practices are nonetheless really distinct, and should not be collapsed into one undifferentiated notion of practice in general. For we shall see in due course that most of the theoretical errors and deviations, within, and outside, Marxism, which constitute the objects of his criticism, are put down in the last analysis to an incorrect understanding of the concept of practice, and, in particular, to a tendency to reduce or negate the distance between the practices. The concept has thus a polemical or negative function which complements its positive function of foundation-stone of the Althusserian system, and its performance of both functions is importantly determined by the distinctions

[17] RC p. 58.
[18] FM p. 229.
[19] See e.g. RC p. 97.

inscribed within it: 'we must recognize that there is no practice in general, but only *distinct practices*', for 'there can be no scientific conception of practice without a precise distinction between the distinct practices'.[20] I shall return in a moment to the principle of distinction.

The General Essence of Practice

It is necessary, first of all, to investigate the principle of unity, referred to by Althusser as 'the general essence of practice',[21] which makes possible a 'general definition of practice'[22] such that the different levels of social existence, whatever their concrete differences, are all equally practices. This principle of unity Althusser expresses as follows: 'By *practice* in general I shall mean any process of *transformation* of a determinate given raw material into a determinate *product*, a transformation effected by a determinate human labour, using determinate means (of "production"). In any practice thus conceived, the *determinant* moment (or element) is neither the raw material nor the product, but the practice in the narrow sense: the moment of the *labour of transformation* itself, which sets to work, in a specific structure, men, means and a technical method of utilizing the means.'[23]

Given this definition, politics, ideology and science (or theory), as well as economic production in the narrow sense, can all be regarded as forms of practice, to the extent that they all entail a transformation of a given raw material or object into a specific product by means of a labour process involving labourers and means of production – to the extent, that is to say, that each exemplifies 'the structure of a production',[24] that, as one of Althusser's critics has put it, they all share this 'homologous form'.[25] Thus in Althusser we find reference not only to the economic mode of production, combining in specific relations of production the elements of the material production process,[26] but also, for example, to 'the *mode* of theoretical production' or '*mode of*

[20] RC p. 58.
[21] FM pp. 188, n.26, 169.
[22] FM p. 167.
[23] FM pp. 166–67.
[24] RC p. 58.
[25] See A. Glucksmann, 'A Ventriloquist Structuralism' below.
[26] RC pp. 170–77.

production of knowledges,'[27] and to the 'mode of production of ideology'.[28] The same thing in Balibar's more extended treatment of this concept. The economic mode of production in every social formation is said to consist of a combination of the same few elements, namely, labourer, object of labour, means of labour, and non-labourer, in specific relations of production.[29] And, by extension, 'all the levels of the social structure have the structure of a "mode" in the sense in which I have analysed the mode of production strictly speaking'.[30] For, every level of the social structure, as the site of a distinct practice, is constituted by a set of similar elements, which are combined in specific social relations. Hence the scattered references to 'political social relations' and 'ideological social relations', as distinct from the economic relations of production.[31] These other relations represent combinations of the elements of political and ideological practice respectively.

We have, then, a general definition covering a number of particular practices by virtue of the formal similarities just discussed. But within this formal similarity there is a real dissimilarity of content separating the four major practices identified by Althusser. The dissimilarity of content consists in the fact that each practice has a different type of initial object or raw material which is transformed into a different type of product, by means, in each case, of a different type of 'labour' with different instruments of labour. Thus, where economic practice involves putting to work labour power and means of material production to transform natural or already worked-up materials into socially useful products, theoretical or scientific practice brings together 'thought power' and means of theoretical labour (the concepts of a theory and its method) to produce from concepts, representations, intuitions, a specific product: knowledges.[32] Political practice works on its own type of raw materials, given social relations, to produce its own type of product, new social relations. Ideological practice transforms the forms of representation and perception

[27] RC pp. 27, n.9, 41.
[28] RC p. 52.
[29] RC pp. 212–16.
[30] RC p. 220.
[31] RC pp. 140, 180, 220.
[32] FM pp. 167, 173; RC pp. 42, 59.

in which the agents of a social formation 'live' their relations with their world.[33] A respect for these real differences is the fundamental precondition for understanding the distinctive processes of the practices, their peculiar mechanisms and rhythms of development. For they all develop on their own sites, which are really distinct levels or instances of social reality: 'It is perfectly legitimate to say that the production of knowledge which is peculiar to theoretical practice constitutes a process that takes place *entirely in thought*, just as we can say, *mutatis mutandis*, that the process of economic production takes place entirely in the economy, even though it implies, and precisely in the specific determinations of its structure, necessary relations with nature and the other structures (legal-political and ideological) which, taken together, constitute the global structure of a social formation belonging to a determinate mode of production.'[34] The science of historical materialism, which is a theoretical practice, has precisely to study the different practices in their specificity, and their relations to one another in the complex unity of social practice which is the social formation.

What then of dialectical materialism? Within this, its own, conceptual universe it defines itself as the theory 'in which is theoretically expressed the essence of theoretical practice in general, through it the essence of practice in general, and through it the essence of the transformations, of the "development" of things in general'. As such, it is the materialist dialectic in person.[35] But if, in its generality, it is simply theory of practice, it has what might be called a principal aspect, thrown into relief by the primary Althusserian definition: dialectical materialism is, as already indicated, the theory of science or, as we are now in a position to say, 'the Theory of theoretical practice'.[36] In this guise, it embodies an epistemology.

2. Epistemological Concepts

'To conceive Marx's philosophy in its specificity is . . . to conceive knowledge as *production*.'[37] This much should already be clear.

[33] FM pp. 167, 175–76, 233.
[34] RC p. 42.
[35] FM pp. 168–69.
[36] FM pp. 171, 173, 256; RC p. 8.
[37] RC p. 34.

Althusser's own epistemology is simply an attempted elaboration of this 'new *conception of knowledge*'[38] disclosed to him by a critical reading of Marx. Its negative reference point, that which has to be rejected and abandoned in favour of this new conception, is empiricism: the conception of knowledge as *vision*.[39] And it is Althusser's radical and unremitting criticism of this latter conception which I shall take here as my point of departure.

The structure of the empiricist conception of knowledge is defined, according to Althusser, by a small number of central concepts: those of subject and object, of abstract and concrete, and of the given. The starting point of the knowledge process is conceived as 'a purely objective "given"', i.e., as something immediately visible and accessible to direct observation. But since what *is* so given is supposed to be the real (object) itself, the concrete, the starting point for knowledge must be concrete reality. The subject must perform on the latter an operation of abstraction in order to acquire thereby a knowledge of it.[40] This is empiricism's first mistake: it takes the initial object or raw material of theoretical practice to be reality itself. The function of the operation of abstraction which is performed by the subject is to disengage or extract from the real object its essence, to eliminate in the process everything inessential or incidental which obscures that essence. For, if the object itself is accessible to direct observation, its essence is not, and the act of abstraction has to render this visible, so that it may be seen, grasped and possessed. The sight and possession by the subject of the essence of the object is what constitutes knowledge. However, this conception of knowledge (and here is the crucial step in Althusser's argument), presupposing as it does a reality with two parts, actually inscribes within the structure of the real object to be known, the knowledge of that object. It does so by equating knowledge with one part of the real object, the essential part. Thus, the knowledge of a reality is conceived as part of that reality, and its only difference from the reality of which it is the knowledge is that it is merely part of it and not the whole of it.[41] This is empiricism's second mistake: it takes the product of theoretical practice, namely, knowledge, to be

[38] RC p. 35.
[39] RC pp. 19, 24.
[40] FM pp. 183–84, 190–91; RC pp. 43, 161, 183.
[41] RC pp. 35–40.

part of the reality known. It 'confuse[s] thought with the real by reducing thought about the real to the real itself'.[42]

From this it should be clear why Althusser rejects, as a contemporary variant of empiricism, the epistemology of *models*. Here again the model is conceived as providing knowledge of a reality by abstracting its essential from its inessential features. Reality, or the concrete, is then said to be 'always-richer-and-more-living' than the theory which attempts to comprehend it.[43] And we are face to face with a third deficiency of empiricism which is perfectly coherent with the first two: abstract theory is, at best, only an approximation of concrete reality. Theoretical concepts by their very nature (i.e., by virtue of being abstract) have a built-in inadequacy, an 'original weakness' which is their 'original sin'. In consequence, the possibility is lost of a knowledge fully adequate to the reality of which it is the knowledge. This deficiency, which marks both the philosophical efforts of Engels[44] and the writings of Feuerbach and the Young Marx,[45] must be banished, along with the other errors of empiricism, from the epistemology of dialectical materialism. We shall see in what follows that the basic concepts of empiricism, where Althusser retains them at all, are radically transformed and given a different content and role.

Thought and Reality

In the first place the distinction between abstract and concrete, representative for empiricism of the distinction between thought and reality, is transposed by Althusser into the realm of thought itself, and abstract and concrete there become raw material and product respectively of the process of production of knowledge. The latter takes place '*entirely in thought*', that is to say, wholly *within* what the empiricist would regard as abstraction, so that it 'never, as empiricism desperately demands it should, confronts *a pure object* which is . . . identical to the *real object*'.[46] This can be elaborated by reference to the three kinds of 'Generalities' discussed by Althusser. He calls Generalities I the concepts and

[42] RC p. 87.
[43] RC pp. 39, 117–18.
[44] RC pp. 82, 113–15.
[45] FM pp. 186–87.
[46] RC pp. 42–43.

abstractions which constitute the raw material of theoretical practice. This raw material to be transformed is never just a given, it is never concrete reality; it is always an already worked-up material consisting of abstract concepts which are the products of a previous practice. These concepts are partly scientific, the products of past theoretical practice, and partly ideological, the products of an ideological practice. And the raw material of ideological practice, in turn, is never reality itself. It always consists of abstractions, ideas, intuitions, which are themselves the results both of previous ideological practice and of other subsidiary practices (empirical, technical), which Althusser mentions in this connection without expatiating upon them. So the raw material from which theoretical practice 'begins' (the process cannot have an origin, strictly speaking)[47] is never reality as such, but always an abstraction of one sort or another. It is transformed by the application of means of theoretical production, Generalities II, into a product, Generalities III. The means of theoretical production are the basic concepts of a science at any given moment, more or less unified within a specific theoretical framework which will determine the problems capable of being posed and resolved by the science. And the Generalities III which are the product of theoretical practice are the scientific concepts embodying knowledge. Following Marx in the 1857 *Introduction* to *A Contribution to the Critique of Political Economy*, Althusser calls this product the *concrete-in-thought*: it is the synthesis of abstract concepts which provides knowledge of the *real-concrete*; but it is also, as a theoretical product, completely distinct from this real-concrete whose knowledge it provides. The process of knowledge 'ends' as it 'begins' entirely within thought.[48]

The distinction between thought and reality (between theoretical practice and the other practices) is, then, irreducible and, as such, it entails two theses which are essential to dialectical materialism: '(1) the materialist thesis of the primacy of the real over thought, since thought about the real presupposes the existence of the real, independent of that thought (the real *"survives in its independence, after as before, outside the head"* – *Grundrisse*, p. 22); and (2) the materialist thesis of the specificity of thought and of the thought

[47] RC pp. 62–64.
[48] Essential references for this paragraph: FM pp. 183–93. Cf. also RC pp. 41, 87–88, 90, 189–90.

process, with respect to the real and the real process'.[49] This is not a reductionist materialism. The point can be reinforced by indicating a shift in the terms by which Althusser attempts to register the distinction between thought and reality. In *For Marx* a distinction is made between the concrete-in-thought and the real-concrete, and the latter is, as that which is known by theory, the *object of knowledge*.[50] In *Reading Capital* this is no longer the case. To be sufficiently sharp, the same distinction now seems to require that the object of knowledge should be not the real-concrete, not the real object, but a different object, itself completely distinct from these. The object of knowledge is now situated within the realm of theoretical practice, and is a theoretical object, a concept or complex of concepts. Thus, 'the *object* of knowledge . . . [is] in itself absolutely distinct and different from the *real object* . . . the *idea* of the circle, which is the *object* of knowledge must not be confused with the circle, which is the *real object*.'[51] What impels Althusser to sunder the identity between real object and object of knowledge is, once again, his concern to emphasize that theoretical practice has its own raw material and its own product, both of them distinct from the reality it aims to know. The object of knowledge in the strict sense, i.e., in the sense of object worked upon and transformed in the process of production of knowledge, is this raw material and this product, which in turn becomes raw material. It cannot be the real object.[52]

There is, for all that, a 'relation between these two objects (the object of knowledge and the real object), a relation which constitutes the very existence of *knowledge*'.[53] This relation will be discussed more fully below. Suffice it to indicate here its essential implication: if the object of knowledge in the strict sense is *not* the real object, the object which is known finally, *via* the object of knowledge, *is* the real object. Theoretical practice achieves, through the object of knowledge, the cognitive appropriation of the real object called knowledge. More accurately, it ensures, by

[49] RC p. 87. I have modified the English translation slightly since it does not accurately reproduce the French text at this point.
[50] FM p. 186.
[51] RC p. 40 and *passim*.
[52] RC pp. 43, 156.
[53] RC p. 52.

means of the continual transformations it effects in the object of knowledge, the 'incessant deepening' of the knowledge of the real object. The latter therefore remains 'the *absolute reference point* for the process of knowledge which is concerned with it'.[54] Is this to say, borrowing a phrase used by Althusser in a different context, that the real object is the object of knowledge, 'but only in the last instance'?

The Role of the Problematic

In any case we must now examine the process of knowledge from the angle of that complex of Generalities II which Althusser calls the *problematic* of a science (or ideology). The term designates the theoretical (or ideological) framework which puts into relation with one another the basic concepts, determines the nature of each concept by its place and function in this system of relationships, and thus confers on each concept its particular significance. Since the concepts are only properly understood in the context of their problematic, they should not be regarded as so many discrete elements which can be isolated by analysis and compared with apparently similar elements belonging to another problematic. For, if the problematics in question are fundamentally different, any similarities established at the level of their respective elements will be, at best, superficial and, at worst, not really similarities at all. So construed, the problematic of a science (or ideology) governs not merely the solutions it is capable of providing but the very problems it can pose and the form in which they must be posed. It is a 'system of *questions*'. However, this problematic rarely exists in explicit and conscious form in the theory which it governs, so 'cannot generally be read like an open book'. It is, on the contrary, the unconscious structure of the theory 'buried but active' in it in the way that, as we have seen, Marx's philosophy is said to be buried but active in his scientific work. To be grasped, it has therefore to be 'dragged up from the depths'.[55]

Buried but active: let us look at these two characteristics of the problematic in turn and elicit their implications.

The problematic, by determining what it includes within its field, thereby necessarily determines what is excluded therefrom.

[54] RC p. 156. The italics here are mine. Cf. also pp. 41, 48, 64, 66, 87, 107.
[55] FM pp. 32, 39, 45–47, 62, 66–70.

The concepts which are excluded (absences, lacunae), and the problems which are not posed adequately (semi-silences, lapses), or posed at all (silences), are therefore as much a part of the problematic as are the concepts and problems that are present. And it cannot for that very reason be grasped by a simple literal or immediate reading of the explicit discourse of a text. Rather it must be reached by a 'symptomatic' reading where the explicit discourse is read conjointly with the absences, lacunae and silences which, constituting a second 'silent discourse', are so many symptoms of the unconscious problematic buried in the text. Like all knowledge, reading, correctly understood and correctly practised, is not vision but theoretical labour and production.[56] This is the theoretical basis, if you like, of Althusser's insistence, alluded to in the introduction to this article, on the need for a critical reading of Marx. It is also the clue to the enigmatic Althusserian 'circle': the problematic of Marx's philosophy, buried in his mature scientific works, is only accessible if one knows how to read correctly, i.e., if one knows that knowledge is production, which is itself a principle essential to the problematic of Marx's philosophy. The elaboration and refinement of Marxist philosophical principles therefore requires that one disposes of them already in at least provisional form and can apply them in the theoretical practice of elaboration and refinement.[57]

As regards the *activity* of the implicit, unconscious, problematic, it is intended in the strongest possible sense. In words which we are enjoined by Althusser to take 'literally', the problematic is assigned those functions which other epistemologies, such as empiricism, attribute to a human subject: 'The sighting is thus no longer the act of an individual subject, endowed with the faculty of "vision" which he exercises either attentively or distractedly; the sighting is the act of its structural conditions, it is the relation of immanent reflection between the field of the problematic and *its* objects and *its* problems. . . . It is literally no longer the eye (the mind's eye) of a subject which *sees* what exists in the field defined by a theoretical problematic: it is this field itself which *sees itself* in the objects or problems it defines . . . the invisible is no more a

[56] RC pp. 15–33, 50, 86, 143–44.
[57] FM pp. 38–39, 165–66; RC pp. 34, 74.

function of *a subject's sighting* than is the visible: the invisible is the theoretical problematic's non-vision of its non-objects, the invisible is the darkness, the blinded eye of the theoretical problematic's self-reflection when it scans its non-objects, its non-problems without seeing them, *in order not to look at them.*'[58] This passage, in which a theoretical *structure*, the problematic, is represented as the determinant element in the process of production of knowledge, so that the human subject ceases to be the subject of the process in the strict sense, is no mere polemical excess on Althusser's part. It is typical. The Althusserian universe is governed by structures and the only subjects that populate it are those subject *to* this government, their places and functions marked out for them by its ubiquitous hegemony. The elaboration of this particular theme will be undertaken in connection with the historical concepts in Althusser's work.

The Epistemological Break

It was intimated above that the problematic is a category as applicable to ideological as it is to scientific practice. But we know that these are two distinct practices, and the distinction can be said, provisionally, to consist in this, that an ideological concept 'designates' an existing reality, but does not, like a scientific concept, 'provide us with a means of knowing' it.[59] For Althusser, this means that there must be a radical qualitative difference between the problematic of an ideology and that of a science, for all that one may be able to discover 'similar' elements by abstracting these illegitimately from their respective problematics. In other words, a science is founded only at the cost of a complete rupture with the ideological problematic which precedes it, a thorough-going mutation of its basic structure. This rupture or mutation which founds a science Althusser calls an *epistemological break*. The role of the human subject in it is, again, subordinate: 'In this process of real transformation of the means of production of knowledge, the claims of a "constitutive subject" are as vain as are the claims of the subject of vision in the production of the visible. . . . The whole process takes place in the dialectical crisis of the mutation of a theoretical structure in which the "subject"

[58] RC pp. 25–26.
[59] FM p. 223.

plays, not the part it believes it is playing, but the part which is assigned to it by the mechanism of the process.'[60] Be that as it may, it is just such an epistemological break which is said to separate Marx, founder of the science of historical materialism, not only from his predecessors (Hegel, Feuerbach, Smith, Ricardo, etc.) but also from the ideological conceptions of his own youth. The break, situated by Althusser in 1845, is not a 'clean' one: 'Indispensable theoretical concepts do not magically construct themselves on command',[61] and ideological concepts survive in the works of Marx's maturity. So we see, once again, the need for a critical reading, able properly to locate the epistemological break in Marx, by distinguishing between the scientific and the ideological *throughout* his writings.[62]

It remains to ask: if science produces knowledge, what are the criteria which guarantee that this knowledge is true, that it is indeed knowledge? The question, according to Althusser, is 'false', and the classical Problem of Knowledge is not a 'real problem'. Any epistemology that sees the relation between the object of knowledge and the real object as a problematic one, i.e., that regards knowledge itself as a problem, is simply ideological and to be rejected for that reason.[63] Rejecting the problem, Althusser rejects the available solutions to it, including pragmatism: 'It has been possible to apply Marx's theory with success because it is "true"; it is not true because it has been applied with success'. The whole matter is a non-problem because '*Theoretical practice* is . . . its own criterion, and contains in itself definite protocols with which to *validate* the quality of its product'. The established sciences 'themselves provide the criterion of validity of their knowledges'.[64] These criteria of validation internal to the theoretical practice of a science are its 'forms of proof' which, unfolding in the ordered discourse of the science, have the specific

[60] RC p. 27.

[61] RC p. 51.

[62] On the epistemological break, see, apart from the references already given, FM pp. 32–37, 167–68, 185, 192–93, and RC pp. 44–46, 90, 131, 133, 140, 146–57. In this connection it should be said that Althusser, stressing Marx's '*blinding*' 'novelty' (RC p. 78), refuses the conception of continuity in discontinuity embodied in the Hegelian notion of supersession ('Aufhebung'). Reasons of space prevent me from going into this. See FM pp. 76–78, 82, 188–89, 198.

[63] RC pp. 52–55; FM p. 186.

[64] RC pp. 56–9.

effect (called by Althusser the 'knowledge effect') of providing a cognitive grasp of reality. And the *mechanism* which produces this effect is the overall conceptual system of the science, since it determines not only the meaning of the concepts but also the 'order of their appearance in the discourse of the proof'.[65] *That* the effect produced is knowledge is no problem; *how* it is produced is. In other words, the only real problem according to Althusser is to understand the precise nature of the aforesaid mechanism.[66] To this real problem he does not claim to give an answer.[67]

3. Historical Concepts

What is the nature of the social formations studied by historical materialism? What are societies? 'They present themselves as totalities whose unity is constituted by a certain specific type of *complexity*, which introduces instances, that, following Engels, we can, very schematically, reduce to three: the economy, politics and ideology.'[68] We know already that each of these instances (levels), being a practice, combines, in social relations specific to itself, a set of formally similar elements, and that the resultant combination exhibits, in each case, the structure of a (mode of) production. We know, in short, that the different instances are *structures*, so that what Althusser refers to as the 'global structure' of the social formation or social whole[69] is itself 'a structure of structures'.[70] We must now examine the complexity of this global structure as conceived by Althusser. I shall approach his conception of complexity via the conception of simplicity he rejects, or – for it amounts to the same thing – I shall approach Althusser's Marx here by way of Althusser's Hegel.

The problematic of Hegelian idealism may be regarded as an 'inversion' of the empiricist problematic discussed earlier. It shares with empiricism a basic structural similarity in that it too 'confuse[s] thought and the real'; but it does so 'by *reducing* the

[65] RC pp. 67–68.
[66] RC p. 56.
[67] RC p. 61.
[68] FM pp. 231–32. It should be noted that *science* is **not** counted here as an instance of the social formation. In other Althusserian formulations it is. The significance of this inconsistency is discussed in Part II of this article.
[69] RC pp. 42, 180.
[70] RC p. 17.

real to thought, by *"conceiving the real as the result of thought"*.[71] This reduction, evidently the exact inverse of that perpetrated by empiricism, is embodied in the Hegelian conceptions of history and of the epochs, or social totalities, into which it can be periodized. All the phenomena of any one epoch (its economy, its polity and law, its philosophy, art and religion, its ethics, its customs, etc.) are merely the externalizations of one moment of the development of the Idea, i.e. of one internal *spiritual* principle which is the *essence* of those phenomena, manifesting itself in each and all of them, and expressed by each and all of them. Thus, for example, the essence of Rome, pervading its whole history and its manifold institutions, is the principle of the 'abstract legal personality'; the essence of the modern world, equally pervasive, is 'subjectivity'. And Hegel conceives every social totality in this manner as having a unique internal spiritual principle to which all the diverse realities can be reduced, since each of them is only an expression of it. Althusser therefore calls the Hegelian totality a 'spiritual' or 'expressive' type of totality, aiming by these designations to underscore the following: its apparent complexity conceals an essential simplicity, in the sense that the complex of diverse phenomena (appearances) is reducible to a single and simple essence. A sort of cross-section through the historical process at any point – what Althusser terms an *essential section* – will always reveal such an essence, one particular moment of the development of the Idea, manifest and legible in the multitude of social phenomena coexisting at that point in time. For, the historical process is nothing but the linear time continuum in which the Idea unfolds its potentialities, its successive moments. And the several totalities which follow one another are merely the successive expressions of these successive moments. As such, they belong, in all their aspects and instances, in all their apparent richness and complexity, to the same unique continuum in which the Idea unfolds. Their history is reducible to its history, in other words to one all-embracing history, which shares the simplicity of the Hegelian social totality, and by virtue of the same reductions. The conception, which reflects this simplicity, of a unique linear time continuum, is one 'borrowed from the most vulgar empiricism' and 'representative of the crude ideological illusions of

---

[71] RC pp. 46–47, 87; FM p. 188.

everyday practice'; the only difference being that where the empiricist sees a series of events deployed on this continuum, Hegel sees the several moments of the Idea. The difference is explained by the inverse nature of the reductions committed by empiricism and Hegel respectively.[72]

Marxism, according to Althusser, breaks once and for all with the reductionism of this idealist/empiricist problematic, and with its conception of the 'simple unity' of an 'original essence', and establishes complexity as its principle: 'Where reality is concerned, we are never dealing with the pure existence of simplicity, be it essence or category, but with the existence of "concretes", of complex and structured beings and processes.'[73] Accordingly, complexity is central to the Marxist conception of the social formation, and this by virtue of the principle, already enunciated, that the various structures (practices, instances) of which it is constituted are irreducibly distinct and different.[74] They cannot, as with Hegel, be regarded as the mere expressions of a single spiritual essence which is immanent in them all without being exclusive to any one of them. But nor should one of them be conceived as the essence to which the others, as its phenomena, can be reduced. Thus, when Marx distinguishes the different instances of the social formation into a structure (the economic base, comprising forces and relations of production), and superstructures (politics, law, ideology, etc.), and assigns to the former the primary determining role, this is not in order to make it an essence of which the superstructures would then be so many phenomena, the mere passive effects of its unique determinism. Such a conception, economism or mechanism,[75] is a 'deviation' foreign to scientific Marxism, simplifying the complexities of the social formation and hence incapable of understanding it.

The Law of Overdetermination

The superstructures are realities which are distinct from the economic structure. Indeed, they are its conditions of existence just as it is theirs, since economic production never takes place in a

[72] FM pp. 101–104, 202–204; RC pp. 93–97, 103.
[73] FM pp. 197–99.
[74] For this and the following two paragraphs, see FM pp. 94–117, 176–80, 200–18, and RC pp. 97–99, 106–107, 177–78.
[75] Cf. RC p. 111.

void; it only ever exists within the matrix of a global social totality comprising instances other than the economic. These non-economic, superstructural instances have their *specific effectivity* which means, first, that they are determining as well as determined; second, and in consequence, that the economy is determined as well as determining; and, third, that every instance contributes in its own right to determining the nature of the overall configuration of which it is a part, as well as being determined by it in turn. By the same token there is not one simple economic contradiction, that between the forces and relations of production, which governs everything. There is rather a multiplicity of contradictions existing at all levels of the social formation and constituting a kind of hierarchy of effectivities within it. So, determination is never simple but always complex and multiple, and this Althusser encapsulates in the concept of *overdetermination*. Is this to replace historical materialism by a sort of methodological pluralism? No. The autonomy of the superstructures is relative and not absolute, and their specific effectivity does not eliminate the primacy of the economy which for Althusser, following Engels, is still determinant 'in the last instance': '[The] specific *relations* between structure and superstructure still deserve theoretical elaboration and investigation. However, Marx has at least given us the "two ends of the chain", and has told us to find out what goes on between them: on the one hand, *determination in the last instance by the (economic) mode of production*; on the other, *the relative autonomy of the superstructures and their specific effectivity*.'[76] We may consider briefly what Althusser himself offers by way of theoretical elaboration.

The different structures of the social formation are themselves related as the constituent elements of a global structure, said to be *decentred* since its elements do not derive from one original essence, their centre, as do those of the Hegelian totality. This global structure contains a dominant element, not to be confused with the element which is determinant in the last instance, viz., the economy, since 'in real history determination in the last instance by the economy is exercised precisely in the permutations of the principal role between the economy, politics, theory, etc.'[77] To

---

[76] FM p. III.
[77] FM p. 213.

dispel the apparent paradox of an economy determinant in the last instance, but not necessarily always dominant, determination in the last instance is defined as follows: the economy determines for the non-economic elements their respective degrees of autonomy/dependence in relation to itself and to one another, thus their differential degrees of specific effectivity. It can determine itself as dominant or non-dominant at any particular time, and in the latter case it determines which of the other elements is to be dominant.[78] In any case, while one element can displace another to assume the dominant role, such variations occur within a structure which is *invariant* to the extent that it always has a dominant element, and this is what Althusser intends by calling the social formation a *structure in dominance.* But, for a Marxist political practice which aims to transform this invariant structure in dominance by revolution, the knowledge of its invariance is not sufficient. It must, if it is to be successful, be based on the most exact knowledge of the variations and the specific situations which they successively produce. The precise relations of domination and subordination between the different levels of the structure, the complex of contradictions which it embodies, their relative importance and reciprocal influence – all this must be grasped as defining the current *conjuncture* in which political action is to occur. The one thing that can be said in general is that successful revolution is never the simple outcome of the economic contradiction between forces and relations of production.[79] It requires the fusion or condensation of a multiplicity of contradictions, since it too is subject to the overriding law: overdetermination.

It may here be added that, with this concept, dialectical materialism reaches the conception 'of the development of things' which is the Marxist or materialist dialectic.[80] The concept has further ramifications which must now be elaborated.

Differential Historical Time

If the simplicity of the Hegelian totality is rejected, then so too is the simplicity of Hegelian history. The different instances of the

---

[78] Cf. FM p. 255; and Balibar, RC pp. 220–24.

[79] In this connection see Balibar's analysis of Marx's notion of the *tendencies* of the capitalist mode of production. RC pp. 283–93.

[80] FM p. 217.

social formation not being reducible to an original essence, the histories of these instances cannot be subsumed under a unique, all-embracing history which is the mere succession of such essences. On the contrary, each relatively autonomous level of the whole has its own relatively autonomous history, marked by its own rhythms of development and its own continuities, and punctuated in its own specific way by those mutations, breaks or ruptures which constitute its revolutionary events. Thus, there is a history of the economic structure, a history of the political superstructure, a history of ideology, a history of science, and so on. These differential histories are said to be *dislocated* with respect to one another in order to stress their irreducibility, the real differences between their respective rhythms, continuities and discontinuities. For Althusser this means in addition that there cannot be a unique linear time continuum common to all these histories, and against which they can all be measured.[81] The ideology of a simple time falls with the ideology of a simple history, to be replaced by the notion of a complex historical time constituted by the 'differential times' of the different levels. However, one must not infer from the irreducibility of these histories and times their absolute independence in relation to one another. They are no more absolutely independent than are the levels of the social formation of which they are the histories and times. In other words, their independence is the *relative* independence compatible with, and complementary to, their determination in the last instance by the economy, i.e., their relative dependence. The complexity of historical time is, thus, a function of the complexity (overdetermination) of the social formation, and it follows that a section through the historical process will reveal, not an original, omnipresent essence, but a particular overdetermined conjuncture of that complex formation. For the authentic Marxist conception of history, the essential section is impossible.[82]

Now we have seen that one form of ignorance of this authentic Marxist conception is economism. Another, which has vitiated the theoretical efforts of many Marxists, from Lukács, Korsch, and Gramsci to Della Volpe, Colletti and Sartre, is historicism.[83]

---

[81] RC pp. 104–105.

[82] RC pp. 99–109.

[83] For the account of historicism which follows, see RC pp. 105–106, 119–43, and FM pp. 22–24, 31, 171 n.7.

I shall not give an exhaustive account of the latter here, since it represents a sort of compendium of all the mistaken notions we have already encountered (which is not suprising, all of them being variants or effects of a common, reductionist sin): its basis is the empiricist reduction of the object of knowledge to the real object; it negates the differences between the practices; it has, in consequence, a Hegelian conception of the social totality, and regards historical time as a linear continuum susceptible to the essential section; etc. I shall therefore limit myself to indicating the element of the historicist interpretation of Marxism on which Althusser himself lays greatest emphasis, defining it as its 'symptomatic point': namely, its conception of scientific and philosophical knowledge, hence of Marxism itself.

The Irreducibility of Science

Because of the reductions it countenances, the historicist inter-pretation tends to deprive theoretical practice, or science, of its specificity, to assimilate it to the other practices, ideological, political and economic, and ultimately to dissolve them all in a single notion of practice in general: historical practice or, simply, praxis. The history of knowledge thus loses its relative autonomy to become one with the unique 'real history' of the social totality. Marxism itself can then be regarded, not as a specific scientific practice developing on its own site, but as 'the direct product . . . of the activity and experience of the masses',[84] of their political and ideological practice, or as the self-consciousness (class consciousness) of the proletariat. For Althusser this is a 'leftist' conception whose political effect is to legitimate spontaneism, and whose theoretical effect is to relate the content and history of science to class conflict as its criterion of explanation – Marxism becomes the 'proletarian science' which confronts and challenges 'bourgeois science'. Against this theoretical effect, which is also a 'theoretical monstrosity', he insists that the criterion of class has its limits and cannot explain the relatively autonomous history of science. He therefore takes Gramsci to task for regarding science as a superstructure: 'This is to attribute to the concept "super-structure" a breadth Marx never allowed, for he only ranged within it: (1) the politico-legal superstructure, and (2) the ideological

superstructure (the corresponding "forms of social consciousness"): except in his Early Works (especially the *1844 Manuscripts*), Marx *never included scientific knowledge in it*. Science can
no more be ranged within the category "superstructure" than
can language, which as Stalin showed escapes it . . . [one must
therefore distinguish] between the relatively autonomous and
peculiar history of scientific knowledge and the other modalities
of historical existence (those of the ideological and politico-legal
superstructures, and that of the economic structure)'.[85] In view
of this, there can be no direct equation between the science of
Marxism and the ideology of the proletariat. And spontaneism is
therefore rejected in favour of 'Kautsky's and Lenin's thesis that
Marxist theory is produced by a specific theoretical practice,
outside the proletariat, and . . . must be *"imported"* into the working class movement'.[86]

There is one other consequence of the historicist interpretation
of Marxism which should be mentioned. By depriving theoretical
practice of all specificity, it deprives of its rationale that discipline,
Marxist philosophy, which takes theoretical practice as its object
of study. The historicist interpretation does not therefore recognize the distinction between dialectical materialism, the theory of
science, and historical materialism, the science of social formations. On the contrary, the former is absorbed by the latter which
does adequate service as a comprehensive theory of history, and a
distinction which is crucial for Althusser is lost.

It is time, however, to take up another distinction, equally
crucial: that between science and ideology. If it has been with us
throughout the course of this exposition – in the notion that
ideology threatens science at its weak points, in the concept of the
epistemological break, in the opposition postulated between
Marxism and the ideology of the proletariat – this is because it is
implicit in the definition of Marxism as a science. To be complete,
the distinction requires some account of the Althusserian definition of ideology, an account which may take as its point of departure what has already been indicated provisionally, namely, that,
unlike a science, an ideology does not provide us with adequate
instruments of *knowledge*.

It fails to do so because 'it is governed by "interests" beyond

[85] RC p. 133.
[86] RC p. 141. Translation modified.

the necessity of knowledge alone', or, to put the same thing slightly differently, because it 'reflects many "interests" other than those of reason.'[87] These interests may be religious, ethical or political, but they are in all cases 'extra-theoretical instances and exigencies' which impose on an ideology both its solutions and its problems and, thus, constitute its real (practical) ends or objectives.[88] So, 'ideology, as a system of representations, is distinguished from science in that in it the practico-social function is more important than the theoretical function (function as knowledge)'.[89] The precise nature of this practico-social function will of course depend upon the nature of the social formation in question. In particular, in a class society it will be such as to legitimate relations of exploitation by concealing them from exploiters and exploited alike. Nevertheless, whatever its nature, it is a function that must be fulfilled in every society, since men must be *formed, transformed and equipped to respond to the demands of their conditions of existence'*. And this requires ideology, a system of ideas, beliefs and values by which men live and experience their world. Ideology is therefore an essential part of every society, not excluding a classless, communist society.[90] For Althusser, moreover, it should not be equated with the ambiguous and idealist category of 'consciousness', since this might tend to suggest that it is a purely subjective phenomenon, freely chosen. But ideology is neither. It is, on the contrary, an objective structure of the social formation, which is imposed on most men by a mechanism they do not understand, a mechanism which determines that structure as the *objective* mode of appearance of reality.[91] This is the mechanism which Marx termed *fetishism* and which is embraced by the Althusserian notion of *structural causality*.

Structural Causality

The latter is meant to describe the determination of its regional structures (ideology being one of them) by the global structure in

[87] RC pp. 141, 58.
[88] RC pp. 52–55, 183.
[89] FM p. 231.
[90] FM pp. 191, 231–36; RC p. 177. Althusser distinguishes different levels of ideology. Its 'reflected forms' (FM p. 233) are pre- or non-scientific 'philosophies'. But the distinction does not affect the basic definition of ideology as dominated by a practico-social, rather than theoretical function.
[91] FM p. 233; RC pp. 17, 66, 191.

dominance of the social formation, as well as the determination by these regional structures of their own constituent elements. It describes, in short, the effect of a whole on its parts, 'the effectivity of a structure on its elements'. This is a new concept of causality, existing in Marx's scientific work 'in a practical state' and requiring theoretical elaboration from Marxist philosophy. Pre-Marxist philosophy had, according to Althusser, only two concepts of causality: linear or transitive causality, able to describe the effect of one element on another, but not of the whole on its parts; and expressive causality, which could describe the determination of the parts by the whole, but only by reducing it to an essence of which they would be the phenomena, i.e., by simplifying the whole. The concept of structural causality is distinct from both. From the first, because the structure is a cause present or immanent in its elements/effects, rather than exterior to them. And from the second, because it exists only in the totality of these elements/ effects and their relations; it is not completely present in any *one* of them but, as Althusser puts it, 'is only present there, as a structure, in its *determinate* absence'. The structure can, in this sense, be described as both present and absent in its effects.[92]

In any case, on the concept of structural causality is based the Althusserian definition of Marxism as a '*theoretical anti-human-ism*', and of humanism as an ideology. It is not men that make history. They are not the subjects of the process. And a scientific knowledge of social reality cannot be founded on an anthropology embodying a concept of human nature or of the essence of man. Rather, the 'absolute precondition' of such knowledge is 'that the philosophical (theoretical) myth of man is reduced to ashes', and that 'we do completely without [its] *theoretical services*'.[93] So, though humanism may still have a role to play as an ideology, its rejection for scientific purposes is complete and unambiguous. Nor is this affected by the centrality of the notion of practice. For, as we know, each practice is a structure, and, as such, exercises its determination over the elements it combines or relates – men, objects of labour and instruments of labour. Men cannot therefore be regarded as the active subjects of the process. They

---

[92] RC pp. 180–93.
[93] FM pp. 36–37, 227–30, 243–44; RC p. 119. As part of the humanist problematic, the concept of *alienation* is also ideological. Cf. FM pp. 158–59, 214–15, 239.

are simply its 'supports': 'The structure of the relations of production determines the *places* and *functions* occupied and adopted by the agents of production, who are never anything more than the occupants of these places, insofar as they are the "supports" (*Träger*) of these functions. The true "subjects" (in the sense of constitutive subjects of the process) are therefore not these occupants or functionaries, are not, despite all appearances, the "obviousnesses" of the "given" of naive anthropology, "concrete individuals", "real men" – but *the definition and distribution of these places and functions. The true "subjects" are these definers and distributors: the relations of production* (and political and ideological social relations). But since these are "relations", they cannot be thought within the category *subject*'.[94] Balibar has expressed this by saying that 'individuals are merely the effects' of the different practices, and that 'each relatively autonomous practice . . . engenders forms of historical individuality which are peculiar to it'.[95]

Thus, the human subject is definitively abolished, and the exposition ends, as it began, with the 'primacy of practice': first and last principle of Althusserian Marxism.

II Assessment

The assessment which follows neither aims nor claims to be exhaustive. It concentrates on certain problems in Althusser's work at the expense of certain others. This calls for a few explanatory remarks.

In the first place, I do not propose to consider the reading of Marx Althusser offers us and to judge it *as a reading of Marx*, endorsing or challenging its various points by reference to some alternative reading of Marx. This is not because such an exercise is entirely fruitless. On the contrary, to the extent that some of the crucial weaknesses in Althusser's work relate, it seems to me, to points where he has seriously misread Marx (and Lenin for that matter), and where Marx (and Lenin) are right against Althusser, it is an exercise which may help to focus on these weaknesses and bring them thoroughly to light.[96] It remains the case, nevertheless,

94 RC p. 180, Cf. pp. 139–40, 174–75.
95 RC pp. 251–53. Cf. Althusser p. 112.
96 See, for example, Michael Löwy, 'L'Humanisme Historiciste de Marx ou Relire Le Capital', *L'Homme et la Société*, No. 17, July/Aug/Sept. 1970, pp. 111–25.

that if Althusser is wrong, it is not simply *because* he departs from Marx. His errors and deficiencies can therefore be exposed for themselves without specific recourse to the classical texts of the revolutionary Marxist tradition. The latter procedure steers clear of judging Althusser in the name of any dogma.[97]

What I do propose to consider are a number of problems relating to Althusser's conceptions of science and scientificity, and of the relations between scientific and the other practices. Since Althusser defines his project as philosophical, and philosophy as the theory of science, it is not surprising that many of the difficulties in his work are concentrated in these conceptions. In particular, I shall argue that he produces an account of science that is idealist, paradoxical as this may sound, and an account of the relation between Marxist theory and Marxist politics that is both theoretically incorrect and politically harmful.

Secondly: I will therefore add that the predominantly critical tone of this assessment should not be taken as an indication that I judge Althusser's work unworthy of serious attention, and, to forestall misunderstandings of this kind, I shall suggest, briefly, the areas in which his theoretical contribution seems to me to be important.

The Positive Achievements

Althusser has tried to forge and refine the concepts which will separate Marxism once and for all from the forms of reductionism (economism, spontaneism, etc.) which have compromised it since

[97] It has the additional advantage that it does not risk being brushed aside as the product of a merely uncritical (literal, immediate, etc.) reading of Marx. That the Althusserian *practice* of critical reading (the *theory*, as I shall argue, deserves serious consideration) leaves much to be desired is a point I do not propose to argue here. The following remarks must suffice: this practice has achieved its *reductio ad absurdum* with Althusser's recent assertion that Marx's only works '*totally and definitively exempt* from *any* trace of Hegelian influence' are . . . the *Critique of the Gotha Programme* and the *Marginal Notes on Wagner* (LP p. 90). Althusser is, of course, perfectly entitled to reject as much of Marx as he finds deficient, arguing the case as best he can. He can reject the whole of Marx if necessary. But to claim that it is *Marx* who definitively breaks with Hegel while admitting that Marx's work, almost in its entirety, is marked by Hegelian influences; more generally, to claim, against the explicit letter of Marx's texts, that Marx is not *really* saying what he manifestly *is* saying (example: Marx on the ahistorical categories of classical political economy, RC, pp. 91–92) – these are claims indeed. Do they not install behind a facade of anti-dogmatism what is in fact merely a very special kind of dogmatism – one which insists on claiming the authority of Marx for all it deems scientific?

its inception. Such forms have always been unable to comprehend the realities confronting the revolutionary socialist movement, realities whose names are: fascism, imperialism, the national question, combined and uneven development, racism, 4 August 1914; but also permanent revolution, the bureaucratization of the Soviet state, the debacle of the Comintern; and they have been unable to do so because these realities are, in every case, complex ones, not adequately explicable by unique reference to a single origin, whether this be the development of the economy or other. In the concept of overdetermination and its related concepts (specific effectivity, relative autonomy, determination in the last instance, structure in dominance) Althusser has tried clearly to pose and to respond to the exigency according to which they must be thought in the complex combination of their economic, political, ideological and theoretical causes and effects if they are to be adequately grasped and adequately dealt with. Of course, these realities have been understood, and well understood, before Althusser produced his work – not only by those whom he reads (Marx, Engels, Lenin) but also by those whom he does not read (Trotsky: symptomatic Althusserian silence). The pages of their works accordingly bear witness to the most acute awareness of the exigency which Althusser has posed.[98] To say this, however, is not to detract from his own achievement, and two reasons may be offered as to why it does not.

The first is a reason adduced by Althusser himself. If Marxist theory is to be freed, and decisively freed, from all traces of reductionism, it is not enough that its most outstanding practitioners should have avoided, in the analyses of the concrete problems and concrete situations they faced, the practice of reductionism. The theory which sustained their practice is also required. The classical texts do not always give us this theory in an explicit and rigorous form, lapsing occasionally, and even in some of their most famous formulations, into a simplistic conception of the social whole. Althusser has tried to provide it by

[98] I cite only Trotsky, since Althusser takes care of the others: see, as a few examples among dozens from his work, *Results and Prospects* (New Park Publications, London, 1962), pp. 194–200; *The First Five Years of the Communist International*, Vol. I (Pioneer Publishers, New York, 1945), pp. 50–63; *Through What Stage Are We Passing?* (New Park Publications, London, 1965), pp. 3–19, 34–36; *The Third International After Lenin* (Pioneer Publishers, New York, 1957), pp. 81–82, 96; etc.

posing, not only in relation to this or that concrete example, but for and of itself, the problem of the specificity of the different practices/instances and of their complex interrelationship. If, as we shall see with his conception of science, he has not answered all the questions he has asked, this does not deprive him of the merit of having asked clearly, without prevarication, and at length, questions which are crucial to the development of Marxist theory.

The second reason relates to the need, signalled in the introduction to this article, to situate Althusser in that theoretical context which makes him define his work as an intervention against Hegelian and humanist Marxism. Measured now, not against the classics of revolutionary Marxism, but against some of the writers who are the specific objects of his criticism, Althusser's achievement is thrown more sharply into relief. Lukács and Korsch, for example, in their very reaction against the economism of the Second International, do not avoid reductionism themselves, offering a conception of the social whole which falls squarely under the Althusserian category of the expressive or spiritual totality.[99] It is also the case, even if one does not share Althusser's view of them, that the great themes at the core of this tradition, of humanism and alienation, are not, *taken by themselves*, adequate to grasping any of the diverse social realities enumerated above. Unless they are specified in the concepts with which Marx thinks the complexity of the social formation, these themes can just as easily lead to interminable philosophical ruminations on, for example, the ethical bases of Marxism as they can to new knowledges of concrete problems – and since the discovery of Marx's Early Works they have done. Bearing in mind, then, that it is this

[99] But one should avoid oversimplification. Take Korsch: in *Marxism and Philosophy* (NLB, London, 1970), he espouses, and in a very explicit form, a conception of totality which is expressive (see, especially, pp. 41–42), and it is this conception which governs his thought. At the same time, and however contradictory this may be, what he denies in this conception he also tries to affirm by insisting on the reality and irreducibility, that is to say, the relative autonomy, of ideology (see, for example, pp. 62–64, 84–85). If the affirmation does not succeed in freeing itself from the weight of the denial, Korsch is still worth the kind of critical reading which may perform that liberation, worth more, in any case, than the off-hand remark with which Althusser dismisses him as one of those who 'were lost later' (RC, p. 120). Lost, in the first instance, to and from the Communist movement: this loss was not unrelated to the descent of that movement into Stalinism. It should also be said that being lost did not prevent Korsch from writing an excellent book on Marx – see his *Karl Marx*, New York, 1963.

tradition and these themes, unilaterally interpreted, that have come to exercise an almost hegemonic influence within Western Marxism, and that this is the context in which Althusser has produced his work, his theoretical efforts in the area under discussion must be given their due.

It is also my view that the concept of the problematic, as elaborated by Althusser, represents a substantial contribution to the Marxist theory of ideology and of science. As has been intimated above, I do not find tenable the particular reading of Marx that Althusser has, by his use of this and related concepts, proposed,[100] although, for the reasons given, this point will not be argued here. It is a concept, nevertheless, which forces us to regard theoretical and ideological ensembles in their unity, and not as arbitrary agglomerations of discrete and self-sufficient elements such that these elements might be torn from their context without this altering their significance. By doing so, it undermines such teleological approaches as are ready to find germs and anticipations of Marx's mature theory even in his most youthful, schoolboy essays, and the superficial argument that, because the term 'alienation' is common to the *1844 Manuscripts* and *Capital*, it is the same concept, with the same role and importance, that is present in those works. Althusser has been perfectly right to challenge notions such as these, to try to isolate the analytical assumptions which legitimate them, and to focus on the eclecticism which they involve. By theorizing, against them, the concept of the problematic, he has laid the basis for a more systematic approach to the study of theories, ideologies, and their histories.

The Contradictions of Althusserian Science

This said, we can proceed to the main point: science. Even here some of the impulses which motivate Althusser's positions must be recognized as fundamentally correct, and these may be enumerated in the form of two, intimately related theses:

(1) Scientific knowledge *in its content* is universal and objective, not dependent for its *validity* on the values and perspectives of this social group or that historical epoch, not therefore merely a matter

---

[100] I have given some indications as to why I do not in 'Essence and Appearance: Aspects of Fetishism in Marx's *Capital*', *New Left Review*, No. 65, Jan/Feb 1971, pp. 69–85.

of opinion or of interest. By emphasizing this, Althusser reasserts knowledge's rights against all forms of relativism, which, 'proving' in their theories of knowledge, of ideology and utopia, that all knowledge is necessarily partial and subjective, cannot escape the contradiction and embarrassment of claiming to be the knowledge of the impossibility of knowledge.

(2) Scientific knowledge is not immediately and directly (i.e. miraculously) *given* in the consciousness of an individual or class, but has its specific *conditions and processes of production*, which involve, among other things, the activity of theoretical labour. By emphasizing this, Althusser reminds us that scientific activity is a *reality* (as real as the realities it studies and on no account reducible to them): to identify its products with what is immediately given in consciousness is to deny its rationale and thereby its very reality.

The difficulties, however, begin from here. In the first place, some of the arguments by which Althusser attempts to sustain these theses lead us straight into the realms of mystery. He rejects, as empiricist, the idea that concrete reality might form part of the raw material of theoretical practice, insisting that the process of production of knowledge takes place entirely in thought: this does not prevent him from arguing that the science of political economy investigates 'a raw material provided *in the last resort by* the practices of real concrete history'.[101] He rejects, as empiricist, the idea that the real object known by science is the object of knowledge, insisting that the object of knowledge is internal to thought: the real object is, nevertheless, the 'absolute reference point' because it is the object known via the object of knowledge; it becomes object of knowledge of the object of knowledge or object of knowledge *in the last resort*.[102] He rejects, as ideological, the theories in which classical epistemology tries to formulate the criteria of validity of knowledge, rejecting their very question, and replacing it by that of the 'mechanism' of production of the knowledge effect: but his failure to answer what is for him the real question gives his rejection the mere status of a gesture.

But, in the second place – and here we reach the main point – Althusser's attempt to give the first thesis all the weight he can

[101] RC pp. 109–10. My italics.
[102] Cf. on this point Glucksmann below.

leads him to an elaboration of the second thesis which is indistinguishable from idealism. For, if he begins by affirming the
universality of knowledge *in its content*, he ends by denying the
historicity of its *conditions and processes of production*;[103] their
autonomy has become, quite simply, absolute. These assertions
will be justified in a moment. Let it first be said that this represents
a very substantial failure on Althusser's part. For the account of
science he thus produces is not the one he wants to produce. He
knows that the conditions of production of knowledge, though
they do not affect its validity, are social and historical conditions
and not, as idealism supposes, absolutely independent of social
formations and their history. He knows it because he says it:
science is *relatively* independent, organically related to the other
social practices, its development crucially affected by that relationship.[104] But that is all he says. The nature of the relationship is not
spelt out, so that we have once again the gesture of an intention
but hardly a substantive theory. At the same time what emerges
time and again in Althusser's text, in its ambiguities and silences
as well as in its sounds, is a view of science which negates his
intention. Lapses of rigour? Perhaps. But the rigour of a text
counts for more than the intentions of its subject-author.[105]

I shall therefore examine four of Althusser's more ambiguous
arguments before proceeding to his view of the relation between
Marxist science and revolutionary politics, for that is the real site
of his idealism.

(i) Science is not a superstructure. It is outside the structure-
superstructure complex. In these propositions Althusser may be
taken to be asserting the first of the two theses set out above. But
he asserts something else as well. For he follows Marx in defining
the social formation as constituted by the structure-superstructure
complex.[106] He therefore excludes science from the social forma-

---

[103] This denial is most explicit in Rancière, who attributes to Marx 'une conception qui fonde la science dans une rupture radicale avec les conditions d'existence des
agents historiques'. *Lire le Capital, op. cit.*, Vol. I, p. 209. In Althusser it never takes
quite this form except perhaps once, when he seems to fault historicism for defining
'as historical the conditions for all knowledge concerning a historical object'. (RC
p. 122).

[104] FM pp. 167, 229; RC pp. 41–42, 58, 60, 99–100, 133.

[105] For Althusser's emphasis on rigour, see FM pp. 37, 116, 164, 193; RC pp. 74, 77,
90, 144: LP pp. 23–25, 76.

[106] FM p. 111.

tion.[107] And he continues to do so in some of his more recent texts,[108] although in other respects he has modified his positions substantially.

(ii) Dialectical materialism is 'the theory of science and of the history of science'. Historical materialism is the theory of social formations and of their history. The distinction must be respected. But it is impossible to find, in Althusser's work, a precise justification for the third of these propositions: one can only construct it. He tells us, it is true, that scientific practice is a specific and irreducible practice. But then so too is every other practice. And this does not prevent Althusser from integrating the theories of ideology, politics and political economy *within* historical materialism as so many component sub-disciplines. For example, he repeatedly insists that the Marxist theory of political economy, since it considers one relatively autonomous region (level or instance) of the social formation, is simply one region of the Marxist theory of history, which considers the social formation as a whole.[109] If the Marxist theory of the history of science is different in this respect, distinct from, rather than a region of, the Marxist theory of history, this can only be because the history of science is absolutely autonomous, outside the history of social formations – because, once again, science is not an instance of the social formation.

(iii) 'Ideology . . . is distinguished from science in that in it the practico-social function is more important than the theoretical function (function as knowledge)'.

(iv) Ideology is 'governed by "interests" beyond the necessity of knowledge alone'.

I take these two arguments in conjunction because it may be that they are simply the same argument and that what they both state is that the (class) interests and values expressed in ideology actually deform the content of the 'knowledge' it claims to provide and deprive it of the status of valid knowledge. They may, in other

---

[107] Cf. above n.68. Ben Brewster's Glossary (FM pp. 249–58; RC pp. 309–24), faithful in almost every detail to Althusser's thought, reproduces this exclusion at several points: see the entries for 'Formation, Social', 'Practice, Economic, Political, Ideological and Theoretical', and 'Superstructure/Structure'. Althusser has himself 'gone over the text of the glossary line by line'.

[108] LP pp. 47, 129–30.

[109] RC pp. 109, 113, 117, 145, 183.

words, simply be reformulations of the science/ideology distinction. But they are ambiguous formulations to say the least. The first, because the very terms in which the distinction is drawn suggest that the theoretical function is not *itself* a practico-social one, and that to function as knowledge is not *itself* to function socially. The second, because it suggests that the only interests at work in the development of knowledge are interests internal to knowledge (the desire for knowledge, the search for truth: knowledge for its own sake), and not also the political and social interests which, if they cannot give knowledge its theoretical solutions, certainly assist in defining its problems. Thus, the ambiguities of these arguments lead in one and the same direction, the direction we are already acquainted with: towards the absolute autonomy in which science celebrates its 'escape'[110] from social formations and their history.

The Final Idealism

But we may leave these ambiguities as they stand, since they are only ambiguities, to take up the investigation of a silence whose meaning is, this time, unambiguous. This silence has a precise location: in his concern to stress the scientificity of Marxism, Althusser fails to provide any account of what distinguishes this particular science from the other sciences. The very recognition that there might be such a distinction only rarely marks his text – once in the following form: 'Hobbes said it long ago: men tear out their hair or their lives over politics, but they are as thick as thieves over the hypotenuse or falling bodies.'[111] It occurs a second time, in almost identical terms, elsewhere.[112] For the rest, his constant emphasis on what Marxism as a science shares with the mathematical and physical sciences,[113] and his simultaneous failure to elaborate the difference which he barely takes the time to register in this Hobbesian aphorism, suggest that it is a difference of little importance.

It is, on the contrary, crucial, as is the problem it poses for any theory claiming to be the theory of science and of its history. This problem is one of the *differential* relations which the *different*

---

[110] Cf. *Lire le Capital, op. cit.*, Vol. II, p. 93.
[111] FM p. 122.
[112] RC p. 185.
[113] See e.g. RC pp. 59, 150–3.

sciences entertain with the other practices in the social formation, of their *differential* relationship to the class interests in confrontation there, hence, of their *differential* conditions and processes of production. Althusser never tackles this problem because he never tackles the problem of the relationship between scientific and the other practices in anything but the most gestural form. When he does not, as in some of the formulations discussed above, actually deny that relationship, he merely asserts it, but he does not theorize its nature. Hence, the purely programmatic character of his utterances on the epistemological break which separates the science of Marxism from its ideological past: the conditions and mechanisms of its occurrence are taken 'for a fact', not analysed, though such an analysis is declared to be an indispensable project.[114] For all, therefore, that we are assured that ideological, political and economic practice can and do contribute decisively to the occurrence of these kinds of theoretical event, Althusser's *effective* practice is to abstract from the precise character of this contribution, and, by concentrating exclusively on the conceptual shifts and restructurations involved, to treat the process as a purely intellectual one, i.e. idealistically. It is only because he does so that he can submerge the difference between Marxism on the one hand, and the mathematical and physical sciences, on the other. Considered independently of the other instances in the social formation, and of the class interests inscribed therein, they are all indifferently valid knowledges. Althusser's silence about the difference is thus part of a deeper silence: an idealist silence about science's mode of dependence in the social formation.

Let us track down this idealism in its last hideout, for there it is neither ambiguous nor silent, but quite explicit. Althusser thinks the relation between Marxist theory and the working class movement as one of exteriority: the former is produced *outside* the latter, and must be *imported* into it, failing which this movement can only arrive at conceptions which are ideological, and bourgeois-ideological at that. These theses, however 'Leninist' one may care to think them,[115] are erroneous. For, where finally is this 'outside'

[114] FM p. 168; RC pp. 27, 45–46, 50–51, 153.

[115] They are Leninist in the sense that Lenin put them forward in *What is to be done?* However, the conceptions developed in his subsequent works are not the same. Cf. on this Lenin's 1907 Preface to the collection 'Twelve Years' in *Collected Works*, Vol. 13, pp. 100–108.

if not on the inside of a purely intellectual process without historical conditions and determinants? To reduce the whole process by which Marxist theory was produced to a theoretical activity *autonomous* of the political practice of the working class, *autonomous* of the class and political conditions which were *its* indispensable, if not sufficient, conditions of production, is to perpetrate a reduction as grave as any of those castigated by Althusser himself. Its final effect is to make the relation between Marxist theory and the working class a unilateral and purely pedagogic one: the intellectuals 'give' the class the knowledge it needs. This is only the final consequence of every idealism: élitism. When knowledge celebrates its autonomy, the philosophers celebrate their dominance.

Marxism and the Working-Class

These arguments will now be elaborated and the threads of this assessment drawn together. Marxist theory was not produced *outside* the working class movement. It was produced *inside* the working class movement. True, it was produced by intellectuals, and these intellectuals were most often of bourgeois or petty-bourgeois origin. But that is another matter. For these were not just any bourgeois intellectuals. They were precisely those who linked their fate with that of the working class, formed organizations to institutionalize that union, and participated in the class struggle for socialism. What they brought to the working class movement was not a well-formed science elaborated elsewhere, but the theoretical training and the elements of scientific culture essential to the production of such a science, things which their position as intellectuals had enabled them to acquire and which cannot emerge spontaneously from experience on the factory floor, or from participation in strikes and demonstrations. At the same time, what they gained from the working class were a number of experiences not readily available to most bourgeois intellectuals and which do not emerge spontaneously from the activity of theoretical work: the experience of exploitation and repression, the experience of the struggle against these realities, the experience of the successes and failures of that struggle. The theoretical practice by which Marxist theory, as such, was founded and developed, and by which these experiences could be transformed into knowledges, was the theoretical practice of intellectuals of *this* type: a theoretical practice interior to the working class movement, and which could only teach the masses something because it also knew how to learn from them.

Marx learned, from the initiatives of the Communards, of the need for the proletariat to smash the bourgeois state. Lenin learned, from the self-organizing initiatives of the Russian proletariat in 1905 and 1917, of the significance of the soviets and of the possibilities of dual power. He learned, through years experience of party organization, both the indispensability and the limitations of party organization. Rosa Luxemburg learned, in the experience of 1905, the importance of the mass strike. Marx learned, in the failure of 1848, and Trotsky learned, in the failure of 1905, the necessity of permanent revolution. In all these cases, of course, they did not just learn. They explained these lessons, theorized these experiences, brought all their theoretical training and abilities to the task of producing new knowledge. Doing so, they founded and developed the corpus of Marxist theory. But they did so as intellectuals engaged in the struggle and the organizations of the working class. It could not be otherwise.

For Marxism is not a science just like any other. Men tear out their lives over it. If it can claim for the knowledges it produces the same validity and objectivity claimed by the other sciences for theirs, it cannot claim for them the same universal recognition. These knowledges are anathema to the bourgeoisie and its ideologues (some of whom are also scientists): by disclosing the mechanisms and contradictions of its power, they call into question the permanence of that power. Since it is precisely permanent power that the bourgeoisie wishes and thinks for itself in one ideological form or another, it cannot but refuse to look at this question and the theory which contains it. The proletariat, on the other hand, can look at this question because it has a direct interest in looking at it. It does so *in its own way* whenever it challenges the foundations of bourgeois power, whenever it proves that its spontaneous political practice is not always and inevitably trade-unionist or reformist. This is not to deny either the fact or the indispensability of the arduous process of theoretical labour and research by which certain intellectuals produced a rigorous knowledge of this question, theorizing its bases and all its ramifications. But it is to say that this was only possible for them because they had ceased to be bourgeois intellectuals, abandoned their class origins and interests, and risked all the refusals and ridicule of official culture to espouse the interests, perspectives and struggles of the working class. It is to point to the political conditions of their theoretical work.

The First Rule of Revolutionary Politics

Lest the meaning of what has been said be misconstrued, a couple of cautions are necessary. First: it is not simply the proletariat's 'point of view' that it is exploited and oppressed. It is exploited and oppressed. But it is only from its 'point of view' that that exploitation and oppression can be comprehended, i.e., known. Second: this is not by virtue of any *logical* necessity. Since it is not *simply* a class point of view that is embodied in Marxist theory, there is no reason in logic which could prove that that theory could not have been founded and developed by intellectuals in complete isolation and detachment from the struggles of the working class. But 'history is not a text in which a voice (the Logos) speaks':[116] it is not Reason which holds sway there. Powerful realities, in the shape of hegemonic interests and the ideologies that universalize them, make this logical possibility historically impossible.

I shall also take the liberty of saying at this stage, that all this has the most direct bearing on the particular way in which Althusser chooses to read Marx. For if Marx's work embodies the knowledge of history produced by his theoretical practice, if it is not *simply* an expression of the interests of the proletariat, it is that *as well*. Once again, this is not by virtue of any logical necessity. In logic, Marx could have produced a work that was value-free. In fact, he did not. Thus, he not only analysed the modalities of exploitation, he also protested against it in the name of those who suffered it. A reading of *Capital* which fails to see this is a guilty reading indeed – guilty of an oversight of inexplicable proportions. No doubt, one could, by a fairly intricate analytical operation, purge Marx's concept of exploitation of its ethical and critical content (one would have, in the first place, to change its name), leaving it only its cognitive function. But then it would no longer be *Marx's concept* of exploitation. The use Marx himself makes of

[116] RC p. 17.

it is a critical as well as a cognitive one, because he expresses in his work the interests of the exploited. Althusser is right to insist that *Capital* should not be reduced 'to an ethical inspiration'.[117] He is wrong to pretend that it contains no values of any kind whatever. Doing so, he merely echoes Hilferding who, with a logic that was flawless and a historical understanding that was limited, believed one could accept the whole of Marxist science without the least commitment to socialism.

To come to the final consequence of Althusser's idealism: the knowledge which Marxism provides and which intellectuals import into the working class movement has, for him, a very specific kind of directive role. It tries to produce 'a *new* form of ideology in the masses'[118] by supporting and using, or transforming and combating the ideologies in which the masses live.[119] But Althusser also tells us, in at least a hundred passages, that ideology is a realm of mystification and deformation, of illusion, falsehood and myth, of confusion, prejudice and arbitrariness, of the imaginary and non-knowledge.[120] He thus cuts off the masses, by a necessity he never explains, from the knowledge of their situation which the intellectuals have produced. How then can the intellectuals brandish what they know to be an ideology without violating the first principle of revolutionary politics – to tell it as it is?

It would not be in order to conclude this article without indicating that Althusser's writings since 1965 represent a 'break', in at least certain respects, with the positions which have been dealt with here, and that the fundamental direction of this break at times seems similar to that of the assessment offered above. The changes in question are signalled in the 'self-criticisms' which Althusser appends to the English translations of *For Marx* and *Reading Capital*.[121] He there suggests a different view of the spontaneity of the masses ('*the most precious* aspect of the workers' movement') and the elements of a new definition of philosophy. He acknowledges his failure to specify the relationship between Marxist

---

[117] RC p. 139.
[118] RC p. 131.
[119] FM pp. 231, 232, 241.
[120] FM pp. 66 n.29, 67 n.30, 74, 76, 79–82, 84, 126, 144, 186, 190; RC pp. 39 n.18, 47, 57, 62–63, 90, 97, 103, 105, 110, 111–12, 117, 172, 179.
[121] FM pp. 14–15, 254, 256, 258; RC pp. 7–8, 318–19, 321, 324.

theory and the working class movement (though what has been identified above as idealism, he chooses to call 'theoreticism'). His subsequent texts return again and again to the nature of this relationship and in terms which appear to be similar to those I have used.[122] Equally, the new conception of philosophy they offer has the precise function of focusing on this same relationship.[123] Of all this readers of Althusser can satisfy themsélves. On the other hand, while it undoubtedly constitutes an attempt to correct some of the major weaknesses in his original positions, whether the new positions reached can be taken for a genuine step forward is to be doubted. Whatever the errors and lacunae of *For Marx* and *Reading Capital*, they embody a systematicity, coherence, and substance, which are lacking in the revised formulations, and this lack is most visible where, perhaps, it matters most given the nature of Althusser's project, namely, in the new definition of philosophy: *not* a science or theory, but representing the class struggle *in* theory; *not* a political practice, but representing science *in* political practice; an 'original instance' representing the one alongside the other; etc. Within these mysterious, negative formulae, an empty space is enclosed.

[122] See e.g. LP pp. 7–9, 16–17, 23, 37, 53–54, 73–74, 95–96, 119.
[123] LP pp. 21–25, 29–67, 105–106.

Introduction to Glucksmann

NLR

The publication of the major philosophical works by Louis Althusser in the mid sixties provoked a wide variation of responses in Europe. In the previous essay, Norman Geras provided a careful account of the general design of Althusser's system, from *For Marx* to *Reading Capital*. Geras subjected this system to a Marxist criticism that focused essentially on the idealism of its conception of science, and hence the inevitable inadequacy of its grasp of the relationship between political theory and class struggle – the complex and vital nexus between the conceptions of historical materialism and the practice of the industrial proletariat which Lenin always insisted was constitutive of the nature of Marxism. Such a critique is based squarely within the classical traditions of revolutionary socialism, from which Althusser's 'theoreticism' is – on his own subsequent admission – a visible and definite departure, with specific effects on its links to working-class struggle. In the article that follows, we publish another critique of Althusser's work that discusses the same system from a very different perspective. André Glucksmann's essay, printed below, appeared in *Les Temps Modernes* in May 1967,[1] a year after the original French edition of *Reading Capital* had been released, and a year before the events of May 1968. Its remarkable power of penetration derives, paradoxically, to a large extent from the fact that

[1] To render the text optimally accessible to English-speaking readers, the following modifications have been made to the French original of Glucksmann's essay in the translation printed below. A mannered and sybilline introductory section has been condensed into one short paragraph, the concluding section has been slightly abridged, and the syntax and sentence-construction has been anglicized throughout, decompressing it to clarify its meaning, and selecting plain rather than precious equivalents wherever necessary. A few other minor simplifications have been made, which can be registered by consulting the original French.

it is not written from the classical standpoint of revolutionary Marxism, but primarily from within the intellectual tradition of European philosophy that pre-dates Marx. For it is precisely this 'exogenous' perspective on Althusser's writings that illuminates, much more clearly than any other critique of them, certain features of his system which have most puzzled Marxists in their encounter with it. For what appears disconcertingly unfamiliar or even indefinably alien to the corpus of previous Marxist thought, conversely becomes readily intelligible and identifiable when viewed against the background of European metaphysical philosophy, from Aristotle to Kant, and Nietzsche to Heidegger. One of Glucksmann's basic achievements is to show how close Althusser's affinities are with his pre-Marxist predecessors, and how intimately his system is related to the 'high' tradition of philosophical discourse that forms the inherited medium of instruction in European universities. This is an especially important service, in so far as the novelty of Althusser's vocabulary, and its loans from other contemporary disciplines, have tended to conceal the homology of many of his concepts with those – not of psychoanalysis or linguistics, so often cited – but of anterior metaphysics.

Glucksmann opens his case against Althusser's theory by levelling the basic preliminary charge that its classification of all social reality into four different types of 'production' – economic, political, ideological and theoretical – is arbitrary and empiricist. It is unsupported by any sustained argument or demonstration, and indeed lacks any precise demarcation of the frontiers between the different types of production.[2] Moreover, Glucksmann argues, this 'empiricist' classificatory schedule is coupled with a 'transcendentalist' epistemology. It is well-known that Althusser goes to great lengths to separate the 'real object' from the 'object of knowledge' in his epistemological theory: the latter is the specific object of theoretical production, and is to be radically distinguished from the different 'real objects' of economic, political and ideological production that together otherwise compose a social formation. The connection between the real object and the object of knowledge, which ensures the correspondence of the one to the

---

[2] Althusser was later, in fact, to have considerable difficulty in fitting art into his initial quadripartite scheme, given his acknowledgement that it was neither ideology nor theory (science); see the 'Letter on Art in Reply to André Daspré' in *Lenin and Philosophy and Other Essays*, London 1971.

other – that any given 'knowledge' is, in fact, a verity – is called by Althusser the 'mechanism' of the 'knowledge effect'. But it is never explored or explained as such: it remains a purely verbal solution to the central problem of his whole epistemology. Glucksmann, however, in a hawk-eyed examination of the letter of the texts in *Reading Capital*, isolates what he claims to be the secret, implicit answer to it presupposed by Althusser's theory: nothing less than an underlying *categorial* correspondence between the order of the world and the nature of thought, that is founded on their common essence as productions. The truth of the practice of theoretical production is thus guaranteed by the ontological 'conditions' which it shares with the various historical productions that provide the 'absolute reference-point' for its object of knowledge. Glucksmann comments that such a philosophical solution is, in fact, a modern translation of Kant's transcendental epistemology. Its direct derivation, however, is from another metaphysical system – Spinoza's monism, for which 'the order and connection of ideas is the same as the order and connection of things', because the universe is of a single substance. Reliance on Spinoza has its necessary effects. Althusser's theory is 'ventriloquist' because in it the ostensible duality between knowledge and the real is a disguise: in the puppet of theory, only one voice speaks, the general conjuror of the world, the 'common essence of production'.

Glucksmann's second focus of criticism is the 'structuralism' of Althusser's and Balibar's substantive theory of modes of production and their elements, developed in *Reading Capital*. Althusser's eloquent attacks on evolutionist and 'historicist' versions of Marxism have attracted much more polemical attention than his own proffered alternative to them: the claim that historical materialism is basically a theory of the variant combinations of five structural items that make up all modes of production. The attempt to demonstrate this claim is the nearest that Althusser's philosophy gets to actual historiographic propositions in *For Marx* or *Reading Capital*: the burden of doing so is discharged mainly by Balibar in his essay 'On the Basic Concepts of Historical Materialism', in the latter volume. Glucksmann proceeds to a logical dissection of Balibar's exposition that reveals insurmountable gaps and contradictions within it. To begin with, he points out, the five-unit grid advanced to define and distinguish all existent or possible modes of production is, in fact, formally inadequate for doing so in Balibar's version of it, because the first of the two 'relations' (that of 'real appropriation') which bind together the three 'elements' (workers, means of production, and non-productive appropriators of surplus labour) to form any given mode of production, is assigned an implicit principle of variation that is too vague and crude to permit of any comparative differentiations between feudal, 'asiatic', slave-owning or other modes of production prior to capitalism. Essentially, Balibar's analysis confines itself to offering the two alternatives of 'unity' or 'separation' between the direct producer and the means of production in the relation of real appropriation (i.e. the production process). In doing so, it remains faithful to the limits of Marx's own fragmentary reflections in *Pre-Capitalist Formations*. But it fails altogether to confront the wealth of historical evidence accumulated since Marx on the diversity of pre-capitalist societies, which makes it impossible to construct a typology that would include, say, Imperial Rome, T'ang China, Capetian France and Ottoman Turkey, along such a simple axis. A much more sophisticated set of concepts is needed to grasp the wide gamut of relationships between the direct producer and the means of production in such modes of production. In other words, the project of a direct theorization of the basic elements of all possible modes of production from the literal texts of Marx risks naïveté: it assumes a finished intellectual corpus where Marx in fact left only preliminary guesses and incomplete signposts. The very fact that the number of modes of production listed in *Pre-Capitalist Formations* (the basic text on which Balibar relies for his essay in *Reading Capital*) is itself oscillating and confused should be enough to warn against any innocent confidence in the letter of Marx's manuscripts.[3]

[3] Marx includes in different passages of *Pre-Capitalist Formations* the Asiatic, Germanic, Slavonic, Ancient, Feudal and Capitalist modes of production. The third of these, however, leads at most a semi-existence in his text, and its differential relationship to the Asiatic or Germanic is never established (see *Pre-Capitalist Formations*, London 1964, pp. 95 and 97). Moreover, the very heteroclite nature of the designations used unmistakeably reveals the impromptu and unorganized character of Marx's manuscripts: the first of the modes cited is given a geographical denomination, the second and third an ethnic, the fourth a chronological, leaving only two out of six denominations with an actual theoretical content, directly denoting the type of object in question, rather than merely gesturing by connotation towards it. There is consequently an extreme indetermination, beyond the limits of feudalism/capitalism, in the texts. Inchoate frontiers to a concept always indicate internal difficulties within it.

Glucksmann next proceeds to the obvious possible line of defence against these criticisms – the insistence of Althusser and Balibar that the three elements and two relations that combine to form any mode of production are themselves not constant items, but alter their very nature according to the total configuration which they compose in any given case. In this sense, 'unity' and 'separation' in the relations of real appropriation would always have to be specified differentially, according to the modes of production in question, and their glancing use by Balibar could be excused as a mere short-hand. But it is just at this point that Glucksmann deals a rapier stroke to the whole theoretical construction of the Althusserian combination. For he points out that, precisely, if it is the case that the very identity of the terms in any given mode of production can only be established once their concrete combination in it is known – if the very notion of what is the 'economy' in primitive or tribal societies, for example, cannot be ascertained until the total structure of the latter is first elucidated – then the whole possibility of a five-term comparative analysis of different modes of production collapses. For the end-result of such a comparison – the delimitation of distinct combinations by analysis of their constituent terms – becomes the circular presupposition of delimiting these terms themselves in the first place. The most patent example of this procedure cited by Glucksmann concerns the second of the two 'relations' in Balibar's theory of the combination – the 'property relation'. Balibar takes great pains to insist that this relation is in no way identical with that of *legal* property. Thus, in the case of the capitalist mode of production, the fundamental property relation is not the juridical ownership of single units of capital by individual entrepreneurs, but the total system of surplus extraction. This, in turn, can by definition only be grasped once the overall, articulated structure of the capitalist order itself is determined.

For Althusser and Balibar, the articulation of this structure depends on the efficacy of what they call the *Darstellung*. The notoriously elusive character of this concept conceals, Glucksmann points out, two contradictory attributes. For it is the 'invisible machinery' that ensures both the real constant reproduction of the total system of capital and the travestied forms of its phenomenal appearance, in the fetishism of commodities. It is thus responsible both for the intricate, shadowy truth and the hypnotic surface mirage of the capitalist mode of production for the social classes distributed within it. Entrusted with both tasks, it becomes incapable of performing either – in other words, of establishing any principle of distinction between the true and the false, the real and the illusory, at all. Consequently, the 'property relation' whose elucidation within capitalism was confided to an ulterior analysis of its system of reproduction, can never be scientifically identified by it. For in the 'theatre' of the *Darstellung*, the criterion of truth necessarily has no place: on the stage, all scripts are fiction. Thus, if Balibar's discussion of the 'relation of real appropriation' in the Althusserian theory of the combination inevitably blurs the differences between pre-capitalist modes of production, his account of the 'property relation' tends symmetrically to submerge the differences between capitalist and non-capitalist (post-revolutionary) modes of production. For once legal property is simply divorced from 'real property', 'private ownership' of the means of production from 'capital', and the *Darstellung* is empowered to transfigure and occlude the latter altogether from sight, the way is open to virtually any *ad hoc* conceptual manipulation to 'discover' capitalism in the contemporary world.[4] The first error is no more than historiographically ingenuous. The second is obviously much graver, because politically confusionist: its ultimate consequences remain to be seen. Nor, meanwhile, does the companion notion which escorts the *Darstellung* substantially improve it. For the 'structural causality' which is held to operate through it, both delegating specific autonomy and efficacy to the different levels of any social formation and determining all of them in the last instance by the economy, itself proves on inspection to be a vacant category. The verbalism of its final unification of the different instances in a social formation matches the empiricism of their initial division into productions. Ironically borrowing a pejorative neologism coined in the original French edition of *Lire Le Capital* to describe the 'empty' transpositions of anthropological into economic

---

[4] Balibar has since taken the step implicitly prepared above; see his collaboration in Bettelheim's *Calcul Economique et Formes de Propriété*, Paris 1970, p. 81ff, a volume devoted to the divination of 'capitalism' in the USSR today (China tomorrow?). It is probably significant that the final formulation harpooned by Glucksmann in his essay – 'the laws of necessary correspondence and non-correspondence' cited in note 66 – should be a quotation from Bettelheim. But it is clear that the general ideological function of the notion of the *Darstellung* is such as to permit operations of this type. A panurgic conception is always liable to give birth to monsters.

vocabulary in Marx's *Economic-Philosophic Manuscripts*, which establish mere ideological equivalences without yielding any new knowledge, Glucksmann dubs the structural causality of Althusser's theory – in its own language – an 'amphibology': a terminological round trip that never leaves its conceptual starting-point except in its own imagination.

Glucksmann ends his essay with some brief reflections of his own on the problems for Marxist theory left unresolved by the answers Althusser has tried to give to them. His cryptic notations on a 'linguistic' reading of *Capital* and the role of 'scepticism' in Marx's thought, with their Heideggerian undertones, need not be taken too seriously. They reflect the necessary limits of any critique of Althusser's work primarily from within the framework of traditional European philosophy, rather than that of revolutionary socialism, and provide no substantial alternative line of exploration. However, it should be noted that Glucksmann does, in passing, make two straightforward and valid comments in the last section of his text, with which any militant can agree. He insists that social classes by no means merely function as the 'supports' (*Träger*) of economic relations of production, since they also obviously operate 'demolitions' of them, in the concrete clash of class struggle for the possession of political power in any social formation. He further reminds those who would study *Capital* of the dangers of poring over *just Capital*, and ignoring the whole, complex international history of the capitalist mode of production since Marx wrote his first theorization of it – a history which includes the systemic reactions of capitalism both to the periodic crises that have gripped it since the mid 19th century and to the successive blows delivered against it by the exploited classes across the world in the 20th century. For it is self-evident that the central, undischarged task of Marxist theory today is not simply to read and re-read the three volumes of *Capital*, but to write the redoubtable, necessary sequels to them.

Glucksmann's critique of Althusser's theory has never been answered in France. But its efficacy can be judged, not only from this circumstance, but from certain curious features attending the new editions of *Reading Capital* brought out after the publication of his essay. Thus it is striking that a large number of key passages in *Lire Le Capital* cited by Glucksmann to drive home his attack, were removed from the 1969 French edition (of which the English

Reading Capital is a translation). Thus all the formulations cited by Glucksmann in notes 41, 45, 47, 52–53, 56–61, and 63–65 below, no longer appear in current versions of the book. In part, this is because of omission of Rancière's long contribution to the original edition from post-1968 editions of *Lire Le Capital*, from which Glucksmann quotes abundantly; but the very elimination of this essay, whose formulations on the *Darstellung* are most flagrantly vulnerable, may have been inspired by the difficulty of modifying it to evade the criticisms made of it by Glucksmann.[5] However, both Althusser and Balibar have also deleted pivotal cognate formulations, which were particularly exposed to Glucksmann's attack, from their own texts. It is thus reasonable to surmise that the silent response to 'A Ventriloquist Structuralism' was a premeditated partial withdrawal, in order to narrow tactical flanks, because of the difficulty of any frontal reply or counterattack. Such a silence, of course, tells its own story.

However, it would nevertheless be wrong to regard the balance-sheet of Althusser's work as definitively drawn up yet. Two considerations preclude this. Firstly, if it is the case – as Glucksmann shows – that Althusser's epistemology is a variant of metaphysical transcendentalism, this does not mean that the alternative epistemologies which he attacks are in any way adequate or scientific either. Gareth Stedman Jones has recently demonstrated that the most celebrated of these alternatives within Western Marxism – that of the young Lukács – leads to no less patent mistakes and contradictions. It should by now, in fact, be clear that no Marxist epistemology as such yet exists, and that the difficult problems posed by the bond between historical materialism and the proletarian class struggle are still far from being solved. Althusser's failure in this respect is not a solitary one. Similarly, the rudimentary character of Balibar's 'combination' is not just a matter of the limitations of his own historical culture. It also reflects a general situation of Marxist theory, which has yet to tackle or integrate systematically the great advances that have been made in the last decades in historiographic study of diverse pre-capitalist social formations, from Antiquity onwards. At the same

[5] It is possible that Rancière's revulsion against Althusser's philosophy after 1968 may have been another contributing factor. Rancière has since attacked Althusser's theory of science with some violence, in an essay published in Saul Karsz (ed), *Lecturas de Althusser*, Buenos Aires 1969.

time, it should be noted that Glucksmann's critique does not concern itself with two crucial 'historical' concepts of Althusser's theory – 'over-determination' and 'differential temporality' – and does not necessarily affect them; Geras has likewise shown considerable respect for these. It seems likely that they will, in fact, prove the most lasting accomplishments of Althusser's 'first period', even if they have yet to be embodied in any documented historical investigations of the first order. Debray is probably right to remark that 'Contradiction and Over-Determination' remains the most useful and viable single text that Althusser has so far produced. Such an assessment would indicate a real residual achievement, if a more modest one than its claims imply. Finally, it must be remembered that Althusser's development is by no means finished. A 'second period' is evident in the writings contained in *Lenin and Philosophy and Other Essays*, which falls outside the scope of the criticisms by either Geras or Glucksmann. It is clear that in this second period, the subterranean *political* currents moving beneath Althusser's work will increasingly come to the surface.* Future assessments of it will accordingly have to deal far more with these – with the great, plain questions of revolutionary socialist struggle that dominate and divide the world today.

---

* See now the astringent account by Valentino Gerratana, 'Althusser and Stalinism', *New Left Review* No. 101–102, February–April 1977.

A Ventriloquist Structuralism

André Glucksmann

The aim of this article is to question the structuralist finery in which Althusser has decked Marxism, and to demonstrate the weakness of its seams. If we find that Althusser's theory comes apart philosophically, it will be by measuring what he says against what he says, and not against what Marx may have said, or what other readings of Marx expound as the truth of Marxism. Hence we shall restrict ourselves to Althusserian texts alone. The focus of our procedure will be the internal consistency of the texts examined; our aim will be to locate the central contradiction under which the whole system can be seen to collapse. In order to do this, an understanding of the Althusserian programme as a whole is needed. Althusser's project (his interrogation of Marx) is to be found in the function that two key concepts – *production* and *theory* – play in it. The realization of his project (how he makes Marx talk) involves two different types of structural analysis. The ensuing 'duplicity' will reveal the lines of fracture in his structuralism, which will furnish the specific object of our criticism. [1]

I The Concept of Production

Althusser's basic concepts have a dual function. The first is polemical. It challenges all other readings of Marx and lays down what it conceives to be the deviations from Marxism. The second is architectonic. It guides Althusser's investigation into the logic of *Capital*. The concept of production is thus central in two ways,

---

[1] The following abbreviations have been used throughout the article: FM = *For Marx*, London 1969. RC = *Reading Capital*, London 1970.

because it both regulates the primordial divisions of the Althusserian universe, and establishes the breaks by which scientific
theory ensures its independence *vis-à-vis* ideology and politics.

The Break between the Productions

Everything is production, and as productions, the productions
have the same status. There are four kinds of production: material,
political, ideological and theoretical. The unity of theory and
practice is not achieved between the different productions but
first of all within each of them. 'So a practice of theory does exist;
theory is a specific practice which acts on its own object and ends
in its own *product*: a *knowledge*.'[2]

Each production obeys its own laws in the sphere in which it
exercises its autonomy: 'It is perfectly legitimate to say that the
production of knowledge which is peculiar to theoretical practice
constitutes a process that takes place *entirely in thought*, just as we
can say, *mutatis mutandis*, that the process of economic production
takes place entirely in the economy.'[3]

This structural autonomy of the different types of production
leads to a strictly theoretical reading of *Capital*, a reading which
does not allow itself any proof by ethics (humanism) or history.
It also rejects straight away an original unity of praxis (labelled
'Hegelian'), whether in its subject (Lukács), in its historical act
(the Italian school) or its mediations (Sartre).

The Breaks in Production

Although there is no original production manifested in the
different types of production, there is a general concept that refers
to a 'general definition of practice'.[4] The productions are not
unified by a common being but by a homologous form ('the
structure of a production').[5] 'By *practice* in general I shall mean
any process of *transformation* of a determinate given raw material
into a determinate *product*, a transformation effected by a determinate human labour, using determinate means (of "production")'.[6]

[2] FM p. 173.
[3] RC p. 42.
[4] FM p. 167.
[5] RC p. 58.
[6] FM p. 166.

The tripartition which separates the raw material (material in one case, ideological and pre-scientific in the other: Generality I), the labour ('means' and 'forces' of labour; the axiomatic and method of a science: Generality II) and the product (object, commodity, object of knowledge: Generality III) is identical not in its terms but only in its form. This formal unity implies more than the use of the same term. By invoking the general essence of 'production', Marxism safeguards itself against two of its greatest temptations: a 'technologistic' understanding of material production and 'Hegelianism' in theoretical production. 'In any practice thus conceived, the determinant moment (or element) is neither the raw material nor the product, but the practice in the narrow sense: the moment of the *labour of transformation* itself, which sets to work, in a specific structure, men, means and a technical method of utilizing the means.'[7]

The fate of this set of the three moments of production is decided in the second moment. In the case of material production, this moment articulates the indissoluble link between force of labour and means of labour and excludes any reference to 'the ahistorical absolute of a "free", "unlimited" growth in the productivity of labour'.[8] It is also the determinant moment of theoretical labour, where it excludes empiricism (in which the first element is determinant) and speculation (in which the third predominates). The second moment has chief place in all the epistemological breaks by which science guarantees its scientificity.

Role of the Concept of Production: Breaks and Joints

The Althusserians have underlined the importance of production by suggesting the possibility 'of formulating a new philosophical concept of production in general'.[9] This intervenes at each crucial moment in their analyses, even in solving the problems of literary criticism. They themselves stress only its critical and architectonic functions. However, its further, philosophical function will allow us to insinuate into Althusser's theory the questions it does not ask.

1. The critical function. This is the principle of all the 'breaks'

[7] FM p. 166.
[8] RC p. 288.
[9] RC p. 268.

which provide a guarantee for the autonomy of theoretical reflection: the structural break that separates it from all other types of production and the epistemological breaks that distinguish between science and ideology within theoretical activity itself.

2. The architectonic function. This is the principle of all the 'joints' of the 'historical materialism' that attempts to reassemble the different real practices within the same mode of *production* as well as of the 'dialectical materialism' that promises a general theory, 'the theory of practice in general, itself elaborated on the basis of the theory of existing theoretical practices'.[10] The concept of production is the supreme principle of unity, the Althusserian idea of reason. Hence the problem of its philosophical function.

First Philosophical Question: Production and Being

The concept of production claims to be both the first and last word of theoretical reflection as well as the original element and definitive form of the structure of the real. It governs the birth and totalization of wisdom, the definition and persistence of social structures. But where does it come from itself? From a simple observation: 'It is therefore a question of producing, in the precise sense of the word, which seems to signify making manifest what is latent, but which really means transforming (in order to give a pre-existing raw material the form of an object adapted to an end) . . .'[11]

The basis for the whole tripartite Althusserian architecture thus arises fully armed from the simple but somewhat forced use of a dictionary. It 'happens' that everything is production, it 'happens' that every production is divided into three. That is how it is. This conceptual empiricism is never questioned in the Althusserian reflection. True, no *a priori* truth is deducible, but it can be examined. This interrogation, however, cannot be undertaken until we have developed the whole Althusserian system and ascertained the role the concept of production plays in it. We shall find that if this concept turns out to fulfil the function of the concept of being in traditional philosophy, Althusser's whole scientific project is in fact displaced towards metaphysics.

[10] FM p. 168.
[11] RC p. 34.

II The Concept of Theory

The concept of theory takes us directly to the very core of the Althusserian project. It explains the first chaplet of Marxism: dialectical materialism. Instead of a Marxist system which discerns in nature the same dialectical 'laws' as in society, here the unity of the theory of nature and the theory of society no longer has an ontological but epistemological basis. There are no longer two theories that find the same laws in 'reality' but a single theoretical activity subject to laws of its own whose generality can be traced in every domain. The universality of Marxism is expanded into a general theory (the dialectic) 'in which is theoretically expressed the essence of theoretical practice in general, through it the essence of practice in general, and through it the essence of the transformations, of the "development" of things in general'.[12] Our construction of the concept of this theory will start from the double use Althusser makes of it.

Theory in its Polemical Use

Like every basic production, theory is an autonomous and articulated practice. In so far as it is autonomous, it has its own sphere of legitimation. Althusser maintains, as against Gramsci, that theory is not a superstructure: 'Science can no more be ranged within the category "superstructure" than can language which, as Stalin showed, escapes it. To make science a superstructure is to think of it as one of those "organic" ideologies which form such a close "bloc" with the structure that they have to disappear with it!'[13] Theory is a thought process that has its own laws and no reference to the real process of society or history can invalidate or justify it. This eliminates the extreme pretensions that might lead a sociology of knowledge, or historicism in general, to judge a knowledge not in the name of knowledge but before the tribunal of a history given as such, without further ado.

Theory is not just autonomous, 'breaking' with the other productions (or structures); it is also 'broken' within itself. Ignorance of these intrastructural breaks is the epistemological

[12] FM p. 169.
[13] RC p. 133. The author altered the last four words to read 'the same history as it does', in the edition from which the English translation of *Reading Capital* was made.

source of the deviations criticized by Althusser. He sees all of them as establishing an illegitimate continuity between the different 'moments' of theoretical activity: ignorance of the first break (G.I/G.II) defines empiricism in particular; ignorance of the second (G.II/G.III) reveals the stamp of speculative dogmatism. In either case it is supposed that the moment chosen to initiate the pseudo-continuity is endowed with an ontological privilege, whereby knowledge touches being, real process and thought process finally fuse.

Theory in its Systematic Use

The positive principle of theoretical activity can be grasped in its second moment: 'theoretical practice produces *Generalities III* by the work of *Generality II* on *Generality I*.'[14] The theoretical corpus of a science (Generality II) is thus constituted by the armoury of concepts, rules and experimental procedures that specify its activity. This corpus enables a science to define the demarcation of its problematic in (pre-scientific) Generality I and by the same stroke to judge the knowledge produced (Generality III) by the form of apodictic certainty it poses: 'the criterion of the "truth" of the knowledges produced by Marx's theoretical practice is provided by his theoretical practice itself, i.e. by the proof-value, by the scientific status of the *forms* which ensured the production of those knowledges'.[15]

Hence the unity of Marxist theory depends on the connection it can establish between the corpuses (G.II) of the different theoretical activities. Althusser, to start with, considers the two possible directions of a 'theory of the history of the theoretical' and finds them both necessary but not sufficient. There is a synchronic connection between the different theoretical activities that raises the question: 'what effective relationship there is between the forms of proof in *Capital* on the one hand and the forms of theoretical proof contemporaneous with it and close to it, on the other'.[16] It is possible in this way to consider the original history of knowledge (Foucault, Bachelard, Koyré).

But the theory of the history of knowledge cannot fully satisfy

[14] FM p. 185.
[15] RC p. 59.
[16] RC p. 49.

Althusser because it remains descriptive and observational, and pre-supposes the central proposition: that the objects whose theoretical history it tells are really knowledge. 'It treats the knowledge *as a fact* whose transformations and variations it studies as so many effects of the structure of the theoretical practice which produces them, as so many products which happen to be knowledge – without ever reflecting *the fact that these products are not just any products but precisely knowledges*. A theory of the history of the production of knowledge therefore does not take into account what I propose to call the *"knowledge effect"*, which is the peculiarity of those special products which are knowledges'. [17]

This is the problem of the *'differential* nature of *scientific discourse'* ('what distinguishes scientific discourse from other forms of discourse') and it is a truly philosophical glance that leads Althusser to pose a question he does not answer and which therefore remains 'in suspense' at the level of epistemological generality at which it was posed. Althusser seems to invite us to look for the elements of a reply in the more specific analyses of *Reading Capital*. But even if it were possible to grasp the scientificity of Marxism in opposition to classical political economy by defining the 'object of *Capital'*, it would still remain to be shown that this established more than the epistemology of one particular science, or that by starting from the scientificity of *Capital* it is possible to reach towards the essence of 'theoretical practice in general' and 'through it' to the essence of 'the development of things in general'. Yet until this is demonstrated, Althusser's claim that dialectical materialism is a general theory remains an empty ambition.

Second Philosophical Question: Theory and Transcendental Correlation

The rigour of Althusser's analysis depends on his keeping the order of knowledge ('thought process') apart from the order of reality ('process of the real'). Hence he is careful to distinguish between the real product of the ensemble of productions (or 'society effect', the object of historical materialism) and the theoretical product of this same ensemble of praxes (or 'knowledge effect', the object of dialectical materialism). [18] In the first case, the production that provides the key to the organized set of

[17] RC p. 61–62.
[18] RC p. 66.

productions is material production, which 'in the last instance' determines the modes of production. In the second case, the key is the theoretical production 'through which' the essence of all production is to be read.

We are obliged to posit between these two basic 'productions' what Althusser calls a 'correspondence of knowledge'. The 'society effect' can only be known in a 'knowledge effect' and, reciprocally, the 'knowledge effect' can only be known in the knowledge of the 'society effect'. But the relation between these two productions is not direct; for the one is not the object of the other.

'As Marx says profoundly, the *real* object, of which knowledge is to be acquired or deepened, *remains what it is*, after as before the process of knowledge which involves it (cf. the 1857 *Introduction*); if, therefore, it is the absolute reference point for the process of knowledge which is concerned with it – the deepening of the knowledge of this real object is achieved by *a labour of theoretical transformation* which necessarily affects the *object of knowledge*, since it is only applied to the latter.'[19]

How are we to understand that the structure of the real is to be the 'absolute reference point' for theory without being its object of knowledge – except by presupposing some more secret correspondence between a theory and its object? This underlying correspondence, everywhere present, is never theorized. It is mentioned once, *vis-à-vis* the modes of production: 'we can set out the "presuppositions" for the theoretical knowledge of them, which are quite simply the concepts of the conditions of their historical existence'.[20]

The simplicity of this 'quite simply' announces the transcendental correlation whose law was formulated by Kant: the conditions of the *possibility of experience* in general are at the same time the conditions of the *possibility of the objects* of experience. The kinship of thought and being is thus not conceived in the immediate relation of thought (theory) and its object, but more mysteriously, between the categories of thought and the elements of reality. This is precisely the minimum basis for any structuralism.[21] While

---

[19] RC p. 156.
[20] RC p. 216.
[21] 'Myths signify the mind that elaborates them by means of the world of which it is itself a part'. Lévi-Strauss, *The Raw and the Cooked*, London 1969, p. xxx.

Kant explored his 'at the same time', the critical question *par excellence*, Althusser's 'quite simply' translates the transcendental *zugleich* only to obliterate the problem as soon as it appears.

The power of the concept of production is thus not limited to scattering over all productions the tripartite demarcation of the 'general essence of all production'. At the same time:

1. It makes possible a double unification of the set of productions. If the logic of all productions can be read 'through' theoretical productions, it is because a kinship is supposed to exist between them which should be visible in theoretical production. Conversely, if the reality of all production can be determined 'in the last instance' by material ('economic') production, this is again because of the kinship of all productions, this time in their material aspect.

2. It makes possible the unification of these two unities in a transcendental correlation, inasmuch as the elementary categories of theoretical production are 'quite simply' the categorical elements of real production. Hence the articulation of 'production' determines both the order of knowledge and the order of the real.

There are other, yet more metaphysical, functions of the Althusserian concept of production with which we shall deal later in our investigation.

III The Articulated Structure in Dominance of the Complex Whole

The 'theory' instructs us to conceive the ensemble formed by a number of 'productions' that are distinct, autonomous and irreducible to one another. The task of the notion of structure and its specifications is to give us the concept of this set and to cure us of the two 'infantile' disorders of Marxism: those which either reduce all practice to economic production, or attempt to 'make history' by describing what happens without theorizing it. In other words, this is 'a *new conception* of the relation between determinant instances in the structure-superstructure complex which constitutes the essence of any social formation. Of course, these specific *relations* between structure and superstructure still deserve theoretical elaboration and investigation. However, Marx has at least given us the "two ends of the chain", and has told us to find out what goes on between them: on the one hand, *determination in the last instance by the (economic) mode of produc-*

tion; on the other, *the relative autonomy of the superstructures and their specific effectivity.*[22] The determinations that specify the Althusserian use of the notion of structure are intended to provide a solution to this problem.

Structure = 'Structure of the Social Whole'

Just as the Marxist theory of knowledge (dialectical materialism) was to be the theory of the ensemble of theories, so the Marxist theory of reality (historical materialism) is designed to think the real production of the ensemble of productions. Professional historians (L. Febvre, Labrousse, Braudel, etc.) have observed the presence of different levels of 'history' and the different temporalities or rhythms of development of these histories. Marxist theory must 'relate these varieties as so many *variations* to the structure of the whole although the latter directly governs the production of these varieties'.[23] Hence it must determine in the whole of the social structure 'the type of dependence which produces relative independence and whose effects we can observe in the histories of the different "levels"'.[24]

Structure = 'Specific Type of Unity', 'Verbindung'

This 'whole' is to be regarded synchronically as an 'articulated combination' (Marx: *Gliederung*). The elements of this ensemble co-exist in a mutual definition, such that the whole cannot be reconstituted by a temporal composition that introduces these elements in succession. Hence the rejection of any genetic explanation of the structure, both from the point of view of knowledge (Marx's critique of Proudhon in *The Poverty of Philosophy*) and from the point of view of reality: 'there is no history in general but only specific structures of historicity, based in the last resort on the specific structures of the different modes of production, specific structures of historicity which, since they are merely the existence of determinate social formations (arising from specific modes of production), articulated as social wholes, have no meaning except as a function of the essence of these totalities, i.e.

[22] FM p. 111.
[23] RC p. 96.
[24] RC p. 100.

of the essence of their peculiar complexity.'[25] The 'meaning of history' does not underlie the meaning of the structure; on the contrary, it is the structures that allow us to assign significations to history.

Structure = 'Articulated Structure' versus 'Expressive Totality'

If we have to say structure and not just totality, it is because the social whole is organized in levels of relative and irreducible independence. These different levels cannot be inter-related by a single internal principle of which they are 'expressions' – whether this principle is spiritual (labelled 'Hegelian') or material (Plekhanov's 'monism'). This independence accounts for the gravity of the contradictions between the different levels. But since these contradictions are themselves regulated, the independence is relative.

Structure = 'Structure in Dominance'

The articulation of the structure prevents any equality of the levels, conceived as parallel expressions of the same principle of unity: among the levels some will play 'major roles' and others 'minor roles'. Hence the two notions of 'dominance' to govern this hierarchized structure. The 'dominant instance' designates the different levels of the structure which may successively play the major roles; 'dominance in the last instance' designates the relations of production (the economic 'base') in so far as they govern every mode of production 'in the last instance'. Thus the double character of dominance corresponds to the double nature of the structure, articulated both into levels of relative independence and as a totality. 'It is economism that identifies eternally in advance the determinant-contradiction-in-the-last-instance with the *role* of the dominant contradiction . . . whereas in real history determination in the last instance by the economy is exercised precisely in the permutations of the principal role between the economy, politics, theory, etc.'[26]

[25] RC pp. 108–109.
[26] FM p. 213.

Structure = Structural Invariant of Concrete Variations

The causality of the economy can only be understood by its place in the social structure. It is the invariant which only appears through the play of variables that govern this structure by turns: 'the economy is determinant in that it determines which of the instances of the social structure occupies the determinant place.'[27]

Hence it is possible to explain why economic causes in history never – or rarely – appear to be directly determinant. The exceptions that seem to disturb the economic determinism of history (e.g. the 1917 revolution) are the rule – both in fact and in principle. The strategically dominant instance in a social structure will rarely be the economy, although it is the relations of production that govern the *mise en scène* and apparition of the different principal roles.

Structuralism: Terminology or Concept?

So far we have only been given some nominal definitions; they indicate a research programme which must be judged by its results. We start with 'the two ends of a chain': the freedom (autonomy) of the different levels and the omnipresent providence (in 'the last instance') of the economy. Between the two, structuralist terminology links a chain of words. Althusser, quite correctly, is not satisfied with this. We know that theology, faced with the same difficulty, and without any chain, has always managed to join the two 'ends' (for Bossuet, the two ends of the chain were human freedom and divine providence). To express the need for a concept is not to provide the concept of this need. It remains to be seen whether structuralist notions paper over the problem or resolve it – in particular since they seek to link two ends of a chain whose existence itself remains a mere presupposition.

Where should we look for a proof of the theoretical efficacy of this vocabulary? Not in the commentaries Althusser proposes of Lenin and Mao, which are in this respect no more than exercises in translation. Given that the primary problem of the function of the economy is a problem common to all Marxists, and that the structuralist vocabulary has been specially moulded to verbalize

[27] RC p. 224.

a solution to it, it is obvious that the latter will correspond para-
phrastically to the words that Lenin and Mao used in order to
resolve problems in their own way. If the structuralist vocabulary
claims to be scientific, it is because it theorizes the science of
Capital. The Althusserians try to prove this by showing that
Marx's analysis in *Capital* is structuralist *ante diem*.

IV The Structuralist Analysis of Modes of Production

Althusser's structuralism claims to be verified by the analyses of
Capital. His reading of *Capital* thus has two goals. Dialectical
materialism is to be founded as a general theory by displaying the
mechanism of a particular 'knowledge effect' (the science of
Capital). Simultaneously, historical materialism is to vindicate its
claim to be the science of the real by providing the formula for
those 'basic forms of unity of historical existence' that are 'modes
of production'.

A first type of structuralist analysis is introduced by Althusser[28]
and developed by Balibar.[29] It appears to be inspired by Lévi-
Strauss's analysis of kinship structures. Just as real and possible
kinships can be deduced from an atemporal typology of exchange
systems (restricted or generalized), so modes of production can be
defined in their form (their 'combination') by a universal and
ahistorical quasi-combinatory of the types of production. Referring to Balibar's exposition, Althusser stresses: 'But it is clear that
the théoretical nature of this concept of "combination" may
provide a foundation for the thesis I have already suggested in a
critical form, the thesis that *Marxism is not a historicism*: since the
Marxist concept of history depends on the principle of the
variation of the forms of this "combination"'.[30]

Comparative Analysis: Definition of the Modes of Production

The problem is to define in some way the elementary structures of
any social production – or mode of production – on the basis of a

[28] RC p. 176ff.
[29] RC pp. 201–308.
[30] RC p. 177.

finite (as it happens, small) number of elements and typical relations between these elements. Each of the modes of production
will then arise from a different way of combining the same terms.
Consequently, the difference between the modes of production 'is
necessarily and *sufficiently* based on a variation of the connexions
between a small number of elements which are always the same.
The announcement of these connexions and of their terms constitutes the exposition of the primary theoretical concepts of historical
materialism.'[31]

This 'completely unprecedented structuralism', the formula for
which Balibar finds in Marx, defines every mode of production as a
combination of three elements:
1. the worker or direct producer (the labour force)
2. the means of production (object and means of labour)
3. the non-worker appropriating surplus labour
These elements are combined by the play of two relations:
4. the relation of real appropriation (production process)
5. the property relation (exploitation process)

The first relation refers primarily to the 'productive forces', the
second to the relations of property in the means of production,
traditionally designated as 'relations of production'.[32] However, all
these terms are structural in that their content varies according to
the mode of production in which they are combined. Thus the
'worker' may be 'individual' or 'collective' according to whether
he is defined in a feudal or capitalist mode of production.

The analysis thus attempted is not a 'real' decomposition of the
mode of production, reducing it to ultimate and invariable
elements (invisible 'atoms of history'). On the contrary, we have a
'comparative analysis' that defines each mode of production by
the original combination of these five terms, and this combination
alone specifies their content. Balibar gives an example of such a
comparative analysis when he distinguishes between the feudal and
the capitalist modes of production. The three component elements
are the same (though their concrete contents are different). The
structural difference is to be found at the level of the relations
between them. The production process unites the labour force
and the means of labour in the feudal regime (the worker is not

[31] RC p. 225.
[32] RC p. 292.

separate from his means of production); in the capitalist regime, on the contrary, the worker is 'free' and the labour force is separated from the means of production (mechanization, heavy industry). Hence different possibilities for the relations of exploitation. In feudalism, a distinction must be made 'in time and space' between the 'necessary' labour process (devoted to the reproduction of the labour force) and the process of surplus labour (producing surplus labour for the non-worker). Consequently a power, which is not directly economic, is required to impose this separation on the producers: 'Thus surplus-labour for the nominal owner of the land can only be extorted from them by *other than economic pressure* whatever the form assumed may be.'[33] In the capitalist regime, on the other hand, where the worker is separated from the means of production, there is 'a term by term coincidence *of the labour process and the process of producing value*'[34] and surplus value 'goes of itself' to the governing classes without it being necessary to resort to the direct intervention of 'extra-economic pressure'. This first type of analysis is intended to define comparatively the specific differences of all possible modes of production. It is coupled with an analysis – called a synchronic analysis – of the functioning of these modes of production.

Synchronic Analysis: the Reproduction of the Modes of Production

Comparative analysis seems to show that the combination of the five terms is necessary to define the mode of production. If we want to show that it is also sufficient we have to prove that the mode thus defined contains – due to this fact alone – the reasons for its persistence. This persistence in existence is analysed only in the case of capitalism, as 'reproduction' of capital. 'Reproduction' contains the secret of the determination in the last instance of a social structure by the mode of production: it brings out the '"consistency" of the structure'.[35]

The mode of production itself reproduces itself: it permanently induces the reappearance of the terms that define it and thereby assures the sufficiency of its definition: 'The capitalist production

---

[33] Marx, cited RC p. 221.
[34] RC p. 222.
[35] RC p. 269.

process, therefore, considered in its inter-connexion (*Zusammen-hang*) or as reproduction, produces not only commodities, not only surplus-value, but *it also produces and eternalizes the social relation between the capitalist and the wage-earner*'.[36] This reproduction by 'virtue of the repetition' of its definition determines an autonomous intra-structural temporality. The encroaching demands of this reproduction are progressively unearthed throughout the analyses of *Capital*. It is they which explain how the demands of reproduction determine the modes of circulation, distribution and consumption – in the last instance, the whole social structure.

The Problem of the Relationship between the Two Analyses

In the case of the capitalist system, the two analyses fit perfectly together. The comparative analysis reveals the distinctive features of capitalism, the synchronic analysis shows their sufficiency as the process of capital perpetually reproduces them. For other modes of production the question is more complex. As in the capitalist case, only reproduction should pose the 'consistency of the structure' and the sufficiency of its differential features. As opposed to the process of capital in capitalism, reproduction here has necessarily to introduce 'extra-economic pressure'. In this case, then, the mode of production reproduces the necessity for its extra-economic determination. In other words, given that the non-capitalist economy needs an extra-economic cause to develop and survive, the idea that the superstructures must necessarily correspond to the economic base conceals the fact that, in doing this, the superstructure corresponds only to itself – since it is the cause of the 'consistency' of the base.

To escape this circle and apply the Althusserian distinction (dominant instance/determination in the last instance) Balibar simply quotes a text by Marx on the feudal regime that develops the following syllogism:[37]

1. if economic activity is to be carried out, 'extra-economic' reasons must intervene;

2. but this economic activity must be carried out;

3. hence the reason behind this extra-economic reason is economic.

[36] Marx, cited RC p. 269.
[37] RC p. 220.

If the 'must' in the minor premise is to lead to the conclusion, another postulate must be introduced: that all the reasons, conscious or not, that a society presents for living and dying count for nothing before the fact that in order to present reasons at all, whatever they are, it must 'first' live in the purely economic sense of the word. Moreover, a second postulate is necessary to establish the first; the words 'live in the purely economic sense' must have a meaning in all societies. This meaning is only possible in thought, for no pre-capitalist society would let itself be isolated in a 'first' life which is purely economic.

Balibar does not explicitly formulate these two postulates, but he does imply them when he uses a phrase of Marx as a justification: 'This much, however, is clear, that the Middle Ages could not live on Catholicism nor the ancient world on politics.'[38] Yet these postulates which govern the universalization of the 'structuralism' in *Capital* are not examined as such by Balibar. It remains to consider whether the terms retained by this 'perfectly unprecedented structuralism' allow us to define the pure demands of production in all modes of production.

Critique: a 'Savage' Structuralism

Two technical questions can be put to this type of structuralism. On the one hand, does it work? Does it make possible the comparative analysis which it pretends to invoke? On the other hand, is it sufficient? Are the terms that it introduces 'pertinent'; do they systematically define themselves without reference to any other terms, or do they form a 'bad infinity'?

1. An Indeterminable Comparativism

In fact, Balibar's comparative analysis is very limited. He distinguishes two modes of production (feudalism and capitalism) and refers in passing to the Asiatic mode of production. Mathematically speaking, it is doubtful whether five terms are sufficient to determine all the possible modes of production without using other implicit differentiating principles. If we restrict ourselves to the three modes mentioned by Balibar, we can already discern a

[38] RC p. 217.

lack of precision in his analyses. He discovers one feature common to the capitalist and Asiatic modes of production in that in both cases the surplus value seems to flow 'naturally' to the ruling class. He finds an explanation of this in the labour process, in 'the joining of the function of control or direction, indispensable to the performance of the labour process . . . with the function of owner-ship of the means of production'.[39] Between these two modes, the originality of feudalism is that it does not separate the worker from his means of production (he exercises the function of control) while it separates him from his surplus labour (hence the extra-economic violence that characterizes the feudal property function).

The obviousness of this distinction is only a result of the imprecision of the terms employed. We may say that the serf is not separated from the means of production and that he controls his production, but we might just as well assert the opposite – in so far as the lord's power maintains the division of labour, permits and organizes economic exchange, protects the economic units against external dangers, i.e. in so far as he exercises control functions analogous to those of the 'Kings of Asia and Egypt' or the 'Etruscan Theocrats' in another type of society. The notions of 'control', of 'separation' or 'non-separation' of the 'direct producer' from the means of production, are essentially ambiguous when pre-capitalist societies are compared with one another.

The comparative analysis is thus reduced to propounding not a theory of all modes of production but a theory of the originality of capitalism: only capitalism radically separates worker and means of production; only capitalism poses a homology between labour process and surplus process; only capitalism makes it possible to pin-point an autonomous (economic) process of value creation.[40] What else can this mean but that the economy, in its autonomous movement (the value-creating process), is the characteristic feature of capitalism, one which distinguishes it from the other modes of production but which does not distinguish between the other modes? The so-called comparative analysis is restricted to the separation of two terms, an insufficient foundation for any kind of structuralism.

[39] RC p. 219.
[40] RC p. 221.

2. An Evasive Analysis

If the system of five 'structural terms' does not permit an analysis of the multiplicity of modes of production, it is because it contains an evasion hidden in the fifth term, the 'property relations'. Balibar correctly remarks that this term cannot have the strictly legal sense: 'It is important, despite the double usage of the term, to distinguish between the "property" whose ("structural") space has been situated here, and its legal expression, the legal form of property. These forms do not enter into the "combination" – they are part of the "superstructure" and not of the "base" with which we are dealing here. This is an essential and indispensable distinction if we are to be able to think the eventual *disjuncture* (*décalage*) between the base and the superstructure, between "property" (concerned exclusively with the means of production) and the legal forms of property.'[41]

But what is property beyond its legal definition? In the case of capitalism the answer is simple but long: it is not the (legal) property of some isolated capitalist but the whole system which ensures the extraction of surplus value. 'Capital' defines property as a whole and only as a whole. In other words, the definition of property implies the analysis of 'reproduction'; the so-called 'comparative analysis' presupposes – and does not precede – the 'synchronic analysis' of the whole of *Capital*. Consequently it is impossible to claim that 'the scientific method of *Capital*, generalizable to all the historical modes of production, is characterized by these few general concepts that constitute in principle the beginning of its exposition'. These general concepts cannot be distinguished from one another until *Capital* has been read and absorbed.

We can now understand, for the same reason, why it is difficult to pin down the other modes of production with these five terms. Here too the 'synchronic analysis' of the reproductive process must take place before it is possible to grasp the five terms with which the comparative analysis claims to deal. If property can be defined in a way other than as a legal category, this is because its concept is suggested by the place of the 'proprietors' in the process

---

[41] *Lire le Capital* II, Paris 1966, pp. 209–10. This passage was omitted by the author from the second edition of 1969 from which the English translation was made. All subsequent references to *Lire le Capital* are to the 1966 edition.

of reproduction – which again presupposes that the analysis of the 'social whole' has been completed. Without realizing that by this he would make any preliminary comparative analysis impossible, Althusser remarks: 'in primitive societies it is not possible to regard any *fact*, any practice apparently unrelated to the "economy" (such as the practices which are produced by kinship rites or religious rites, or by the relations between groups in "potlatch" competition), *as rigorously economic*, without first having constructed the concept of the differentiation of the structure of the social whole into these different practices or levels'.[42]

Could it be more strongly stressed that an intra-structural analysis of each mode of production necessarily precedes any possibility of a comparative, inter-structural analysis? Yet precisely the opposite order is adopted by Althusser and Balibar in *Reading Capital*, in the hope of isolating 'the basic concepts of historical materialism' via a comparative analysis situated 'at the beginning of the exposition'. If we then inquire into the origin of these 'basic' concepts (basic precisely because they cannot be produced by a comparative analysis) we find the same conceptual empiricism that introduced without qualms 'the general essence of production': 'it happens' that all modes of production are articulated by five terms.

Two consequences follow immediately from the failure of a comparative analysis of the modes of production.

1. It has not been proved that the object of *Capital* is modes of production in general and not the capitalist mode of production alone. Similarly, the presence in *Capital* of a universal theory of the 'basic forms of unity of historical existence' remains a gratuitous hypothesis; this classic problem for Marxism remains unsolved.

2. It has been proved even less that the method of *Capital* implies a comparative analysis of a structuralist kind. All the terms that were supposed to articulate this analysis are in fact derived from the 'synchronic analysis' of the process of capital which preserves existing social relations and produces their terms. This 'synchronic' analysis presupposes the understanding not of a diversity (of modes of production) but of a *development* (of the capitalist mode of production in *Capital*).

This introduces the second chaplet of Althusser's 'structuralism'.

42 RC, p. 179.

V The Analysis of 'Structural Causality': The 'Darstellung'

The secret of the comparative analysis lies in the 'synchronic' analysis of reproduction. A second theoretical path is thereby opened to the Althusserians: to show that Marx reveals the secret of capitalist reproduction throughout the development of *Capital* and then regard this as automatically giving us the secret of the reproduction of all modes of production. Here the order is inversed: the universalization of the Marxist concepts follows rather than precedes the analysis of *Capital*. In this enterprise one and the same concept will have to explain four types of determination.

1. The self-determination of the capitalist reproduction process, or how the economic base poses its own end and persists in its existence.

2. The determination, in the last instance, of the superstructures by the base, or how the capitalist superstructure fulfils the aims of its base.

3. The determination of the 'region of the economic' and of the movement of reproduction in non-capitalist modes of production.

4. The determination of the superstructure by the base in non-capitalist societies in so far as 'in all forms of society it is a determinate production and its relations which assign every other production and its relations their rank and influence'.[43]

Althusser discharges the burden of this quadruple secret onto the single concept of *Darstellung*: 'the key epistemological concept whose object is precisely to designate the mode of *presence* of the structure in its *effects*, and therefore to designate the structural causality itself'.[44] *Darstellung* means 'presentation', 'exposition', and this term becomes the key to Althusserian structuralism because it denotes 'at its deepest "positing presence", presence offered to the visible'.[45] It is in the *Darstellung* that the structure is to appear. Whereas the 'combination' of comparative analysis was intended to establish anti-historicism positively, the purpose of the *Darstellung* is to found anti-humanism, since reproduction appears in it as 'a process without a subject'. Marx described the capitalist

[43] Marx, quoted in RC p. 187.
[44] RC p. 188.
[45] *Lire le Capital* II, p. 170. This passage was omitted by the author from the second edition, and hence also from the English translation.

system as a 'mechanism', a 'machinery', a 'machine'. 'Now we can recall that highly symptomatic term *'Darstellung'*, compare it with this 'machinery' and take it literally, as the very existence of this machinery in its effects: the mode of existence of the stage direction (*mise en scène*) of the theatre which is simultaneously its own stage, its own script, its own actors . . . since it is in its essence *an authorless theatre'*.[46] There is nothing behind this *mise en scène* except the rules of *mise en scène* present in this *mise en scène*. Hence the *Darstellung* must provide Althusserian structuralism with its first and last word.

1. 'Darstellung': Mode of Existence

Rancière[47] has analysed the use Marx makes of this expression and its derivatives. We find that Marx employs it both to designate the way capital reproduces itself[48] and to indicate how the social system transforms labour into commodities: 'it is only at a definite historical epoch in a society's development that such a product becomes a commodity, viz., at the epoch when the labour spent on the production of a useful article becomes expressed (*darstellt*) as one of the objective qualities of that article, i.e. as its value'.[49] Hence the strategic importance of this word which is introduced as a pointer both to the mechanism of the self-reproduction of the base and to that mechanism in the base which determines the social whole. It is necessary now to show that 'this word is a concept'.[50]

2. 'Darstellung': Development

The *Darstellung* becomes a methodological concept if we comprehend its place in Marx's dispute with his predecessors. The *Darstellung* is not a grasp of the manifest as such. It becomes a method of knowledge only if it implies setting the appearance in motion. Its point of departure is not the contemplation of 'that

---

[46] RC p. 193.
[47] *Lire le Capital* I, pp. 95–210. Rancière's contribution was omitted from the 1969 French edition, and hence is not included in the English edition of *Reading Capital*. An English translation of – so far – half of it is available in *Theoretical Practice*, Nos 1 and 2, January and April 1971, pp. 35–52 and pp. 31–48.
[48] ibid., p. 190.
[49] ibid., p. 134. The quotation is from Marx, *Capital* Vol. 1.
[50] RC p. 29.

money form that stares everybody in the face' but the construction of its (conceptual) genesis: it discovers in the appearing the mechanism of apparition. Marx attacked the 'analysis' of classical political economy for being too empirical, for sticking to the immediate fixed form of wealth, and hence also for being too abstract, for radically separating the essence from its 'forms of manifestation'. 'Political economy . . . has never once asked the question: why this content adopts this form, why labour is represented (*sich darstellt*) by value?'[51] If the *Darstellung* enables us to avoid the split between form and content, essence and existence, it is because it presents the *development* of the form, and Marx attacks Ricardo and other economists for not being able to see this. The conceptual movement, the progression of *Capital*, is thus inscribed in the development of the *Darstellung*.

3. 'Darstellung': Formation of Forms

This development must be understood as the necessary movement whereby we pass from one form to another. The necessity of this movement is conceivable if we note that even the 'simplest' form which Marx discusses, the commodity form, is inhabited by a contradiction: 'The development of forms is thus the development of contradiction. . . . The more complex and more developed forms are those in which the contradictions of the simpler forms can be developed and resolved. This is the case for exchange with respect to the contradictions inherent in the commodity form, for the forms of capitalist production with respect to the forms of simple commodity production.'[52] Thus the simple exchange of two commodities presupposes that two perfectly heterogeneous objects can be equated. The possibility of this equation is not present in the simple exchange but is reflected in another form (the 'double nature' of labour). The *Darstellung* appears as 'the space that makes possible an impossible equation'.[53]

This logic of concepts, whose peculiar features have still to be specified, enables us to understand that the simplest form of commodity 'contains the whole secret of the money form and hence *in nuce* the secret of *all bourgeois forms of the product of*

[51] *Lire le Capital* I, p. 129. The quotation is from Marx, *Capital* Vol. I, p. 80.
[52] Rancière, ibid., p. 143.
[53] Ibid., p. 131.

labour.[54] If we are attached to the idea of describing this type of logical development as structuralist, then it would be more appropriate to compare it with the analysis of myth than with that of kinship systems. The initial contradiction in the commodity form would then play an analogous role to the asymmetrical matrices (the nature/culture opposition, the culinary triangle) which organize the development of mythological forms.[55] But this comparison can only serve as a commentary, for in any case a veritable *coup d'état* in the concept is about to make the *Darstellung* incapable of sustaining any analysis, whether logical or structural.

4. The Duplicity of the 'Darstellung'

Capital presupposes not only a theory of the true appearance of the process of capital but also a theory of its false appearances (the fetishism of commodities, etc.). The Althusserians' whole problem stems from the fact that they make the *Darstellung* responsible for falsity as well as for truth: it is simultaneously '*Schein*' and '*Erscheinung*' in Kantian terminology. 'These forms of manifestation are just as much forms of dissimulation.'[56]

The Althusserians attribute the error of the 'vulgar' economists to their application of the economic categories of everyday life without any grasp of their systems, and the error of the 'classical' economists to their inability to 'develop' the systems. The insurmountable difficulty arises when they attempt to base this double misrecognition on the very same mechanism that governs our accession to theoretical truth: 'The mechanism of transformation of the forms is thus determined by the relations of production which manifest themselves in the *Erscheinungsformen* by concealing themselves'.[57]

---

[54] Ibid., p. 152. The quotation is from a letter of Marx to Engels, of June 22 1867, *Selected Correspondence*, Moscow 1965, p. 189.

[55] 'Even when (this) structure is transformed or complemented to surmount an imbalance, it is always at the price of a new imbalance; the structure owes to this ineluctable asymmetry its aptitude to engender myth, which is simply an effort to correct or conceal its constitutive asymmetry'. Lévi-Strauss, *L'Arc* no. 26. 'The myth is there to show us the balancing in a significant form of a problematic that by itself must necessarily leave something open, that responds to the insoluble by signifying the insolubility and the protrusion rediscovered in its equivalence, which provides (as in the function of myth) the signifier of the impossible.' J. Lacan, *Bulletin de la Société Française de Philosophie*, July–September 1956.

[56] *Lire le Capital* I, p. 148.

[57] Ibid., p. 148.

Clearly, it is possible in this way to claim 'simultaneously to theorize the process and its misrecognition',[58] but the *Darstellung* by the same stroke assumes all the contradictory attributes of the imagination in classical philosophy as well: it becomes '*la folle du logis*'. This is why the truth of the *Darstellung* lies outside it: 'it refers us to the absent cause, the relations of production'. But this reference is itself ambiguous for, when the phenomena manifest 'the effectiveness of the relations of production', they do so 'in a specific distortion'.[59] The relations of production are 'the hidden motor' of the development. It is precisely because they are not only hidden *in* but also *by* the *Darstellung* that they must be 'truly' grasped elsewhere.

We can now see the solidarity of the two wings of *Reading Capital*. Since the *Darstellung* is a deceptive power, it cannot establish the (synchronic) analysis of the development of the concepts of *Capital*, except by presupposing a successful analysis of 'the basic concepts of historical materialism', in particular the concept of the mode of production as presented by the comparative analysis itself. Unfortunately, however, while the synchronic analysis finds itself paralysed by the deception of the *Darstellung*, the comparative analysis has already proved itself blind. La Fontaine could have written a fable on the solidarity of these two 'structuralisms'. The Althusserians, caught in this circle, believe that they can exorcize its vice by invoking the concept of 'structural causality'.

The Amphibology of Structural Causality

The *Darstellung* has not given us the key to the quadruple secret of Marxist determination. It arose from a contradiction and presents 'those forms of motion in which this contradiction is as much realized as resolved'.[60] But why 'must' the contradiction be developed? What is the 'hidden motor' of its development?

'Thus the contradiction might well designate nothing else but the mode of effectiveness of the structure. . . . Using the Hegelian concepts of contradiction and development of contradiction, Marx thought something which was radically new and whose concepts he

[58] Ibid., p. 203.
[59] Ibid., p. 151.
[60] *Lire le Capital* I, p. 143. This is a quotation from Marx, *Capital* Vol. 3, p. 104.

did not succeed in formulating: the mode of action of the structure as the mode of action of the relations of production that govern it.'[61] Thus the concept of structural causality fuses the difficulties that surround the determination of modes of production in general with those that block the conception (via the *Darstellung*) of the self-determination of the process of capitalist production.

The reading we have made of Althusser shows that the two types of structural analysis he proposes are inadequate as a foundation for the concept of structural causality, since this concept is intended precisely to make *them* possible by removing the basic deadlocks that have jammed them up. Each analysis by itself admits to its own impossibility and refers to the other for the condition of its possibility. Althusser attempts to save himself by installing between the two his special concept of cause, that obscurely central point from which the whole system is supposed to become legible.

In structural causality the two ends of the hypothetical chain of the Althusserian programme reappear: it is neither transitive causality (externally mechanistic) nor expressive causality (with a 'Leibnitzian' internal essence or a 'Hegelian' principle).[62] But this double negation is not as yet the equivalent of a positive concept; it is an expression of a need to salvage both the relative autonomy of the structures and the determination in the last instance by the 'base'. By discovering these two 'ends' of the chain in structural causality, Althusser is hardly offering us the possibility of conceiving their unity. Such a unity would be precisely the *concept*: 'understood as the concept of *the effectiveness of an absent cause*, this concept is admirably suited to designate the absence of the structure in person in the effects considered from the erasive perspective of their existence. But we must insist on the other aspect of the phenomenon, which is that of the *presence*, of the immanence of the cause in its effects, in other words, of the *existence of the structure* in its effects'.[63]

When they use this concept, the Althusserians stress either one or the other of its aspects. Thus the commodity form 'takes us back

---

[61] Rancière, *Lire le Capital* I, p. 143.

[62] RC p. 187.

[63] Althusser, *Lire le Capital* II, pp. 170–71. This passage was omitted by the author from the second French edition, and hence the English edition of *Reading Capital*.

to the absent cause, to the relations of production'[64] where the cause is again absent because it is present elsewhere, in the 'social relations'.[65] In other cases, e.g. in pre-capitalist societies, the absent cause is not present anywhere else. There 'the economy is determinant in that it determines which of the instances of the social structure will occupy the determinant place' – which includes some difficult postulates and which a simple allusion to 'structural causality' does not magically remove.

The unity of the concept lies entirely in its function, which is to explain that the determination by the economic is present/absent in pre-capitalist economies and that it is 'manifestation/concealment' in the *Darstellung* of the process of capital. Its aim is to formulate generally 'the law of necessary correspondence or non-correspondence between the relations of production and the nature of the forces of production'[66] – which no one will ever challenge, since saying simultaneously black and white cuts short all possible objections. Not merely does the concept of structural causality tell us nothing of its origins, for no structural analysis really founds it, but it actually says nothing itself, just because it can say everything or anything – it inaugurates no actual type of analysis. It is possible to appeal to 'correspondence' or 'non-correspondence', cause or absence of cause. In this way structural causality will always be the blessing of the Marxist explorer; at his departure as well as his return he will always be safely at home – but so much the worse for his exploration, which will be a vacant journey.

VI Readings of Marx

This ends the strictly technical critique of the texts presented in *Reading Capital*. Having shown that the Althusserian framework contains two structural analyses, we need no longer listen to them call to one another in a vocabulary that names the difficulties without providing any resolution of them. The time has come for the critique to make way for a commentary that will try to hear the silences in Althusser and reflect upon the reasons for them. Leaving behind us the strictly methodological problems, what would Althusser have achieved if he had succeeded?

[64] Rancière, *Lire le Capital* I, p. 146.
[65] Ibid., p. 189.
[66] RC p. 304.

Metaphysics in 'Capital'

The last difficulty we discussed, the inability of the *Darstellung* to justify simultaneously both a theory of truth and a theory of error, indicates Althusser's basic ambition: to explain everything, to make a system which would be as much the system of the whole (the mode of production as a production of productions) as the whole of the system (dialectical materialism as a theory of theories). Nothing, of course, leads us to suspect a naïve system. Dialectical materialism is no longer a system of nature but a system of knowledge (theory, epistemology); similarly, historical materialism is not a system of history but the unique system of concepts that allows various histories to be thought ('there is no history in general', there are only modes of production and the plurality of historical processes that they determine). The search for a system is displaced from the real to the theory of the real. We can call this displacement *metaphysical* – not in the pejorative sense of a duplication of the real world in a world of ideas, but in the classical sense in which a 'primary' philosophy develops the initial concepts (*a priori* transcendentals) that enable us to think the real as real. The *a priori* conditions for all possible history are the 'basic concepts of historical materialism'.

The Althusserian reading parallels not only the project of metaphysics, but also its systematic organization. Unity is not naïvely sought between thought and being, but in a transcendental correlation that identifies the concepts of thought with the 'conditions of existence' of the real.[67] This unity is the duplex unity of the 'general essence of production', in so far as it is this unity that divides to produce a 'knowledge effect' and a 'society effect'. The simple opposition of 'theoretical production' and 'material production' does not exhaust the essence of production. Theoretical production contains the essence of all production since 'through it' one must read 'the essence of practice in general' and of 'the development of things in general'; for its part, 'material' production is also the production of the knowledge effect as *Darstellung*. The knowledge aspect and the real causality aspect are thus present in all forms of production: it is not the factual distinction between theory and real production that explains the double aspect of all production; on the contrary, it is the internal

[67] RC p. 216.

division of the essence of production that gives rise to the factual distinction. This internal difference defines production meta-physically.

Production – first and last thought of Althusserianism – is the being that is both the positing of the copula in the proposition (knowledge effect) and of the object in reality (society effect). *That a thing is and that it is thus*: the double face traditionally represented by metaphysics as *existentia et essentia*, existence and essence. The role of the 'mode of production' is to provide the form (essence, structure) of all historical existence – what general metaphysics reflects in the *essentia*. In the *Darstellung* we rediscover the *existentia* whose explanation tradition delegates to theology. It comes therefore as no surprise that for Althusser it is the location of the fall, where truth (positing 'presence') and error ('absence of the structure in person from the effects *considered from the erasive perspective of their existence*') mingle in confusion. The unity of production is then decked out in the attributes which qualify the primary substance (subject) conceived by modern metaphysics: will and understanding, *appetitio* and *perceptio*; here, knowledge and real causality.

A supplementary pointer to Althusser's metaphysical position can even be found in the initial definition he proposes for production, giving priority to its second meaning ('to transform in order to give a pre-existing raw material the form of an object adapted to a purpose') over what 'seems' to be its first meaning ('to render what is latent').[68] This choice, apparently taken for granted, is the choice by which Heidegger sums up the whole of Western metaphysics; it translates Greek truth ('unveiling', the apparent meaning of the word 'production') into the language of Roman and Christian activity.[69] 'The general essence of production' thus claims to be the source simultaneously of the unity, the division, the correlation and even the whole articulation of Althusser's structuralist reading.

The Language of 'Capital'

Another reading is possible, suggested by the synonym with

[68] RC p. 95.
[69] Thus Heidegger has written of Marx: 'The essence of materialism does not consist in the claim that everything is elementary matter (*Stoff*), but rather in a metaphysical determination according to which all being appears as the raw material (*Material*) of labour.' *Letter on Humanism.*

which the Althusserians abortively refer to structural causality: 'metonymic causality'. Metonymy is a figure of speech (the part for the whole, the sail for a ship), regarded by linguistics as one of the two essential dimensions of all language: it governs 'syntagmatic' relations, relations of contiguity, i.e. the concatenation of the elements in the chain of a discourse. In the 'fixed forms' which Marx accuses his opponents of not developing, we might register a number of 'parts' that the classical economists have taken for the whole of the capitalist system and whose metonymic character, their place in the general process of production, they have not been able to read. Jacques Lacan has brilliantly demonstrated that such an extension of the categories of language is possible – but by first postulating that his object, the unconscious, is 'structured like a language'.

Only such a justification would allow us to talk of metonymic causality, but not only do the Althusserians fail to give it (for them being is production), they even forbid it. To say that each fixed form of the economic process, each 'part', is metonymically equivalent to the whole system is to say that in each fixed form it is possible to read '*in nuce*' the pre-supposition of the totality of the system and that the *Darstellung* must present the succession of these forms. Here the truth of the 'development' cannot lie at the end of its exposition-*Darstellung* (vulgar Hegelianism) nor 'beneath' it (the Althusserian break between the fallacious *Darstellung* and the true reality of the modes of production). It is in the order of succession of the figures of the process in so far as this order is presupposed by each figure, which is thus *located* in the process, metonymically. Each form, starting from the simplest, the commodity form, includes the premise that the process as a whole will be traversed, i.e. that the capitalist system exists.

This is then an 'anticipated certainty' – for the commodity form precedes the capitalist mode of production. The commodity is 'theological' because it is not only pregnant with its contradiction but also with the presumption that this contradiction can only be resolved in the coherence of a purely economic (capitalist) system. Marx is 'midwife' to the commodity; he makes these presumptions explicit and develops the forms so that they can answer the initial question – on what conditions can a purely economic system resolve the contradiction in the commodity?

Jacques Lacan has demonstrated the constitutive presence of this 'assertion of the anticipated certainty' in the order of discourse: it presupposes that each form of the process is determined by a 'future anterior'.[70] Here it would be a Kantian postulate of the coherence of the economic system by means of which the commodity would have been coherent ever since the beginning. In such a conception, the economic enunciate engulfs more and more of the world in search of its own coherence. Marx allows us to perceive the upheavals provoked by the theology of the commodity in its attempt to assure itself, through the different forms of its assumption, that it will have been true because it is simply the coherence of the reproduction of the (capitalist) system.

Let us follow such an 'anticipated assertion' through. Marx is not obliged to adopt it for himself; he can state the secret enunciate of the theology of the commodity without having to believe in the divine coherence it postulates. If we hold firmly to the idea of the economy conceived as a discourse, we are not obliged to end up with a structuralism without subject and history. Only because they sustained the economic discourse by referring to an *enunciate* alone did the classical economists have to postulate the necessary coherence of this enunciate and come to grief in economism. If the economy is basically not a relation between things, but a social relation, it is because the commodity is not the enunciator of the discourse enunciated in it. For the social classes intervene here not only as supporters (*Träger*) of economic intercourse, as the Althusserians maintain,[71] i.e. as the subject of the enunciate, but also in so far as they also maintain this intercourse as the subject of the *enunciation* – or of the denunciation. Hence there is no need to distinguish what is historical in *Capital* (primitive accumulation, transitional forms) from what is structural (the 'mechanisms' of capital). On the contrary, it is the system of 'shifters' from the register of the enunciate ('economy') to the register of the enunciation ('history', 'sociology'), and vice versa, which organizes the incomplete development of *Capital*. Hence we can understand the privilege granted to the two basic classes of *Capital*, the only classes Marx regards as capable of sustaining the discourse of the

[70] 'the retroversion effect whereby the subject at each stage becomes what it was as if from before, and only announces itself: it will have been – in the future anterior'. Jacques Lacan, *Ecrits*, p. 808. It is this determination in a future anterior that Althusser rejects in the very case of the young Marx's itinerary (FM p. 75); a more general negation of this kind of temporalization (dubbed 'Hegelian') leads Althusser to 'break' the development of the *Darstellung*. Hence its logical leakage.

[71] RC p. 252; ibid., pp. 183ff.

economy as a whole; of supporting not only its coherence but also its incoherences, the one proclaiming a benediction on the whole, the other a curse on it.

Philosophy in 'Capital'

That linguistics can explain Marx's decoding of the economic language, and psychoanalysis the isolation of this language's incoherence, does not necessarily imply that we can discover beneath *Capital* a completed 'general' science which – with respect to the ensemble of all theories and the ensemble of all historical and social realities – enjoys the epistemological status postulated for general linguistics with respect to the ensemble of all possible languages. To 'read' classical political economy, Marx does not need to muster the metaphysical attributes of a system – even in scientific translation – and in this Marx is not only a good reader but also a philosopher.

Marx does not borrow from philosophy its eternal truths, nor its metaphysical demarcation of the world into a system, but its scepticism. Althusser correctly remarks that the critical discourse is used to discover the *mise en scène* behind the actors' play. To do this, however, there is no need to postulate a positive system of 'all modes of production', of the direction in all the world's theatres. The critical gaze (*Skepsis*: view) is the gaze that tries to catch apparition in its appearing 'so that it ceases to be a simple entrance on to the stage'.[72]

Marx the philosopher is not the man of a higher learning but the unlearned: he only needs to take classical economics *at its word*. Marx was a revolutionary because he assigned to the capitalist system the sole basis of its mortality. He has been turned into a Statue of the Commander, before whom incense is burned in expectation of a sign of the final date of its decease, while all about the banquet of life continues in the joys of profanity. The Althusserians have remarked that, in his scrutiny of the symptoms of its mortal disease, Marx does not define any crisis as the final catastrophe for capitalism. But neither does he present us with a comparison of the set of all possible modes of production, in order to pose in simple otherness the certain sign of an imminent death for imperialism. Marx is no Enlightenment *Aufklärer* for whom

---

[72] Heidegger, 'Hegel and his concept of experience', *Holzwege*.

history progresses by choosing the best in the light of comparison. If death is to be registered neither within the system nor between the systems, this is because it has no place – it gives place, alone, in closing a system as a system. Marx knew, with philosophical knowledge, that no absolute justifies and that every stage of reality is formed by defending itself against the movement that carries it away. The truth of this knowledge he discovered in the stone banquet of the 'fixed' forms of the process of capital, by showing 'in the positive understanding of the existing state of things (*Bestehende*) at the same time also the understanding of its negation, of its necessary destruction'. The capitalist system now knows that it is mortal, not by having read it, but by having experienced it in the dimensions in which death registers its power, traumas like the 1929 crisis and the birth of one or more non-capitalist systems. The objective transformations of it induced by this new awareness of mortality must be deciphered today from the work of contemporary economists. Althusser is right to refer us to *Capital* for the principles of a critical reading of them. But his metaphysical passion for a system threatens to obliterate this new body of knowledge, over which the Marxist critique of political economy must exercise its permanent power.

A Political and Philosophical Interview

Lucio Colletti

Can you give us a brief sketch of your initial intellectual origins, and entry into political life?

My intellectual origins were similar to those of virtually all Italian intellectuals of my generation. Their starting-point during the last years of fascism was the neo-idealist philosophy of Benedetto Croce and Giovanni Gentile. I wrote my doctorate in 1949 on Croce's logic, although I was already by then critical of Croceanism. Then between 1949 and 1950 my decision to join the Italian Communist Party gradually matured. I should add that this decision was in many ways a very difficult one, and that – although this will perhaps seem incredible today – study of Gramsci's writings was not a major influence on it. On the contrary, it was my reading of certain of Lenin's texts that was determinant for my adhesion to the PCI: in particular, and despite all the reservations which it may inspire and which I share towards it today, his *Materialism and Empirio-Criticism*. At the same time, my entry into the Communist Party was precipitated by the outbreak of the Korean War, although this was accompanied by the firm conviction that it was North Korea which had launched an attack against the South. I say this, not in order to furnish myself with an *a posteriori* political virginity, but because it is the truth. My attitudes even then were of profound aversion towards Stalinism: but at that moment the world was rent into two, and it was necessary to choose one side or the other. So, although it meant doing violence to myself, I opted for membership of the PCI – with all the deep resistances of formation and culture that a petty-bourgeois intellectual of that epoch in Italy could feel towards Stalinism. You must remember that we had lived through the experience of fascism, so that all the paraphernalia of orchestrated unanimity, rhythmical applause and charismatic leadership of the international workers' movement, were spontaneously repugnant to anyone of my background. Nevertheless, in spite of this, because of the Korean conflict and the scission of the world into two blocs, I opted for entry into the PCI. The left-wing of the PSI did not provide any meaningful alternative, because at that time it was essentially a subordinate form of Communist militancy, organically linked to the policies of the PCI. It is important to emphasize the relative lateness of my entry into the Party – I was about 25 or 26 – and my lack of the more traditional illusions about it. For the death of Stalin in 1953 had a diametrically opposite effect on me to that which it had on most Communist or pro-Communist intellectuals. They felt it as a disaster, the disappearance of a kind of divinity, while for me it was an emancipation. This also explains my attitude towards the Twentieth Congress of the CPSU in 1956, and in particular towards Khruschev's Secret Speech. While most of my contemporaries reacted to the crisis of Stalinism as a personal catastrophe, the collapse of their own convictions and certitudes, I experienced Khruschev's denunciation of Stalin as an authentic liberation. It seemed to me that at last Communism could become what I had always believed it should become – an historical movement whose acceptance involved no sacrifice of one's own reason.

What was your personal experience, as a young militant and philosopher, within the PCI *from 1950 to 1956?*

My membership of the Party was an extremely important and positive experience for me. I can say that if I were to relive my life again, I would repeat the experience of both my entry and my exit. I regret neither the decision to join nor the decision to leave the Party. Both were critical for my development. The first importance of militancy in the PCI lay essentially in this: the Party was the site in which a man like myself, of completely intellectual background, made real contact for the first time with people from other social groups, whom I would otherwise never have encountered except in trams or buses. Secondly, political activity in the Party allowed me to overcome certain forms of intellectualism and thereby also to understand somewhat better the problems of the relationship between theory and practice in a political movement. My own role was that of a simple rank-and-file militant. From 1955 onwards, however, I became involved in the internal struggles over cultural policy in the PCI. At that time, the official orientation of the Party was centred on an interpretation of Marxism as an 'absolute historicism', a formula which had a very precise meaning – it signified a way of treating Marxism as if it were a continuation and development of the historicism of Benedetto Croce himself. It was in this light that the Party also sought to present the work of Gramsci. Togliatti's version of Gramsci's thought was, of course, not an accurate one. But the fact is that Gramsci's writings were utilized to present Marxism as the fulfilment and conclusion of the tradition of Italian Hegelian idealism, in particular that of Croce. The objective of the internal struggles in which I became engaged was by contrast to give priority to the knowledge and study of the work of Marx himself. It was in this context that my relationship to Galvano Della Volpe, who at that time was effectively ostracized within the PCI, became very important for me.[1] One outcome of the theoretical struggle between these two tendencies was the entry of Della Volpe, Pietranera and myself into the editorial committee of *Società*, which was then the main cultural journal of the Party, in 1957–58.

To what extent was the change in the composition of the editorial committee of Società at that time a consequence of the Twentieth Party Congress in the USSR *and of the Hungarian Revolt?*

It was a consequence of Hungary, for a very simple reason. After the rising in Budapest, the majority of Italian Communist professors abandoned the Party, which was left virtually without university luminaries. One of the few professors who remained in the Party was Della Volpe. The new situation induced Mario Alicata – who was then in overall charge of the Party's cultural policy and who, it must be said, was a highly intelligent man – to change his attitude towards Della Volpe, who had hitherto been intellectually proscribed within the Party. The result was that Della Volpe was finally accepted on to the editorial board of *Società*, and with him a good part of the Della Volpean tendency,

[1] For an introduction to the work of Della Volpe, see NLR 59, January–February 1970, pp. 97–100.

including Giulio Pietranera (who died today) and myself. This lasted until 1962. In that year, the Party then decided to dissolve *Società*, for reasons which were not only ideological but political. The suppression of the journal was basically motivated by the fact that after the composition of the editorial committee had changed, the review became steadily radicalized, if only on an ideological level: Marxist and Leninist articles were becoming predominant, and this theoretical turn to the left disquieted the Party leadership for a very good reason. The PCI had for many years previously ceased to recruit young people. But from 1959–60 onwards, it started to register gains amongst youth once more – especially after the popular demonstrations which overthrew the Tambroni government in 1960. There now started to emerge a new levy of young Communist intellectuals – some of whom occupy comparatively important positions in the PCI today, while others have left it – influenced by Della Volpean positions. Alarmed by the leftward shift of these younger intellectuals, who soon dominated the Youth Federation of the Party, the PCI leadership decided to suppress *Società* as the source of their theoretical inspiration.

Yet within the editorial committee of Società there were other currents – represented for example by Spinella or Luporini, who joined the journal at more or less the same time as Della Volpe and yourself. Wasn't there a plurality of contending influences on Società, consequently?

No, there were no real debates as such in the pages of the review. Spinella was in principle the chief editor; but after the entry of Della Volpe onto the editorial board, some of its members – while remaining formally on the masthead – simply ceased to collaborate with the journal. So in practice there was no public confrontation of views in *Società*. Moreover, you must remember that the journal was a publication produced by the Party, which meant that the preparation of its issues was tightly controlled from above, in particular by Alicata. In practice, most of the contributions came from the so-called Della Volpean group, but more for reasons of inertia and boycott by its antagonists on the journal. Thus, without a true political debate, *Società* eventually came to reflect – within its own ideological-cultural limits – a new commitment to themes proper to Marxism and Leninism.

Surely towards the end of this period there were some quite important debates on political questions in the review : for instance, the polemic between yourself and Valentino Gerratana on the nature of the representative State?

It would be misleading to call this episode a debate within the review. It occurred within the Party. For some years back, I had been attacking the notion of the 'constitutional State' (*Stato di diritto*), to some extent also in the journals of the Left of the PSI like *Mondo Nuovo*. The theme of my polemics was that it was strange for the PSI to call for the advent of a 'constitutional State', since in my view this already substantially existed in Italy – it was none other than the liberal-bourgeois State. I failed to understand how the status quo could become a future objective of the Party. To organize a reply to such criticisms, the Party convoked a conference on the 'concept of the constitutional State', at which Gerratana delivered a report rebutting positions expressed in an article of mine. The two texts were published in *Società*, but the debate did not derive from within the journal.[2]

You left the Party two years after the closure of Società, in 1964. What were the reasons for your depature? Was it mainly inspired by a persistent Stalinism, or by a growing reformism, of the PCI?

My decision to leave was the result of the overall evolution of the Party. In one sense, the process of renovation for which I had hoped after the Twentieth Party Congress had failed to occur – but in another sense it had occurred, in a patently rightward direction. I slowly came to realize in the period from 1956 to 1964 that both the Soviet regime itself, and the Western Communist Parties, were incapable of accomplishing the profound transformation necessary for a return to revolutionary Marxism and Leninism. It had become structurally impossible for either the CPSU or the Western Parties to undergo a real democratization – in other words, not in the sense of a liberal or bourgeois democracy, but in the sense of revolutionary socialist democracy, of workers' councils.

[2] See L. Colletti, 'Stato di Diritto e Sovranità Popolare', *Società*, November–December 1960; and V. Gerratana, 'Democrazia e Stato di Diritto', *Società*, November–December 1961 – the last issue of the journal. For Gerratana's work, see his important essay 'Marx and Darwin', NLR 82, November–December 1973.

This conviction gradually matured within me during the experience of these years. I found myself ever more marginalized within the Party, where I was permitted to pay my dues, but little else. Thus when I finally came to the conclusion that there was no chance even of a slow transformation of either the Soviet regime or the Western Communist parties towards a renewed socialist democracy, membership of the PCI lost any meaning for me, and I left the Party silently. There was no dramatic scandal or rupture in my departure. I left in 1964, the year of Khruschev's fall. There should be no misunderstanding about my attitude towards this. I was naturally aware of all the criticisms to be made of Khruschev, whom I never idealized. Nevertheless, Khruschev did represent a crucial point of no-return in post-war history. For his Secret Speech was a formal denunciation of the sacred character with which all Communist leadership had surrounded itself for four decades. This desacralization of Communist bureaucratic leadership remains an achievement that cannot be cancelled. Thus Khruschev's importance for me was that he did symbolize an attempt – however inadequate and debatable – to unleash a process of transformation of Soviet society, by a radical and violent indictment of Stalin. If this process had succeeded, it would have transformed the Western Parties too. In the event, as we know, it failed.

So far as Italian Communism is concerned, the PCI does possess certain traits that are distinct from those of other parties of classical Stalinist formation, and which are in some ways more rightist and revisionist. However, in essence – in its mechanisms of policy-making, its selection of leadership, the whole way in which the political will of the organization is formed – the PCI has remained a fundamentally Stalinist Party. The expulsion of the *Manifesto* group in 1970 shows how limited the real margins for political debate and struggle in fact are within the Party. Naturally, this does not mean that there is no political conflict within the Italian Communist Party. There is: but it is masked and hidden from the base of the Party, which remains ignorant even of the terms of the stealthy struggles at the summit. The rank-and-file consequently remains confined to a perpetually subaltern and atomized condition. The ordinary Communist militant is converted from a vanguard to a rearguard element, whose function is simply to execute political directives determined over his head. My rejection of this type of party can be summed up in a single formula. The real mechanisms of power in contemporary Communist parties are these: it is not the Congress that nominates the Central Committee, but the Central Committee that nominates the Congress, it is not the Central Committee that nominates the Executive Committee, but the Executive Committee that nominates the Central Committee, it is not the Executive Committee that nominates the Political Bureau, but the Political Bureau that nominates the Executive Committee.

The major early influence on your philosophical work was Galvano Della Volpe, with his concern for the nature of scientific laws, his notion of the role of specific-determinate abstractions in cognition, and his stress on philological precision in the study of Marx. What is your assessment of Della Volpe today?

The essential lesson I learnt from contact with the writings of Della Volpe was the need for an absolutely serious relationship to the work of Marxism based on direct knowledge and real study of his original texts. This may sound paradoxical, but it is important to remember that the penetration of Marxism in Italy in the first post-war decade, from 1945 to 1955, was intellectually and theoretically very superficial and exiguous. Let me explain. The official Marxism of that epoch, as it remains today, was Soviet-style dialectical materialism. Now, Togliatti was cultivated and intelligent enough to be aware that this Stalinist compendium was too blatantly crude and dogmatic to have much attraction for the Italian intellectuals whose adhesion to the PCI he was anxious to obtain. Consequently, there were few orthodox dialectical materialists in Italy: compatriot charity forbids me to mention names. What Togliatti sought to substitute for Soviet orthodoxy in his cultural policy was an interpretation of Marxism as the national heir to the Italian historicism of Vico and Croce – in other words, a version of Marxism that did not demand any real break of these intellectuals from their former positions. Most of them were Crocean by formation. The Party simply asked them to take one small step more, to adopt a historicism that integrated the basic elements of Croce's philosophy, repudiating only the most patently idealist propositions of Croceanism. The result was that up to 1955–56 Marx's work itself, above all *Capital*, had a minimal diffusion in the cultural ambience of the Italian Left. It was in these conditions that Della Volpe came to symbolize a commitment to study Marxism rigorously, where it is actually to be found, namely in Marx's writings themselves. For Della Volpe, Marx's early *Critique of Hegel's Philosophy of Right* was a central starting-point. But this naturally represented only the beginning of a direct knowledge of the work of Marx, which necessarily had as its conclusion an intense study and analysis of *Capital* itself.

Would it be true to say that in the period after 1958, Della Volpeanism as a theoretical current within the PCI – *by its emphasis on the paradigmatic importance of* Capital, *and the necessity of determinate abstractions for the formulation of scientific laws – implied a covert political opposition to the very moderate goals officially pursued by the* PCI, *the 'democratic' objectives which were justified by the Party on the grounds of the relative backwardness of Italian society? Some of your 'historicist' adversaries at the time argued that the real meaning of Della Volpeanism was a denial of the hybrid and retarded character of the Italian social formation, which dictated democratic rather than socialist demands, for a fixation with the general laws of pure capitalist development as such, to justify inappropriately 'advanced' objectives for the working-class in Italy. How valid was the interpretation?*

It is certainly true that the diffusion of Della Volpean positions – a phenomenon whose dimensions should not be exaggerated, incidentally – was combated in the Party, with the accusation that they were pregnant with political sectarianism and ultra-leftism. For it was evident that while the historicist tradition tended to give priority to the peculiarities of Italian society, playing down the fact that despite all its particularities it was still a capitalist society, the systematic study of Marx that was central to Della Volpeanism gave priority precisely to the concept of the capitalist socio-economic formation and the laws of motion of capitalism as such. In the latter perspective, Italy was analysed essentially as a capitalist country. Naturally, there was no question of denying that Italian capitalism had idiosyncratic characteristics of its own, but merely of affirming that despite these peculiarities, the predominant characteristic of Italian society was that it was capitalist. The opposing theoretical trends of the time thus could well lead to divergent political conclusions.

If this was so, how is the subsequent political role of some of the lead-ing members of the Della Volpean school to be explained? Della Volpe himself was always unquestioningly loyal to the official line of the Party, even exalting the Stalin Constitution of 1936 in the USSR as a model of radical democracy. Pietranera went on to theorize and justify 'market socialism' in Yugoslavia and Eastern Europe generally. What explains the apparent combination of methodological rigour and political weakness or complaisance?

Firstly, Della Volpe himself was an intellectual of the old style, who always worked on the assumption that there should be a division of labour between theory and politics. Politics could be left to professional politicians. Secondly, it is important to stress that the Della Volpean school proper was a very circumscribed phenomenon; it involved a few collaborators, among whom, as events were rapidly to show, there was no basic identity of political views at all. Della Volpeanism was a phenomenon limited in both space and time, of very short duration, after which the members of this so-called 'school' went their separate ways. Most of them have remained in the PCI to this day.

Turning to your own philosophical writings, you have expressed an increasingly marked respect and admiration for Kant in them – a preference unusual among contemporary Marxists. Your basic claim for Kant is that he asserted with the greatest force the primacy and irreducibility of reality to conceptual thought, and the absolute division between what he called 'real oppositions' and 'logical oppositions'. You argue from these theses that Kant was much closer to materialism than Hegel, whose basic philosophical goal you inter-pret as the absorption of the real by the conceptual, and therewith the annihilation of the finite and of matter itself. Your revaluation of Kant is thus complemented by your devaluation of Hegel, whom you criticize implacably as an essentially Christian and religious philosopher – contrary to later Marxist misconceptions of his thought. The obvious question that arises here is why you accord such a privilege to Kant? After all, if the criterion of proximity to material-ism is acknowledgment of the irreducibility of reality to thought, most of the French philosophers of the Enlightenment, La Mettrie or Holbach for example, or even earlier Locke in England, were much more unambiguously 'materialist' than Kant. At the same time, you denounce the religious implications of Hegel – but Kant also was a profoundly religious philosopher (not to speak of Rousseau, whom you admire in another context), yet you appear to pass over his religiosity in polite silence. How do you justify your exceptional esteem for Kant?

The criticisms you have just made have been levelled at me many times in Italy. The first point to establish is the difference between the Kant of the *Critique of Pure Reason* and the Kant of the *Critique of Practical Reason.* . . .

Isn't that the same sort of distinction that is commonly made between Hegel at Jena, and Hegel after Jena – which you reject?

No, because the difference between knowledge and morality is a central one for Kant himself. He explicitly theorizes the difference between the ethical sphere and the cognitive-scientific sphere. I cannot say whether Kant is important for Marxism. But there is no doubt whatever of his importance for any epistemology of science. You have remarked that La Mettrie, Holbach or Helvetius were materialists, while Kant fundamentally was not. That is perfectly true. But from a strictly epistemological point of view, there is only one great modern thinker who can be of assistance to us in constructing a materialist theory of knowledge – Immanuel Kant. Of course, I am perfectly aware that Kant was a pious Christian. But whereas in Hegel's philosophy there is no separation between the domain of ethics and politics and the domain of logic, because the two are integrally united in a single system, in Kant there is a radical distinction between the domain of knowledge and the domain of morality, which Kant himself emphasised. Thus we can leave Kantian morality aside here. What is important to see is that the *Critique of Pure Reason* is an attempt by Kant to arrive at a philosophical comprehension and justification of Newton's physics: the work is essentially an inquiry into the conditions that render possible true knowledge – which for Kant was represented by Newtonian science. Naturally, there are many shades and contradictions in Kant's epistemological work, with which I am perfectly familiar: I have used only certain aspects of it. But there is one basic point that must always be remembered, nevertheless. While Hegel died at Berlin delivering a course of lectures on the proofs of the existence of God, and reaffirming the validity of the ontological argument (which a century later was still being upheld by Croce), Kant – despite all his contradictions – from his text of 1763 on the *Beweisgrund*³ to the *Critique of Pure Reason*, never ceased to criticize the ontological argument. His rejection of it was founded on the qualitative (or as Kant says, 'transcendental') gulf between the conditions of being and the conditions of thought – *ratio essendi* and *ratio cognoscendi*. It is this position that provides a fundamental starting-point for any materialist gnoseology, and defence of science against metaphysics. The problem of an overall interpretation of Kant is a very complex one, which we cannot resolve in an interview. I have singled out and stressed one particular aspect of his work – the Kant who was the critic of Leibniz, and the scourge of the ontological proof. In this respect, although Kant was not a materialist, his contribution to the theory of knowledge cannot be compared to that of La Mettrie or Helvetius.

Thus my interest in Kant has nothing in common with that of the German revisionists of the Second International, Eduard Bernstein or Conrad Schmidt, who were attracted to Kant's ethics. I have tried, on the contrary, to revalue Kant's contribution to epistemology, as against the legacy of Hegel. In fact, my own interpretation of Kant is precisely that of Hegel himself – except that whereas Hegel rejected Kant's position, I have defended it. For Hegel, Kant was essentially an empiricist. In his Introduction to the *Encyclopaedia*, Hegel classifies Kant together with Hume as examples of the 'second relation of thought to objectivity'. There is no need to remind you of the stature of David Hume in the history of the philosophy of science. One could say, indeed, that there are two main traditions in Western philosophy in this respect: one that descends from Spinoza and Hegel, and the other from Hume and Kant. These two lines of development are profoundly divergent. For any theory that takes science as the sole form of real knowledge – that is falsifiable, as Popper would say – there can be no question that the tradition of Hume-Kant must be given priority and preference over that of Spinoza-Hegel.

Finally, I believe that my attempt to separate the Kant of the *Critique of Pure Reason* from the Kant of the *Critique of Practical Reason* has a real basis in history. For bourgeois thought and

---

³ Colletti's reference is to Kant's work *The Only Possible Ground for a Proof of the Existence of God.*

civilization succeeded in founding the sciences of nature; whereas bourgeois culture has been incapable of generating scientific knowledge of society and morality. Of course, the natural sciences have been conditioned by the bourgeois historical context in which they have developed – a process which raises many intricate problems of its own. But unless we are to accept dialectical materialism and its fantasies of a 'proletarian' biology or physics, we must nevertheless acknowledge the validity of the sciences of nature produced by bourgeois civilization since the Renaissance. But bourgeois discourses in the social sciences command no such validity: we obviously reject them. It is this discrepancy between the two fields that is objectively reflected in the division within Kant's philosophy between his epistemology and his ethics, his critique of pure and of practical reason.

But is there such a complete separation between the two? Marxists have traditionally seen the Kantian notion of the thing-in-itself – Ding-an-sich – as the sign of a religious infiltration directly into his epistemological theory, surely?

There is a religious overtone to the notion of the thing-in-itself, but this is its most superficial dimension. In reality, the concept has a meaning in Kant's work that Marxists have never wanted to see, but which Cassirer – with whose general interpretation of Kant, based on careful textual studies, I am in considerable sympathy – has rightly emphasized. When Kant declares that the thing-in-itself is unknowable, one (if not the only) sense of his argument is that the thing-in-itself is not a true object of cognition at all, but a fictitious object, that is nothing more than a substantification or hypostasization of logical functions, transformed into real essences. In other words, the thing-in-itself is unknowable because it represents the false knowledge of the old metaphysics. This is not the only meaning of the concept in Kant's work, but it is one of its principal senses, and it is precisely this that has never been noticed by the utterly absurd reading of Kant that has prevailed among Marxists, who have always reduced the notion of the thing-in-itself to a mere agnosticism. But when Kant states that it is an object that cannot be known, he means that it is the false 'absolute' object of the old rationalist metaphysics of Descartes, Spinoza and Leibniz; and when Hegel announces that the thing-in-itself can be known, what he is in fact doing is to restore the old pre-kantian metaphysics.

Your work often appears to define materialism essentially as acknowledgment of the real existence of the external world, independent of the knowing subject. But has materialism not traditionally meant something more than this, both for Marxism and for classical philosophy as well – a specific conception of the subject of knowledge itself? In Italy, for example, you have been reproached by Sebastiano Timpanaro with ignoring the 'physicality' of the knowing subject and its concepts : he has accused you, in effect, of reducing materialism to realism by your silence on the latter score.[4] Would you accept this criticism?

No, in my view Timpanaro's argument is completely mistaken. For a number of reasons. First of all, my own concern has been above all with materialism just in *gnoseology*. Now, on the one hand, it is not true that a gnoseological materialism can be reduced merely to acknowledgment of the reality and independence of the external world. This is, of course, a fundamental thesis, but it in turn provides the basis for the construction of an experimental logic, and the explanation of scientific knowledge. Scientific experiments signify that ideas are only hypotheses. Such hypotheses must be checked, verified or falsified, by confronting them with data of observation, which are different in nature from any logical notion. If this diversity of the material contents of knowledge is denied, hypotheses become hypostases or ideal essences, and sensible and empirical data become purely negative residues once again, as in Leibniz or Hegel. On the other hand, Timpanaro's writings reveal a type of naturalism that remains somewhat ingenuous with its single-minded insistence on the sheer physicality of man as the main basis for a philosophical materialism. Of course, once one acknowledges the existence of the natural world, there can be no disagreement that man too is a natural entity. Man as a physico-natural being is an animal. But this particular natural

---

[4] Timpanaro's criticisms of Colletti have been developed in an essay entitled 'Engels, Materialismo, "Libero Arbitrio"', included in his volume *Sul Materialismo*, Pisa 1970 (English translation, *On Materialism*, NLB, London 1976). For Timpanaro's general philosophical positions, see his essay 'Considerations on Materialism' in the same volume.

species is distinguished from all others by its creation of social relationships. To use Aristotle's formula: man is a *zoon politikon*, a political animal. Men live in society and have a history, and it is this level of their existence that is essential for historical materialism. The specificity of man as a natural being is to refer to nature in so far as he refers to other men, and to refer to other men in so far as he refers to nature. This dual relationship is precisely what is grasped in Marx's concept of 'social relations of production'. For Marx, there can be no production – that is, relationships of men to nature – outside or apart from social relationships, that is relationships to other men; and there can be no relationships between men that are not a function of relationships of men to nature, in production. The peculiarity of the 'nature' in man is to find its expression in 'society'. Otherwise, any discourse on man could equally be applied to ants or bees. The distinguishing characteristic of man as a natural-physical species is his generation of social relations of production, rather than honeycombs or cobwebs. It is in the nature of man to be a social-historical subject.

Within historical materialism it was, of course, Engels who classically insisted most on the physical structure of man, and on the relationships between man and nature, in his later writings. You have tended to counterpose Marx against Engels in an extremely radical way in your work. For example, you attribute the entire responsibility for the notion of 'dialectical materialism' to Engels. Elsewhere, you suggest that it was Engels who introduced the first deleterious elements of political fatalism into Marxism, in the Second International. By contrast, you absolve Marx of any errors in either of these directions. Indeed, in one passage you have gone so far as to speak of 'the gulf between the rigour and complexity which characterize every page of Marx, and the popular vulgarization and at times dilettantism of the works of Engels'.[5] Would you really maintain such a formulation today? Marx, after all, not only read and approved, but collaborated on the Anti-Dühring; *and in his introductions to* Capital, *there are*

---

[5] This passage occurs in the long Introduction which Colletti wrote to an edition of Lenin's *Philosophical Notebooks* in 1958. The Introduction was then reprinted a decade later as the first part of the Italian volume *Il Marxismo e Hegel*, Bari 1969. The English edition of *Marxism and Hegel* (NLB 1973) is a translation of the second part of the Italian volume, which was written as a book of its own by Colletti in 1969. The passage above is to be found in *Il Marxismo e Hegel*, p. 97.

surely statements implying a fatalism and mechanism at least as equivocal as anything in the later Engels? Above all, does not any over-dramatic polarization of this type between Marx and Engels contain the grave danger not merely of at times unjustly criticizing Engels, but also of creating by contrast a kind of sacred zone about Marx, who conversely becomes above criticism?

I absolutely agree with your last comment about the creation of a sacred zone about Marx. You mustn't forget that the passage you quote was written 17 years ago. My view of the relationship between Marx and Engels is now much less rigid and more nuanced, in the sense that I have become aware that in Marx too there are critical areas of uncertainty and confusion about the dialectic. I am currently preparing a study that will deal with this question. Thus I fully accept your objection: it is shameful to confer a sacred aura on any thinker, including Marx. I now utterly reject such an attitude, although I admit that I may have encouraged it in the past. This is a self-criticism. Having said this, however, I continue to maintain that the traditional image of the theoretical twins who presided over the birth of the labour move-ment, is infantile and absurd. The facts, after all, speak for them-selves. Everyone knows that Marx spent a large part of his life studying in the British Museum, while Engels was working in a cotton-business in Manchester. Twin souls are miracles that do not exist in the real world; no two minds think exactly alike. The intellectual differences between Marx and Engels are evident, and have been discussed by many authors besides myself: Alfred Schmidt, George Lichtheim, or Sidney Hook when he was still a Marxist, among others. Then, too, there is no historical malice in recalling the letters which Marx wrote against Engels in his life-time, and which were destroyed by his family after his death. So far as the dialectics of nature are concerned, while I concede cer-tain exaggerations in my writings, I would still insist that in the end all Marx's work is essentially an analysis of modern capitalist society. His basic writings are the *Theories of Surplus-Value*, the *Grundrisse* and *Capital*: all the rest is secondary. While in the case of Engels, one of his major writings is indubitably the *Dialectics of Nature* – a work 90 per cent of which is hopelessly compromised by an ingenuous and romantic *Naturphilosophie*, contaminated by crudely positivist and evolutionist themes.

But what about the supposed political contrast between the two men – an allegedly proto-reformist Engels set off against an unswervingly radical Marx? Engels, after all, never committed such involuntary blunders as Marx's prediction that the mere introduction of universal suffrage – bourgeois democracy – would ensure the advent of socialism in England, a far more parliamentarist statement than anything to be found in Engels?

I concede this point. I would merely say that in the space of this interview I cannot develop all my present critical reflections on the question.

You have accorded an exceptional importance to Rousseau, as the central precursor of Marxism in the field of political theory. You have argued, in particular, that it was Rousseau who first developed a fundamental critique of the capitalist representative State, of the separation of the citizen from the bourgeois, and a counter-theory of popular sovereignty, direct democracy and revocable mandates – all themes directly inherited by Marx and Lenin. You sum up your emphasis on these ideas in a formulation which recurs in your writings, and appears to be a very shocking one : 'So far as "political" theory in the strict sense is concerned, Marx and Lenin have added nothing to Rousseau – except for the analysis (which is of course rather important) of the "economic bases" of the withering away of the State'.⁶ It is the reduction of Marxist political theory solely to a critique of the bourgeois representative State and a model of direct popular democracy beyond it, that appears very strange or outré in this judgment. For it seems to ignore entirely the strategic side of Marxist political thought, above all as developed by Lenin : his theory of the construction of the party, of the alliance between proletariat and peasantry, of the self-determination of nations, of the rules of insurrection, and so on – in other words, the whole theory of how to make the socialist revolution itself. Moreover, even confining political theory in the 'strict sense' to analysis of the capitalist State, this century has seen important types of bourgeois State never dreamt of by Rousseau – above all the fascist States, which were classically analysed by Trotsky. How can you exclude all this from Marxist political theory?

---

⁶ *From Rousseau to Lenin*, NLB 1972, p. 185.

Let me reply in this way. Firstly, the formulation you have quoted obviously refers only to political philosophy proper, in the sense of the most general questions of principle in the theory of Marx and Lenin, which are derived from Rousseau – those you have mentioned: critique of the representative State and of the separation of civil society from political society, non-identification of government and sovereignty, rejection of parliamentary representation, notion of revocable delegates of the people, and so on. In this connexion, we must realize that Marx's own discourse on the State never developed very far. His basic texts on the question are the *Critique of Hegel's Philosophy of Right* of 1843 and the *Jewish Question* of 1844; then much later the pages on the Paris Commune in the *Civil War in France* of 1871. These writings all reiterate themes to be found in Rousseau. Naturally, my statement has no validity in the field of revolutionary strategy – party-building, class alliances or fascism. It was more limited in scope. At the same time, however, I should make it clear that it contained an element of deliberate provocation. It was intended to draw attention to a particular fact – the *weakness* and sparse development of political theory in Marxism. In other words, you can also read it as a way of saying that Marxism lacks a true political theory. All the elements of Lenin's work to which you have pointed – his writings on the party, the peasantry, the national question and so on – are of great importance: but they are always tied so closely to particular historical events, that we can never extrapolate them to a level of generalization where they are simply transferable to an historical environment profoundly different from that in which Lenin thought and acted. Thus the real meaning of my statement was a polemical one. The development of political theory has been extraordinarily weak in Marxism. There are doubtless many reasons for this debility. But a crucial one is certainly the fact that both Marx and Lenin envisaged the transition to socialism and the realization of communism on a world scale as an extremely swift and proximate process. The result was that the sphere of political structures remained little examined or explored. One could formulate this paradoxically by saying that the political movement inspired by Marxism has been virtually innocent of political theory. The absurdity and danger of this situation are manifest, now that it has become clear that the so-called phase of transition to socialism is actually an extremely protracted, secular process whose length was never foreseen by Marx or Lenin, during which Communist leaderships today exercise power in the name of Marxism, in the absence of any real theory of this power – let alone any control by the masses over whom they rule.

What is your judgment of Althusser and his pupils? The Della Volpean school in Italy was the first radically anti-Hegelian current in Western Marxism since the First World War. It developed a whole complex of themes whose aim was to demonstrate Marx's rupture with Hegel by the constitution of a new science of society, which was then compromised by the reintroduction of Hegelian motifs into historical materialism after Marx. A decade or so later, many ideas very close to these were developed by Althusser in France, where they have gained a wide intellectual influence. How do you view Althusser's work today?

It is not easy to reply to this question. I knew Althusser personally, and for some years corresponded with him. Then I would fail to reply to him, or he to me, and gradually the letters between us ceased. When we first met in Italy, Althusser showed me some of the articles he later collected in *For Marx*. My initial impression on reading them was that there was a considerable convergence of positions between ourselves and Althusser. My main reservation about this convergence was that Althusser did not appear to have mastered the canons of philosophical tradition adequately. Della Volpe's discourse on Hegel was always based on a very close knowledge and analytical examination of his texts, not to speak of those of Kant, Aristotle or Plato. This dimension was much less visible in Althusser. On the contrary, it was substituted by the intromission of simplifications of a political type. For example, in these essays there would be a series of references to Mao, which appeared to be an intrusion of another sort of discourse into the philosophical text itself. Politically, it should be added, none of the Della Volpeans had any weakness towards Maoism. At any rate, with these reservations, the articles which later made up *For Marx* otherwise seemed to show a pronounced convergence with the classical themes of the Della Volpean current in Italian Marxism. Then Althusser sent me *Reading Capital*. I started to read it, and found – I say this without any irony – that I could not understand the presuppositions and purpose of the work. What perhaps struck me most was something that Hobsbawm later remarked, in an otherwise very laudatory review of Althusser in the *Times Literary Supplement*: that *Reading Capital* did not actually help anyone to read *Capital*. I had the impression of a lengthy theoretical construction erected, so to speak, behind the back of *Capital*. I did not find it particularly interesting as such, and did not pursue it any further.

Subsequently, the essays in *Lenin and Philosophy* appeared, including 'Lenin Before Hegel', and it became increasingly obvious that Althusser was intent on salvaging 'dialectical materialism', at least in name. Now, so far as I am concerned, dialectical materialism is a scholastic metaphysic whose survival merely indicates the deep inadequacy hitherto of the attempts by the working-class movement to come to terms with the great problems of modern science. It is an evening-class philosophical pastiche. Although Althusser interpreted it somewhat idio-syncratically, I could never understand why he still clung to the notion of dialectical materialism. More recently, however, I think I have grasped the real function it fulfils in Althusser's work, and which situates the latter more readily within the prior history of Marxism. There is a passage in a polemic of Godelier with Lucien Sève which is very revealing in this connexion. Godelier cites a letter from Engels to Lafargue of 1884[7] which anticipates a thesis that was later developed by Hilferding in his preface to *Finance Capital*. This is the idea that there is a fundamental difference between Marxism and socialism, and that you can accept the one while rejecting the other: for Marxism is value-free science, without any ideological orientation or political finalism. In Althusser, the same theme takes the form of his recent discovery that Marx did, after all, directly inherit a central notion from Hegel – the idea of a 'process without a subject'. Philologically, of course, this claim is absurd: it could only be made by someone who had read Hegel a very long time ago, retaining the dimmest memory of him. For the Hegelian process emphatically does have a subject. The subject is not human, it is the Logos. Reason is the subject of history in Hegel, as his famous expression *Der List der Vernunft* – 'the cunning of reason' – makes clear. But apart from

[7] See the polemic, published in Italian, between Maurice Godelier and Lucien Sève, entitled *Marxismo e Strutturalismo*, Turin 1970, pp. 126–27.

questions of scholarship, what does it mean to say that for Marx history is a process without a subject? It means that history is not the site of any human emancipation. But for the real Marx, of course, the revolution was precisely this – a process of collective self-emancipation.

In his latest work, the *Reply to John Lewis*, Althusser once again restates at length his thesis of the process without a subject. But for the first time, he is also forced to admit that the theme of alienation is present in *Capital*. In fact, the truth is that the themes of alienation and fetishism are present not only in *Capital*, but in the whole of the later Marx – not only in the *Grundrisse*, but in the *Theories of Surplus Value* as well, for hundreds of pages on end. The *Grundrisse* and *Theories of Surplus Value* merely declare in a more explicit terminology what the language of *Capital* states more obliquely, because Marx was resorting to a greater extent to the scientistic vocabulary of English political economy itself. But the problems of alienated labour and commodity fetishism are central to the whole architecture of Marx's later work. Althusser's admission, however reluctant, of their presence in *Capital*, in fact undermines his whole previous formulation of the 'break' between the young and the old Marx; it also disqualifies the notion of history as a process without a subject. But it is this component of Marxism that Althusser essentially rejects. I think that this is what explains his organic sympathy with Stalinism. In his *Reply to John Lewis*, of course, Althusser tries to establish a certain distance from Stalin. But the level of this brochure makes one throw up one's arms, as we say in Rome, with its mixture of virulence and banality. Nothing is more striking than the poverty of the categories with which Althusser tries to explain Stalinism, simply reducing it to an 'economism' that is an epiphenomenon of the Second International – as if it were a mere ideological deviation and a long familiar one at that! Naturally, Stalinism was an infinitely more complex phenomenon than these exiguous categories suggest. Althusser is certainly a highly intelligent person, and I have a great human sympathy for him. But it is impossible to escape the impression that his thought has become increasingly impoverished and arid with the passage of time.

In your Introduction to Lenin's Philosophical Notebooks, *written in 1958, you end by saying that the young Lenin of 1894 had not read*

Hegel when he wrote Who are the Friends of the People?, *but nevertheless managed to understand him better than the older Lenin of the* Notebooks, *who did study him in 1916, but misunderstood him. Then, in a cryptic conclusion, you add that this paradox indicates 'two divergent "vocations" which still today contend within the soul of Marxism itself. To explain how and why these two "vocations" became historically conjoined and superimposed would be a formidable task : but it must nevertheless be confronted'.*[8] *What did you mean by this?*

You must remember that I was young and enthusiastic when I wrote those lines. I was given to exaggeration. It is true that Lenin did not know Hegel at first-hand when he wrote *Who are the Friends of the People?*. But this text is marked by the positivist culture of the time : the esoteric meanings I sought to attribute to it I would firmly repudiate today. The occasionally positivist overtones of my 1958 *Introduction* are, I think, corrected and overcome in my 1969 study on *Marxism and Hegel*. However, through these successive divagations and oscillations, I was groping towards a real and serious problem, which has now pre-occupied me directly for a number of years. There are two possible lines of development in Marx's own discourse, expressed respectively in the title and subtitle of *Capital*. The first is that which Marx himself advances in his preface to the first edition, and post-script to the second edition, in which he presents himself simply as a scientist. Marx, according to his own account here, is performing in the field of the historical and social sciences a task that had already been performed in the natural sciences. This too was Lenin's interpretation of Marx in *Who are the Friends of the People?*, and my own *Introduction* of 1958 went in the same direction. The title of *Capital* itself spells this direction out. It promises that political economy, which started with the works of Smith and Ricardo but remained incomplete and contradictory in them, will now become a true science in the full sense of the term. The sub-title of the book, however, suggests another direction: a '*critique* of political economy'. This notion found little echo in the Second or Third Internationals. Lenin would certainly have rejected the idea that Marxism was a critique of political economy: for him it was a

[8] *Il Marxismo e Hegel*, pp. 169–70.

critique of *bourgeois* political economy only, which finally transformed political economy itself into a real science. But the sub-
title of *Capital* indicates something more than this – it suggests that
political economy as such is bourgeois and must be criticized
tout court. This second dimension of Marx's work is precisely that
which culminates in his theory of alienation and fetishism. The
great problem for us is to know whether and how these two divergent directions of Marx's work can be held together in a single
system. Can a purely scientific theory contain within itself a
discourse on alienation? The problem has not yet been resolved.

*The original Della Volpean school interpreted Marx's work as
something like a strict analogue of that of Galileo. There are obvious
difficulties, however, in transferring the experimental procedures of
the natural sciences into the social sciences. History is notoriously not
a laboratory in which phenomena can be artificially isolated and
repeated, as they can in physics. Lenin would often say: 'This
moment is unique : it can pass, and the chance it represents may never
return . . .' – just the opposite of repeatability. There is a striking
passage in your Introduction to his* Philosophical Notebooks,
*however, in which you say: 'Logic and sociology are constituted
simultaneously, in the same relationship of unity-distinction as obtains
between the consciousness they represent and social being : thus logic
falls within the science of history, but the science of history falls in
its turn within history. That is, sociology informs the techniques of
politics, and becomes a struggle for the transformation of the world.
Practice is functional to the production of theory ; but theory is in
turn a function of practice. Science is verified in and as society, but
associated life in its turn is an experiment under way in the laboratory
of the world. History is thus a science of* historia rerum gestarum,
practice-theory ; but it is also a science as res gestae *themselves,
theory-practice ; or in the words of a great maxim of Engels, "history
is experiment and industry". We can thereby understand the deep
nexus between the "prophet" or politician, and the scientist, in the
structure of the work of Marx himself.'*[9] *Do you still find this solution
satisfactory?*

You have selected the best page of that text – the one in which I

9 *Il Marxismo e Hegel*, pp. 126–27.

strove most to square the circle! I no longer agree with it, because what then seemed to me a solution I now realize is still an unanswered problem. I am currently in a phase of radical rethinking of many of these questions – whose outcome I cannot yet wholly foresee. I will probably publish a short work soon on the theory of capitalist contradictions in Marx. In this, I will take a still further distance from Della Volpe's work, and try to show through a study of Kant's *Attempt to Introduce the Notion of Negative Quantities into Philosophy* in 1763, that Marx's concept of a capitalist contradiction is not the same as Kant's notion of a 'real opposition'. I am confident of this point, but it remains a limited one, of whose implications I am still uncertain. However, in reply to your question, my answer would be that the sense of my argument in this forthcoming study is that Marx cannot simply be equated with Galileo; he would only be so, if capitalist contradictions were real oppositions in Kant's meaning of the term.

One of your most central themes in Marxism *and* Hegel *is that contradictions exist between propositions, but not between things. Confusion between the two is for you the hallmark of dialectical materialism, which defines it as a pseudo-science. Yet in the last essay of your* From Rousseau to Lenin, *written a year later, you repeatedly speak of capitalist reality itself as 'upside-down', a system that 'stands on its head'.*[10] *Isn't this simply a metaphorical way of reintroducing the notion of a 'contradiction between things' – by a literary image rather than a conceptual axiom? How can the idea of an 'upside-down reality' be reconciled with the principle of non-contradiction, which you insist is central to any science?*

That is the very problem on which I am working: you are absolutely correct to point out the difficulty. For I stand firmly by the fundamental thesis that materialism presupposes non-contradiction – that reality is non-contradictory. In this respect, I agree with Ajdukiewicz and Linke, and I fully reiterate my critique of dialectical materialism. At the same time, re-reading Marx, I have become aware that for him capitalist contradictions undeniably are dialectical contradictions. Della Volpe tried to save the day by interpreting the opposition between capital and wage-labour as a

[10] See *From Rousseau to Lenin*, pp. 232–35.

real opposition – *Realrepugnanz* – in Kant's sense: that is, an opposition without contradiction, *ohne Widerspruch*. If the relationship between capital and labour were a real opposition of the Kantian type, it would be non-dialectical and the basic principle of materialism would be safe. But the problem is actually much more complex. I continue to believe that materialism excludes the notion of a contradictory reality: yet there is no doubt that for Marx the capital/wage-labour relationship is a dialectical contradiction. Capitalism is a contradictory reality for Marx, not because being a reality it must therefore be contradictory – as dialectical materialism would have it, but because it is a capsized, inverted, upside-down reality. I am perfectly conscious that the notion of an upside-down reality appears to jar with the precepts of any science. Marx was convinced of the validity of this notion. I do not say that he was necessarily right. I cannot yet state whether the idea of an inverted reality is compatible with a social science.

But I would like to comment on the problem of the relationship between the social and natural sciences, which you raised earlier. I no longer uphold the optimistic position of my *Introduction* of 1958, which was too facile in its assumption of a basic homogeneity between the sciences of nature and the sciences of society. On the other hand, I can see that of the two broad positions that are generally adopted on this problem, both raise acute difficulties. The first position is that which I took up in my *Introduction*, and which derived from Della Volpe; it effectively identified the social and natural sciences – Marx was 'the Galileo of the moral world' for us then. Today, this formula strikes me as highly debatable: apart from anything else, it presupposed that the capital-labour relationship in Marx was a non-contradictory opposition, which is not the case. On the other hand, there is a second position which insists on the heterogeneity of the social and natural sciences. The danger of this alternative is that the social sciences then tend to become a qualitatively distinct form of knowledge from the natural sciences, and to occupy the same relationship towards them, as philosophy used to occupy towards science as such. It is no accident that this was the solution of the German historicists – Dilthey, Windelband and Rickert. It was then inherited by Croce, Bergson, Lukács and the Frankfurt School. The invariable conclusion of this tradition is that true knowledge is social science, which because it cannot be assimilated to natural science, is not science at all but philosophy. Thus either there is a single form of knowledge, which is science (the position I would still like to defend) – but then it should be possible to construct the social sciences on bases analogous to the natural sciences; or the social sciences really are different from the natural sciences, and there are two sorts of knowledge – but since two forms of knowledge are not possible, the natural sciences become a pseudo-knowledge. The latter is the ideologically dominant alternative. Continental European philosophy in this century has been virtually united in its attack on the natural sciences – from Husserl to Heidegger, Croce to Gentile, Bergson to Sartre. Against the dangers of this spiritualist idealism, I personally would prefer to incur the opposite risks of neo-positivism. But I am divided on the issue, and have no ready solution to the problem.

Turning to Capital *itself, as an exemplar of scientific method, you once wrote that 'the conclusive verification of* Capital, *which we can call external, has been provided by the ulterior development of history itself : a verification to which Lenin referred when he wrote that "it is the criterion of practice – that is, the evolution of* all *the capitalist countries in the last decades – that demonstrates the objective truth of* all *the economic and social theory of Marx in general". Let it be noted – all the theory : which means that it is not just this or that part, but the entire work of Marx, that constitutes an ensemble of verified hypotheses, and thus of laws to be continuously controlled and adjusted in the light of real historical experience.'* [11] *What is your attitude to these claims today?*

Youthful errors, pure and simple.

In a recent text, you seem to accept that there is a theory of 'collapse' in Capital, *although your analysis is a prudent one which suggests the presence of counter-elements in Marx's work. You identify the main strand of 'collapse' theory as the postulate of the falling rate of profit in* Capital.[12] *Do you regard this as a scientific law that has been 'conclusively verified by the ulterior development of history itself'?*

[11] *Il Marxismo e Hegel*, p. 160.
[12] See Colletti's Introduction to L. Colletti and C. Napoleoni, *Il Futuro del Capitalismo – Crollo o Sviluppo?*, Bari 1970, pp. c–cv ff.

Absolutely not. Indeed I believe there is something much graver to be said about the predictions contained in *Capital*. Not only has the falling rate of profit not been empirically verified, but the central test of *Capital* itself has not yet come to pass: a socialist revolution in the advanced West. The result is that Marxism is in crisis today, and it can only surmount this crisis by acknowledging it. But precisely this acknowledgment is consciously avoided by virtually every Marxist, great or small. This is perfectly comprehensible in the case of the numerous apolitical and apologetic intellectuals in the Western Communist Parties, whose function is merely to furbish a Marxist gloss for the absolutely unMarxist political practice of these parties. What is much more serious is the example set by intellectuals of truly major stature, who systematically hide the crisis of Marxism in their work, and thereby contribute to prolonging its paralysis as a social science. Let me cite two instances, to make myself clear. Baran and Sweezy, in their introduction to *Monopoly Capital*, inform their readers in a brief note that they are not going to utilize the concept of surplus-value, but that of surplus, nor that of wage-labour, but that of dependent labour. What does this actually mean? It means that Baran and Sweezy decided that they were unable to use the theory of value and of surplus value, in their analysis of post-war US capitalism. They had every right to do so; they may even have been correct to do so – we need not enter into that question here. But what is significant is their way of doing so. They effectively blow up the keystone of Marx's construction: without the theory of value and surplus-value, *Capital* crumbles. But they merely mention their elimination of it in a note, and then proceed nonchalantly as if nothing had happened – as if, once this minor correction were made, Marx's work remained safer and sounder than ever.

Let us take another case, of a great intellectual and scholar for whom I have the highest respect, Maurice Dobb. Presenting an Italian edition of *Capital* a century later, Dobb has written a preface in which he gives out that everything in it is in order, except for a very small blemish, a tiny flaw in the original. This little error, says Dobb, is the way in which Marx operates the transformation of values into prices in Volume III of *Capital*: fortunately, however, the mistake has been rectified by Sraffa, and all is now well again. Dobb may well be right not to content himself with Marx's solution of the transformation problem, just as it is possible that Sweezy has good grounds for rejecting the theory of value. For the moment, we can suspend judgment on these issues. But where they are certainly wrong, is in believing or pretending to believe that the central pillars on which Marx's theoretical edifice rests can be removed, and the whole construction still remain standing. This type of behaviour is not merely one of illusion. By refusing to admit that what it rejects in Marx's work is not secondary but essential, it occludes and thereby aggravates the crisis of Marxism as a whole. Intellectual evasion of this sort merely deepens the stagnation of socialist thought evident everywhere in the West today. The same is true of the young Marxist economists in Italy who have adopted most of Sraffa's ideas. I do not say that Sraffa is wrong; I am willing to admit as a hypothesis that he may be right. But what is absolutely absurd is to accept Sraffa, whose work implies the demolition of the entire foundations of Marx's analysis, and at the same time pretend that this is the best way of shoring up Marx.

Pivotal questions for contemporary Marxism do not, of course, concern only its economic theory. They are also political. In two recent texts, you have made a distinction between the notion of a 'parliamentary road' and a 'peaceful road' to socialism. Thus in the penultimate essay of From Rousseau to Lenin *you argue that* State and Revolution *was not directed by Lenin merely against reformism as such, and is not centred on any assertion of the necessity for physical violence to smash the bourgeois State – but is rather concerned with a much profounder theme, namely the need to substitute one historical type of power for another: the parliamentary representative State by direct proletarian democracy, in workers' councils, that are already no longer in the full sense a State at all.*[13] *In a more recent article on Chile, you have repeated that violence is essentially secondary for a socialist revolution – something which may or may not occur, but never defines it as such.*[14] *You cite Lenin's article of September 1917 in which he said that a peaceful accession to socialism was possible in Russia, in both of these essays, to support your argument. But surely this use of a passage from Lenin is very superficial? By September 1917, there had already occurred a colossal historical violence in the*

[13] *From Rousseau to Lenin*, pp. 219–27.
[14] Colletti's article on the lessons of Chile was published in *L'Espresso*, 23 September 1973.

First World War, which had cost millions of Russian lives and essentially broken the whole Army as a repressive apparatus of the Tsarist State. Moreover, the February Revolution had overthrown Tsarism itself by violent riots: a popular explosion that was in no sense a peaceful process. It was only in this context, after the liquefaction of the Tsarist military machine and the nation-wide establishment of Soviets, that Lenin said that for a brief moment a transition to socialism without further violence was possible, if the Provisional Government transferred its power to the Soviets. In practice, of course, the October Revolution proved necessary all the same – an organized insurrection for the seizure of power. The whole of Lenin's work is surely saturated with insistence on the necessity and inevitability of social violence to break the army and police apparatus of the ruling class. In general, you seem to pass too casually over this fundamental theme of Lenin's revolutionary theory. Has the need which you have obviously felt to resist the whole tradition of Stalinist nihilism towards proletarian democracy, and its massive utilization of police violence against the working class itself, not perhaps led you involuntarily to minimize the proletarian violence inherent in any mass revolutionary rising against capital?

You may be right in saying that I have tended to underestimate this dimension of any revolution. But what was my basic aim in writing my essay on *State and Revolution*? You have indicated it yourself. It was to confront and attack a conception that Stalinism had entrenched in the workers' movement, that simply identified revolution with violence. For this tradition, it was only violence that was the real hallmark of a revolution: everything else – the transformation of the nature of power, the establishment of socialist democracy – was of no importance. The difference between Communists and Social-Democrats was simply that the former were for a violent revolution, while the latter were against a revolution because they were pacifists. If Communists created a bureaucratic political dictatorship after the revolution anywhere, or even a personal tyranny like that of Stalin, it was of minor significance: the regime was still socialism. It was against this long tradition that I sought to demonstrate that revolution and violence are by no means interchangeable concepts, and that at the limit there could even be a non-violent revolution. This is not just an isolated phrase in Lenin; there is a whole chapter of *State and Revolution* entitled 'the peaceful development of the revolution'.

The only important passages where Lenin affirms the possibility of a peaceful revolution as such are those in which he envisages a phase of history in which the ruling class has already been expropriated by violent revolutions in the major industrialized countries of the world, and the capitalists of the remaining smaller countries capitulate without serious resistance to their working classes, because the global balance of forces is so hopelessly against them. This is not a very relevant scenario yet.

I don't think we disagree on the substance of the issue. The really important question is the political nature of the power that emerges after any revolution, whatever the coercive force of the struggles that precede it. My main preoccupation has been to combat the heritage of Stalinist contempt for socialist democracy.

This concern remains very understandable. Still, the Communist Parties of the West themselves have now long since ceased to speak of violence in any form, let alone exalt it : on the contrary, they speak only of peaceful progress toward an 'advanced democracy', within the constitutional framework of the existing bourgeois State today. At most, they will say that if the bourgeoisie does not respect the constitutional rules of the game after the election of a government of the Left and attacks it illegally, then the working class has a right to defend itself physically. Whereas in Engels, Lenin or Trotsky, proletarian insurrection is envisaged essentially as an aggressive *weapon of revolutionary strategy, in which the essential rule is to take and keep the initiative – Danton's watchword of 'audacity'. You do seem to play down this central heritage of Marxist thought. Surely polemical confrontation with the Italian Communist Party today cannot avoid it?*

It is true that, as you say, the Western Communist Parties no longer mention violence today. But unfortunately small groups have arisen on the far Left in the same period, which reproduce Stalinist fixations on violence, and whose influence, especially on youth, cannot be ignored; it is often greater on the younger generation of Marxists than that of the Communist Parties themselves. You have cited my article on Chile. In it, I wrote that there can be no socialism without the freedom to strike, freedom of the press, and free elections. These were widely regarded here as outrageously parliamentarist statements. Why? Because in the deformed Stalinist mentality of most of these groups, freedom of the press or the right to strike are simply equated with parliament: since a socialist revolution will abolish parliament, it must also suppress all free elections, newspapers and strikes. In other words, install a police regime, not a proletarian democracy. Against this disastrous confusion it is necessary to remind socialists again and again that civic liberties – of election, expression and right to withhold labour – are not the same thing as parliament and that the mere exercise of violence is not the same thing as the revolutionary transformation of social relationships, and does not guarantee it.

True. But this was not the problem in Chile. No-one on the Left there was threatening to suppress the right to strike. The central problem, on the contrary, was just the opposite: trusting confidence in the neutrality of the repressive apparatus of the bourgeois State. It was that which led to disaster in Chile. Moreover, it was not just the groups on the far Left who spoke of the Chilean situation. The Communist Parties were also vocal in their commentaries. Wasn't it necessary to say something about them too?

You are right. What happened was that I had to write a very short article quickly, in a very brief space of time. I now realize that I exposed my flank towards the Communists. I admit this.

But isn't it possible that there are theoretical – not just conjunctural – reasons for your underestimation of the importance of the coercive apparatus of the capitalist State? For all your interest in the bourgeois State has been essentially concentrated on what the whole Marxist tradition since Marx has largely neglected (Lenin included) – that is, the reality of parliamentary democracy, as an objective historical structure of bourgeois society, and not as a mere subjective trick or illusion created by the ruling-class. The political and ideological efficacy of the bourgeois-democratic State in containing and controlling the working class in the West has been enormous, especially in the absence of any proletarian democracy in the East. Nevertheless, the duty to take the whole system of the parliamentary-representative State with the utmost seriousness, and to analyse it in its own right as the foreground of bourgeois political power in the West, should not lead one ever to forget the background of the permanent military and police apparatuses arrayed behind it. In any real social crisis, in which class directly confronts class, the bourgeoisie always falls back on its coercive rather than its representative machinery. The Chilean tragedy is there to prove the consequences of forgetting it.

I accept the justice of these criticisms. You are right to make them.

In this connexion, it is the particular merit of Gramsci to have started to try to think through some of the specific strategic problems posed by the social and political structures of the advanced countries, with their combination of representative and repressive institutions. You have never referred much to Gramsci in your major writings. Presumably in your Della Volpean phase you regarded him as a dangerously idealist influence in Italian culture, viewing him essentially in a philosophical context, rather than as a political thinker. Is this still your attitude?

No, I have changed my opinion of Gramsci completely. Your assessment of my earlier attitudes is accurate. It was difficult for us in our situation as a minority with an extremely weak position inside the PCI to be able to separate Gramsci from the way in which the Party leadership presented Gramsci. This is completely true. However, since then, I have reflected on Gramsci a great deal, and I now understand his importance much better. We should be quite clear about this, keeping a sense of proportion and avoiding any fashionable cult. I continue to believe that it is folly to present Gramsci as an equal or superior to Marx or Lenin as a thinker. His work does not contain a golden theoretical key that could unlock the solution to our present difficulties. But at the same time there is an abyss between Gramsci and a thinker like Lukács, or even Korsch – let alone Althusser. Lukács was a professor, Gramsci was a revolutionary. I have not yet written on Gramsci, in part because I am waiting for the critical edition of his *Prison Notebooks* to appear;[15] I think it is important to have fully accurate texts before one when writing on an author. In this case, I doubt whether there will be any major surprises in the definitive edition. However, the way in which the *Prison Notebooks* have been published

[15] The critical edition of Gramsci's *Prison Notebooks* has sinced appeared in Italy in 1976, published by Einaudi. Its general editor is Gerratana.

hitherto in Italy has been completely aberrant. For example, the first volume was entitled 'Historical Materialism and the Philosophy of Benedetto Croce', as if Gramsci intended to construct a philosophy. Actually the *Prison Notebooks* are really concerned with a 'sociological' study of Italian society. This was precisely the whole difference between Gramsci and Togliatti. For Gramsci, cognitive analysis was essential to political action. For Togliatti, culture was separated and juxtaposed to politics. Togliatti exhibited a traditional culture of a rhetorical type, and conducted a politics without any organic relationship to it. Gramsci genuinely fused and synthesized the two. His research on Italian society was a real preparation for transforming it. This was the measure of his seriousness as a politician.

In fact, I believe that we can appreciate Gramsci's stature better today than it was possible to do 20 years ago, because Marxism is now in a crisis which imposes on us a profound self-examination and self-criticism – and Gramsci's position in the *Prison Notebooks* is precisely that of a politician and theorist reflecting on an historical defeat and the reasons for it. Hobsbawm has put this very well in a recent article in the *New York Review of Books*. Gramsci sought to understand the reasons for this defeat. He believed that the 'generals' of the proletariat had not known the real nature of the whole social terrain on which they were operating, and that the precondition for any renewed offensive by the working-class was to explore this terrain fully beforehand. In other words, he undertook an analysis of the peculiar characteristics of Italian society in his time. The great fascination and force of his work in this respect lies for me, paradoxically, in his very limitations. What were Gramsci's limitations? Basically, that he had an extremely partial and defective knowledge of Marx's work and a relatively partial one even of Lenin's writings. The result was that he did not attempt any economic analysis of Italian or European capitalism. But this weakness actually produced a strength. Just because Gramsci had not really mastered Marxist economic theory, he could develop a novel exploration of Italian history that unfolded quite outside the conventional schematism of infrastructure and superstructure – a couplet of concepts that is very rare in Marx himself, and has nearly always led to retrograde simplifications. Gramsci was thus liberated to give a quite new importance to the political and moral components of Italian history and society.

We have become so accustomed as Marxists to looking at reality through certain spectacles, that it is very important that someone should now and again take these spectacles off: probably he will see the world somewhat confusedly, but he will also probably perceive things that those who wear spectacles never notice at all. The very deficiency of Gramsci's economic formation allowed him to be a more original and important Marxist than he might otherwise have been, if he had possessed a more orthodox training. Of course, his research remained incomplete and fragmentary. But Gramsci's achievement and example are nevertheless absolutely remarkable, for all these limitations.

You have singled out Gramsci from his contemporaries in Western Europe after the First World War, as on a level apart. How would you summarize your judgment of Trotsky?

My attitude to Trotsky is such that I am generally considered as a 'Trotskyist' in Italy, although I have never actually been one. If you go into the University here in Rome, you will see signs painted by students – Maoists and neo-Stalinists – which demand: 'Hang Colletti'. Anti-Trotskyism is an epidemic among Italian youth: and so I am commonly considered a Trotskyist. What is the fundamental truth expressed by Trotsky – the central idea for whose acceptance I am quite willing to be called a Trotskyist? You could condense it very laconically by saying that in any genuinely Marxist perspective, the United States of America should be the maturest society in the world for a socialist transformation, and that Trotsky is the theorist who most courageously and unremittingly reminds us of that. In other words, Trotsky always insisted that the determinant force in any real socialist revolution would be the industrial working class, and that no peasantry could perform this function for it, let alone a mere communist party leadership. The clearest and most unequivocal development of this fundamental thesis is to be found in the work of Trotsky. Without it, Marxism becomes purely honorific – once deprived of this element, anyone can call themselves a Marxist. At the same time, so far as the Soviet Union is concerned, I consider Trotsky's analyses of the USSR in *The Revolution Betrayed* to be exemplary, as a model of seriousness and balance. It is often forgotten how extraordinarily measured and careful *The Revolution*

Betrayed is in its evaluation of Russia under Stalin. Nearly 40 years have passed since Trotsky wrote the book in 1936, and the situation in the USSR has deteriorated since then, in the sense that the bureaucratic caste in power has become stabilized and consolidated. But I continue to believe that Trotsky's fundamental judgment that the Soviet State was not a capitalist regime remains valid to this day. Naturally, this does not mean that socialism exists in the USSR – a species of society that has still not been properly catalogued by zoologists. But I am in basic agreement with Trotsky's position that Russia is not a capitalist country. Where I diverge from his analysis is on the question of whether the USSR can be described as a degenerated workers' State: this is a concept that has always left me perplexed. Beyond this doubt, however, I cannot propose any more precise definition. But what above all I respect in Trotsky's position is the sober caution of his dissection of Stalinism. This caution remains especially salutary today, against the facile chorus of those on the Left who have suddenly discovered 'capitalism' or 'fascism' in the USSR.

How do you now view your personal development as a philosopher to date: and what do you see as the central problems for the general future of Marxism?

We have discussed the Della Volpean school in Italy, in which I received my early formation. What I would finally like to emphasize is something much deeper than any of the criticisms I have made of it hitherto. The phenomenon of Della Volpeanism – like that of Althusserianism today – was always linked to problems of *interpretation* of Marxism: it was born and remained confined within a purely theoretical space. The type of contact which it established with Marxism was always marked by a basic dissociation and division of theory from political activity. This separation has characterized Marxism throughout the world ever since the early 20s. Set against this background, the Della Volpe school in Italy is necessarily reduced to very modest dimensions: we should not have any illusions about this, or exaggerate the political differences between the Della Volpeans and the historicists at the time. The real, fundamental fact was the separation between theoretical Marxism and the actual working class movement. If you look at works like Kautsky's *Agrarian Question*, Luxemburg's

Accumulation of Capital, or Lenin's *Development of Capitalism in Russia* – three of the great works of the period which immediately succeeded that of Marx and Engels – you immediately register that their theoretical analysis contains at the same time the elements of a political strategy. They are works which both have a true cognitive value, and an operative strategic purpose. Such works, whatever their limits, maintained the essential of Marxism. For Marxism is not a phenomenon comparable to existentialism, phenomenology or neo-positivism. Once it becomes so, it is finished. But after the October Revolution, from the early 20s onwards, what happened? In the West, where the revolution failed and the proletariat was defeated, Marxism lived on merely as an academic current in the universities, producing works of purely theoretical scope or cultural reflection. The career of Lukács is the clearest demonstration of this process. *History and Class Consciousness*, for all its defects, set out to be a book of political theory, geared to an actual practice. After it, Lukács came to write works of a totally different nature. *The Young Hegel* or *The Destruction of Reason* are typical products of a university professor. Culturally, they may have a very positive value: but they no longer have any connexion with the life of the workers' movement. They represent attempts to achieve a cognitive advance on the plane of theory, that at the same time are completely devoid of any strategic or political implications. This was the fate of the West. Meanwhile, what happened in the East? There revolutions did occur, but in countries whose level of capitalist development was so backward that there was no chance of them building a socialist society. In these lands, the classical categories of Marxism had no objective system of correspondences in reality. There was revolutionary political practice, which sometimes generated very important and creative mass experiences, but these occurred in an historical theatre which was alien to the central categories of Marx's own theory. This practice thus never succeeded in achieving translation into a theoretical advance within Marxism itself; the most obvious case is the work of Mao. Thus, simplifying greatly, we can say that in the West, Marxism has become a purely cultural and academic phenomenon; while in the East, revolutionary processes developed in an ambience too retarded to permit a realization of socialism, and hence inevitably found expression in non-Marxist ideas and traditions.

This separation between West and East has plunged Marxism into a long crisis. Unfortunately, acknowledgment of this crisis is systematically obstructed and repressed among Marxists themselves, even the best of them, as we have seen in the cases of Sweezy and Dobb. My own view, by contrast, is that the sole chance for Marxism to survive and surmount its ordeal is to pit itself against these problems. Naturally what any individual, even with a few colleagues, can do towards this by himself is very little. But this at any rate is the direction in which I am now trying to work: and it is in this perspective that I must express the most profound dissatisfaction with what I have done hitherto. I feel immensely distant from the things that I have written, because in the best of cases they seem to me no more than an appeal to principles against facts. But from a Marxist point of view, history can never be wrong – in other words, mere *a priori* axioms can never be opposed to the evidence of its actual development. The real task is to study why history took a different course from that foreseen by *Capital*. It is probable that any honest study of this will have to question certain of the central tenets of Marx's own thought itself. Thus I now completely renounce the dogmatic triumphalism with which I once endorsed every line in Marx – the tone of the passages of my *Introductions* of 1958, which you have quoted. Let me put this even more strongly. If Marxists continue to remain arrested in epistemology and gnoseology, Marxism has effectively perished. The only way in which Marxism can be revived is if no more books like *Marxism and Hegel* are published, and instead books like Hilferding's *Finance Capital* and Luxemburg's *Accumulation of Capital* – or even Lenin's *Imperialism*, which was a popular brochure – are once again written. In short, either Marxism has the capacity – I certainly do not – to produce at that level, or it will survive merely as the foible of a few university professors. But in that case, it will be well and truly dead, and the professors might as well invent a new name for their clerisy.

Interviewer : Perry Anderson

INDEX

DATE DUE

DEC 2 0 1980			
JAN 2 7 1984 7 '89			